The Deportation Machine

# THE DEPORTATION MACHINE

America's Long History of Expelling Immigrants

## ADAM GOODMAN

Princeton University Press
Princeton and Oxford

Requests for permission to reproduce material from this work should be sent to permissions@press.princeton.edu

Published by Princeton University Press
41 William Street, Princeton, New Jersey 08540
6 Oxford Street, Woodstock, Oxfordshire OX20 1TR

press.princeton.edu

ISBN 978-0-691-18215-5
ISBN (e-book) 978-0-691-20199-3

Library of Congress Control Number: 2020931366

British Library Cataloging-in-Publication Data is available

Editorial: Eric Crahan and Thalia Leaf
Production Editorial: Karen Carter
Jacket/Cover Design: Chris Ferrante
Production: Jacqueline Poirier and Danielle Amatucci
Publicity: Kate Farquhar-Thomson and Alyssa Sanford
Copyeditor: Julia Kurtz

This book has been composed in Freight Text and Alternate Gothic

Printed on acid-free paper. ∞

Printed in the United States of America

10 9 8 7 6 5 4 3 2 1

For Hilda

and

in memory of Gerald R. Gill and Michael B. Katz

And they have come for us, two of us and four of them
and I think, perhaps they are still human
and I ask them     *When do you think this all began?*

—ADRIENNE RICH, "DEPORTATIONS," 1994

# CONTENTS

# The Deportation Machine

# Introduction

## Understanding the Machine

What kind of nation is the United States? Although celebrated in popular mythology as a nation of immigrants that has welcomed foreigners throughout its history, the United States has also deported nearly 57 million people since 1882, more than any other country in the world. During the last century, federal officials have deported more people from the land of freedom and opportunity than they have allowed to remain on a permanent basis. Yet we know little about the vast majority of these expulsions, which have taken place far from public view and without due process. The most visible of these have been the so-called formal deportations, often by order of an immigration judge. Barack Obama's administration formally deported some 3 million people in eight years, and during the 2016 presidential election Donald Trump promised to remove all of the undocumented immigrants who remained after taking office. But formal deportations represent only a small sliver of the total. More than 90 percent of all expulsions throughout US history have been via an administrative process euphemistically referred to as "voluntary departure." Similar to prosecutors in the criminal justice system relying on plea bargains, immigration authorities have depended on voluntary departure, making it seem like the best of all the bad options facing people who have been apprehended. Local, state, and federal officials have also waged concerted fear campaigns, causing an unknown number of others to "self-deport," or pick up and leave, without ever coming into contact with an immigration agent.[1]

Together, voluntary departures and self-deportations have minimized the federal government's deportation-related expenses and restricted immigrants' rights while achieving the same end: terrorizing communities amid what amounts to mass expulsion. Although scholars and the public have paid scant attention to these other means of deportation, these seemingly less severe methods have been central to immigration enforcement policy for most of the United States' history.[2]

This book explores the history of expulsion and exposes the various ways immigration authorities have forced, coerced, and scared people into leaving the United States from the late nineteenth century to the present. It reveals how public officials have assembled a well-oiled deportation machine, propelled by bureaucratic self-interest as well as the concerns of local communities and private firms. It is a book about how authorities have used the machine's three expulsion mechanisms—formal deportation, voluntary departure, and self-deportation—to exert tremendous control over people's lives by determining who can enter the country and regulating who the state allows to remain. The machine has not always functioned smoothly or at peak capacity, but when it has run on all cylinders undocumented immigrants, and even some authorized immigrants and US citizens, have found themselves under an all-out physical and psychological assault. This, however, is also a book about how undocumented immigrants and their allies have endured, adapted, and resisted, taking to the streets and the courts to demand their constitutional rights and challenge what they have considered to be unjust laws and inhumane treatment. Ultimately, this is a book about power, about how people have exercised it and contested it, and about how both citizens and noncitizens have leveraged struggles over power to define what it means to be American.

Expulsion has long served as a way for communities and nations to assert control over populations that fall within their borders. During the last two millennia, localities and countries around the world have banished foreigners, indigenous people, criminals, the poor, individuals with communicable diseases, and entire religious groups.[3] Since its founding, the US federal government has expelled people across international boundaries and violently relocated others within the nation. In 1798, the Alien and Sedition Acts gave the president the power to deport "alien enemies" in times of war, especially supporters of the French Revolution and anyone else believed to be a political radical. For more than a century after the nation's founding, state governments also had the authority to banish people. In the 1850s, the nativist Know-Nothing Party called for, and in some cases implemented, state-level legislation authorizing the removal of Irish Catholics and paupers. From 1855 to 1857, Massachusetts authorities deported more than 4,000 people to Liverpool and different parts of British North America.[4]

The deportation of foreigners forms part of a longer continuum of projects of empire, exploitation, and forced migration throughout US history. Over the course of the nineteenth century, the federal government repeatedly removed Native Americans from their lands, pushing more than 70,000 west of the Mississippi River as part of a settler colonialist project characterized by Anglo expansion and the subordination of indigenous people and Mexicans. Many thousands of Native Americans perished from famine and disease, among other hardships. Around the same time, the Fugitive Slave Act of 1850 authorized the forcible return of runaway slaves and levied fines on anyone who tried to hide them or help them escape. And from its establishment in 1816, the American Colonization Society advocated for the emigration or expulsion of the free black population from the United States—a cause promoted by founding father Thomas Jefferson and later Abraham Lincoln.[5]

Only in the last decades of the nineteenth century did a series of consequential congressional acts and Supreme Court decisions create the framework for a deportation machine under the exclusive control of a newly created federal immigration bureaucracy.[6] Granting immigration officials the authority to formally expel also meant that they could use the threat of deportation to push people into the shadows or, in some cases, out of the country altogether. This implicit power, as much as the ability to remove someone, constituted a key component of the expulsion apparatus. While federal authorities have formally deported more than 8 million people since 1892, the year they started recording statistics, they have expelled six times as many people via voluntary departure (see figure 1).[7]

What exactly are voluntary departures? In reality, there has been nothing voluntary about them. Rather, they have built upon the United States' long history of using coercion as a basic governing strategy.[8] Unlike people who leave the country on their own volition, individuals who leave via voluntary departure do so in response to a direct administrative order from the

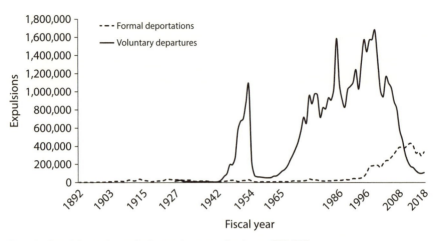

Figure 1. Formal deportations and voluntary departures, fiscal years 1892–2018.
DHS, *YOIS: 2018*, 103. Graph by author.

federal government. The immigration bureaucracy started counting voluntary departures in 1927, when many scholars believed they began. Yet previously undiscovered archival records reveal that the strategy dates back to the first decade of the twentieth century.[9]

Voluntary departures have typically occurred after an agent apprehended someone, coerced the person into agreeing to leave, and then physically removed the individual from the country soon thereafter or confirmed their departure within a set period of time. Unlike formal deportations, which usually have entailed expensive hearings and extended detention stays for people charged with more serious crimes, voluntary departures have enabled low-level officials to use administrative orders to expedite the expulsion of people charged with immigration violations and other minor infractions. They have empowered agents on the border and investigators in immigrant communities to act as both judge and jury. They have allowed officials to deport people on the cheap and prevent immigration courts from getting backlogged. Immigrants have agreed to voluntary departure because the legal repercussions are not as harsh and entail fewer, if any, obstacles to reentering the United States. Until recently, voluntary departures might not have even been recorded on a person's immigration record. By agreeing to leave, people have also minimized their time spent in detention, although doing so has come at a high cost, resulting in the restriction of their rights and precluding them from fighting their case before an immigration judge. Also, in many instances immigrants coerced into leaving have had to pay their own way out of the country. When people have resisted signing a voluntary departure form, authorities have sometimes threatened them or tricked them into doing so, or even forged their signatures.[10]

Self-deportation, the machine's third expulsion mechanism, has received much attention in recent years, but it too is far from new. In fact, self-deportation's roots are older than the nation itself. In the middle of the eighteenth century, towns in colonial New England implemented a practice known as "warning out" to avoid having to provide for people in need of assistance and to exclude people who might be carrying infectious diseases like smallpox. A precursor of sorts to later self-deportation campaigns, warning out involved officials notifying newcomers that they had to leave town by a certain date or be subject to forcible removal by the constable. In some cases, people ignored these notices and remained in their communities. Others, however, decided to depart preemptively. One family unfamiliar with the practice of warning out before moving to Massachusetts was "very much astonished" when officials served them with a notice to leave. The following morning, after a sleepless night of deliberation, the husband told his wife, "I am going to pack up our things and go somewhere else, for this is no great of a place after all." Hundreds of others met a similar fate.[11]

Since the United States declared its independence, individuals in positions of power—as well as ordinary citizens—have continued to use fear in order to define who belongs to their communities and to determine who must leave. They have deployed dread to rally support for nativist policies and draconian enforcement actions based on a supposed Anglo, Protestant, law-abiding US citizen "us" and a non-Anglo, non-Protestant, criminal-illegal-alien "them." Much of the fear has served as a tool of overt social control. Officials have long used everyday policing, immigration raids, and mass expulsion drives to remove unauthorized immigrants from the country, but they have also relied on the rumors and publicity blitzes surrounding these initiatives to spur self-deportation. Similar to other examples of racial violence in US history, these campaigns may have targeted specific individuals or a relatively small number of people, but they have been meant to terrorize entire groups. Even when the threat of expulsion has not scared people into leaving, it has cast a shadow over much of the daily lives of millions.[12]

How important has expulsion been to the history of the United States? Most scholars' attention has gone to formal deportations during particular periods, limiting our ability to grasp deportation's magnitude and changing nature over time.[13] This book is an attempt to see the deportation machine as a whole, looking at all of the forms of expulsion together with the bureaucratic, capitalist, and racist imperatives that have driven them over nearly a century and a half. My work connects historical scholarship on the legal and policy foundations of expulsion to journalistic accounts and social scientific studies of the contemporary enforcement regime and resistance to such policies and practices. And perhaps above all, *The Deportation Machine* argues that these various means of expulsion have been a central feature of American politics and life since before 1900, and particularly in the post–World War II era. The machine's contribution to the growth of state power is remarkable, as is its legacy of creating an exploitable immigrant labor force. Moreover, the malign energies that the machine has unleashed have fueled xenophobia and demonized Asians and Europeans, Mexicans and Central Americans, Arabs and Muslims.[14]

Yet examining expulsion over an extended time span makes something clear: Although Democratic and Republican administrations have targeted different immigrant groups, the history of deportation from the United States has been, for the most part, the history of removing Mexicans. Mexicans make up around half of the undocumented immigrant population in US history, but they account for nine out of every ten deportees. This of course has much to do with the two countries' geographic proximity and intertwined histories of conquest and violence, labor recruitment and migration, economic relations, and family ties. But it also has to do with the distinctive method for deporting most Mexicans.[15]

Even though Mexicans removed through formal deportation far outnumber any other nationality, the expulsion of the overwhelming majority of Mexicans—most of whom had done nothing more than enter the country without inspection or overstay a visa—has come via voluntary departure and self-deportation. Many Mexicans have returned north after expulsion, in part because of the labor demand and higher wages offered in the United

States, and in part because of their long-standing personal connections as well as, until recently, the border's relative porousness. Immigration officials have deported many individuals on multiple occasions, sometimes while they attempted to cross the border, other times as they went about their business in a place they had lived for years or even decades. Some historians have described voluntary departures and self-deportation drives as part of a nod-and-wink agreement between immigration authorities and agricultural business interests that, for most of the twentieth century, made it seem like the former was doing its job, while keeping the latter happy by enabling a steady flow of disposable Mexican workers. However, these other means of deportation have been anything but superficial enforcement tactics. Repeated apprehensions, detentions, and deportations have affected Mexicans' material and psychological well-being, as has living in the United States under the constant threat of forcible separation from one's family. Over time, the machine has helped create and solidify the stereotype of Mexicans as prototypical "illegal aliens."[16]

When I began working on this book a decade ago, the first person I went to see was Marian Smith, chief of the Historical Research Branch of the Department of Homeland Security's US Citizenship and Immigration Services. That morning, in her office in a generic building located north of Washington, DC's Union Station, Smith told me what a historian embarking on a new project hopes to never hear: despite the wealth of materials documenting the immigration service's history, there were no records on voluntary departures, much less on self-deportations. There was nothing for me to look at. "That was the whole point," she explained. The government's effort to streamline expulsions and cut enforcement expenses depended not only on reducing the use of detention and bypassing removal hearings, but also on minimizing the processing of apprehended immigrants—and the voluminous records that would generate.[17]

How does one write a history of something designed to leave no paper trail? Compounding this challenge was the fact that the available federal immigration records at the National Archives only cover the period up to March 1957. Some agency files dated after that were destroyed, others are missing, and most of the rest remain unprocessed and therefore inaccessible.[18] In any case, official accounts do not shed much light on expulsion's impact on those most affected: deportees and their families. Their voices and perspectives are largely absent from institutional records. Yet in the years that followed my meeting with Marian Smith, I discovered fragments of this undocumented history scattered across North America. Some popped up in frequently consulted collections in well-known archives, albeit usually in folders that at first glance didn't have anything to do with deportation. I found other key sources in obscure, far-flung places, from a storage unit in a building along the 110 freeway in downtown Los Angeles and the basement of the US federal district court a few blocks away, to the cramped sixth-floor office of a legal aid organization next to the state capitol in Boston; from the backrooms of a century-old church on the South Side of Chicago, to the folksy National Border Patrol Museum in El Paso, Texas; from the plaza of a small town in the central-western Mexican state of Jalisco, to a tightly controlled government repository in an unmarked warehouse in Mexico City. I conducted archival research, crunched numbers from dozens of internal statistical reports, filed Freedom of Information Act requests, and interviewed migrants and deportees, their family members, lawyers, union organizers, and immigration officials. Eventually, the workings of the deportation machine and the experiences of the people it targeted came into view.

The pages that follow illustrate the great—and often unrecognized—lengths the country has gone to purge recent arrivals and long-term residents alike. They also show how people have fought back by identifying the machine's weak points and pressing on them. This is therefore a history of considerable consequence for citizens and noncitizens, families and local communities. It is a history that has shaped individuals' lives and the nation's trajectory. Both timely and timeless, it is a history we all must reckon with in order to understand the making of modern America.

# ONE

# Creating the Mechanisms of Expulsion at the Turn of the Twentieth Century

Charles Fayette McGlashan lived what some might call an exemplary nineteenth-century American life. The sixth child and first son of a French Canadian schoolteacher mother and a Scottish immigrant farmer father who loved music, Charles was born in Black Hawk country in Wisconsin Territory on August 12, 1847, less than a year before the area became the thirtieth state of the Union. He spent part of his infancy in the 581-person town of Plymouth in Rock County. But the family soon loaded themselves and their possessions into an ox wagon and headed west, arriving in California in 1854. The Gold Rush having passed them by, the McGlashans lived modestly. Charles swept the floors of his Sonoma County school to help pay for his education. In 1872, at age twenty-four, he married and moved to Truckee, a raucous railroad and logging town just north of Lake Tahoe near the summit of the Sierra Nevada. McGlashan quickly became one of the town's most prominent citizens and remained so for the next six decades. When he died in January 1931, residents mourned the passing of the man they considered Truckee's patriarch. Today, he is celebrated as a hero and Renaissance man, an attorney and elected official, newspaper owner and editor, well-known historian and author, educator and inventor, and astronomer and entomologist with a personal collection of more than 20,000 butterflies. Most remembrances, however, make no mention of the fact that during his lifetime Charles McGlashan was best known, not just locally but throughout California, as a leading figure in the anti-Chinese movement—a nativist who pioneered a new method of effecting mass expulsion through self-deportation.[1]

McGlashan had many companions in his efforts to restrict immigration and remove people considered undesirable. From the 1880s to 1920s, industrialization and new transportation technologies facilitated the migration of 25 million Europeans and hundreds of thousands of Asians and Latin Americans to the United States, in addition to another 75 million people around the world. Though some people fled violence or moved to reunite with family, most crossed oceans and traversed continents in search of a better life. Employers did not simply need immigrant workers; they sought them out, dispatching recruiters to foreign countries in hopes of meeting the rapidly expanding labor demand in factories and mines, in fields and on the railroads. The US population more than doubled, going from 50 million to 106 million, in just four decades. Unprecedented migration from places like China, Japan, Italy, Poland, and Russia along with war against Germany contributed to a surge in xenophobia and increased calls to control both entry into the country and who was allowed to remain.[2]

Over the course of the late nineteenth and early twentieth centuries, the United States, in concert with other nations around the world, took administrative, legislative, diplomatic, and judicial action to harden international borders and assert sovereignty. While states and localities had enforced immigration up until then, a series of congressional acts and Supreme Court decisions in the 1880s and 1890s gave the federal government exclusive authority and created a bureaucracy instilled with the singular power to admit, exclude, and expel. Officials soon began using photography, fingerprinting, and other technologies to standardize identification practices and admission procedures, and they established a passport system to document migrants and regulate movement. The United States also initiated a system of "remote control," under which consular officials stationed abroad screened potential emigrants and prevented some people from ever leaving their country of origin.[3]    .

Though the federal government had the power to formally deport foreigners by 1891, doing so proved both cumbersome and expensive. Over time, concerns about the "quality" of new immigrants and their impact on the country led Congress to expand the number and types of deportable categories, making more people subject to expulsion and stretching the immigration bureaucracy beyond its limited capacity. Before long, individual officers took matters into their own hands, finding a variety of other ways to deport people from the United States. And not just officials. Ordinary people across the country continued to deploy violent and nonviolent means to coerce people into leaving as well, just as McGlashan and the residents of Truckee had.

This chapter shows how citizens, immigration authorities, and legislators created and institutionalized the deportation machine's three interrelated expulsion mechanisms—self-deportation, formal deportation, and voluntary departure—during the formative decades around 1900. The machine did not always run efficiently or coherently, and sometimes immigrants' active resistance to deportation or officials' executive decisions to halt removals caused breakdowns. But the new means of expulsion expanded the fledgling immigration service's authority and reach in ways that scholars have yet to fully recognize. They also instilled low-level and high-level bureaucrats with the power to shape ideas about what it meant to be American along the lines of race and class, politics and culture.[4]

## Mechanism 1: Self-Deportation

### The Anti-Chinese Expulsion Campaigns of the Late Nineteenth Century

To understand the making of the modern deportation machine, we must start by examining the history of Chinese migration to the United States, the anti-Chinese campaigns of the late nineteenth century, and the actions of people like Charles McGlashan. Chinese migrants first arrived in large numbers after the discovery of gold in California in 1848. In the years ahead, growing demand for cheap labor in the West brought tens of thousands of people across the Pacific Ocean. Between 1850 and 1870, the Chinese population in the United States increased from around 750 to more than 63,000; a decade later it topped 105,000. Nearly all of the Chinese in the country, 95 percent of them men, lived on the Pacific coast, mostly in California. They toiled as miners, cooks, cigar makers, lumberjacks, and laundrymen. They also laid tracks for the transcontinental railroad.[5]

Although Chinese labor proved essential to the growth of the United States during the second half of the nineteenth century, many Americans saw Chinese immigrants themselves as posing an existential threat to the

11

nation. As early as the 1830s, the penny press, mass-produced newspapers that sold for a cent, described and depicted Chinese people as a distinct race of unassimilable "heathens." By the time migration picked up in the 1850s, this stereotype was both firmly entrenched and pervasive. The Chinese "are uncivilized, unclean and filthy beyond all conception, without any of the higher domestic or social relations; lustful and sensual in their dispositions; every female is a prostitute, and of the basest order," Horace Greeley's *New-York Daily Tribune* asserted in 1854. "If the tide continues," the newspaper warned, the Chinese—"clannish in nature" and "pagan in religion"—would soon outnumber the white population on the West Coast. The supposed danger the Chinese represented had much to do with the widespread belief that "coolie" contract laborers were "virtually, if not nominally slaves" and the fear, as the article put it, that the "horrors of the African slave-trade [would] be renewed on the shores of California." Underlying such concerns was uncertainty about what these changes would mean for white Americans' own tenuous status as free laborers in the antebellum United States.[6]

Anxieties about ongoing Chinese migration and unfree labor persisted in the coming decades. When the Thirteenth Amendment abolished slavery in 1865 in the aftermath of the Civil War, questions arose about the prevalence of Chinese contract labor and its meaning for American democracy. In 1868, the United States and China signed the Burlingame Treaty, facilitating trade and migration between the two countries. The agreement further stoked "anti-coolie" sentiments throughout the nation, especially as companies began hiring Chinese contract laborers to do jobs once reserved for white men and women. When wages dropped and unemployment rose in 1873 and amid the prolonged economic depression that followed, white workers blamed the Chinese. Sustained pressure from Californians, animated by both antislavery and anti-Chinese politics, led the US Congress to pass the Page Act in 1875. Even though the law excluded Asian contract laborers and women suspected of being prostitutes, its limited scope satisfied neither trade unionists nor members of anti-coolie clubs, who continued to push for broader restrictions.[7]

By 1876, the Democratic and Republican presidential candidates had both adopted an anti-Chinese platform. And while anti-Chinese activists continued to organize locally, the formation of the Workingmen's Party of California the following year brought the movement a new level of statewide prominence. Denis Kearney, an Irish orphan, had only been in the United States for nine years and had just recently naturalized when he became the party's leader. A renowned orator, Kearney delivered fiery sandlot speeches attacking both rich capitalists and their "Chinese pets." "Are you ready to march down to the wharf and stop the leprous Chinamen from landing?" he emphatically queried a San Francisco crowd. Kearney also called for more than just exclusion. He captured popular white sentiment with a demand that quickly became a rallying cry up and down the Pacific coast: "The Chinese Must Go!"[8]

Anti-Chinese activists saw their mobilizations as a way to pressure legislators. In 1882, Congress passed the Chinese Exclusion Act, barring the immigration of Chinese laborers for ten years and establishing grounds to deport "any Chinese person found unlawfully within the United States." Three years later, President Chester A. Arthur signed the Foran Act, which prohibited the importation of "alien contract labor," irrespective of country of origin. Despite these restrictive measures, some Americans continued to insist that the nation needed even more stringent laws that excluded and expelled all Chinese immigrants, not just laborers and individuals who had entered the country illegally.[9]

Building on these activist and legal origins of the American deportation machine, people scattered across the West soon took matters into their own hands. During 1885 and 1886, at least 168 communities carried out Chinese expulsion and self-deportation campaigns, relying on a combination of force and coercion in hopes of accomplishing what the federal government could not, or would not, do. Many of these purges involved violence; some concluded in massacres.[10]

In February 1885, after a gunfight between two Chinese men unintentionally killed a white city councilman in Eureka, California, hundreds of outraged townspeople gathered, proposing to "Hang all the Chinamen!" and declaring, "Let's go and burn the devils out!" The mob went door to door, telling Chinese residents to gather their belongings and go to the docks by 3:00 p.m. the following day. They constructed gallows in front of Chinatown and suspended an effigy of a Chinese man from it. A nearby sign read, "ANY CHINESE SEEN ON THE STREET AFTER THREE O'CLOCK TODAY WILL BE HUNG TO THIS GALLOWS." The vigilantes coerced more than 300 Chinese men and women to leave Eureka in less than forty-eight hours.[11]

That September, a group of Chinese miners in Rock Springs, Wyoming Territory, refused to join a strike organized by the Knights of Labor. In response, an armed mob of 150 white (mostly European immigrant) miners killed twenty-eight Chinese workers, wounded fifteen others, and scared hundreds more, causing them to flee. Then they set Chinatown ablaze.[12]

Two months later, in Tacoma, Washington Territory, more than 500 men wielding clubs and pistols took to the streets after many Chinese residents failed to heed a warning to leave. The mob kicked down doors, smashed windows, looted stores, and dragged Chinese men and women from their homes before forcing them on a nine-mile march out of town in the driving rain and mud. As one resident wrote in the aftermath, "The Chinese are no more in Tacoma. . . . Tacoma will be *sans* Chinese, *sans* pigtails, *sans* moon-eye, *sans* joss-house, *sans* everything Mongolian."[13]

While workers in many places across the West resorted to physical violence and extralegal justice to spark mass expulsions, town leaders and businesspeople in Truckee, California, developed another way of coercing Chinese residents into packing up and leaving.

## The Truckee Method

Chinese workers first arrived in Truckee in 1864, four years before the town received its name. As the primary labor force for the Central Pacific Railroad in the Sierra Nevada, the Chinese endured brutal work and weather conditions as they cleared roads, bored tunnels, and laid tracks over, and sometimes through, the mountains. They toiled year-round, despite subzero temperatures, avalanches, and snow accumulation of thirty feet or more. Fatalities were common. When the Central Pacific completed the line at the end of the decade, around 1,400 Chinese decided to stay in Truckee, which by then had grocery and clothing stores, saloons and gambling houses, and ample employment opportunities in service industries and with lumber companies. The Chinese, who lived in the same neighborhoods as white residents during these early years, made up close to 40 percent of the town's workforce.[14]

The history of anti-Chinese violence in Truckee is as old as the town itself. In May 1869, innkeeper Charles Nuce forced an unnamed Chinese man accused of raping his six-year-old daughter to admit to the crime. Nuce then took the man to the Truckee River, shot him, and threw him into the current.

When the man tried to crawl out of the water, Nuce struck him with a rock before pushing him back in. "Public opinion is that Nuce did his only duty," the local newspaper reported. That same day someone shot another unnamed Chinese man in the back and robbed him.[15]

Six years later, in 1875, a fire of questionable origin destroyed Truckee's Chinatown, causing $50,000 in damages, the equivalent of more than $1 million today. "Lucky Truckee. Chinatown Holocausted," the headline read, failing to specify whether the town's good fortune stemmed from white properties remaining mostly untouched, the near-complete devastation of Chinatown, or perhaps both.[16]

By 1876, some 300 of the town's residents, from workers to its most prominent citizens, had formed a local chapter of the Order of the Caucasians, also known as the Caucasian League, to drive out the Chinese. Truckee gained statewide notoriety that summer when late one night seven of the group's members, clad in black, surrounded and set fire to two cabins full of Chinese woodcutters who had refused to leave the area. The vigilantes shot at the Chinese men as they ran out of the cabin, killing forty-five-year-old Ah Ling. That fall, in a closely watched and highly publicized trial in nearby Nevada City, Charles McGlashan represented the accused men and put fifty witnesses on the stand to provide alibis for them and vouch for their innocence. The all-white jury took just nine minutes to acquit the man accused of murdering Ah Ling, at which point the prosecution dropped the arson charges against the others. Upon learning of the outcome, Truckee's white residents rejoiced, firing a cannon for each exonerated man. McGlashan returned to town as a hero as well as an emerging figure in what would quickly become a much broader anti-Chinese movement.[17]

The decline of the silver industry in the late 1870s hit Truckee hard since the town had been the principal supplier of lumber to the Comstock mine in neighboring Nevada. Silver production fell from a high of $36 million in 1877 to $19 million the following year, resulting in a drop in sawmilling and the closure of five local mills.[18] The economic fallout contributed to additional anti-Chinese scapegoating and violence. After a fire devastated Truckee's Chinatown in May 1878, white men marched through the streets yelling, "The Chinese must go!" Less than half a year later, another blaze once again burned Chinatown to the ground. This time white residents threatened the Chinese and gave them one week to leave.[19] Instead, with winter fast approaching, the Chinese began to rebuild. They also armed themselves. But on November 9, a couple of weeks after the fire, hundreds of white men descended on Chinatown and used axes, hammers, and crowbars to break down all of the recently reconstructed houses. The local newspaper reported that as the men went about the demolition work, sympathetic onlookers let out "vigorous cheers" with each "graceful caving in of a roof" or "musical crash of a house." Within a week and a half, the Chinese had relocated to the other side of the Truckee River just south of town.[20]

By late 1885, Chinese people throughout the West knew from decades of firsthand experience that the danger of imminent, apocalyptic violence was real. Truckee's Chinese residents had endured more than fifteen years of vicious organized opposition to their presence. They also had a keen awareness of the recent events in places like Eureka, Rock Springs, and Tacoma. We can only understand grassroots activists' campaigns to push Chinese men and women out of Truckee against this historical backdrop. Their efforts, which became known as the "Truckee method," relied in part on economic boycotts and the public shaming of anyone who defended or employed Chinese workers. Yet their supposedly peaceful, lawful anti-Chinese campaign also depended on incendiary scare tactics, pervasive psychological violence, the strategic use of the newspapers, and the long history and ever-present threat of bodily harm ranging from the routine to the murderous.

The man responsible for designing and implementing this prototypical self-deportation strategy was Charles McGlashan, by then a Nevada County assemblyman and coeditor and copublisher of the *Truckee Republican* (see figure 2). Aware that the Chinese had defended themselves in the face of expulsion and even brought lawsuits against other towns, McGlashan sought out alternative legal, or quasi-legal, means of removing them from Truckee. "If the Chinese do not leave when so ordered, what are the anti-coolie leagues going to do?" McGlashan and his coeditor (a judge who also happened to be his father-in-law) asked in a November 1885 editorial. They ruled out murder since "it would embarrass the average Californian to have to murder any considerable number of Chinamen" and could also lead to "prison, hanging, encounters with United States troops, and war with China." Also, they continued, "the blood of a Chinaman would stain one's hands just like the blood of a more human being." Arson was not an option either, since it constituted "a grave crime" and could result in "riots, and martial law, and heavy claims for damages."[21]

**Figure 2. Charles F. McGlashan, circa 1880.**
Clyde Arbuckle Collection, California Room, San José Public
Library.

The editors then floated another idea: Cut off the queues—the long-braided hair—of every Chinese man who remained in Truckee past a prede-termined deadline. "The crime of cutting off a Chinaman's head is a felony, of cutting off his cue is simply a misdemeanor," a *Republican* editorial ex-plained, before adding, "but most Chinamen would rather lose their heads than their cues." As a result, they argued, this approach would be both fea-sible and effective.

Let the heathen know that their cues are forfeited to the first man who meets them in the darkness, and there will be a stampede. Few men will commit murder, but nine Californians out of ten would go on a cue-cutting crusade. It would be ducks for hoodlums, and this unde-sirable element would become positively serviceable. Pigtails would ornament lamp-posts, be festooned over the doors of business houses, and would form a girdle of bloodless scalps at the belt of every

Caucasian-leaguer. Every Chinaman, rich or poor, mandarin or coolie, merchant or slave, male or female, would leave the State in abject terror, if the cue-cutting edict should go forth and its enforcement commence. It will rid the State of the presence of the Chinese more speedily and effectually than fire and sword, and legions of revolutionists.[22]

A few days later, in a follow-up article titled "The Cue Klux Klan," McGlashan proposed offering a reward for queues, "as is the case with pelts of wolves, cayotes [*sic*] and like vermin when they become a pest." Even though the plan never went into full effect, six weeks later a drunk man severed the queue of a Chinese doctor near the Truckee post office and pinned it to a sign in the center of town for all to see.[23]

From late November 1885 through February 1886, McGlashan and other "conservative, law-abiding property holding citizens" spurred and led Truckee's "peaceful" anti-Chinese movement. At the group's first public meeting, those in attendance approved a resolution declaring, "We will use every means in our power, lawfully, to drive [the Chinese] from our midst, and to assist the white laborers of California in forcing them back across the Pacific ocean." They decided the most effective means of encouraging self-deportation would be to pressure businesses and individuals to fire their Chinese employees by threatening to boycott them if they did not comply. The Chinese would leave if they no longer had jobs and could not feed themselves, the well-to-do activists reasoned.[24]

Two days ahead of the January 15 boycott deadline, McGlashan made clear the stakes. "Either the whites will rule Truckee and the Chinese must leave, or the Chinese must rule and the whites will leave. . . . There will be no compromise, no flag of truce, no cessation of hostilities until the final surrender is made." McGlashan claimed that "no unlawful means will be employed, but such blows will be struck at pocket-books and bank accounts as will prove more telling than violence or incendiarism." However, the threat of physical force was never far from the surface. Organizers also made clear that they would boycott and publicly name and shame any white resident who opposed the movement.[25]

Truckee's Chinese community fervently rallied in response to defend themselves. They acquired weapons, organized pickets and boycotts of their own, and called on the Chinese Six Companies, a benevolent association in

San Francisco, and state and federal officials to intervene and protect them from what one white ally referred to as "McGlashan's mob." Little, though, came of their efforts. In the coming weeks, employers fired their Chinese laborers and banks called loans made to Chinese merchants and cut off their access to capital. The result: the departure of hundreds of Chinese from Truckee. When Sisson and Crocker, a large regional firm that supplied laborers to the Central Pacific Railroad, refused to rescind its contracts with Chinese workers, McGlashan and his supporters ramped up their efforts against the company. They sent out circulars calling for a boycott to newspapers and anti-Chinese leagues in cities across the West. Another group threatened to tar and feather the company's local manager. Finally, on February 11, the firm surrendered. After it did, Chinese merchants requested transportation funds so that Truckee's "unemployed and destitute" Chinese residents could leave town. White citizens rejected the request, however, and instead offered to pay for transportation if "all the Chinamen in the Truckee basin would depart in a body." They even promised to throw in an extra $500.[26]

Two nights later, McGlashan and a large group of white men built bonfires on Truckee's main plaza, danced to the music of drums and fifes, and marched through the streets, yelling and brandishing burning torches. People held signs and hung banners from their homes and businesses reading "Law and Order" and "Boycotting Is Victory." They celebrated "Our Next Governor, C. F. McGlashan, White Labor's Champion." While the torch-lit procession proclaimed the power of the Truckee method, McGlashan made clear that it also reinforced the fear campaign against the small number of Chinese people remaining in town. "Every shout will drive a nail to convince [the Chinese], more and more, that their day is ended in the Sierra," he wrote. "Every burning torch will be a warning that they will not fail to heed, that they must go."[27]

However, McGlashan aspired to do more than just expel Chinese people from Truckee—he hoped to remove them from the country altogether. He telegraphed "How to Boycott" instructions to newspapers across California and promoted supposedly nonviolent means of deportation at statewide conventions and conferences, where representatives elected him president of the state convention of the Anti-Chinese Leagues and chairman of the executive committee of the California Anti-Chinese Non-Partisan Association. In San José, some one hundred delegates from nine counties endorsed the Truckee method, resolving that the Chinese represented "a mental, physical, moral and financial evil" and must be forced to go using lawful means. They proposed establishing local committees to organize boycotts in every city and ordered the printing and distribution of 50,000 circulars in support of the measures. McGlashan threatened to single out individuals who did not sign the circulars and newspapers that did not publicly endorse the movement. If enough towns implemented the boycott, McGlashan posited, the Chinese would keep "moving on" until their only option was "to depart for [their] native shores." And the expulsion campaigns across the West during 1885 and 1886 did push more than 15,000 Chinese men, women, and children out of the United States. Not to mention: When the drives finally concluded, Truckee's white residents had succeeded in forcing out the vast majority of the town's Chinese community, a sign of self-deportation's effectiveness as an expulsion strategy.[28]

## Mechanism 2: Formal Deportation

### The Transition to Federal Control over Immigration

While much of the anti-Chinese movement was designed to affect the local and state levels, activists also sought to influence federal immigration policy and US–China relations. McGlashan claimed the prevailing laws were "full of holes through which Chinamen will creep" and urged Washington to close such gaps. He and other anti-Chinese crusaders organized rallies to protest the Burlingame Treaty and call for an amendment to the 1882 Chinese Exclusion Act that would prevent Chinese people who left the United States from ever returning. Eventually, their efforts also contributed to the creation of the machine's second mechanism: formal deportations.[29]

During the late 1880s, ongoing mob violence and expulsions in the West combined with general anti-Chinese sentiment across the nation pushed Congress to act. In 1888, after negotiations with China stalled in the lead-up to US elections, legislators and President Grover Cleveland took unilateral action, enacting a law excluding all Chinese laborers, including those who had previously been in the United States. Named for its sponsor, Pennsylvania congressman William L. Scott, the act resulted in the immediate nullification of more than 20,000 return certificates US officials had issued to departing Chinese migrants.[30]

When laborer Chae Chan Ping arrived in San Francisco on October 7, 1888, less than a week after the Scott Act went into effect, authorities did not recognize his return certificate and prohibited him from landing. Chae, who had lived in the United States for twelve years before making a brief trip to China, fought his case in court with the support of the Chinese Six Companies. He claimed that the new law violated an earlier treaty between the two countries that guaranteed his and other Chinese laborers' right to come and go. He also argued that Congress lacked the constitutional authority to exclude aliens. The courts ruled against Chae Chan Ping. In a landmark 1889 decision, the US Supreme Court found that the federal government's exclusive authority to regulate immigration derived from the United States' status as a sovereign nation, rather than from an explicit provision of the Constitution. In the years and decades ahead, the court reaffirmed and expanded the "inherent sovereign powers" doctrine, limiting noncitizens' constitutional rights and giving Congress and the executive branch "plenary power" over not only whom to admit and whom to exclude, but also whom to expel.[31]

Federal control over immigration emerged as part of the broader centralization of power under the Progressive Era administrative state around the turn of the twentieth century. In addition to prevailing anti-Chinese sentiments, rising nativism in response to unprecedented numbers of "new" immigrants from southern and eastern Europe and frustrations stemming from alleged corruption and lax enforcement at New York's Castle Garden immigration station led to calls for legislative reform. However, rather than restricting immigration entirely, a joint congressional committee recommended the best approach would be "to sift it, to separate the desirable from the undesirable immigrants, and to permit only those to land on our shores who have certain physical and moral qualities."[32] But who would do the sifting and sorting? Who would decide what constituted a "desirable" immigrant? And what would happen to the "undesirable" immigrants already in the country?

In 1891, Congress passed a law that began to provide answers to these questions. The act, which applied to all immigrants except Chinese laborers, created a new superintendent of immigration within the Department of the Treasury, marking an important shift from piecemeal state-by-state immigration policies to federal control within a single office. It also called for the deportation of aliens in the United States who had been in the country for less than a year and had been excludable when they entered. At the same time, the law expanded the list of excludable—and thus deportable—categories to include people "likely to become public charges," individuals with contagious diseases, and polygamists. (Previous laws had already excluded convicts, "lunatics," "idiots," people judged unable to care for themselves, and contract laborers.)[33]

Moreover, another provision of the 1891 act gave immigration officials tremendous power by exempting them from judicial review, thus making their decisions final. This consequential stipulation emerged for at least two distinct reasons. First, "finality" was not new; state authorities in places like Massachusetts and New York had exercised similar powers under the prefederal immigration control system. When the federal government took over, the new bureaucracy simply adopted the status quo.[34] Second, Chinese immigrants' success in using the courts to challenge exclusion and deportation orders made lawmakers more inclined to instill administrative officials with the ability to prevent other immigrants from relying on similar strategies. The Supreme Court upheld the finality provision in *Nishimura Ekiu* in 1892, concurring with a lower court's decision not to hear the appeal of a Japanese woman officials excluded after finding her likely to become a public charge. By limiting the judiciary's role, the ruling expanded immigration officials' broad discretionary authority.[35]

In 1892, Congress passed legislation specifically targeting Chinese laborers. The Geary Act extended exclusion for an additional ten years. The law also required Chinese laborers already in the United States to obtain a certificate of residence from federal authorities. To qualify for such a certificate, people had to prove they had been in the country prior to 1892 and include an affidavit from at least one white witness. Anyone who failed to register within a year faced possible arrest, imprisonment, and deportation.[36] The act's emphasis on expulsion led one newspaper to declare that "the title of the law should be changed from 'the Chinese exclusion act' to 'the Chinese deportment act.'"[37]

The Chinese community in the United States protested and organized legal challenges to the Geary Act. In San Francisco, the Chinese Six Companies challenged the deportation machine by running an effective campaign that encouraged people not to comply with the law and to instead donate toward litigation expenses against it. When the deadline passed, fewer than 2 percent of Chinese in the city and 20 percent across the nation had registered. They also put forward a test case challenging the constitutionality of the law's registration and white witness requirements. In 1893, the Supreme Court ruled against them in *Fong Yue Ting*, finding that "the right of a nation to expel or deport foreigners . . . rests upon the same grounds and is as absolute and unqualified as the right to prohibit and prevent their entrance into the country." Congress's power to exclude and expel, for reasons of national security or otherwise, were two sides of the same coin—with neither subject to judicial review. The court also determined that deportation was not "a punishment for crime" but simply "a method of enforcing the return to his own country of an alien" that the government decided no longer met the requirements for residence. Some members of the court offered forceful dissents. "Deportation is punishment," Justice David Brewer wrote. "Everyone knows that to be forcibly taken away from home and family, and friends, and business, and property, and sent across an ocean to a distant land, is punishment; and that oftentimes most severe and cruel." But the majority disagreed with him. Its finding had broad implications, still felt today, that stripped noncitizens facing expulsion of basic constitutional safeguards, like the right to due process.[38]

By the mid-1890s, congressional acts and Supreme Court decisions had established the federal government's primacy over immigration and created a rough division of labor. Congress would determine who could enter the United States, stay in the country, and become a citizen, and who was inadmissible, deportable, and therefore inherently un-American. The new federal immigration bureaucracy, in turn, would enforce these laws, admitting and naturalizing immigrants considered desirable, excluding and expelling those deemed undesirable.

However, a considerable gap existed between the law on the books and its implementation on the ground. Removing the estimated 85,000 Chinese laborers who found themselves subject to expulsion after *Fong Yue Ting* would have cost an estimated $7.3 million, but the Geary Act allocated only $60,000 and the secretary of the treasury had an annual budget of just $25,000. Congress's failure to appropriate adequate funds or indicate how the process for expelling people would work led executive branch officials to simply ignore the law's deportation provision. The federal government's lack of action outraged many Californians, prompting calls for President Cleveland's impeachment and sparking renewed anti-Chinese violence and expulsion campaigns. The administration had little choice in the matter, a scholar later explained, since Congress had provided "neither money nor machinery for executing the law."[39]

Yet in reality, what happened in the aftermath of *Fong Yue Ting*—itself the culmination of a decade-long battle over Chinese immigration—revealed both the basic framework and inner workings of the modern deportation machine.

### Making Immigrants Deportable

In the decades after the federal government took over immigration control, Congress steadily expanded the list of excludable and deportable classes, narrowing the legal definition of what it meant to be American. The immigration bureaucracy, for its part, opened new stations on Ellis Island in New York Harbor (1892) and Angel Island in San Francisco Bay (1910) to screen, admit, detain, and expel immigrants (see figures 3 and 4).[40] But who did federal authorities target for formal removal? And why?

Despite the fact that the United States depended on immigrant labor to fuel industrial and agricultural growth, ongoing migration from southern and eastern Europe and parts of Asia raised fears—similar to those that intensified the anti-Chinese movement—about foreigners' economic impact on the nation. Rising levels of xenophobia often coincided with economic downturns. A dire four-year depression in the mid-1890s spurred widespread claims that immigrants stole Americans' jobs and undercut wages and working conditions. Over time, organized labor solidified its restrictionist position and used its political clout to pressure politicians to act. (Unions also had direct ties to the Bureau of Immigration: three former labor leaders sat at the helm of the federal agency from 1897 to 1913.) Anxiety that foreigners would become dependent on public coffers resulted in legislators and immigration officials dedicating considerable resources to single out people deemed likely to become public charges. This gendered policy, which accounted for nearly two-thirds of all exclusions and expulsions by 1915, disproportionately affected women, whom authorities treated as male breadwinners' dependents rather than economic actors in their own right.[41]

Scientific racism and the proliferation of eugenics also played an important role in the push to curtail immigration and expel foreigners. On the East Coast, the Immigration Restriction League (IRL), founded by a group

Figure 3. Immigrants awaiting deportation pass time in a detention pen on the roof of the main building on Ellis Island, 1902.
Library of Congress.

of Harvard graduates in 1894, sought to reduce immigration from southern and eastern Europe that "lower the mental, moral, and physical average of our people." On the West Coast, the Asiatic Exclusion League, formed in San Francisco in 1905, aimed to combat the "Yellow Peril" by ending Asian immigration, segregating children in schools, and advocating for new laws that limited Asians' ability to buy land. (The league primarily targeted Japanese, Korean, and Indian immigrants because a 1904 law had indefinitely extended Chinese exclusion.) Around the same time, social scientists at the nation's leading universities popularized the idea that different racial, religious, and national groups possessed innate, immutable biological characteristics. The intersection of eugenics, immigration, and public health led authorities to declare some people inadmissible or unfit for citizenship based on physical or mental disabilities, or their supposed susceptibility to carry and spread communicable diseases. In 1911, a congressional commission chaired by

25

Figure 4.  Authorities interrogating an immigrant at Angel Island, 1923.
File 90-G-124-479, RG 90, Records of the Public Health Service,
Still Picture Branch, NARA2.

Republican senator William P. Dillingham of Vermont offered additional support to these assertions when it released an authoritative forty-two-volume report meant to demonstrate "new" immigrants' inferiority, inability to assimilate, and responsibility for myriad social problems. Books such as Madison Grant's *The Passing of the Great Race*, published in 1916, further amplified nativist fears about the existential threat immigration posed to white Anglo-Saxon Protestants.[42]

Nativist preoccupations with immigrants' purported proclivity toward crime and immorality shaped policy as well. Progressive Era officials tried to regulate noncitizens' sexual lives and behavior by cracking down on prostitutes and "perverts," a broad category that included "homosexuals," "degenerates," "pederasts," and "sodomites."[43] Rather than excluding or expelling people for prostitution or perversion, authorities often invoked the capacious and difficult-to-refute "likely to become a public charge" clause. While they focused much attention on Asian women and women traveling alone, they also worried about "white slavery," or the trafficking of European women for sex. Immigration officials conducted investigations in Europe, New York City, and along the Mexican border with the intention of better understanding and eventually solving the problem of white slavery. In 1910, Congress made it a felony to transport "any woman or girl for the purpose of prostitution or debauchery, or for any other immoral purpose" across state lines or national borders. That same year, the Immigration Act of 1910 made prostitution a deportable offense regardless of how long someone had lived in the United States, marking an important shift toward deporting immigrants based on their actions after entering the country, rather than as people who should have been excluded upon arrival. This new emphasis on what legal scholar Daniel Kanstroom has called "post-entry social control" would only increase in the years and decades ahead, drawing an ever-harder line between citizens and noncitizens in the eyes of the law.[44]

Restrictionists and government officials also had a long history of targeting political radicals for formal removal. The bombing in Chicago's Haymarket Square during a Knights of Labor strike in 1886, the assassination of President William McKinley by an anarchist in 1901, and the founding of the militant Industrial Workers of the World labor union in 1905 heightened concerns about subversive foreigners. Congress had called for the exclusion and deportation of anarchists as early as 1903, but fears about radicals and so-called hyphenated Americans reached new heights during World War I. Presidents Theodore Roosevelt and Woodrow Wilson demanded loyalty to the country and "100 per cent Americanism." States enacted laws making it illegal to teach German in schools and renaming hamburgers "liberty sandwiches." Educators, employers, ethnic organizations, and local, state, and federal agencies all participated in a national movement to Americanize immigrants. And Congress passed the 1917 Immigration Act, a law that expanded the number of excludable and deportable classes to include people convicted of "a crime involving moral turpitude," and increased the statute of limitations on expulsion to five years for some offenses while eliminating time limits altogether for others. The act also implemented a literacy test and an $8 head tax on immigrants that the IRL had pushed for since the late nineteenth century, and simultaneously established a "barred zone" that extended exclusion to most of Asia. The campaign against political radicals continued after the war ended. In 1919 and 1920, a series of bombs mailed to public officials, including one that detonated outside the home of Attorney General Mitchell Palmer, prompted a unit within the Department of Justice (led by a young J. Edgar Hoover) and the Bureau of Immigration to carry out mass raids that resulted in the apprehension of some 10,000 suspected anarchists and the deportation of at least 500 people.[45]

## The Process of Formal Deportation

At the same time Congress gave the immigration bureaucracy broad authority to deport people for any number of reasons related to economics, race, politics, health, gender, sexuality, or ability, federal officials also established a standardized procedure to formally expel noncitizens. Local immigration commissioners appointed boards of special inquiry—consisting of an inspector, an interpreter, and a stenographer—that conducted investigations and held closed-door administrative hearings to determine someone's potential eligibility for deportation. Inspectors received tips from police, charitable organizations, hospitals and institutions, and individuals with motives sometimes known but mainly unknown. Foreigners faced deportation proceedings where they typically had neither the right to counsel nor the ability to call witnesses in their defense. The board's recommendation then went to the commissioner general of immigration for a warrant of removal. Immigrants had the ability to appeal rulings against them. These cases went to the secretary of labor for a final decision. If federal authorities ordered someone deported, they then had to arrange and pay to transport the person first to a port on the East or West Coast or the northern or southern land border and, finally, out of the United States.[46]

Officials within the immigration bureaucracy enjoyed tremendous discretionary power. In some cases, even low-level officers without any special legal training or knowledge served as inspector, interpreter, and stenographer, single-handedly deciding immigrants' fates.[47] A variety of authorities on the ground had such a broad mandate that one critic of the bureau described them in 1936 not as law enforcers, but as "self-constituted, lawmaker[s]."[48] As a federal judge put it, "If the Commissioners [of immigration] wish to order an alien drawn, quartered, and chucked overboard they could do so without interference."[49] Rhetorical flourish aside, the judge's statement reflected a larger truth: The deportation machine that legislators and immigration bureaucrats established during these decades prioritized speed and economy over people's constitutional right to due process.[50]

This fact bothered Louis F. Post, a populist lawyer and editor who, as assistant secretary of labor in the early 1920s, lamented that "whereas a citizen cannot be punished without substantial cause and after conviction at a judicial trial, an alien may be banished for frivolous causes and by autocratic 'administrative process.'" During the "Red Raids" and "deportation deliriums" of 1920, Post used his authority to lower or waive exorbitant bail for detained immigrants and cancel what he saw as 2,700 arbitrary and unlawful expulsion orders against alleged communists.[51] These bold actions, unpopular with much of the public and among legislators (who held hearings and called for his impeachment), led one newspaper columnist to write: "In the machinery which the United States government has set in motion to rid the nation of those strangers within its gates ... there has been tossed a wrench which damages the whole mechanism. That wrench is Assistant Secretary of Labor Louis F. Post."[52] On rare occasions, discretion worked in immigrants' favor.

Despite the streamlined procedure that officials depended on to formally deport people from the United States, the agency found itself stretched beyond its limited capacity as expulsions increased. Between 1892 and 1907, officials removed fewer than 500 people per year under general warrant proceedings and 300 per year via Chinese exclusion. Deportations paled in comparison to the 584,000 annual admissions during the same period. Over the course of the next dozen years, changes to immigration law, augmented enforcement appropriations, and growing xenophobia during World War I resulted in formal deportations rising to around 3,000 per year.[53] As they did, new organizations like the American Civil Liberties Union, Hebrew Immigrant Aid Society, and Foreign Language Information Service organized in defense of noncitizens, mounting legal challenges to authorities' arbitrary decisions. Altogether, investigations, hearings, appeals, and the detention and transportation of deportees both internally and internationally took time and required considerable federal resources.[54]

Complications related to foreign relations sometimes gummed up the machine's gears as well because officials first had to establish immigrants' nationalities, obtain travel documents, and confirm that people's countries of origin would accept them before they could be formally deported. During the height of the Red Scare in the aftermath of World War I and the Russian Revolution, removing radicals to Russia proved problematic since the United States had no diplomatic relations with the new postrevolutionary government. To sidestep this obstacle, officials searched for third-party countries willing to accept Russian expellees and facilitate their return. Such was the case in December 1919, when US officials deported well-known anarchists Emma Goldman and Alexander Berkman, along with 247 others, on the SS *Buford* (also known as the Russian Ark) after securing their removal via Finland. If authorities failed to find another nation willing to take immigrants, people ended up stuck in limbo. From 1916 to 1919, questions of international relations, safety, and transportation during the war forced officials to suspend more than 3,200 removals to Europe. But challenges stemming from deportation's bilateral nature continued long after the armistice. Asked during a 1926 congressional hearing whether authorities "ever have any difficulty in securing the approval of the country to which you intend to send" a deportee, Assistant Secretary of Labor Robe Carl White responded: "Oh, yes; we have questions arising all the time. We have two or three aliens in custody now who have been in custody for some time, waiting passports, because the country to which they are going refuses to issue the passport on the ground they have no record of his having been born there."[55]

Scholars have examined this history in depth, charting the evolution of deportation law and policy, the steady expansion of expellable classes, and officials' attempts to exclude and remove immigrants from Asia and southern and eastern Europe from the 1880s to the 1920s.[56] But a different story of deportation emerges if we broaden our perspective beyond formal expulsions and reckon with the various mechanisms officials have relied on throughout US history to push people out of the country.

## Mechanism 3: Voluntary Departure

The financial and legal restrictions limiting the immigration bureaucracy's ability to formally deport people led officers to develop an alternative, ad hoc means of expulsion: voluntary departure. Under voluntary departure, immigration officials across the country permitted or coerced apprehended immigrants to leave "on their own." The mechanism proved to be expeditious because it allowed officials to sidestep the rigid legal process that formal deportations entailed and made deportation a unilateral decision, rather than a question of international relations. Voluntary departure reduced both the number of arrest warrants issued and the number of people awaiting administrative hearings, thus saving the bureaucracy money and minimizing or eliminating the time immigrants spent in detention as cases worked their way through the system. Immigrants also benefited from avoiding legal bars on reentry after formal deportation.[57]

The federal government began tracking voluntary departures in 1927, but a close reading of the archival record reveals that authorities relied on them as early as 1907—two decades earlier than most historians previously thought and thirty-three years before the immigration bureaucracy gained the statutory authority to carry them out. The 1907 annual report of the commissioner general of immigration noted that authorities had carried out "336 deportations and an unknown number of voluntary departures." Officials used this informal expulsion mechanism to expel people to China, Japan, and countries across Europe. But more than anything, they relied on voluntary departure to deport Canadians and especially Mexicans who had entered the United States without inspection.[58] Authorities, of course, found it much easier to send immigrants across the northern or southern land border than to ship them across the Atlantic or Pacific Ocean.[59] The earliest recorded voluntary departure of a Mexican immigrant that I found occurred in 1908 or 1909 after a man facing formal deportation in El Paso grew restive during his prolonged detention. He contacted the local Mexican consul general and made clear "that he would be glad to go to Mexico without awaiting the Department's action if the immigration officers would permit him to do so." US authorities granted the detained man's "urgent request" and allowed him to voluntarily depart.[60]

Voluntary departure's rise to prominence as officials' go-to expulsion mechanism in the years ahead has inextricable connections to the history of large-scale Mexican migration to the United States. Until the mid-nineteenth century, most of the US Southwest was part of Mexico. The Mexican–American War of 1846–48 changed that. The United States' conquest of nearly half of Mexico's territory coincided with the discovery of gold in California. In the years that followed, a small number of Mexicans joined the throngs of people who traveled to California from around the world in search of the precious metal.[61] But Mexicans did not start heading north in large numbers until after the 1907 Gentlemen's Agreement between the United States and Japan put an end to significant labor migration from Asia. As US employers came to depend on Mexican labor as never before, Mexican immigration shot up, going from an average of just a few hundred per year between 1899 and 1907 to around 15,600 in 1909.[62] Ongoing labor demand and US companies' active recruitment of Mexican workers, combined with the two countries' economic disparities and geographic proximity, caused migration to the United States to grow even more after 1910. At the same time, some Mexicans fled north to escape the violence and political and social unrest of the Mexican Revolution. And tens of thousands of Mexican agricultural guest workers toiled in the United States during World War I. The extensive railroad network crisscrossing North America facilitated this migration. From 1910 to 1921, an average of nearly 20,000 Mexicans immigrated each year, including more than 51,000 in 1920 alone.[63]

As authorized Mexican migration increased, the number of people who entered the country surreptitiously did too, quickly overwhelming federal officials in the Southwest. Entry without inspection became a deportable offense during the first decade of the 1900s. A proposed amendment to the Immigration Act of 1903 would have made deportable any immigrant who did not cross into the United States at a designated port of entry. Although legislators seem to have struck the amendment from the final version of the law, the immigration bureaucracy began arresting people for "attempting surreptitious entry" as early as August 1903, indicating that the act of that year gave officials the authority to deport people for entry without inspection.[64] By 1915, voluntary departures outnumbered formal deportations in the border region. The following year, the supervising inspector overseeing the nearly 2,000-mile international divide reported that "no inconsiderable number of Mexican aliens found unlawfully resident in the immediate vicinity of the border—whose only offense is the technical one of entry without inspection—were permitted of their own volition . . . to return to Mexico." This, he explained, "sav[ed] time, expense, and labor, and greatly ameliorat[ed] hardships to the aliens involved."[65]

The years 1917 and 1918 marked a turning point in the history of Mexican migration and immigration enforcement policy. In late January 1917, fears of typhus and other contagious diseases led US immigration and public health officials to quarantine and disinfect all people crossing the border from Ciudad Juárez to El Paso.[66] A couple of weeks later, Congress implemented the literacy test and head tax as part of the Immigration Act of 1917, although legislators also created a loophole for wartime guest workers.[67] The following year, another act aimed at excluding subversives required anyone arriving to the United States to present a passport at an official port of entry. (Protests soon pushed officials to create ways for many local border residents to come and go.) Around the same time, the Bureau of Immigration sent additional officers to the southwest border "as a war measure to protect the country against the ingress and egress of enemy agents and intermediaries." But many of these agents ended up policing unauthorized Mexican migration instead.[68]

While formal deportations along the southwest border increased by nearly 50 percent between fiscal years 1917 and 1918, voluntary departures surged by more than 1,200 percent. During fiscal year 1918, voluntary departures to Mexico (3,811) outpaced formal expulsions across the nation for all nationalities combined (1,569) by more than two to one. A similar gap persisted in the years ahead.[69] In 1921, an economic recession, an unemployment crisis, and the expiration of wartime waivers on Mexican labor migration caused informal expulsions to jump to 7,482. That year, officials in the Southwest deported more than 80 percent of all apprehended immigrants via voluntary departure.[70] As an inspector in Douglas, Arizona, explained two years later, "Practically all of the aliens that can be handled from jail are permitted to voluntarily return to Mexico from this Port."[71] In these cases, simple arrests resulted in deportation—no conviction necessary. Authorities' exploitation of this other means of expulsion expanded the power and reach of both individual officers and the bureaucracy as a whole.

Immigration historians argue that federal officials did not make the regulation of unauthorized Mexican migrants a central focus of their efforts until after 1924, the year Congress passed the Johnson-Reed Act. The law indefinitely extended Asian exclusion and implemented a system of national origins quotas that severely restricted southern and eastern European immigration, but did not apply to the Western Hemisphere. That same year, legislators appropriated money to create the Border Patrol.[72] This is well-trodden ground, and rightfully so given the lasting impact the Immigration Act of 1924 had on the composition of the United States in the decades to come. But seeing the machine and its multiple expulsion mechanisms in

| Fiscal year | LPC[1] | Unable to read[2] | Diseases[3] | Anarchists[4] | Criminals[5] | All formal deportations | EWI (Mexican)/ Vol. departure[6] |
|---|---|---|---|---|---|---|---|
| 1918 | 401 | 67 | 15 | 2 | 57 | 1,569 | 3,811 |
| 1919 | 1,150 | 466 | 54 | 37 | 175 | 3,021 | 4,466 |
| 1920 | 808 | 171 | 80 | 314 | 229 | 2,751 | 4,096 |
| 1921 | 1,293 | 328 | 113 | 446 | 316 | 4,517 | 7,482 |
| 1918–21 | 3,652 | 1,032 | 262 | 799 | 777 | 11,858 | 19,855 |

Figure 5.  Formal deportations by reason and voluntary departures to Mexico after entry without inspection, fiscal years 1918–21.

1. "Likely to become a public charge";
2. "Unable to read (over 16 years of age)";
3. "Loathsome or dangerous contagious diseases";
4. "Anarchists," before or after entry;
5. "Criminals," before or after entry; and
6. Mexicans who entered without inspection, deported via voluntary departure.

Commissioner General of Immigration (CGI), AR 1918, 152–55; CGI, AR 1919, 184–87; CGI, AR 1920, 200–203; CGI, AR 1921, 120–23; Harris to CGI, Aug. 10, 1921, 53244/1C, Entry 9, RG 85, INS, NARA1. Table by author.

the whole allows us to see that federal immigration authorities did not just execute 11,858 removals between 1918 and 1921. In fact, they carried out a total of 31,713 expulsions—nearly two-thirds of them voluntary departures (see figure 5).[73] Immigration officers throughout the country still dedicated much of their energies to excluding and formally expelling Asians and undesirable Europeans, but the typical deportee was no longer a Chinese or Japanese laborer, Italian or Russian political radical, or foreigner deemed likely to become a public charge. According to the aggregate data, by the late 1910s the typical deportee was a Mexican who had entered the country without inspection.[74]

In the late nineteenth century, violence- and fear-fueled self-deportation drives against the Chinese contributed to the creation of a federal immigration bureaucracy instilled with the power to formally deport. Even though the number of expulsions remained relatively low, a shortage of funding and a lack of political will curbed authorities' ability to remove people. As a result, rather than obviating the need for self-deportation campaigns, federal control over immigration came to depend on them. Tactics similar to those used in Truckee soon became core components of the deportation machine. Periodic immigration raids, the persistent targeting of Chinese people, and the "crusades" during the Red Scare of 1919–20 caused alarm and created a "psychology of fear" in immigrant communities.[75] Armed mobs and other non–state actors also continued to use vigilante violence (or the threat of violence) to force and coerce people into leaving.[76] And the very existence of the newly created federal bureaucracy tasked with policing the nation's borders scared some people out of the country. The Border Patrol, a Los Angeles official reported in 1925, "has not only been the means of apprehending and deporting, or causing the voluntary departure under supervision of the aliens shown in the reports submitted." Even more, this perceptive bureaucrat observed that "the influence of this service has been felt by hundreds of aliens who, being illegally in the United States and hearing of the patrol activities, have hurriedly departed to Mexico."[77]

Low- and mid-level immigration officials throughout the country also used their discretionary authority to circumvent the fledgling agency's limitations since the power to formally deport contained within it the ability to remove people via voluntary departure. This informal expulsion mechanism would prove essential to the machine's basic functionality, the immigration bureaucracy's growth, and even the United States' claim to legitimacy as a sovereign nation. But in the early twentieth century, the central office policy regarding these ad hoc, administrative expulsions wavered. In August 1921, George Harris, the acting supervising inspector of the US–Mexico border region, wrote to the commissioner general asking him to lift an injunction that prevented local immigration officers from granting voluntary departure to people awaiting removal hearings. The injunction, he argued, "was rather more rigid than necessary and that on this Border in particular, discretion might very well be allowed . . . without harmful results." In some cases, administrative hearings were neither necessary nor fiscally feasible, according to Harris. "If the alien does not want his day in court, why not let him return to Mexico instead of holding him anywhere from two or three weeks to a month or more? Why insist in such cases that the alien shall remain locked up at the expense of the Government until the Department has had opportunity to act on the record?" Harris, who expected his district to run a deficit as high as $37,500 in the coming year (more than $500,000 today), noted that removing the injunction would "without doubt result in the saving of many thousands of dollars."[78]

Inspectors increasingly relied on voluntary departures in the years ahead, but sometimes questioned their decision to do so. In February 1925, John P. Johnson, an immigration official in Boston, Massachusetts, reported several instances in which people facing formal expulsion proceedings who "would be deported to Canada eventually" requested to leave voluntarily. "In one case," Johnson wrote, "the alien was in an advanced stage of pregnancy and our Doctor ordered her to the hospital, where she might remain the greater part of the time until confinement, which would of course be a very heavy drain on our none too large allotment." He granted the woman voluntary departure, as he had with numerous other immigrants, "merely as a matter of economy." Yet, he confessed, "I am not entirely satisfied in my own mind whether my action is proper or not."[79]

Just how far did individual immigration officials' authority extend? Did their considerable discretionary power allow them to act autonomously? Or did they have to run deportation decisions through the centralized bureaucracy? The answers to these questions lay somewhere in the middle. Inspectors could take unilateral action in cases in which the apprehended migrant posed no threat and could be easily returned. However, if authorities had already issued a warrant for someone, then low-level officials had to send their decisions up the chain of command. That is why the commissioner general thanked Johnson for acting with the bureau's interests in mind, but also asked the Boston-based officer to check with the central office in the future before extending voluntary departure to an immigrant already in deportation proceedings.[80]

Ultimately, however, immigration officials cared most about maximizing the number of expulsions. As Johnson himself noted, "the sole purpose in deportation proceedings is to effect the departure from the United States of inadmissible aliens, under warrant."[81] *How* that happened was of secondary importance to authorities. Such hardheaded, and soon-to-be brutal, pragmatism continued to hold sway in the decades ahead, as officials across the nation tried to control unprecedented Mexican migration by any means necessary.

# TWO

# Coerced Removal from the Great Depression through Operation Wetback

Grover Cleveland Wilmoth was never anything more than a mid-level bureaucrat. Born near Denton, Texas, in 1884 and raised in Virginia, Wilmoth started working for the Post Office Department in Washington, DC, at the age of fifteen, after a short stint with the Weather Bureau. But he spent most of his career in Texas, working for the Immigration Service, first as a stenographer and typist and then as an immigration inspector tasked with breaking up rings that smuggled Chinese migrants. He excelled in his work, displaying "unusual interest" and "zeal." "This employee," his supervisor wrote in 1917, "typifies almost the ideal, and his value to the Service is in many ways incalculable." Around a decade later, Wilmoth was named district director in El Paso, a post he held for the next quarter century. Overseeing immigration and enforcement in one of the busiest border crossing regions of the Southwest afforded Wilmoth rare insights into the implementation and making of policy on the ground—insights that would not have been possible had he continued to ascend the ranks of the federal agency.[1]

Much of what Wilmoth observed in El Paso concerned him. The most significant challenge facing the service had to do with budgetary constraints that limited immigration officials' ability to carry out their mission. In January 1926, two months before Wilmoth became district director, his predecessor declared that the financial situation was so bleak that for the second half of that fiscal year "no expense of whatsoever character shall be incurred unless vitally and urgently necessary." To stretch the region's funding, he ordered his charges to rely on "voluntary returns in the cases of Mexicans in lieu of [formal] deportation proceedings." Wilmoth continued this policy when he took over and went a step further when he gave patrol inspectors on the line the power to execute voluntary departures at the nearest border point. "No money should be spent for the maintenance or detention of any Mexican alien, or of any Canadian alien, or any able-bodied alien seaman of whatever nationality, if such can possibly be avoided," he wrote in March 1927. "With the exercise of the most rigid economy, we may be able to handle the majority of European and Asiatic aliens, but it is impossible to get sufficient funds with which to do more than that. . . . A real emergency in the matter of finances now confronts the entire Service as well as this district."[2]

The pressures on the Immigration Service grew worse in the years ahead as officials shifted their energies and resources to controlling Mexican migration. Whereas Mexicans represented 17 percent of all formal deportees in 1924, they constituted 63 percent of that group four decades later. During the same period, Europeans went from making up 44 percent to only 13 percent of all formal deportees. Mexicans also accounted for more than nine out of every ten voluntary departures and total deportations.[3]

Voluntary departure and anti-immigrant fear campaigns became the dominant mechanisms of expulsion during the middle decades of the twentieth century. This chapter shows how and why this happened—and how and why immigration officials came to primarily target Mexicans—through a fine-grained analysis of the repatriations of the 1930s and Operation Wetback of the mid-1950s. Few formal deportations occurred during these campaigns, despite the fact that both efforts resulted in hundreds of thousands of Mexicans leaving the United States. In fact, between 1927 and 1964, voluntary departures outnumbered formal deportations nearly nine to one, representing more than 90 percent of the nearly 6.4 million expulsions the federal government recorded (see figure 6).[4] An unknown number of others left in response to concerted self-deportation efforts at the local, state, and national levels.

Unlike formal removals, these coercive mechanisms enabled authorities to unilaterally execute mass expulsions on an unprecedented scale and on a shoestring budget, all while bolstering the fledgling agency's institutional legitimacy within the growing federal bureaucracy. These other means of

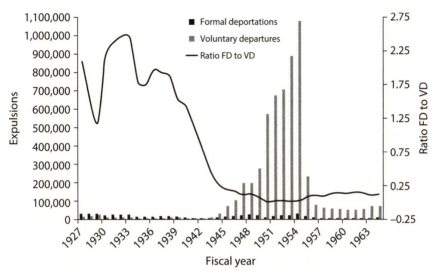

**Figure 6. Expulsions by type and ratio of formal deportations to voluntary departures, fiscal years 1927–64.** On the left Y-axis is the number of expulsions by type. On the right Y-axis is the ratio of formal deportations to voluntary departures. The number of repatriations and self-deportations are unknown and incalculable, and therefore not included. DHS, *YOIS: 2017*, 103. Calculations and graph by author.

deportation served to fashion state power as much as control migration.[5] They also effectively denied due process rights to citizens and noncitizens alike and inflicted trauma on individuals, families, and communities. Examining two of the most notorious deportation drives in US history side by side offers insights not only into the machine's inner workings, but also into the future of immigration enforcement for the remainder of the century and beyond.

## Demonizing and Deporting Mexicans during the Great Depression

Though immigration officials began singling out Mexicans who entered the country surreptitiously in the 1910s, authorities placed an even greater emphasis on controlling the nation's borders after the mid- to late 1920s. In addition to implementing a numerical restriction on immigration, the Johnson-Reed Act of 1924 called for the deportation of anyone who had violated the law by entering the United States without inspection or by overstaying a visa—regardless of how long the person had lived in the country. That same year, Congress's decision to establish the Border Patrol resulted in extra attention on regulating the nation's land borders. Five years later, the Immigration Act of March 4, 1929, made unauthorized entry a misdemeanor and reentry after deportation a felony, each punishable by a fine of up to $1,000 and a one- or two-year prison sentence.[6]

Yet after Congress approved and new president Herbert Hoover signed the 1929 act, insufficient allocations prevented the Immigration Service from fully implementing its provisions and forced the agency to increasingly rely on alternate, cheaper means of deporting the vast majority of Mexicans. "The Assistant US Attorney in charge at El Paso does not contemplate authorizing the institutional or criminal proceedings in all cases under the Act of March 4, 1929, but will select the strongest cases from those presented to him," Grover Wilmoth explained. All other apprehended migrants would continue to be expelled via voluntary departure, even though Wilmoth later expressed concern that "some day an immigration officer will erroneously extend the voluntary departure privilege to an American citizen of alien appearance, and one incident of the sort, with a claim of coercion, given sufficient publicity may do this Service irreparable injury."[7]

Despite these reservations, Wilmoth and other officials in the cash-strapped agency had little to no choice in the matter. Formally deporting someone entailed an elaborate process consisting of ten or more steps, including formal questioning, additional investigation, a hearing, and a review of each case by at least a handful of officials up and down the bureaucracy and a review board. At that point, if the assistant secretary decided to issue a warrant of deportation, people had the right to challenge the case in court through a writ of habeas corpus. And even if immigrants' legal appeals failed, US authorities still had to determine their nationality and confirm that their country of origin (or a third-party country) would accept them. Voluntary departures, by contrast, could be carried out after the arresting officer asked some informal questions and conducted a perfunctory examination.[8] There were no bureaucratic hoops to jump through, no courts involved, no burdensome paperwork to complete, and no need to make immigration enforcement a matter of international relations—just streamlined, expedited, unilateral expulsions without which the deportation machine would have come to a grinding halt.

After the 1929 act went into effect, authorities also became increasingly aware of the power of scare tactics to exert control over noncitizens, and especially Mexicans. The act, an immigration official observed, had "put the fear of God in their hearts." Fear of apprehension and deportation became so pervasive in Mexican communities across the country that it changed the bureau's enforcement strategy. Whereas the Bureau of Immigration used to send undercover agents into dance halls to collect intelligence in hopes of building cases against people, under the new law authorities realized that all they had to do was send in a couple of uniformed officers. As one agent explained, "In a few minutes, the people who are here illegally begin to sneak out only to fall into the arms of a cordon who are waiting for them. A guilty conscience does the job." Though such fear may have been impossible to quantify, it was very real and caused a considerable number of people to preemptively leave the country.[9]

That fall, the stock market crash of October 1929 and the onset of the Great Depression led to spiking unemployment, heightened anxiety levels, and the widespread scapegoating of immigrants. The beliefs that foreigners stole US citizens' jobs, drained public coffers, carried diseases, committed crimes, and harbored communist and radical political views resulted in a rising chorus across the country calling for their expulsion. William Randolph Hearst, the nation's most powerful media mogul, repeatedly used the pages of his twenty-eight newspapers (which reached 5.5 million daily subscribers and 7 million people on Sunday) to call for deportations and harsher immigration laws. "The farmer rids his barn of rats, his hen house of weasels. Good housekeepers wage ceaseless war against vermin. And employers, will not have dishonest people about them," read an August 1930 editorial in the *San Antonio Light*, a Hearst paper. "No man keeps in his own house those that are enemies of his family or for any other reason harmful. Uncle Sam should clear his house, clear it thoroughly of all 'undesirables.'"[10]

Citizens expressed similar opinions—and outrage—in letters to public officials. "Despite our disastrous experience since colonial days creating race problem after race problem, Negro, Chinese, Japanese, Filipino and now the Mexican Indian, have we learned anything as a nation?" J. C. Brodie, head of the Democratic Committee of Superior, Arizona, asked his senator. During the 1930s, Brodie gained a reputation of "flooding prominent persons with communications of [this] nature," claiming that Mexicans had pushed millions of citizens out of jobs and into bread lines, lowered the country's morale and living standards, and infected the "white American population" with everything from smallpox and meningitis to typhoid and venereal diseases. Though it would have been easy to dismiss Brodie as a crank or an extremist, authorities recognized that a sizable portion of the population supported his positions. People in Arizona and other states formed "America for Americans" nativist societies, based in part on the Ku Klux Klan (which itself had experienced a resurgence during the previous decade), that advocated policies and actions similar to those that Brodie preached. What he preached was mass deportation. "The way to cure a disease is to remove it's [sic] cause, not treat the symptoms and we are treating symptoms," he wrote to an immigration official. "The cause is Mass alien employment and mass alien indigence; the cure is . . . the deportation of alien indigents."[11]

In early January 1931, William N. Doak, the newly appointed secretary of labor who oversaw the Bureau of Immigration, told Congress that some 400,000 people resided in the United States without authorization. Estimating that as many as a quarter of them could be deported immediately, Doak set out to remove "every evader of our alien laws, regardless of nationality, creed or color." During his tenure, a contemporary commentator observed that "alien hunting . . . became a gladiatorial spectacle" in which agents raided homes, churches, picket lines, public spaces, bars, dance halls, and pool halls, sometimes without a warrant. Though immigrant communities, academics, government commissions, and rights groups like the American Civil Liberties Union (ACLU) denounced and vehemently protested the arbitrariness and harshness of such practices, the secretary of labor stood defiant. "If we can't raid these places, where the hell do you expect we are going to get these fellows?" It was the federal government's responsibility to "protect its own citizens against illegal invaders," Doak said, and he made clear that he would use "every weapon in [his] power" to do just that. "The gates of the promised land have been closed," he wrote in an op-ed later that summer. "Our self-preservation has demanded it."[12]

Fear campaigns and immigration raids that ran roughshod over citizens' and noncitizens' rights proved to be two of Doak's favorite "weapons" to expel people. Local officials collaborated in organizing and carrying out these large-scale self-deportation drives and roundups, which frequently worked in unison. In Los Angeles, Charles P. Visel, head of the city's Citizens Committee on Coordination of Unemployment Relief, developed a multipronged expulsion plan after learning about the secretary of labor's intentions. Visel wrote to Doak, describing how the presence of a small number of federal agents would serve as a "psychological gesture" that, accompanied by a well-orchestrated publicity campaign complete with photographs of apprehensions, might "scare many thousand alien deportables" into leaving Los Angeles. Walter Carr, the local district director of immigration, agreed. He acknowledged that "the machinery set up for deportation would be entirely inadequate on a large scale," but reasoned that "with a little deportation publicity, a large number of these aliens, actuated by guilty self-consciousness, would move south and over the line on their own accord, particularly if stimulated by a few arrests."[13]

On January 26, Visel put his "scareheading" strategy into action when he sent a press release to all of the major English- and Spanish-language newspapers in Los Angeles announcing that federal immigration officials, with the assistance of the local police and county sheriff, would be conducting immigration raids throughout the area. In the days that followed, the *Los Angeles Times*, *Illustrated Daily News*, *Express*, and *La Opinión* ran long articles publicizing the upcoming operation. A front-page article in *La Opinión*, published under the sensational headline "The Next Mexican Raid," instructed anyone in the country without authorization to turn themselves in to authorities (see figure 7a–d). Rafael de la Colina, the Mexican consul in Los Angeles, reported that such coverage "caused considerable alarm among the large Mexican population here." US and Mexican officials' statements denying that the operation targeted any one group did little to quell the pervasive fear that enveloped the city's Mexican neighborhoods.[14]

The second phase of Visel's plan commenced a week later, on Monday, February 3, when federal agents began apprehending immigrants. Over the course of the next few weeks, officials fanned out across Los Angeles and the surrounding area, apprehending people in a piecemeal fashion and carrying out blanket raids in a part of the city known as Sonora Town because of its high concentration of Mexican residents. As the raids continued and word spread about mass deportations without regard to individuals' rights or possible legal remedies, people soon decided it was better to stay home than risk apprehension. The local merchants' association, whose members

**LA OPINION**
DIARIO POPULAR INDEPENDIENTE

# PROXIMA RAZZIA DE MEXICANOS

**LA OPINION**
DIARIO POPULAR INDEPENDIENTE

# SE ACTIVAN LAS DEPORTACIONES

**LA OPINION**
DIARIO POPULAR INDEPENDIENTE

# 11 MEXICANOS PRESOS EN UN APARATOSO RAID A LA PLACITA

# PASAJES GRATUITOS A MEXICO!

**LA OPINION**
DIARIO POPULAR INDEPENDIENTE

# RAID A 6 CASAS DE PRESTAMOS
## 600 Deportados Salen de Mexicali

Figure 7.  Sensational headlines announce immigration raids and report on mass deportations to Mexico.
*La Opinión*, January to March 1931, CSRC.

started a legal defense fund for apprehended immigrants, complained to the Mexican consul that the sweeps had resulted in the virtual "incarceration of foreigners," who had "stopped buying all but [the] barest necessities." Visel, for his part, was thrilled. As he wrote to Colonel Arthur Woods, national coordinator of the President's Emergency Committee for Employment, the joint effort had been "functioning 100% efficiently, quietly, with what we feel is probably the maximum result."[15]

A couple of prominent, large-scale operations further stoked fears within the community. On Friday, February 13, federal and local authorities stopped and questioned some 300 people in suburban El Monte, apprehending thirteen people, all but one of them ethnic Mexicans, including at least four who had lived in the United States for at least seven years and another described as an "American-born Mexican."[16] Two weeks later, on February 26, 1931, six immigration agents in olive green khaki uniforms and a couple dozen Los Angeles police officers carried out another raid on La Placita in downtown Los Angeles. The officials converged on the crowded public plaza at 3:00 p.m., sealing it off and forcing all present to remain seated, which "caused tremendous panic" according to the front-page article that ran the next day in *La Opinión*. They held hundreds of people for over an hour as they interrogated everyone while a large crowd gathered and watched. Authorities apprehended just seventeen people that afternoon: a Japanese man, five Chinese immigrants, and eleven Mexicans, including a legal US resident who presented his papers but was taken anyway. Officials in Los Angeles deported more than 400 people and stopped and questioned ten times that many during the first month of the campaign.[17]

Apprehension and deportation statistics did not include the vast majority of people who left the United States in the decade after 1929. As the Depression dragged on, cities and counties across the nation came to the conclusion that they could save hundreds of thousands of dollars by repatriating people instead of keeping them on the relief rolls.[18] Acting as de facto immigration agents, local welfare officials and social workers tried to coerce people into departing by threatening to cut off their unemployment benefits and offering to pay for their travel out of the country. Authorities also relied on the power of rumor and exaggeration to do some of the work for them. As sociologist Emory Bogardus noted in 1933, "It takes only an insinuation from a welfare official in the United States to create widespread fear among Mexican immigrants."[19] The repatriation program proved so successful and cost-effective in Los Angeles, where around one-third of the city's ethnic Mexican population packed up and left, that residents came to regard it "as a piece of consummate statescraft," according to writer Carey McWilliams.[20] Though some localities also targeted Filipinos and Europeans for repatriation, they directed most of their energies and funds toward expelling ethnic Mexicans (regardless of legal status or citizenship), whom they considered unassimilable in addition to being a drain on the economy.[21]

The Mexican state, steeped in postrevolutionary nationalism and eager to spark economic growth, encouraged this southbound migration by announcing that it would waive duties on automobiles, appliances, and other household items, as well as provide free land and transportation from the border to those who returned. Though some people who wanted to return to Mexico took advantage of this unique opportunity to do so, most repatriations fell into what one scholar described as the "huge twilight zone between voluntary and forced migration." And despite the nationalist rhetoric, Mexican society greeted repatriates with ambivalence, rather than open arms.[22]

Although it is impossible to determine exactly how many people left the United States during the Great Depression or pinpoint what influenced each individual's decision, one thing is clear: The collective efforts of local, state, and federal officials caused or contributed to the repatriation of as many as half a million Mexicans and Mexican Americans between 1929 and 1939. Federal deportation statistics do not account for these self-deportations, but the pressure officials put on people and the coercive environment they created is not in question. Fear campaigns served as the primary expulsion mechanism in the 1930s. Government officials repatriated more than twice as many Mexicans in 1931 alone (138,500) as they formally deported during the entire decade (64,000).[23] Authorities' simultaneous reliance on formal deportations, voluntary departures, and self-deportation drives showed what the machine was capable of, even in these early years, when operating on all cylinders. And, whether intentional or not, these officials provided a blueprint for how to churn out mass expulsions on the cheap. Officials would turn to this strategy frequently in the decades ahead.

## Operation Wetback and the Mass Expulsion Campaigns of the Bracero Era

The start of World War II in 1939 sparked economic growth that helped pull the United States out of the decade-long Great Depression. The international conflict also led to heightened concerns about internal security and the four million foreign-born people living in the country. The following year, Congress transferred the Immigration and Naturalization Service (INS) from the Department of Labor to the Department of Justice. Legislators also passed the Alien Registration Act, which required noncitizens to provide their fingerprints and addresses to federal officials. Yet authorities did not treat all immigrants equally. Throughout the 1930s and 1940s, US officials used their administrative discretion to cancel the formal deportations of people with long-term residence, individuals without a criminal record whose expulsion would cause economic hardship to their families, and anyone judged to have an "exceptionally meritorious" case. Authorities used these seemingly race-neutral policies to "unmake the illegality" of European immigrants, while denying the same benefits to Mexicans and Asians.[24]

The Alien Registration Act of 1940 also gave the immigration bureaucracy the statutory authority, for the first time, to do what individual officers had long handled on an ad hoc basis: offer voluntary departure to noncitizens of "good moral character" facing deportation and willing to pay their own way.[25] Although Congress formalized this power as a privilege for migrants who posed no threat (and as a cost-saving measure), voluntary departure proved punitive in practice.

The war also ushered in a new era of Mexican migration. In 1942, the United States and Mexico agreed to a wartime measure that ended up being the first in a series of binational labor agreements between the countries. From 1942 to 1964, the two governments issued more than 4.6 million short-term contracts to more than 400,000 Mexican men who went to the United States as agricultural guest workers as part of what came to be known as the Bracero Program. (The word *bracero*, from the Spanish word *brazo*, referred to the strong arms of Mexican laborers.) During the war years, some braceros also worked on the railroads. While the two countries initially decided on the terms of the program together, the US government and growers gained increasing control with each successive renegotiation and extension.[26]

In the postwar years, hundreds of thousands of Mexicans—both with and without contracts, and oftentimes in response to active labor recruitment from north of the border—continued migrating to the United States in search of work. The "wetback crisis" arose out of this context and came to define enforcement policy in the early 1950s. (The derogatory term "wetback" derived from migrants who entered the country without authorization by wading or swimming across the Rio Grande, though immigration officials and media outlets frequently used it to refer to any undocumented Mexican.) In 1954, the annual report of the INS described unauthorized migration as if it was a natural disaster that required immediate attention. "The influx of aliens illegally entered from Mexico appears like an incoming tide," noted the report in an attempt at metaphorical lyricism, "with mounting waves of people entering the country, and being sent back, and returning again but in ever greater volume, and always reaching further inland with each incoming wave."[27] News outlets disparaged unauthorized migrants and essentialized their physical and psychological beings. A May 1951 *LIFE* magazine article titled "Wetbacks Swarm In" noted the supposed "inexhaustible perseverance of the wetback" and concluded that because of "the patient invasion force" even the Border Patrol's "most valiant efforts" would prove to be "exasperatingly futile." The "wetback," the article continued, undercut domestic wages and would never be unemployed, "because he can weed a 1,000-foot furrow without once straightening up, and he willingly works with the short-handled hoe which, so much more efficient around delicate plants, tortures American spines."[28]

Organizations and private citizens also scapegoated unauthorized migrants. Dr. Hector P. Garcia, founder of the American GI Forum (AGIF), a Mexican American veterans' organization, wrote to Attorney General Herbert Brownell in August 1953 to "urge that whole border from California to Texas be effectively patrolled and closed to wetback invasion which is undermining our American standard of living."[29] Others wrote to Brownell with specific ideas for how to address the problem. A Phoenix man suggested offering "a $50.00 reward for information leading to the arrest and conviction of persons illegally in this country." He recommended placing those apprehended in "two very large Prisoner of War camps in Arizona" (with a total capacity of around 50,000), and then sentencing them to hard labor. "If these 'Wet-backs' had to work one year at hard labor without being paid for it, I am quite certain that this would be a deterrant [*sic*] in so far as any new

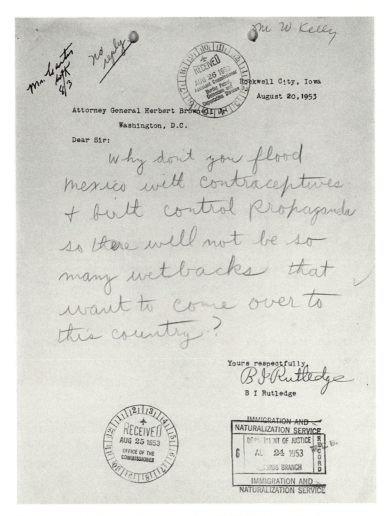

Figure 8. One citizen's suggestion for how to deal with the "wetback problem."
56364/45.7, Folder 2, Entry 9, RG 85, INS, NARA1.

arrivals are concerned."[30] And, in a handwritten note to the attorney general, Burtch I. Rutledge, a sixty-year-old farmer from a Republican stronghold in northwest Iowa, asked, "Why don't you flood Mexico with contraceptives + birth control propaganda so there will not be so many wetbacks that want to come over to this country?" (see figure 8).[31]

Although officials did not act on Rutledge's recommendation, they did target Mexican women, children, and entire families for expulsion (see figure 9).

Figure 9. A family deported from McAllen, Texas, begins the 400-mile trek home to the central Mexican state of San Luis Potosí, 1953.
56364/45.7, Folder 2, Entry 9, RG 85, INS, NARA1.

The Bracero Program's exclusion of women and children made them more likely to enter without inspection, whether in search of work or in order to reunite with relatives.[32] Women's deportation cases often differed from those of men. If authorities expelled men to control exploitable labor, they oftentimes removed women to regulate morality and social boundaries. Officials distinguished between "good" and "bad" women and specifically singled out those they deemed prostitutes. In some cases, Mexican authorities continued to monitor women's postdeportation actions. In 1948, a Mexican official in Matamoros wrote the chair of the civil service board to inform him that two young, recently expelled women had returned "without resources or any kind of protection." He asked the chair to "have the goodness to intervene" on behalf of the women on their trip home to ensure that "they don't take the wrong path, and do honorable work, so that they can return to their mother's side."[33]

But officials also targeted women, like men, for doing nothing more than entering the country without inspection. Their deportation frequently divided families and separated people from their material possessions. In February 1942, while detained in a Brownsville, Texas, jail, María Fernanda Prieto pleaded with authorities to reunite her with her three-year-old daughter and some of her clothes—all she had to her name. This was, she thought, "a request that I honestly never thought they were going reject on humanitarian grounds." Instead, immigration officials deported her. A month later Prieto wrote to Mexican migration officials, lamenting that "neither my first efforts, nor my later begging, nor prayers while they carried out my deportation had the slightest effect on [the US] authorities."[34] Something similar happened to Durango native Elena Gómez. She and her family entered the United States without authorization in 1944. Her husband died shortly thereafter, and for the next five years Gómez worked hard to provide for her five school-aged children and buy and furnish a humble home in Edinburg, Texas. One day in October 1949, US immigration officials apprehended and deported Gómez while her children were at school. She also turned to Mexican officials seeking their help in securing the return of her children and the sale of her property.[35] Some American citizens criticized immigration policies' cruelty. "I have seen mothers deport[ed] and leave on this side their nursing babies," an indignant South Texas resident wrote to the US attorney general in 1953. "What is the matter with this country any way?"[36]

Even when Mexican women themselves were not expelled, they sometimes played an active role in their family members' cases. Mexican mothers sought the release and return of detained family members. When fifty-eight-year-old Magdalena Navarro found out US authorities were holding her nineteen-year-old son Guillermo in the Lower Rio Grande Valley for crossing without authorization, she traveled to the border to seek his release. The head of Mexican migration at Reynosa noted Navarro's persistence and plan to return to the migration office daily "until his return so that they can go back to Monterrey together and be with their family."[37]

In some cases, people used deportation in unexpected ways. Mexican women called for the apprehension and expulsion of their husbands, usually after discovering that they had found new partners in the United States. In 1948, Juana Estévez de Llano, of Monterrey, Nuevo León, wrote to Mexican officials asking them to have US authorities deport her husband from Harlingen, Texas, where she said he was living illegally. He initially went in search of work, she wrote, "but what he earns is for him and he doesn't send anything, because according to him he lives with a woman he says passes for his wife but that's not true." She continued: "Knowing that he has good work and doesn't send us anything I don't think it's right that that woman is stealing food from my children." Estévez asked authorities to return her husband so he could provide for his family and "not laugh in the face of the law." In hopes of expediting the matter, she sent authorities a photograph and the exact address where they could find him.[38]

Beyond personal motivations and those related to the regulation of Mexicans' labor and morality, Cold War–era national security concerns also animated calls for restrictive immigration measures. Fears of a communist infiltration led lawmakers to pass the McCarran–Walter Act of 1952, reaffirming the national origins quota system and excluding people who espoused radical political views. Though aspects of the law conflicted with the United States' self-professed ideals of civil liberties and freedom of expression, by the early 1950s, according to historian Carl Bon Tempo, anticommunism "had become a central aspect of national identity, national politics, and partisan electoral strategies, which, in turn, made it central to the immigration issue."[39] After Attorney General Brownell made a special trip to California in August 1953 to assess the state of affairs on the border, he reported that "the flow of illegal aliens into California from Mexico is critical and endangering the national security." "The most serious aspect of the situation," he continued, was that it "provide[d] an easy avenue of entrance of aliens of the most dangerous subversive classes, not only from Mexico but from any part of the world." For Brownell, the porous southwest border represented "an emergency of national importance" that demanded an immediate solution.[40]

The following April, President Eisenhower nominated Lieutenant General Joseph M. Swing, his former West Point classmate, to be the new commissioner of the INS. Swing had just retired from the army after serving for more than forty-four years. During his career he took part in the 1916 Pershing Expedition that set out to capture Pancho Villa in northern Mexico, served as a field artillery officer in France during World War I, and commanded troops in World War II and the Korean War. Swing officially became commissioner in May, just as planning accelerated for a mass expulsion campaign to rid the country of undocumented Mexicans.[41]

Launched in the summer of 1954, Operation Wetback sought to regulate the flow of Mexican agricultural laborers by reducing the number of unauthorized migrants and increasing the number of braceros. It built on previous deportation efforts mounted throughout the 1940s and early 1950s, including an aborted secret plan that called for 3,500 to 4,000 army troops to execute deportation drives and patrol the California portion of the US–Mexico border twenty-four hours a day, seven days a week for three to six months.[42] Rather than just a deportation drive along the US–Mexico border, the operation targeted people living in established communities in the interior of the country as well. Though it began as a plan to deport some 25,000 Mexicans from California over the course of thirty to forty-five days, the INS expanded the drive to Texas in July and to Midwest industrial centers like Chicago in September, as the pages that follow show. The campaign depended not only on hundreds of Border Patrol agents organized in special mobile task forces, but also on local and state authorities and law enforcement officers, farmers and ranchers, and the media. It stoked and mobilized public fears that "wetbacks" propagated disease, committed crimes, drained the tax base, and degraded the labor standards and living conditions of domestic workers. Whereas the service relied on hundreds of Border Patrol officers and the use of light planes to locate large numbers of immigrants and jeeps and buses to apprehend them in the southwestern border region, in Midwestern metropolitan areas a relatively small number of agents conducted investigations and relied on tips from citizens and informants to carry out piecemeal deportation campaigns.[43]

The history of Operation Wetback is inextricably intertwined with the histories of the Bracero Program and the mass expulsion of migrants via voluntary departure. It is no coincidence that voluntary departures first outnumbered formal deportations in fiscal year 1942, the year the guest worker program began and both documented and undocumented migration increased. Whereas INS apprehensions numbered just 11,000 that year, they ballooned to more than one million a little over a decade later. In total, the INS carried out nearly six million expulsions between 1942 and 1964—almost all to Mexico, and roughly six times as many as in the previous half-century. Nearly all of these additional deportations occurred via voluntary departure. By 1945 voluntary departures outnumbered formal deportations five to one, and by 1950 the ratio had increased to fifty-six to one. The one-million-plus voluntary departures during fiscal year 1954 dwarfed the slightly more than 30,000 formal deportations recorded during the same period.[44] Though scholars have pointed out that the vast majority of these expulsions actually occurred *before* the INS had even announced the special drive, voluntary departures still played an integral role during the campaign.[45] Indeed, as a July 1954 INS press release noted, voluntary departures "were a planned part of the overall purpose of the Operation."[46] Officials' inability to carry out formal deportations should not, however, be mistaken for a lack of power. As in the 1930s, the INS's reliance on voluntary departures and self-deportations revealed the state's capacity to effect expulsion through other means.[47]

## California

Operation Wetback began weeks before immigration officers started apprehending or deporting anyone as part of the official drive. The agenda for a preliminary meeting to discuss the "Special Patrol Force" listed publicity as the first item on the advance plan.[48] The INS's carefully planned, large-scale publicity campaign led an undetermined number of Mexicans (and possibly Mexican Americans) to leave the United States. On June 10, the Border Patrol sent a press release announcing the operation to 150 newspapers in Southern California. Los Angeles officials stated that the news "was carried by practically every radio station." They also prepared "special announcements" for local television stations, and arranged "to have releases published in the newspapers of Baja California and the communities along the border." The Los Angeles district director reached out to the national media and reported to Commissioner Swing that NBC and other major media outlets planned to cover "the activities of the 17th and propose to arrive at El Centro on the evening of the 16th." He added that he had informed the head of the Border Patrol "of the desired coverage and [was] certain that it [would] be arranged so that very favorable publicity will be attained, not only on the local but national level."[49]

In some cases, US officials did not have to seek out news outlets to publicize Operation Wetback. On June 21, the director of news and public affairs at a San José radio station contacted Brownell and informed him that the station's two daily Spanish-language programs had the widest reach in the area. "Is it possible you may wish to send us a statement of instructions to be read by our Spanish-speaking announcer to direct Mexican Nationals on ways and means of co-operating at this time?" He continued, "If you believe a statement of this sort will help your Department in its work, we will be most happy to broadcast it as a public service."[50]

US authorities waged a simultaneous open and behind-the-scenes campaign in Mexico. Border Patrol officials proposed a number of ways to inform the Mexican public and potential unauthorized migrants of the forthcoming drive. Marcus T. Neely, district director at El Paso, recommended giving deportees handbills and putting up large signs at points of expulsion that read, in Spanish and English:

**NOTICE**
THE UNITED STATES NEEDS LEGAL FARM WORKERS!
THE MAYOR OF YOUR TOWN CAN ARRANGE FOR YOUR CONTRACTING.

**WARNING**
THE ERA OF THE WETBACK AND THE WIRE CUTTER HAS ENDED!
FROM THIS DAY FORWARD ANY PERSON FOUND IN THE UNITED STATES ILLEGALLY WILL BE PUNISHED BY IMPRISONMENT.

Neely added that he would contact Mexican authorities "for the purpose of making such 'propaganda' arrangements." The INS also tried to reach Mexicans other than deportees. After officials decided to buslift people from California to Arizona for removal at Nogales, Sonora, the INS planned to give local radio stations in Nogales "a short news release they can, and we think perhaps they will, use as a spot announcement." Moreover, Neely suggested a "plan to use the Cessna aircraft from Marfa, Texas, with an observer who speaks and understands the Spanish language fluently and who will be able to talk over the plane's loudspeaker, for such other 'propaganda' purposes we may work out."[51]

US officials noted that Mexican support was key to Operation Wetback's success and strategized about how to win over Mexican officials and the public. One strategy the INS employed was distinguishing braceros from "wetbacks" and encouraging the continued migration of the former.[52] On May 20, Secretary of State John Foster Dulles wrote that the US Information Agency in Mexico should "initiate [a] campaign immediately on [the] difference between braceros and wetbacks and on United States problems with wetbacks in order to lay [a] basis for rebuttal of anti-United States propaganda which can be expected when mass movement starts."[53] State Department officials ensured that the US Information Agency would be "thoroughly briefed at the appropriate time concerning the program so as to disseminate information to offset any adverse propaganda in Mexican papers."[54] According to US officials in Mexico City, the Mexican press was willing to "carry quotes of US officials" about the differences between braceros and "wetbacks," but was "reluctant [to] handle much other material."[55] The day before the United States officially announced Operation Wetback, a confidential internal memo reasserted the importance of Mexican support and stressed that the emphasis on more braceros and fewer unauthorized laborers "must be accomplished through expression [of] this idea by Mexicans themselves," which "will require fullest use [of] personal contact for discreet placement materials and to stimulate useful Mexican commentary."[56] The US cared about Mexican support, but only so far as the lack of it threatened Operation Wetback's overall effectiveness.[57]

With the end of fiscal year 1954 fast approaching, US officials wanted to start the drive "as early as possible to use this year's funds." Authorities proposed June 1 as a start date. Despite its delay of a couple of weeks, as soon as Brownell announced the operation on June 9, the 240-man Southern California Border Patrol force, joined by 491 officers sent from around the country in addition to local law enforcement officials, began setting up roadblocks and started apprehending migrants the following morning (see figure 10). Over the course of the next week, the special task force apprehended more than 12,300 Mexicans and buslifted some 7,000 people to Nogales for deportation.[58]

On June 17, Operation Wetback officially began. The special task forces raided agricultural fields and industrial places of employment in addition to private homes and public areas. The INS leased the Elysian Playground Recreation Center from the Los Angeles Department of Recreation and Parks for $125.00 per day and converted it into a makeshift, open-air detention center for people awaiting deportation.[59] Within a week, the operation had expanded to Northern California, where members of the special task force were supposed to take people to their homes or places of employment to collect their wages and belongings before being processed for deportation. The INS, however, deported "a number of aliens" immediately, without any

Figure 10. Border Patrol officials brief agents for Operation Wetback, Sacramento, California, 1954.
Courtesy of the National Border Patrol Museum, El Paso, Texas.

consideration of what they left behind.[60] By the beginning of July, Commissioner Swing observed that the results "show that splendid headway is being made to rid [the Los Angeles] area of illegal entrants. But," he added, "lasting benefits can only be derived in this work by continuing to seal the border so that it can't be penetrated beyond a mere trickle." Swing stressed that "illegal crossings . . . must be held in check at all costs," and recommended that Border Patrol officers work nights and off hours to ensure success.[61]

The INS was well aware of its own limitations. Although Brownell stressed in his initial press release that the operation would "not be a hit and run project," that same day he wrote a letter admitting that it was merely "a temporary expedient" that "must be limited to a brief period because of a lack of funds and the need to return the personnel to their regular posts."[62] The INS planned to buslift up to 1,000 deportees per day (which would drop to 500 per day over time) from California to Nogales, Arizona. And between June 10 and July 14, the special task force apprehended 44,876 Mexicans in California, and shipped 37,170 people to the border—including more than 33,000 to Nogales, where US officials transferred them to their Mexican counterparts for removal into the Mexican interior in hopes of discouraging reentry into the United States.[63]

Although it is impossible to say how many Mexicans left the United States in response to the INS's scare tactics, officials and some Southern California residents celebrated the supposed success of the self-deportation campaign. "It would be, of course, premature at this time to pass judgment upon the success of this operation," Border Patrol Chief Harlon B. Carter wrote the day before Operation Wetback officially started. "I should say, however, that since the Attorney General's announcement, followed as it has been by the physical show of force here, illegal aliens by the hundreds are beginning to sneak southward."[64] B. D. Diaz, a man from Brawley, California, a town in the Imperial Valley located twenty-five miles north of the Calexico–Mexicali border, wrote a six-page, handwritten letter lauding the INS for its fear-driven publicity campaign.

> Whoever originated the idea is a "psycohologist [sic] of the first magnitude." You have not only save [sic] the Government of the expenses involve [sic] in the apprehension, the ill feelings created on the side of the "wets" but educated them to obey the Law voluntarily. For the first time in the History of these wetbacks in a grove of date trees across other side of the canal east of the place where I live for over a quarter century—the "Place" becomes a "Ghost Town."

Referring to the drive as "'head work' rather than 'hard work,'" he then related a metaphor in which he compared self-deportation campaigns to scaring rabbits while hunting so that the animals would have a chance to run instead of being shot without any warning. "So there we are as 'the Omnipotent Judge.' 'Shoot or not to shoot?'" he wrote. "You scared [them] and they did run to save yourselves the trouble of enforcing and the cash for our Government."[65]

The INS concurred with this assessment. An *INS Information Bulletin* article at the end of June celebrated the California operation and claimed that "an indication of the success of the program is that 'wetbacks' laden down with their belongings are heading south across the border on their own initiative in many instances, rather than waiting to be apprehended by the Border Patrol." As it also pointed out, "This is saving the Government money for it means we do not have to bear the cost of gathering them and then transporting them to the border."[66] A month into the drive, the INS claimed that total apprehensions, "slightly lower than the apprehension rate in California in recent months, reflect the voluntary exodus of thousands of 'wetbacks' to Mexico when the campaign was announced June 10, and an apparent cessation in the traffic northward."[67]

## Texas

The INS's publicity onslaught continued as Operation Wetback shifted to Texas. Despite receiving the full support of local law enforcement, the special task force sent to implement the drive in South Texas faced considerable resistance from ranchers and other residents of the Lower Rio Grande Valley.[68] Similar to the California operation, the Department of Justice tried to stem some of the blowback by putting out a press release two weeks ahead of time. In a July 2 statement, Swing declared that the Texas operation would start around July 15 and "an advance party to man rail and road blocks [would] arrive in McAllen, Texas, about July 6." He also reiterated the Department of Labor's promise to "insure [*sic*] the availability of legal labor," and added that he was "hopeful that out of this effort the illegal entry and subsequent employment of these aliens [would] be discouraged."[69] The service also stressed that the Rio Grande Valley drive would not be "a hit and run affair, but on the contrary . . . a feature of the new but continuing policy for effective law enforcement marked by new methods and a bolder concept in regard to public relations."[70]

The INS made a concerted effort to enlist the aid and support of influential Mexican American organizations in South Texas, including AGIF and the League of United Latin American Citizens (LULAC). A week before the Rio Grande Valley operation launched, the INS asked the president of AGIF in Del Rio, Texas, to bring the upcoming drive to the attention of his members and friends, "in order that they will know that we are working in their behalf, and if they are questioned regarding their citizenship, they will understand the motive behind our actions."[71] Ed Idar Jr., leader of the Texas AGIF, spoke highly of the service and Swing's work in ridding the country of "illegal resident aliens." According to the INS, Idar "was working on press and radio releases," in both English and Spanish, to be distributed and aired in areas "where our operation will be most intensive." Officials "believed that information released in this manner will materially hold down some complaints against this Service."[72]

But it was not easy to win over growers in the area who had long relied on undocumented workers to maintain their cotton fields and feared that the crackdown would jeopardize their crops. While the INS tried to use local media to its benefit as the drive neared, officials worried that many newspapers in the Rio Grande Valley would not support Operation Wetback since their owner had "a reputation of fighting against all law enforcement agencies."[73] Their fears proved prescient: a week before Operation Wetback commenced, one newspaper offered a tongue-in-cheek solution to potential labor shortages: "putting 700–800 invading Border patrolmen into the cotton fields, picking."[74] Another ran an editorial that referred to Border Patrol officers as "Armed Young Gringos with full bellies and tin badges." Many local residents and establishments were less than welcoming as well. A candy store in Harlingen put up a sign stating, "Prices Double to Border Patrolmen until Cotton is Picked"; some officers found that people would not rent them rooms, and a number stated that locals made snide remarks about them at cafes and banks.[75]

Men and women across the Lower Rio Grande Valley wrote letters to President Eisenhower and his wife, Mamie, that used Cold War–era language to convey their displeasure and disgust with Operation Wetback. "If all the other countries, where American officials have been sent, are being treated like the poor innocent wetback is being treated it is no wonder they have turned against the Western Power and are looking towards the Iron Curtain," the head of a farmers' association in Mercedes, Texas, wrote to the president.[76] Another man who feared that Operation Wetback would push Mexicans toward communism pleaded, "Above all PLEASE DO SOMETHING TO ERASE FROM THE MINDS OF THE POOR MEXICANS THAT WE ARE WORSE THAN THE RUSSIANS, WHICH THEY NOW MAY WELL BELIEVE."[77]

Some South Texas residents went so far as to explicitly compare the INS to Nazis. A Harlingen woman suggested that the president "should try [picking cotton] some time" so that he "would know then how hard [Mexicans] work," only to be "robbed of it at gun point, the gun being held by the immigration officer, who is no better than Hitler's gestapo." She concluded, "Americans fought and died to stay such precautions in foreign countries, yet it happens here, is even supported by the Federal government. How inhuman can the U.S. be? I hope that you, in common decency can stop these terrible happenings."[78] In hopes of combating such negative opinions, the INS conducted its own surveys and interviewed "persons believed to be favorable

Figure 11. Packing apprehended migrants into trucks after mass roundups in McAllen, Texas, 1954.
Courtesy of the National Border Patrol Museum, El Paso, Texas.

towards the wetback drive for the purpose of securing written comment"
that the agency could use for purposes of publicity.[79]

Despite public opinion, Operation Wetback forged ahead in South Texas.
During the first two weeks, US officials claimed that the special task force
apprehended more than 44,000 Mexicans (see figure 11). As the McAllen
*Valley Evening Monitor* reported in August 1954, officials frequently crowded
apprehended men, women, and children onto the flatbeds of trucks and
packed them into buses, "then forced [them] to sit for hours in the hot sun
while the patrol unit completes a load." Similar to California, nearly all of
these apprehensions resulted in voluntary departures since, as the district
director reported to the central office on August 6, "it is not believe[d] that
formal deportation proceedings can be further accelerated."[80] The Mexican
government agreed to receive between 500 and 1,000 deportees per day at El
Paso–Juárez, and another 1,200 to 1,500 per week at Presidio–Ojinaga. While
Mexican authorities agreed to then move deportees into the interior aboard
trains, they also planned to transport thousands back to Reynosa, Matamoros, and Valle Hermoso in order to work 250,000 hectares of cotton, worth
more than 520 million pesos, that needed tending.[81] The INS also claimed
that its scare tactics and publicity campaign resulted in more than 60,000
people returning to Mexico to avoid arrest during the first thirty days of

the Texas drive, while "others simply fled across the Rio Grande."[82] Attorney General Brownell hyperbolically described it as "the greatest migration of people ever witnessed on this continent, at least in modern times."[83]

When the Texas campaign wound down in September, Swing offered an assessment of Operation Wetback up until that point in a report to the American Section of the Joint Commission on Mexican Migrant Labor. He described it as "a well-planned, large-scale, and energetic campaign . . . to stamp out the wetback practice and all its attendant evils," and added that "sight was not lost of the need of protecting the interests of the employers and workers and the national interests of the two Republics." The work of some 750 INS and Border Patrol officers, using 300 cars and buses and seven planes, had supposedly "netted over 140,000 wetbacks" during the previous three months. The commissioner asserted that "every effort was made to make the drive as humane as possible," adding that "families were not separated" and "aliens with long residence in the United States who had established roots were not molested." These claims, however, were false. Deportation's punitive nature would become even more apparent in the coming weeks and months as Operation Wetback moved further into the interior of the country.[84]

### Chicago

Although there is much less of a record of the Chicago phase of Operation Wetback, it offers important insights into the deportation machine and the history of interior enforcement.[85] Mexicans started migrating to the Second City in large numbers in the early to mid-twentieth century, drawn by high wages in industry and later by a combination of job opportunities and social networks. Some reached Chicago by riding freight trains north through the Mississippi Valley, while others paid smugglers $50 to $150 to transport them from the Texas–Mexico border. Immigration officials estimated that 75,000 Mexicans, including 10,000 who were in the country without authorization, lived in Chicago in 1951. In response, the following year the INS opened a five-person Border Patrol station on the ninth floor of the old Post Office building "for the express purpose of apprehending Mexicans and smugglers of Mexicans." The inauguration of the new station coincided with a nationwide campaign "against aliens in large populated centers," for which the service sent twenty Spanish-speaking officers to Chicago. Their six-week 1952 drive resulted in more than 1,200 apprehensions and deportations to Mexico, but "made no appreciable hole in the numbers present in the city, in spite of the fact that great numbers fled the city to escape apprehension during the period." By 1954, the INS estimated—without providing any supporting evidence—that Chicago's Mexican population had grown to 125,000, including some 20,000 to 40,000 unauthorized migrants.[86]

Even though the INS did not launch Operation Wetback's interior phase until the fall, the service started planning for it before the California drive even began. In mid-June, the central office solicited a confidential "plan of operation, to rid the Chicago area of Mexican aliens, utilizing a special mobile force of 100 men."[87] Before the month ended, Commissioner Swing made the informal announcement that starting in the fall "Chicago, Illinois, would be the first major United States city to be cleaned out."[88] Forty-eight-year-old Walter A. Sahli, the son of Swiss and Austrian immigrants and a career civil servant with a background in law who had just become the Chicago district director after a stint in Miami, would oversee the Midwest campaign.[89]

In a letter to Sahli at the end of July, General Frank H. Partridge, an army buddy of Swing's whom the commissioner had appointed as his special assistant, stated that the service's "experience in California and the Lower Rio Grande Valley of Texas has shown that an intensive information campaign is an effective means of causing voluntary departure at no expense to the Government." According to Partridge, "latest reports indicate that those departing of their own accord as a result of the news of the drive, have exceeded those arrested by officers nearly three times." Thus, he recommended that Chicago officials solicit the help of Chicago-area media outlets, organizations, Mexican social clubs, and the Catholic Church in Chicago to advertise the upcoming drive. "By such methods many hundreds of aliens would no doubt choose to return to Mexico of their own accord rather than to await their eventual arrest and removal by this Service," Partridge concluded, adding that "it would be well to encourage voluntary departures now rather than at a later date."[90]

On July 30, US officials doubled down on the advanced publicity campaign when Attorney General Brownell announced "that Chicago would be a focal point of a federal immigration service drive to return 'wetbacks' to Mexico."[91] Yet local officials would not provide details about the operation or even corroborate its existence. In hopes that rumors of a possible drive would scare people into leaving regardless if it ever materialized, Sahli put out a press release: "Without confirming or denying the possibility of any drive, I should like to offer advice to all aliens illegally in the United States . . . obviously the simplest way to avoid formal deportation is for the individual to depart from the United States on his own accord." The statement continued, "This he is permitted to do and even encouraged to do. In fact, we offer our assistance to enable such departing aliens to return without difficulty." Sahli concluded with the following lines:

> I cannot stress too highly the importance of aliens leaving the United States of their own accord rather than await deportation, particularly in the case of any individual who hopes some day to return to the United States legally for permanent residence. Those who depart by themselves are virtually in as good as position as though they had never entered illegally and have an excellent opportunity of returning some day, but in the case of an alien who is formally deported, the law requires that before he is permitted to apply to enter, he must first obtain special permission from the Attorney General, and I can assure you this permission is sparingly given. Once an individual is formally deported, he has an obstacle to overcome which will prevent him from ever entering the United States again.

> Hence, I whole-heartedly and sincerely suggest to all aliens illegally in the United States to think in terms of leaving the United States voluntarily before any formal action is commenced against them.[92]

The *Chicago Tribune* and *Chicago Daily News* picked up the story, reporting that Mexicans could avoid apprehension, detention, prosecution, and deportation if they agreed to depart "on their own accord." They also noted that Sahli recommended that before leaving people should stop by the Chicago Border Patrol office to pick up letters that "would guarantee the safe passage of the bearer to Mexico and explain that he was doing so voluntarily" (see figure 12).[93]

During Operation Wetback, INS officials across the interior of the United States strategized about how to convince migrants to accept voluntary departure. As the Seattle district director told his subordinates, "Aliens are more likely to accept [voluntary departure] if the matter is broached at the time of apprehension rather than some days later. Therefore, they should be

Figure 12. Waiting for voluntary departure letters at the Chicago Border Patrol office on the ninth floor of the Post Office building.

INS District Director Walter Sahli (in suit) stands at right. September 1954. IChi-59815, CHM.

interrogated regarding voluntary departure immediately [so that] a prima facia case of deportability is established." Moreover, "the advantages of voluntary departure may be explained to them clearly and forcibly; for example, probable shorter detention and avoidance of having a deportation against their record." And, he continued, if the person accepted voluntary departure the apprehending officer should have him or her sign the required forms—"particularly the portion authorizing use of their funds in Service possession for purchase of transportation to the appropriate Mexican border port or for any stage of the journey that they are able to pay." If a person refused voluntary departure then officials, Sahli wrote in a letter to Harlon B. Carter, "had no alternative but to institute deportation proceedings."[94]

In the early planning stages of the Chicago operation, Sahli had actually recommended holding removal hearings, even if that meant paying for an extra day or two of detention, and then deportation. He reasoned that holding hearings would place "the Service in a much stronger position to deal with that individual should he again enter the United States illegally," and reported to central office officials that the Chicago district had "been most successful in obtaining convictions and actually sentences for a year and a day and these cases have been given considerable publicity." Formal deportation accompanied by an extended prison sentence would send a message, Sahli argued. "Those who know Mexicans clearly concede that a sentence of two to three months means nothing to the Mexican but where he is given a sentence of a year, then it does begin to mean something."[95]

Whereas Sahli had the long term in mind, central office officials focused on the short term rejected his suggestion and argued that formal deportation proceedings did not align with the goals of Operation Wetback. In the margin of Sahli's memo an official commented, "Costly detention point not necessary if processing is streamlined," and later added, "Hearings not necessary if idea is to clean out volume—not make records."[96] The acting chief of the Border Patrol also weighed in on Sahli's proposal in a letter to Partridge: "I feel that this plan would be too slow and cumbersome to be effective. That part of the plan which deals with according hearings to all aliens apprehended, I feel, in such an operation, would be out of place."[97] Despite misgivings from local officials, Operation Wetback was not a campaign grounded in hearings, formal proceedings, and the airing of Mexicans' cases and rights; it was mass deportation on the cheap, by whatever means necessary, in hopes of establishing the INS's authority and pushing unauthorized laborers into the Bracero Program.

Throughout July and into August rumors about the potential deportation campaign in Chicago led some organizations to contact the INS with concerns about how such an operation would affect Mexicans' and Mexican Americans' rights. The director of the Council Against Discrimination of Greater Chicago wrote to INS officials in early July, noting that "an operation of this size, announced as it was in The Daily News, can lead to panic and unreasoned action." When he asked how his organization could help immigration officials "in making an orderly deportation," the central office suggested that Sahli ask the Council Against Discrimination and its 143 affiliates "to urge . . . all illegal aliens in the area return at this time to Mexico on their own accord."[98] The ACLU also contacted INS officials and, as a result of its concerns about the impact of a potential deportation campaign, came to the conclusion "that all illegal aliens in the area should be advised that it would be to their best interest to return to Mexico voluntarily rather than to await any drive such as the Union anticipates." While the ACLU published "Latin Americans and the Immigration Service," a brochure meant to inform people of their rights, it also told Mexicans to leave the United States in order to avoid deportation. Despite whatever intentions it might have had, by sending a press release about the brochure to all Illinois newspapers and promising to "give considerable publicity" to the deportation drive, the ACLU helped propagate the INS's fear campaign.[99]

The combination of INS press releases, media coverage, and the assistance of local organizations in spreading the word had the effect the INS desired, at least by some accounts. The ACLU stated that news of the operation had "created the anxiety primarily among the Spanish-American population in Chicago."[100] An information officer in the Illinois Department of Labor's Employment Service reported that "about 50% of their Mexican help had left the area when the Wetback Drive was first publicized" and "stated that he had been advised that the number which had departed from the area under these conditions amounted to about 4,000." Romana R. Fierro, acting director of the Mexican American Council of Chicago, told an INS investigator "when publicity concerning the proposed wetback program was first given out . . . many wives and other relatives of illegally resident Mexicans started coming to see her for advice on how to legalize the status of such illegal aliens." Fierro also mentioned "that all such persons who came to talk to her told her that their husbands or other relatives illegally in the United States sent them to talk to her because they were afraid to be on the street for fear of being apprehended by Immigration Officers." In her opinion, "undoubtedly a great number of illegal Mexicans have left the area to evade apprehension," not counting those who left under voluntary departure. The INS investigator noted that Fierro and a social worker informed him "that there has been a marked increase in the number of marriages" between undocumented Mexican men and US citizen Puerto Rican women. The director of the Hull-House, a prominent settlement house on the city's Near West Side founded by Jane Addams in 1889 and dedicated to serving immigrant communities, also related to the service that the number of Mexicans asking about legalizing or naturalizing had increased in recent months, "coincid[ing] with the publicity given to the wetback program and the beginning of the drive in this area."[101]

While the advanced publicity in Chicago was similar to the strategy the INS had adopted in California and Texas, officials pointed out that the Chicago operation would differ from the previous campaigns in important ways. It would "not be a blitzkrieg but an infiltration," one official declared.[102] This was partially because the extended advanced publicity campaign had pushed some people into hiding, but also because many Mexicans in Chicago were established members of the community, rather than recent arrivals or seasonal labor migrants. Indeed, the long history and recent growth of Chicago's Mexican community had caused friction in some parts of the city and led citizens to contact the INS and urge it "to correct the situation as it is seen by them in their own neighborhoods." A March 1954 report on the history of Mexicans in Chicago noted that most of these complaints "reflect the growing competition for jobs, for living space and for women" and a growing resentment of an "alien group—almost entirely a youthful male group—swaggering in gangs through the streets and openly contemptuous of the laws of our country."[103] However, some Chicago-area residents complained about Mexicans decreasing neighborhood property values and Democrats winning Chicago ward elections by "buying votes from Spanish speaking people."[104]

The INS also noted that the Mexican community's deep roots in Chicago meant that Mexicans were "no longer easily rounded up in large gangs, nor are they concentrated in definite areas for housing purposes." When INS officials did apprehend Mexicans in Chicago, it was only after "painstaking questioning" to establish deportability since "many of the aliens now being apprehended have a thorough knowledge of the English language." Officials also claimed that Mexicans' integration "into Negro and Porto [sic] Rican social circles" and the fact that "some Mexicans have married Negroes" made it more difficult to deport them.[105] And, according to Sahli, many Mexicans in Chicago had been in the city long enough to have bought cars, opened bank accounts, and signed public utility contracts. They had, he said, "become economically involved in the neighborhood, thereby complicating immensely the process of removal after apprehension." Moreover, he continued, "and perhaps more important from our standpoint, they have acquired associations with citizens and resident aliens which results in demands for release on bond, representation by counsel and in many cases applications for discretionary relief."[106]

In hopes of avoiding such problems, the chief patrol inspector in New Orleans suggested the INS heighten enforcement efforts in the South to stop migrants from reaching Chicago in the first place, thus preventing their integration into established communities and the service's subsequent costly efforts to deport them. "If these aliens are apprehended immediately, while still in the New Orleans Sector and in transit, they can be expelled from the United States at a minimum cost in both money and manpower, since they are handled in the same manner as if they had been caught within a few miles of the border," he wrote to the chief of the Border Patrol.[107]

Even if the INS had acted on the recommendation to crack down on northward migration within the United States, it would not have resolved the issue of deporting the thousands of Mexicans already living in Chicago without authorization. In Sahli's opinion, a "'dragnet' type of operation" would only result in a small number of apprehensions and might lead some thousands to "temporarily leave the area." But, he went on, "no great percentage would voluntarily depart the United States." And after the first days of any comprehensive drive "the sources which usually provide group apprehensions would be exhausted and the operation would necessarily revert to a process of combing literally thousands of small factories, nurseries, golf courses, restaurants and small rooming houses."[108]

In early September, the INS recalled all Chicago Border Patrol agents who had been detailed to California and South Texas. Less than two weeks later, on September 17, District Director Sahli notified officers that the "accelerated program of removing Mexicans illegally in the United States from Chicago area and vicinity" had commenced.[109] Before the campaign started the INS had indicated that it hoped to deport one hundred Mexicans per day during the first week, seventy per day during the second week, fifty per day during week three, and then forty per day thereafter for a period of six months. The service estimated that it would need all Chicago officers plus fifty extra officers for the drive, which would target Chicago in addition to parts of Wisconsin, Indiana, and Michigan.[110] When the campaign officially began, the *Chicago Daily News* reported that "a small army of immigration officers searched throughout the city for offenders."[111] By the end of the first week it became clear that the INS would come nowhere near meeting its apprehension goals: the service had arrested fewer than 150 people. By the end of the month apprehensions only totaled 510. Men made up the vast majority of apprehensions. Nearly half of the people officials rounded up worked in manufacturing, while another third labored on the railroads or in hotels, restaurants, and "metal industries."[112]

Deportations remained low in part because some apprehended Mexicans rejected voluntary departure and fought their cases. At least sixteen people requested hearings during the first ten days of the Chicago operation. Lawyers sometimes served as counsel for people facing deportation, though having legal representation did not necessarily provide any guarantees. Nathan Caldwell, the executive secretary of the Midwest Committee for Protection of Foreign Born, opined that many defense attorneys felt that "any Mexican person arrested for 'illegal entry' must automatically be returned to Mexico even though we fight for due process in the arrest procedure and hearings. This in itself may be diluting all our efforts to halt mass deportations and the accompanying terror," he lamented. In another instance, to his shock and dismay, Caldwell noted that an attorney for the packinghouse workers' union was going to let a man be deported "without even trying to obtain his release and a stay of deportation on a writ of habeas corpus." "It didn't occur to him to demand that a hearing be held," Caldwell wrote to a colleague. "Good God!" Over time, he became "more convinced that [lawyers] must not stipulate this point, particularly when realizing that the majority of so-called illegal entrants arrive in the US with the open connivance of the INS—or at the least through a look the other way."[113]

Although formal deportations remained low, authorities' scare tactics led a considerable number of Mexicans to self-deport, or at least leave the area. On October 6, Sahli wrote to Swing that the number of "aliens" in Chicago had "decreased substantially. The distribution has become more diffuse." Furthermore, he continued, "there is strong evidence of a general exodus of Mexican aliens during recent months," which he attributed to the publicity campaign, the accelerated program itself, and the "moderate decline" in job opportunities. The priest at Our Lady of Guadalupe on the South Side of Chicago, the city's oldest Mexican parish, reinforced these conclusions, telling INS officials that attendance had been down since the last week of July. Moreover, traffic checks at Chicago-area bus terminals indicated a "substantial Southward movement of Mexican aliens," including many with voluntary departure letters. "Many Mexican aliens are apparently under cover," Sahli told the commissioner, and "several . . . who surrendered voluntarily said that they failed to report to work over a period of several days in an effort to avoid deportation." He also made a point of stating that the advanced publicity campaign "produced several positive results," including that the number of "voluntary surrenders" (1,246) exceeded apprehensions (1,193). The publicity, he added, had also caused "large numbers of Mexican aliens" to self-deport "without voluntary departure letters."[114]

The Chicago phase of Operation Wetback continued throughout the fall and into the new year, albeit in a reduced capacity. By the spring of 1955, there were "only two Patrol Inspectors engaged in full time wetback work," in addition to a handful of officers overseeing detention, deportation, and parole. During the last months of the drive investigators targeted "firmly entrenched individual aliens," turned to confidential informants for tips, and offered rewards for information leading to the apprehension of unauthorized immigrants. Removing such individuals was a slow and drawn-out process that required considerable resources, offering a glimpse into some of the challenges related to interior enforcement that the INS would face in the future. By late July 1955, claiming that the number of unauthorized Mexicans in Chicago had dropped to 600, officials announced that the drive had ended.[115]

More than just a deportation drive, Operation Wetback also amounted to a yearlong INS self-promotion campaign that served as a way for the agency to boost its reputation, build morale among its officers, and solidify its place within the federal bureaucracy.[116] Commissioner Swing touted the service's achievements to the press and sent out certificates recognizing and congratulating officers' participation in the historic drive that resulted in the deportation of around 200,000 Mexicans—though the INS claimed that it had yielded more than five times as many expulsions.[117] The campaign was such a success, supposedly, that in its wake Swing declared that "the so-called 'wetback' problem no longer exists. . . . The border has been secured."[118]

Although the commissioner's claim would not hold up over time, there was some truth to it in the operation's immediate aftermath. The deportation drive seemed to push Mexican migrants into the Bracero Program, in turn reducing unauthorized migration. The number of guest worker contracts rose from some 309,000 in 1954 to a record high of more than 445,000 in 1956, in part because of the expulsions, but also because the INS and Department of Labor promised to provide southwestern growers with a sufficient number of braceros to replace the unauthorized labor force. The number of braceros the United States admitted would remain above 400,000 per year until the end of the 1950s before tapering off. At the same time, apprehensions—an imperfect measure of unauthorized migration—dropped dramatically from more than one million in fiscal year 1954 to an average of around 78,000 per year during the program's final decade.[119] But after the Bracero Program drew to a close on December 31, 1964, Mexicans who had been migrating for years or decades with contracts continued to do so—only now the authorities considered them undocumented. In the years ahead, whatever control the INS had managed to achieve proved fleeting.[120]

Examining Operation Wetback alongside the repatriation drives of the 1930s offers important insights into how the deportation machine operated. In many ways, the two most notorious expulsion campaigns in US history tell a story of continuity, rather than change over time. Unable to formally expel the increasing number of Mexicans considered undocumented, the INS turned to voluntary departures and self-deportations to purge millions of people from the country by whatever means necessary. Officials' success in using these mechanisms reflected the state's ability to exert control over ethnic Mexicans' lives and labor irrespective of fiscal limitations. A close analysis of the history of expulsion from the late 1920s through the late 1950s reveals that, despite their euphemistic names, voluntary departures and self-deportations had more to do with overt government planning, force, and coercion than with migrants' autonomous decisions. The machine only functioned because of these alternate and expedited means of expulsion that stripped migrants of any rights they had. Simply put, US officials could not have carried out mass expulsions without them.

That would remain the case for the next forty-plus years.

# THREE

# The Human Costs of the Business of Deportation

In January 1928, I. M. Adler, owner of a steamship and tourist agency in New Haven, Connecticut, wrote a letter to his senator. "It occurred to me that the United States Government can save itself quite a sum of money and annoyance each year in the matter of deportation of aliens." Noting that the government purchased "a large number of steamship tickets each year" for deportees rejected at Ellis Island and those already in the country whom officials considered to be "undesirable," Adler offered his services. As "the authorized agent for all steamship lines" and someone who spoke "seven different languages including Russian, Polish, Hungarian, German, Yiddish, and all Slavonia languages," he suggested that this was a win-win proposition: the government would save money by outsourcing and centralizing the purchase of deportation fares, and he would benefit from the windfall of new business. The Immigration Service decided to pass on Adler's proposal, but his story is instructive. By the 1920s, deportation had become a business, and there was money to be made.[1]

Immigration historians know little about *how* authorities have forcibly removed people, and even less about the US government contracting private companies to effect expulsions. Yet, examining the physical process of deportation offers important insights into both the history of the immigrant experience and immigration policy. Scholars have focused on domestic politics and foreign affairs as the driving forces behind immigration policy and its implementation. The history of the business of deportation reveals that interpenetrating—and not infrequently corrupt—public–private relations have also decisively shaped enforcement practices, with devastating consequences for migrants.

The United States federal government has long relied on third parties for public purposes, so it is not surprising that deportation has both facilitated and fed profit-making ventures.[2] This has only been possible, however, because of lawmakers' and national elites' active exclusion of entire groups of people from citizenship throughout US history and their belief that certain racialized migrants represented nothing more than a source of disposable labor. Moreover, over the course of the twentieth century, changing immigration laws and enforcement practices resulted in a growing number of people—and especially Mexicans—considered to be undocumented.[3] These state policies created a market in deportable persons, turning expulsion into a lucrative business. Shipping companies and entrepreneurial individuals such as Adler that had profited from transporting immigrants and goods to and from the United States now sought to capitalize on the removal of deportees from the country.[4] In many cases, national imperatives and the economic incentives of private firms interacted to create a mode of expulsion that treated people not as human beings, but as cargo. This was neither accidental nor incidental. The commodification of people allowed the federal government to minimize its expenditures and enabled companies to maximize profits by only providing migrants with what they needed for bare survival.

Abysmal onboard conditions and precarious journeys also served another fundamental purpose: to punish deportees, including those expelled via voluntary departure. Despite the Supreme Court's 1893 declaration in *Fong Yue Ting* that expulsion of noncitizens was not a punishment but an inherent power essential to the security of sovereign nations, the following history leaves little doubt about deportation's retributive and disciplinary nature. Bringing this violent past to light reveals how bureaucratic rationality led authorities to use the process of removal to inflict trauma on migrants' bodies and minds with the explicit goal of discouraging them from returning to the United States. This strategy, a precursor to later "prevention through deterrence" efforts, did not stop future immigration. But it did deliberately cause substantial, often overwhelming, physical and psychological suffering and material hardship. Not only was deportation punishment; frequently, punishment became the point. The federal immigration agency cared more about its institutional objective of controlling the nation's borders and employers' desire to maintain a well-regulated, exploitable migrant labor force than the particular means utilized to achieve those ends. By examining the *how* of the expulsion process, this chapter uncovers the web of public and private actors driving the deportation machine and the human costs of policies that prioritize punishment and profits over the well-being of people.[5]

## Boats, Trains, Buses, and Planes

Since the late nineteenth century, when immigration enforcement became the sole domain of the federal government, authorities have relied on a variety of local, state, and federal facilities to detain people awaiting expulsion, and a combination of publicly and privately owned buses, trains, boats, and planes to forcibly move deportees both within the United States and across international borders. Before deportation became a big business, shipping firms were already making money by transporting millions of emigrants from Europe and Asia to the United States. The proliferation of steam-powered ships in the 1860s facilitated the expansion of transatlantic and transpacific travel. Whereas the trip from Europe to the east coast of the United States had taken forty to forty-five days by sail, it took less than two weeks by steam. Likewise, the trip from Hong Kong to San Francisco was cut from a minimum of forty-five days to less than twenty-five days by 1900. As transoceanic travel became easier, the profit margins increased, along with the number of shipping companies—from Britain, Germany, Holland, Japan, Canada, and the United States, among other countries—that sought to capitalize on the burgeoning business of migration.[6]

Return migration, whether by choice or force, was an important source of revenue for shipping companies as well, and became even more so after the Chinese Exclusion Act of 1882 and immigration acts of 1917, 1921, and 1924 restricted immigration and expanded the population of deportable people in the United States. At first, however, immigration restriction cut into shipping companies' profits. This was not only because it limited the number of people who could migrate, but also because it interrupted shipping schedules and, under the 1891 Immigration Act, made the companies financially responsible for inadmissible migrants' detention and return trip. As an immigration official at the time put it, "We treat a Chinaman just as if he was a chest of tea, or a box of opium. . . . We hold him until we get authority to set him free, and the company, meanwhile, is responsible for his safe-keeping."[7]

Shipping companies' desire to minimize their losses came at migrants' expense. Some companies made migrants purchase return tickets in advance if it was thought they were likely to be excluded or deported under the "likely to become a public charge" provision. Firms oftentimes held people waiting to hear whether they would be allowed to enter the country on the ships themselves, which functioned as "floating detention facilities." In 1898, the US-based Pacific Mail Company, one of the largest transpacific shipping lines, created a detention shed on its docks. As one detained man described it, "The detention shed is another name for a 'Chinese jail.' I have visited quite a few jails and State prisons in this country, but have never seen any place half so bad. . . . We were treated like a group of animals, and we were fed on the floor. Kicking and swearing by the white man in charge was not a rare thing. I was not surprised when one morning, a friend pointed out to me the place where a heartbroken Chinaman had hanged himself after fourth [sic] months' imprisonment in this dreadful dungeon, thus to end his agony and the shameful outrage." The conditions were not notably different at the federally run Angel Island immigration station, which opened in the San Francisco Bay in 1910.[8]

While shipping companies were responsible for maintaining detained immigrants who had arrived on their ships, the federal government picked up the bill when the enforcement of firms' financial responsibility was not possible or when someone had entered the United States via the northern or southern land border. Both companies and the federal government pushed to streamline deportations in hopes of reducing their detention expenses. In December 1906, the New England superintendent of the Dominion Atlantic Railway, which operated steamships between Boston and Nova Scotia, wrote to officials "to see if some arrangement cannot be made so that your department can notify us the moment a person applies to you for relief, and that we may deport such persons immediately without awaiting the long formality of person becoming an inmate of an institution."[9] The following month, the chief immigration inspector in Tucson, Arizona, urged the commissioner general of immigration to expedite the process of issuing deportation warrants to people found to be in the country without authorization.

Doing so, he wrote, would "save the Government a great deal of expense which is incurred for subsistence, etc., in detaining the aliens pending the receipt of deportation orders."[10] In 1919, immigration officials in the northeast near the Canadian border complained about a group of eleven Mexicans who were "in jail eating their heads off" while waiting for the rendering of decisions on their deportation cases. In a letter to the central office, the local district director pleaded: "Can't you please hurry decision in these cases, so that we can get rid of these aliens, and cut out the expense incident to detention?" It was another six weeks until the authorities finally deported the group back to Mexico.[11] The prospect of extended periods of detention sometimes led officials to change when, how, and to where deportations took place. After an unexpected interruption in shipping service left authorities with the prospect of having to cover the cost of detaining a group of Mazatlán-bound Mexicans for an additional month in 1926, the Bureau of Immigration made alternate arrangements to have them deported to Manzanillo at an earlier date, albeit at a slightly higher fare.[12]

The Bureau of Immigration's mandate to minimize overall enforcement expenses created opportunities for and competition between private transportation companies. In June 1920, during a time of heightened nativism after World War I, the bureau created the Deportation and Transportation Division to formalize a network of cross-country deportation trains. Systemizing deportation allowed the bureau to expel large, diverse groups of Chinese, European, and Mexican immigrants officials considered to fall into deportable categories such as anarchists, diseased, or likely to become public charges.[13] For more than a decade, hundreds of deportation parties, including dozens that traversed the entire United States, operated under the supervision of Officer E. M. Kline "on a fast and comprehensive schedule," picking up deportees and dropping them off at a port on the east or west coast or along the Mexican or Canadian border.[14] Hoping to land these lucrative government contracts, railroad companies vied with one another and offered reduced rates and additional benefits. As a representative of the Southern Pacific Company noted in 1926, "We have decided that we do not care to offer to furnish free guards to the Government, but we are willing, in order to meet competition to reduce our rates for the service of guards and meals."[15] In exchange for these concessions, including the discounted rate of $80 per deportee (around $1,150 today) to transport groups of at least twenty-five people between New York and California, and vice versa, Southern Pacific, which operated many of the internal trainlifts, sought out an exclusive contract. While the bureau was "pleased to avail itself of the reduced rates and concessions," which it estimated would add up to as much as $10,000 in annual savings, it reserved "the right to patronize other common carriers in the event it may find it advisable to do so."[16]

Officials' insistence on retaining the power and flexibility to contract whichever lines and rely on whatever mode of expulsion was most cost-effective sometimes led the service to contract foreign firms.[17] This, in turn, led some US-based companies to make arguments based on economic nationalism in hopes of winning deportation contracts. In 1928, a representative of the San Francisco–based Panama Mail Steamship Company wrote to the commissioner general of immigration to express his frustration with the government's decision to rely on Mexican and Japanese shipping lines to carry out deportations to Mexico. "Recently, quite a large portion of the United States government deport business has been going on vessels of these two foreign lines, and we are hoping that you will find it in order to instruct your offices on the Pacific coast to route all of their deports [*sic*] to our vessels (or other American vessels when available)." In his response, Commissioner General Harry E. Hull made clear that "while the Bureau would be glad to patronize American Lines in deporting aliens, it must of necessity effect deportations at the lowest rate and unless you can compete with foreign lines, it is regretted that nothing can be done in the matter."[18]

How authorities deported people and which company they contracted to do it depended not only on cost but also on the effectiveness of a particular mode of deportation as a deterrent to future unauthorized migration. This took on particular importance in the case of Mexicans, given Mexico's geographic proximity to the United States and the relatively unguarded 2,000-mile border between the two countries. As early as 1923, people like R. B. Sims, the superintendent of the Arizona State Prison, considered deporting people just over the land border to be "an absolute farce." In his opinion, Mexicans convicted of crimes should be "deposited in Veracruz, Yucatan, or some other far interior point," adding that otherwise deportation "just might as well be abolished."[19] Immigration officials generally agreed. For example, inspectors in Phoenix, Tucson, and El Paso pushed for Mexicans in the western United States to be deported via steamship down the Pacific coast to remote places like Salina Cruz in the southern Mexican state of Oaxaca. From there, a deportee "would have to cross to the east side of the Isthmus of Tehuantepec and work his way up through the entire length of the Republic, which would be a difficult undertaking."[20] As the number of apprehensions and deportations increased, limited congressional funding forced officials to deport many Mexicans over the land border. Budget permitting, they also continued to contract private shipping lines to deport people via water.[21]

In the 1940s and 1950s, the Immigration and Naturalization Service began using airplanes to transport deportees both within the United States and to their home countries. The first airlift took place on a sunny morning in the fall of 1946, when an Air Force B-25 aircraft ("originally designed for much more lethal cargo") transported a group of apprehended migrants from Tucson, Arizona, to Texas for deportation. After just a few flights, immigration officials turned to private contractors to carry out the lift.[22] The most infamous airlift in US history, the January 1948 flight that crashed near Coalinga, California, killing all thirty-two people aboard, including twenty-eight Mexicans—memorialized by Woody Guthrie's song "Deportee (Plane Wreck at Los Gatos)"—was run by Airline Transport Carriers, Inc.[23] The service fielded a wide range of offers, including proposals from a California-based helicopter company, a large "clearing house" association representing more than a dozen charter airlines, and a Mexican pilot offering to fly more than 1,300 deportees each month from Arizona and California to Guadalajara, Jalisco, in central-western Mexico, at $10 and $15 per person ($95 and $143 today).[24] Although it is unclear whether the INS ever enlisted the services of Mexican pilots, officials investigated whether the law allowed for it and concluded that it was permissible as long as the individual acquired a "permit for the transportation of non common carrier goods such as personal property and other things not carried by common carriers." Whether or not deportees fit into this category was another question, but the opinion of one of the INS officials in charge of the lift spoke volumes about how the service understood its work and viewed deportees: "Our contention is that the Mexican aliens are, in a sense, personal property in that they make no decisions as to the means of transportation or destination."[25]

While it received numerous proposals from private individuals and companies, the INS directed most of the airlift business to the Flying Tiger Line of Burbank, California. Founded in 1945 by a group of Air Force pilots who had

Figure 13. Mexicans waiting to board a privately contracted Flying Tiger deportation flight, 1950s.
Courtesy of the National Border Patrol Museum, El Paso, Texas.

flown as part of the Flying Tigers fighter squadron in East Asia, the line would eventually become "the world's largest air cargo carrier" (before being bought by Federal Express in 1988).[26] In its early years, the airlift business helped launch the Flying Tiger Line, which initially just flew deportees from the US interior to the Mexican border and laterally along the border. But starting in June 1951, up to three sixty-passenger, twin-engine C-46 Flying Tiger planes began making nightly seven-hour deportation runs from Southern California to Guadalajara. Similar to the boatlifts before them, the goal was to deter future migration to the United States. Explaining the rationale behind the air-lift, an INS memo described it this way: Deporting people just across the land border was "like trying to empty a tub of water by continually stirring—and never pouring or siphoning any off. The airlift siphons off." In its first year of operation, the Flying Tiger Line transported more than 34,000 deportees to Guadalajara on behalf of the service (see figure 13).[27]

Though the INS found the airlift effective, budgetary constraints forced the agency to use it only intermittently in the early 1950s. The service soon found alternative ways to cut back on costs while still discouraging future unauthorized migration. In June 1953, an article in *The Laredo Times* revealed that the Border Patrol had adopted a policy of dumping Mexican men over the border in the depopulated Zapata, Texas area, forty-five miles away from the closest city. Deportees with enough money could buy a bus ticket, but a considerable number of them could not afford transportation. Despite claims by Ed Idar Jr., head of the American GI Forum, that deportees' rights and human dignity had never been violated, independent investigations by the newspaper and the Mexican government found that each morning US officials forced as many as 200 men and boys to make the march in 100 to 110 degree Fahrenheit heat with no food, water, or shelter along the way.[28] "They call it the 'hot-foot lift' today," the author of the article wrote, adding that "tomorrow it may carry the sinister brand of 'The Death March of Zapata.'"[29] Responding to what it called the INS's "truly inhumane" policy, the Mexican government agreed to provide transportation and assistance to destitute deportees at Zapata.[30]

The following year, during Operation Wetback, the service embraced a cheaper way to deport people away from the border than the airlift: It contracted Pacific Greyhound bus line to transport Mexicans apprehended in California to Nogales, Arizona, at which point Mexican officials would use chartered trains to take them away from the border.[31] Though Mexican authorities might have agreed to assist the United States in principle, in many cases deportees never made it very far south. Desertions from the trainlifts "occurred in large numbers," with some deportees "bribing the train guards to turn their backs" when they disembarked at transportation hubs that facilitated their return to the border. On one trip, Gilbert P. Trujillo, a Border Patrol inspector sent undercover to investigate the matter, reported that only two of the sixty deportees remained on the train when it arrived at its final destination. Mexican transportation companies, for their part, actually profited from this arrangement. Yellow Line, a bus company, "believed that such aliens should be permitted to go where they chose" and told US officials that "bus lines in Mexico would transport [deportees] where they wished to go at reduced rates if necessary to secure the business." On one occasion, Yellow Line sent at least six buses, each with a fifty-person capacity, to San Luis, Sonora, to take deportees who had left the trainlift back to Mexicali and Tijuana.[32] Given the buslifts' and trainlifts' ineffectiveness, INS officials were eager to find another way to deport people deep into the Mexican interior. Soon they did.

## Bananas North, Deportees South

Sometime in late 1954, James Hockaday, a physician and two-time mayor of Port Isabel, Texas, spent a day at the beach with his family. His camera in tow, Hockaday shot a home movie, the first four minutes of which documented the loading and departure of a hulking ship named the *Emancipación*. In the clip, multiple truckloads and busloads of people, most of them men, pull up alongside the vessel. Some of the younger ones hop down from the trucks with a spring in their step, while older men carefully make their way down before joining hundreds of others already on board the crowded boat. The last load is only women and children: some carrying bags, one with a box tucked under her arm. Officials supervising the process pass babies from one officer to the next until they reach the deck. As a boy marches up the stairs, Hockaday's son appears in the background, cutting between the buses and freely roaming about. Once all are on board, a middle-aged man with graying hair and a cigarette dangling from his mouth appears in the frame and waves goodbye to the people on the ship, first with one hand and then with both. He looks back at the camera twice, fully aware of being filmed. Finally, the visibly weighed-down vessel sets off with black smoke billowing. Onlookers on the beach watch the ship leave; one person appears to be looking through binoculars. Then, suddenly, the picture cuts to a woman and two children playing in the water, jumping waves. The last minute and a half is banal footage of boys goofing around for the camera and the amused adults watching them.[33] What we see more than a half-century later appears to be an ordinary, relaxing day at the beach for the Hockaday family. The same, however, could not be said for the 800 people on the *Emancipación*—all Mexican deportees—who had just begun the grueling voyage, up to forty-eight hours, across the Gulf of Mexico (see figure 14).

From September 3, 1954, to August 24, 1956, immigration officials contracted two Mexican companies, Transportes Marítimos y Fluviales (TMF) and Transportes Marítimos Refrigerados, S.A. (TMR), to transport their compatriots 550 miles south, from Port Isabel, Texas, to Veracruz, Mexico. Initially, Attorney General Herbert Brownell recommended the use of US Navy ships, but concerns about the Mexican public's potential reaction to "the arrival in Mexican port of a United States warship discharging Mexican nationals" led officials to instead use privately contracted Mexican flag ves-

Figure 14. Route used to boatlift deportees across the Gulf of Mexico.
Map by Daniel Immerwahr.

sels.[34] The first boat to transport deportees was the SS *Emancipación*, the TMF-owned "1800-ton riveted steel construction passenger-cargo vessel" seen in Hockaday's home movie. The US and Mexican governments approved the ship to carry up to 800 deportees per trip. Starting in June 1955, increasing demand and frequent mechanical and weather-induced delays resulted in the SS *Veracruz* joining the *Emancipación* in making weekly deportation runs. The impetus for the boatlift came from the United States, but the Mexican government collaborated on the selection and inspection of vessels, shared responsibility for the custody of deportees, and helped pay for the operation.[35]

For private shipping companies already hauling bananas, cement, and other cargo from Mexico to the United States, deportees represented a potential moneymaking opportunity for the return trip south. But to win the boatlift contract, TMF, and later TMR, had to make offers to transport as many people as possible at as low a cost as possible. In doing so, they created conditions on board that, though approved by the US and Mexican governments, led some to refer to them as "hell ships" comparable to "black slavers."[36] The Mexican government received numerous complaints about the *Emancipación* as early as January 1955 and became "increasingly concerned about [the ship's] continued use" and the "possibility of a disaster." That summer, after the passenger vessel *La Flecha* sank during a storm and some thirty people drowned, the Mexican government called for the inspection of all flagships and sent José T. Rocha, the official in charge of the Bracero Program, to examine the *Emancipación* at Brownsville. Rocha found the concerns about the vessel justified and reported back to Secretary of the Interior Gustavo Díaz Ordaz that using the ships would be dangerous in bad weather. Other officials also expressed serious doubts about the *Veracruz*. On the eve of its first trip, the Mexican ambassador to the United States sent a cautionary letter to the US secretary of state warning against integrating the *Veracruz* into the boatlift. Citing the "bad conditions and small dimensions . . . which must inevitably occasion crowding and unjustified inconveniences," the ambassador described the ship as "unsafe" and the conditions as "inhumane." He made it clear that the Mexican government would not take responsibility in the event of an accident and, moreover, "such responsibility would fall upon the American authorities that ordered this form of deportation."[37]

Critiques of the *Emancipación* and *Veracruz* in the Mexican press became more biting and more frequent during the summer of 1955, eventually leading the Mexican government to act. A July 25 article in *La Prensa* described the trip aboard the *Emancipación* as "painful and inhuman," adding that the deportees are treated like prisoners and "transported like cattle." The article concluded by warning that "it is feared . . . that the *Emancipación* will suffer the same tragedy as '*La Flecha*.'"[38] On August 29, 1955, the Mexican government refused to clear the *Emancipación* and *Veracruz* for passenger transport. Neither ship made any trips for the next six weeks, forcing the INS to rely on other methods to deport thousands of people. Detainees who had been transported to McAllen from El Paso were sent back to El Paso, and the INS had little choice but to expel them just across the border or by trainlift to Monterrey.[39]

Factors other than negative press coverage were also at play. Mexican officials may have had less power than their US counterparts, but they still exer-

Figure 15.   The *Mercurio*, 1956.
56364/43.36 pt1, Boatlift8, Entry 9, RG 85, INS, NARA1.

cised considerable control over the boatlift. Some Mexican bureaucrats even enriched themselves from the deportation machine. The Mexican government did not call for the end of the entire operation in response to the public outrage about the boatlift; it called for the termination of TMF's contract. As a possible replacement, Rocha suggested TMR. What he did not mention, but INS officials soon learned, was that "Mr. José T. Rocha [was] a member and stock-holder of the firm Transportes Marítimos Refrigerados, S.A."[40]

The Mexican navy finally cleared the *Emancipación* and *Veracruz* and the boatlift resumed on October 16 with TMF still the provider. Just over a week later, however, INS Commissioner Joseph M. Swing expressed his desire to utilize the SS *Mercurio* and SS *Frida*, owned by TMR. Swing officially claimed that the ships were "smaller and better conditioned," but the six-week hiatus, ongoing negative press in Mexico, and pressure from Mexican government officials "who would apparently like to get their ships in business" also pushed the INS to act. "The Mexican Ministry of the Interior has assured us that it desires and endorses the change," Swing noted.[41]

By the end of the year TMR had prevailed. After TMF's boats had expelled 32,797 people on forty-one different trips, the *Mercurio*, a vessel originally built for use by the Canadian navy in World War II, left Port Isabel bound for Veracruz on New Year's Eve 1955 with 450 deportees on board (see figure 15).

Although the INS's agreement with TMR stipulated that "no member of or delegate to Congress, or resident Commissioner, shall be admitted to any share or part of this contract, or to any benefit that may arise therefrom," that seems to have only applied to US officials. The INS was fully aware of Rocha's conflict of interest and the corruption involved in pushing the agency to drop TMF in favor of TMR. But that did not matter: The service cared much more about the continuation of the boatlift and buy-in from the Mexican government than about which contractor carried it out or that a Mexican official stood to financially benefit. The boatlift was indispensable to the INS, based on Swing's and other officials' conviction that deporting Mexicans "to points distant from their place of employment and apprehension in the United States is the most effective means of preventing their unlawful return to this country."[42]

Although INS officials may have been indifferent as to which company carried out the boatlift, the terms of the new contract with TMR shaped immigration policy in consequential ways. The two sides initially agreed that the *Mercurio* would carry between 400 and 450 deportees per voyage, but after the first trip the maximum number increased to 500. Seeing as that meant more profits for TMR and more deportations for the INS, both parties were amenable to the modification. By guaranteeing to provide a minimum of five trips per month with at least 400 deportees per trip, the INS set a quota of boatlifting 2,000 people per month, regardless of need.[43]

Hoping to avoid delays similar to those encountered with the *Emancipación* and *Veracruz*, the INS insisted on exclusive use of the *Mercurio*. Prior to the agreement with the INS, TMR had dedicated its ships to transporting bananas from the Mexican state of Tabasco. But when tropical storms devastated Tabasco's banana plantations in 1955, the company's only source of income disappeared. TMR saw the boatlift as a stopgap while banana production recovered and as an opportunity to diversify and expand its business. Even though TMR's vessels were cargo ships not meant or approved for passenger transport, the company hoped to transport bananas north and deportees south.[44]

TMR may have initially agreed to enter into an exclusive contract with the INS when it had no bananas to transport, but when the banana business picked up again the company promised to use two ships to make eight trips per month for the service while also fulfilling the needs of its "steady banana customers." As way of explanation, a TMR representative told US officials that the *Mercurio* and *Frida* had long been used to haul bananas and he did not want to "neglect his former customers completely for a short term contract [with the INS]."[45] Though US officials did not want to enter into a nonexclusive contract, they eventually did. The new arrangement led to routine delays related to the *Mercurio* picking up Tabasco bananas and hauling them to customers in places like Alabama. The ship also had to be scrubbed down on either end "after unloading bananas and after unloading *gente*." But the US government's overriding desire to maintain uninterrupted boatlift service, Rocha's personal financial interest, and the firm's goal of maximizing returns resulted in the continuation of the operation. Soon thereafter, TMR installed air-conditioning in the between deck: not for the deportees, but to ensure that the bananas arrived in good condition.[46]

In addition to their willful neglect of Mexican migrants' physical welfare aboard the ships, US officials also made deportees provide financial support to sustain the boatlift. The INS paid TMF and TMR $8 or $9 per deportee ($77–$86 today), but soon after the operation commenced the service defrayed part of this cost by collecting money from people deemed able to pay—although not all who were able to pay did. In total, the INS paid TMF and TMR nearly $400,000 ($3.84 million today) over the course of seventy-six boatlifts. At the same time, they collected $32,850 ($315,000 today) from deportees on forty trips, defraying 8 percent of the overall cost and nearly 20 percent of the cost of the trips in which money was collected. Forcing Mexicans to subsidize their own expulsion enabled the INS to apprehend, detain, and boatlift even more people. This in turn benefited private firms eager to profit off migrants' misfortune.[47]

US officials also had other reasons for wanting to extend the boatlift. The ships involved in the operation functioned, as William Walters has argued about all vehicles used to deport people, as "mobile sites of power" and "mobile zones of governance."[48] Although the Justice Department claimed that the boatlift "wasn't punishment for the wetbacks but only served to teach them a lesson," Commissioner Swing's testimony before the House Appropriations Committee in February 1955 left little doubt about the operation's real purpose. "They [the Mexicans] hate the boat trip like a devil hates holy water. They get out and they get seasick and the boat lift is the most salutary thing that we have hit on yet."[49] By the middle of the twentieth century, *how* the INS deported people mattered, and officials hoped the conditions on the ships, along with the destination deep in the Mexican interior, would traumatize migrants and deter future unauthorized migration.

## The Human Costs of Commodifying Deportation

What did deportation as punishment and profit-making enterprise look like to migrants on the ground or, in this case, on the sea? What was it like to be boatlifted? What were the human costs of the business of deportation?

After apprehension, whether along the border or in the interior, the government moved migrants to South Texas for expulsion. Transportation companies vied with one another to win these internal contracts. Until late March 1954, the Border Patrol used trains to move Mexicans from Chicago to San Antonio, where they then took the deportees to Laredo by bus. The trip took five to seven days and required three officers to serve as guards. But then, to the railroad companies' dismay, the service started using commercial airplanes to convey deportees from different interior points to the border. In an attempt to win back the removal contract, railroad officials made a counteroffer: "We are very anxious to again participate in the handling of this Mexican deport business, and hope that with the reduced rate we are quoting, and the furnishing of guards to relieve your man-power situation, that we will again be privileged to participate in this very nice business." In the end, the INS decided to continue using the airlift since it streamlined the process by taking deportees directly to the border without any intermediary stops.[50]

Aboard the planes an INS officer armed with a pistol guarded the deportees, who were given an in-flight meal. As a reporter who accompanied a July 1954 airlift noted, "It's not filet mignon but every returning wetback being flown back to Mexico was given a box lunch by the plane stewardess." While the airlift helped the INS deport Mexicans from the interior of the country, it raised questions for others, including one of the pilots for the contract transportation company: "This Mexican business mystifies me. We just hauled a load of contract laborers from Mexico to Michigan. Now we're hauling a load of other Mexicans back to Mexico. Well, I just fly the plane."[51]

During the Chicago phase of Operation Wetback, the increased volume and frequency of flights led the INS to temporarily use three C-46-D airplanes on loan from the Air Force to transport people to the Lower Rio Grande Valley for the boatlift. (The Air Force told the INS that the planes were not certified for passenger service and understood that the service would make sure the Civil Aeronautics Administration cleared them.) The switch to government-owned and -operated planes angered private carriers. In a letter to the attorney general, the president of the Flying Tiger Line accused the INS of engaging in competition with private airlines. "As a corporate citizen in the United States business community we are appalled by this usurpation of our right to do business." A representative of the Air Transport Association of America, a clearinghouse that represented numerous carriers, agreed and argued that they had "been unable to discover any justification in the national interest why government aircraft must be used on these moves." He continued, "As a matter of fact, it seems entirely likely that a study of this traffic would reveal that commercial airlines cannot only move this traffic efficiently, but that they can do so to the financial benefit of the United States." However, in the end none of the private carriers' offers could compete with the lower cost of using the Air Force planes.[52]

Upon arriving in the Lower Rio Grande Valley, officials took the men, women, and children slated for the boatlift to the McAllen Detention Camp (see figures 16–18). The facility had an official capacity of 500, but often filled to more than twice that amount and sometimes held as many as 2,000 people. "The matter of excess numbers and prolonged detention," an official reported in early 1955, "has caused unrest among the prisoners and has resulted in escape attempts and, on one occasion, a mass demonstration." In the middle of the night on March 1, three teenage migrants tried to scale the fence in the northeast corner of the camp. Two of the boys stopped after Officer Carl G. Cole fired a warning shot, but seventeen-year-old Porfirio Flores Pruneda kept climbing. As he reached the top and attempted to navigate his body through the concertina wire, Cole took aim with his shotgun. Flores dropped to the ground after two shotgun pellets struck him in the back and another two lodged themselves in his leg. A doctor removed the round, metal masses, dressed what he described as "very slight" wounds, and told officials they

Figure 16. The McAllen Detention Camp, 1954.
Courtesy of the National Border Patrol Museum, El Paso, Texas.

Figure 17. The cafeteria at the McAllen Detention Camp, 1953.
TM-27-29, AHSRE.

Figure 18. Families held at the McAllen Detention Camp, 1953.
TM-27-29, AHSRE.

could send Flores on the next boatlift. Responding to such escape attempts, the INS recommended taking measures to tighten up security at the camp, from having agents be more vigilant about searching detainees to repositioning the watch towers and illuminating the external fence.[53]

Approximately two hours before the scheduled departure of the *Emancipación*, *Veracruz*, or *Mercurio*, INS officials loaded detainees onto as many as ten or twenty buses, while their baggage and personal effects were loaded onto separate baggage trucks for transfer to Port Isabel. When a bus broke down the INS forced deportees to "double up." Crowding twice the number of people onto a bus as were meant to fit violated laws and regulations but was a common practice. On an inspection trip to McAllen in 1953, Harlon B. Carter noted, "Our officers call this the 'Border Patrol Pack,' and comment facetiously upon the extent they have improved upon the sardine canning industry." Despite being aware that it was unsafe, the Border

Patrol preferred to overload buses instead of cutting back on apprehensions, releasing detainees, or spending more money.[54]

Authorities deported nearly all Mexicans bound for the boatlift, including individuals and families who had long lived in the country, via voluntary departures. The vast majority of them never went before an immigration judge and never had the chance to fight to stay.[55]

At Port Isabel deportees were loaded onto the boat and forced to descend into the forward below deck, their place of confinement until the ship departed (see figures 19–21). As soon as the boat cast off, most, if not all, deportees returned to the top deck. For some to jump overboard was "not at all unusual." During the first month of the boatlift two deportees did so. "Two wetbacks lived up to their name," read the lede to a *Valley Morning Star* story, adding that it "was unreported whether the men left the boat in a swan dive or half-gainer, or whether they used the Australian crawl or a free-style stroke to reach shore." Despite an extensive search by Border Patrol boats and observation airplanes the men were never found, which "threw the Border Patrol in a tizzy, although one high B.P. Official said the US Government's responsibilities ended when the wetbacks were loaded aboard." To prevent such an event from recurring in the future, a Border Patrol boat followed the ships full of deportees until they cleared the channel.[56]

On board the ships, US and Mexican immigration officials and Mexican shipping company representatives cooperated in the administration of the boatlift. Generally, an INS officer, Mexican migration official, and Mexican doctor joined the captain, crew, and deportees. The doctor vaccinated all deportees and tended to any sick or injured passengers, while the US and Mexican officials maintained general order, broke up fights, mediated accusations of theft, and stopped illicit gambling. INS officers also acted as intelligence gatherers, questioning deportees about their experiences and future plans.[57]

Gender norms and expectations influenced how officials policed deportees aboard the ships. Reporting on the second boatlift ever on September 9, 1954, a US newspaper noted, "In contrast with the first cruise, which was strictly stag, the trip of the S.S. *Emancipación* which began today was co-educational."[58] Adult men comprised the vast majority of boatlift passengers, but the *Emancipación* and *Veracruz* also deported a considerable number of women and children, who at times represented more than 10 percent of the 800 deportees.

Figure 19. Loading deportees onto the *Mercurio* for the treacherous trip across the Gulf of Mexico, 1956.
56364/43.36 pt1, Boatlift8, Entry 9, RG 85, INS, NARA1.

Figure 20. The spare below-deck area of the *Mercurio*, not designed for passenger transport, 1955.
56364/43.36 pt1, Boatlift2, Entry 9, RG 85, INS, NARA1.

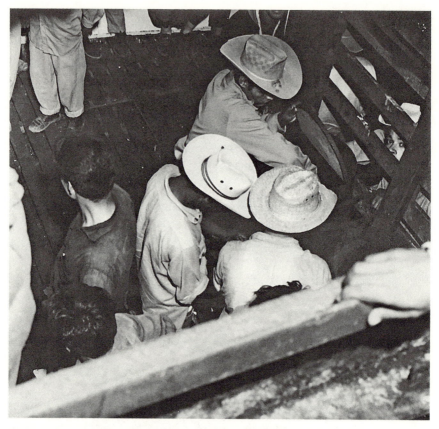

Figure 21. Mexican deportees in the *Mercurio*'s forward hold, August 1956.
56364/43.36 pt1, Boatlift8, Entry 9, RG 85, INS, NARA1.

In some cases boatlifts swept up entire families.[59] Women and children usually stayed in the passenger-class cabins. When cabins were not available they received reclining canvas deck chairs and cots on a separate deck of the ship. The women and children's quarters were almost always off limits to men and, in some instances, the crew took extensive measures to regulate contact between the sexes. On an August 1955 boatlift aboard the *Veracruz*, officials roped off all points leading to the women's deck and then stood guard. The patrol inspector on that trip reported that "these steps proved very effective and as a result, indications of prostitution were not present."[60]

Business interests and socioeconomic status also shaped the experiences of boatlifted deportees. Whereas cabins on the *Emancipación* and *Veracruz* were initially reserved for women and children at no cost, TMF's desire to maximize profits led them to start renting cabins for $5–$10 per night ($48–$96 today) to "aliens having the necessary funds." In theory, this was only supposed to happen if extra cabins were available upon the accommodation of all women and children. However, exceptions occurred. On a December 1954 boatlift carrying sixty-three women and twenty-two children, four-person cabins packed in six adult women. TMF's desire to ramp up profits exceeded its desire to provide deportees comfortable facilities.[61]

Authorities usually relegated men to the hold and the open deck, where tarps blocked the sun and rain. Deportees often had to contend with inclement weather. Passengers on the January 2, 1955, boatlift complained about a lack of blankets and said they were "too cold to sleep at night." Patrol Inspector Marvin L. Butler Jr., who accompanied the *Emancipación* on that trip, largely dismissed these complaints. "While cool nights, and in some cases, insufficient clothing did serve to make them more or less uncomfortable, I do not believe there was any real suffering from the cold." But deportees who stayed on the open deck had to contend with adverse climactic conditions. When the *Mercurio* encountered rough waters soon after leaving Port Isabel on March 19, 1956, "the bow-splash kept those who stayed on deck wet and cold."[62]

Still, most deportees stayed on the ships' open decks since the holds were "hot and crowded," "very filthy and foul-smelling." A South Texas newspaper noted that even the *Mercurio*, whose below-deck area was air-conditioned for the transport of bananas, "is undoubtedly messy and must be crowded when from 400 to 500 wetbacks pile aboard." A political cartoon that ran in the government-aligned *Excélsior*, one of Mexico's two major national daily newspapers, critiqued the boatlift by depicting Mexican laborers as sardines packed into a tin labeled "Mercurio I" (see figure 22). While one government inspection found that several overhead floodlights illuminated the *Mercurio*'s hold around the clock, another claimed there were only two lights, one forward and one aft, and darkness "for over 170 feet amidships." A couple of small barrels of potable water sat at each end of the hold. Although the INS's contracts with TMF and TMR stipulated that the service would provide mattresses or install bunks, that implied additional costs, and it never did. On the *Mercurio* deportees used lifejackets as pillows and bedding.[63]

The boatlift also offers insights into the intersection of social control, public health, and the state's coercive efforts to regulate immigrants deemed

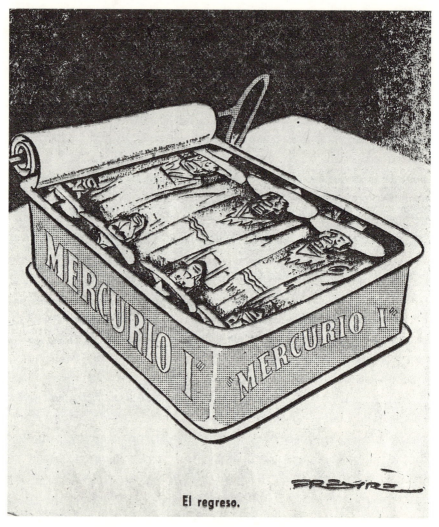

El regreso.

Figure 22. Freyre, "El regreso" ("The return"), *Excélsior*, August 28, 1956.

dangerous.[64] Soon after leaving Port Isabel, the ship's doctor began administering smallpox vaccinations to deportees. Officials sometimes stamped meal tickets as proof of vaccination, which migrants then had to present in order to receive a meal. Authorities kept track of who had already received food in hopes of preventing people from getting more than one portion. Someone caught trying to do so was denied another meal as punishment. Feeding occurred in shifts since just thirty to fifty people could be accommodated at once. Long lines were common, and the crews often served food al-most all day and night. Gabriel Esquivel, a twenty-six-year-old apprehended in California, flown to Brownsville, and boatlifted in 1955, described his des-peration from hunger but having to wait until night to eat because there were so many people in line ahead of him. During the *Veracruz*'s first boatlift on June 11, 1955, a bottleneck occurred when men began crowding to the front. According to the patrol inspector, "This situation was alleviated and cor-rected for subsequent meals by the rigging of firehoses and threatening to turn them on the aliens in a state of semi-riot."[65] In addition to the lengthy waits and violent treatment at the hands of immigration officials monitoring the meals, deportees also complained about the food's quality. "The food is the worst," one man told a Mexican newspaper. "Poorly done and under-cooked rice, beans without salt, and watery coffee." On a May 1956 boatlift, deportees complained that "the beans were spoiled and the rice was sour" and people "seemed to think that they were sick from the food rather than being seasick."[66]

Seasickness was a real problem, though, and affected a considerable num-ber of deportees. On one trip the patrol inspector reported that "seasickness was prevalent," adding that "most cases were not serious, however a few ap-peared desperately ill." From March to August 1956, the *Mercurio*'s ship logs indicated that, depending on the conditions, anywhere from 5 to 60 percent of the 500 passengers were seasick. Rough seas caused as many as three-quarters of the deportees to fall ill on some runs. As a twenty-five-year-old Michoacán native recounted, "I was seasick the entire voyage and decided that I would not return to the United States illegally because I never wanted to get on another ship." Even if a deportee did not become seasick, the seasick-ness of others and the "resulting mess" affected the conditions for all.[67]

The US and Mexican governments and private Mexican contractors did not—to put it mildly—prioritize onboard safety. The INS's contract with TMF specified that the *Emancipación* and *Veracruz*, which each transported 800 deportees plus the crew, should carry "four (4) seaworthy lifeboats each with a capacity of thirty-seven (37) adult passengers." It also called for 800 lifejackets, but even that would not have been enough for the deportees plus captain, crew, doctor, and migration officials aboard the ships. Upon in-specting the *Mercurio* prior to its enlistment in the boatlift, a Mexican naval official called on TMR to place an adequate number of life rafts on board in addition to lifeboats to account for the total number of crew and passengers. The Mexican government later approved the ship for use provided that it carry an additional ten to fifteen life rafts. However, it seems that TMR never complied. The company's contract with the US government required the *Mercurio* to carry only two lifeboats, each with a twenty-four-person capacity. The patrol inspector accompanying the vessel on April 11, 1956, reported that it carried two lifeboats and five rubber rafts, in addition to "an undetermined amount of life jackets which, considering the amount of passengers, seemed hardly adequate in case of an emergency." An official inspection later concluded that the total capacity of the lifeboats and rafts was 356. But US and Mexican officials repeatedly approved the *Mercurio* to carry up to 500 passengers, in addition to twenty-six crewmembers.[68]

The INS purposefully attempted to evade US safety inspection laws in hopes of expediting deportations and continuing the boatlift. Though its initial petition to the secretary of defense to waive "safety-of-life at sea requirements" for the *Mercurio* was unsuccessful, it seems as if officials later approved the exemption. The United States argued that waiving inspection requirements was "in the interest of national defense" because, in the context of the Cold War, the "constant presence of such a large number of [Mexican] aliens whose loyalty could not be determined constituted an ever present and serious security threat." By waiving US inspection requirements the *Mercurio* only had to comply with Mexican safety standards. As a US official pointed out in a draft of a letter later amended to omit this section, "Mexico is not a signatory nation to the International Convention for Safety of Life at Sea, 1948, and while its vessels are adequate for its own standards, they do not generally conform to the United States inspection requirements."[69] Safety was not a priority for any of the parties carrying out the boatlift since, in financial terms, adhering to lesser requirements meant the governments could deport more people at a lower cost and the companies could maximize their profits.

Most boatlifted deportees arrived safely in Veracruz, but on at least two occasions deportees aboard the *Emancipación* died of heart attacks. At the end of January 1955, General Frank Partridge, a special assistant to the commissioner, inquired about whether the United States was "bound to acknowledge [the first death] with Mex. Govt." The second man, Manuel Arroyo Hernández, died of a heart attack at 3:30 a.m. on August 23, 1955, and was "buried at sea as per instructions" of the public health office at Veracruz. It is unclear whether US or Mexican officials contacted either man's family, or if legal action was taken against either government. What is clear, however, is that INS leaders considered covering up these tragedies in hopes of avoiding a diplomatic standoff or negative press coverage that might have jeopardized the entire operation.[70]

Upon arriving at Veracruz, Mexican migration officials met the ship and transferred deportees to a large warehouse near the dock, where they were processed, examined by a doctor, and given sandwiches, fruit, and the chance to exchange dollars for pesos. There were usually between twelve and twenty "repeaters"—people who had been deported before—on each trip, plus others who avoided detection by using false names or other means. Mexican authorities separated repeaters from other deportees, lectured them, and, at the behest of the US government, took them to Allende Prison in hopes that a short jail stint would discourage future migration. In some instances, rumors spread about repeaters receiving harsh prison sentences, but in reality they usually ranged from a few days to a couple of weeks. On occasion, Mexican immigration officials released them without requiring jail time. The motivation of the authorities ranged from bribery to pity, as when they chose not to imprison any of the seventeen repeaters who arrived on Christmas Eve 1954.[71]

For the vast majority, arriving at Veracruz was an intermediate, rather than terminal, point of their deportation. Despite the US government's claim that expelling people via boatlift would put them closer to their homes, the vast majority of deportees came from the historic migration region in central-western Mexico or from the border region. From Veracruz officials sent deportees to Mexico City. Those who had money could pay for a ticket aboard chartered buses run by Mexican companies like ADO. Others bribed Mexican officials to stay in Veracruz. Deportees who could afford neither a bus ticket nor a bribe were herded onto boxcars aboard freight trains that the Mexican government funded. By slow freight train the trip to the capital took forty hours, considerably longer than by bus or the twelve-hour trip on the first-class Pullman trains. Upon arriving in Mexico City deportees continued by bus, train, or on foot to their homes. Eustacio Maldonado Martínez, who arrived without any money, described the difficult journey home to the northeastern border state of Tamaulipas: "The trip was very hard since I had to walk a long distance each time in order to reach my home. . . . I wore out my shoes and had to walk from Mexico, D.F. to Mantes without shoes." Leopoldo Belmontes Ramos, from the central-western state of Michoacán, had a similarly trying experience. "I had no money for transportation and had to walk all the way to my home. I begged for food from houses along the way and did whatever work I could find to do." Others returned directly to the northern border to try their luck once more, but some decided that they had had enough. As one man declared, "The boat trip was very bad for me and if I ever got on land again I would never get on another boat or take the chance of being sent to Veracruz again."[72]

None of this was unintentional. The dreadful onboard conditions, the rough waters, and the removal of deportees to points not only far from the border but also far from their homes were all a product of the operation's punitive, for-profit nature. The boatlift across the Gulf of Mexico was grueling—by design. And immigration authorities and company officials tried to maximize the number of deportees subjected to this traumatic form of expulsion. In fiscal year 1956, the INS used the boatlift to expel more than 40 percent of all Mexicans apprehended in the Border Patrol's southwest region, and during some months that figure topped 60 percent.[73]

In early August 1956, Representative Robert H. Mollohan (Democrat, West Virginia), chairman of the Legal and Monetary Affairs Subcommittee under the House Committee on Government Operations, called for an investigation into the operation and whether the *Mercurio* met the US Coast Guard's safety and sanitation standards. He found reprehensible the US and Mexican governments' approval of the vessel's use and compared it to an eighteenth-century slave ship, opining that it "seems shameful to subject these aliens to penal conditions and practices that Western civilization abandoned over a century ago." In addition, Mollohan wondered how 500 deportees could possibly fit onto a ship that previously carried seventy to ninety people. "I am sure that the people of this Nation will not countenance the transportation of human beings on a standard which appears to be below that required for the hauling of livestock."[74]

In response to growing criticism and pressure resulting from Mollohan's investigation, Navy Captain John D. Reese Jr. was called upon to inspect the *Mercurio*. Strong accusations notwithstanding, INS officials believed themselves on firm ground. "I'm not *preocupado* . . . about the inspection," Charles Beechie, the INS attaché in Mexico City, wrote. "We can't (and shouldn't try) to make a luxury liner out of a ship that has been operating out of Mexico with a Mex crew for years, but I think she'll be plenty presentable." Moreover, he continued, "now that I have learned that the hold <u>IS</u> air-conditioned, I'm convinced that we couldn't do better. Sure hope we come out on top." Reese inspected the ship on August 24, 1956, accompanied by other INS officials, the local Mexican consul, and other Mexican immigration officials. Responding to Mollohan's accusations of overcrowding, Reese explained that although the *Mercurio* had held ninety to one hundred people during its use by the Canadian navy, TMR converted the ship after purchasing it. "The wetbacks now are berthed," he stated, "in the 'tween decks which periodically are used as cargo space for bananas." In other words, 500 people now occupied the same space as ninety before, squeezed in like the yellow fruit for which the ship's hold had been designed. Echoing Beechie, Reese told reporters, "It is no luxury liner, but it appears to do the job."[75]

Reese and other migration officials' perceptions of Mexican migrants shaped the process of expulsion and cruel treatment of deportees. As he explained in an attempt to justify onboard conditions, the boatlift's accommodations "must take into consideration the character and type of individual being transported." He then proceeded to describe the "character of the wetback." His conclusions, among others, included:

The wetback, by and large, has never been accustomed to the necessities of life, much less luxuries.

Most wetbacks have never known what it is like to sleep in a modern bed, most of them living in the open, sleeping on the ground and living in general not much better than animals.

Many of the wetbacks are not used to such modern conveniences as wash basins and toilet facilities. . . . It was explained by the officer in charge of the [McAllen] camp that the wetbacks frequently make their toilet in the wash basins, and wash their hands and face in the toilet bowls.

Many wetbacks do not sleep in the same position as the average American, but squat on their haunches and bury their heads in their arms.

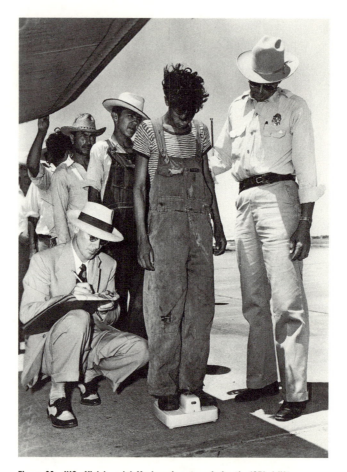

Figure 23.   INS officials weigh Mexican deportees during the 1951 airlift operation.
Courtesy of the National Border Patrol Museum, El Paso, Texas.

During 1951, the Immigration and Naturalization Service weighed approximately 10,000 wetbacks to determine an average weight [see figure 23]. The figure, complete with personal belongings, was 110 pounds.[76]

These findings supported a patrol inspector's earlier assertion that the "conditions on the [*Emancipación*] were reasonably good considering the type of persons being handled."[77] At the end of his inspection, Reese and Mexican migration officials concluded that the *Mercurio* was in compliance with its contract and announced that the vessel would sail that same day, August 24, with a full load of deportees.[78]

What they did not know then was that it would be the ship's final trip—and the last boatlift ever.

## The End of the Boatlift

In the early hours of August 26, 1956, a mutinous uprising led by deportees upset about their treatment and the boatlift's conditions forced Captain Jorge Noval Espinosa to reroute the Veracruz-bound *Mercurio* to Tampico. As a man who had been apprehended eleven times and boatlifted four times told INS officials, even before the last trip deportees felt that "the *Mercurio* was not fit to haul human beings, that it was alright for cargo, but not for human beings."[79] Once the ship anchored near the dock, around forty deportees jumped overboard. Those who did may have done so in hopes that reaching Mexican soil would void any jurisdiction or power boatlift officials had over them. Some insisted that they jumped after the captain refused to accede to their demand to be let off at Tampico instead of Veracruz. A written petition later circulated, with supposedly more than three hundred signatures of those who also insisted on a Tampico disembarkation. After making it to shore, a few deportees contacted the Mexican press and encouraged others to describe the boatlift's conditions, as well as how they were treated.[80]

Some deportees who jumped overboard never made it ashore. Reports in the press varied, claiming either four or five had drowned. At first, the INS denied that anyone had died, but a couple of days later three bodies were found. A *Noticias de Tampico* article that conjectured that the men were "probably devoured by sharks that abound in these waters" proved to be somewhat prophetic. When the US vice consul at Tampico and a local clerk went to identify the bodies, they could only take thumbprints because of their "rapid decomposition" and missing body parts. In spite of their physical state, two of the men were wearing Levi's pants, which led the US consul to conclude "that the three men were very possibly 'wetbacks' who were traveling aboard the SS MERCURIO."[81]

The Tampico incident resulted in INS investigations and denunciations in the US and Mexican press. A US newspaper editorial stated that the conditions aboard the *Mercurio* "ought to be made the object of an investigation by an international tribunal." The Mexico City–based *Zócalo* placed the blame on Mexico. "We should be ashamed that we do nothing effective to prevent them from going to provide their services elsewhere." The *Excélsior* described the *Mercurio* as "old and unsafe" and opined that the conditions were worse than those endured by Chinese "culíes." Another *Excélsior* article lamented that "not a single Mexican voice protested, until now, that 500 Mexicans were treated like animals."[82]

In the wake of the incident, members of the Mexican Congress voiced strong opinions and called for an investigation. "It's inhuman what happened. Extremely unfortunate. Necessary steps should be taken so that it doesn't happen again," said one congressman. Two of his colleagues described the incident as "profoundly painful for Mexico" and noted that although the United States had the right to deport people, "the deportations should be humane. Our emigrants are men, not animals."[83]

Yet in the weeks leading up to the Tampico incident, Mexican officials defended the conditions on board the *Mercurio*. In mid-August, Mexican migration officials reported on the satisfactory nature of the food, safety and sanitary conditions, medical attention, and general treatment of deportees. The Mexican consul in Brownsville insisted his government would not allow the ship to sail if they deemed it unsafe. But, like their US counterparts, Mexican officials also used degrading stereotypes to describe deportees. After the Tampico incident, the Mexican migration chief at Matamoros dismissed deportees' complaints as "typical." His comments reflected his privileged socioeconomic position within Mexican society and racist view of migrant laborers. "They will never be satisfied, with any food or any treatment," he asserted. "As for not having beds, they would have torn them apart. I tell you, you don't know these people. They are my people, but they are bad some of them, and they would complain if you fed them a banquet."[84]

Other Mexican government officials felt that the bad press surrounding the Tampico incident was politically motivated since it fell less than a week before the president's state of the nation address. The Partido Revolucionario Institucional (PRI), the ruling party, was "extremely embarrassed and upset." The opposition Partido Acción Nacional (PAN) seized the opportunity: "The events in Tampico constitute a national embarrassment," the PAN proclaimed, and went on to lay the blame on the PRI for ignoring the inhumane treatment of Mexican migrants.[85] Captain Noval also harbored stereotypes about deportees and used them to discredit critics and clear himself—and in turn the PRI—of any wrongdoing. He slandered the deportees in the press, asserting that among those aboard the *Mercurio* during the Tampico incident "were numerous bad actors, thieves, homosexuals, escaped prisoners from Mexico and agitators that dedicated themselves to provoke discontent that ended in the uprising." Elsewhere he claimed that the group also included many thugs, delinquents, and drug traffickers.[86] But records prove that these characterizations did not accurately describe the vast majority of Mexicans aboard the last boatlift.[87]

By describing deportees as criminals, and worse, US and Mexican government officials and TMR representatives attempted to justify their treatment of migrants and deflect blame from themselves in hopes of continuing the boatlift. Their efforts failed. At the end of August the Mexican government terminated the boatlift in response to investigations and growing criticism in the US and Mexican press, as well as throughout Mexican society. The following week a Mexican official announced that migrants "will never again be transported like beasts."[88]

The INS made multiple attempts to reinitiate the boatlift, believing that deporting Mexicans into the interior of the country had "prove[n] to be an effective weapon in [its] all-out campaign to rid the country of the wetback menace."[89] Swing, for his part, warned that "in order to maintain continued control of the border, steps should be taken immediately to resume the repatriation of wetbacks by sea," and urged State Department officials to pressure the Mexican government.[90] Despite the INS's and TMR's desire to extend the boatlift, that required the approval of all involved parties, and in the aftermath of the Tampico incident the Mexican government was no longer willing to do so.

The boatlift's termination may have hurt TMR, but it opened up new opportunities for other transportation companies both in the immediate aftermath and in the decades to come. The INS first turned to charter bus companies and Mexican government–operated trainlifts, and then reinitiated the airlift to León, Guanajuato, in November 1957 in an effort to avoid deporting Mexicans just over the land border.[91]

In the following decades, private US and Mexican carriers would go on to deport millions of Mexicans. People on both sides of the border have been critical of the for-profit interior lifts, albeit for different reasons. For example, in the mid-1970s, US companies hoping to capitalize on the burgeoning deportation business could not have been pleased with immigration authorities' conscious effort to contract Mexican companies in hopes that doing so would "make the program more palatable" to the Mexican government.[92] The INS went so far as to allow representatives of Mexican bus companies and airlines to enter detention facilities in the San Diego sector to sell tickets to deportees, which sometimes led to kickback schemes that lined the pockets of US and Mexican officials.[93] During a six-month period around the same time, five different contract airlines, including at least some based in the United States, transported more than 23,000 people from the border to the interior at a cost of $2.75 million ($12.3 million today). In Mexico, rumors spread that US officials were deporting people "under sub-human conditions (e.g. in 'chicken coop' cages on freight air planes) and deprived of earnings and other rights." Upon arriving in Mexico City, deportees from different parts of the country frequently found themselves stranded and without the help of the Mexican government. Meanwhile, in the United States, newspapers' exaggerated reports described the airlifts as luxurious to a fault, noting that deportees were "just like any tourist taking the 'Fiesta Flight' to Mexico," during which they would be "served dinner and, if they wanted it, California champagne" on the US government's dime. In spite of these controversies and the substantial expense to the US government, immigration authorities' conviction that interior repatriation was a "significant and cost effective deterrent to illegal reentry" led them to rely on the lifts whenever possible.[94]

But such enforcement efforts did not stop people from coming to the United States. Nor would they in the future. They did, however, exact an incalculable toll on migrants. The combination of government policies meant to punish and private companies only interested in turning a profit proved devastating for deportees. Although we can hardly quantify the extent of the suffering these policies caused, it is clear that, for many people, enduring state-sanctioned violence and trauma was—and continues to be—a central element of the immigrant experience.

# FOUR

# Manufacturing Crisis and Fomenting Fear at the Dawn of the Age of Mass Expulsion

Juan Olivarez was twenty-four when he first went to the United States in 1966. He entered as a tourist—but he really went to work. After returning to his small town in the central-western Mexican state of Jalisco the following year, he headed north again, finding work picking beets, tomatoes, and cherries in California. Four months later, he and a few friends went to Oregon, where they repaired train tracks until one night after dinner an immigration officer knocked on their door and asked to see their papers. "We told him, almost in unison, 'We don't have any,'" Olivarez recounted. So the agent took them to the county jail, where they spent three days before being flown to Santa Rita, California. After four days in a large detention center there, the authorities flew the men to El Paso, Texas, where Olivarez described the jail as "deplorable," with "bad barracks, lots of disorder, . . . horrible food." Then, three days later, the service flew them back to California. Olivarez and his friends spent less than an hour at the El Centro detention center before the officers transported them to Calexico and deported them to Mexicali. "We went to eat Chinese food, we went to shower, and then I came [home], promising not to return to the United States," Olivarez remembered. "But a year later I went again."[1]

Olivarez's expulsion was one of thirteen million deportations the INS carried out between 1965 and 1985. From the mid-1970s on, deportations averaged nearly 925,000 per year, or more than 2,500 each day.

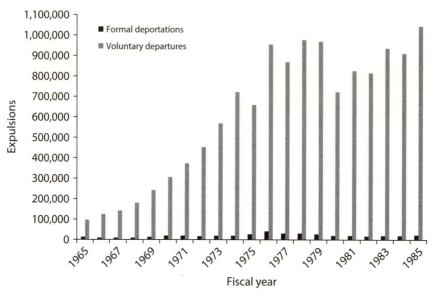

**Figure 24. Formal deportations and voluntary departures, fiscal years 1965–85.**
1976 includes a fifteen-month period because the fiscal year changed. DHS, *YOIS: 2017*, 103. Calculations and graph by author.

Unlike the episodic deportation campaigns during the Great Depression and early years of the Cold War, the unprecedented magnitude and regularity of enforcement actions marked a break from the past and the dawn of a new era: the age of mass expulsion.[2]

Like Olivarez, almost all of the people pushed out of the country during this period were Mexicans deported via voluntary departure (see figure 24). And, like Olivarez, many of them returned to the United States after their expulsion. The INS's near-exclusive reliance on voluntary departure helped produce a public narrative of perpetual crisis that depended on the criminalization of Mexicans.[3] While most apprehensions occurred at or near the border, which became a "revolving door" of sorts, agents—with assistance from local police officers—also relied on immigration raids to target hundreds of thousands of people, many of them long-term residents, who lived in established communities throughout the country. This created widespread anxiety among Mexican immigrants and Mexican Americans, establishing internal borders that circumscribed the physical spaces people inhabited and, in some cases, confined them to their homes.

This chapter argues that the nation's ongoing demand for cheap migrant labor and the INS's increasing dependence on voluntary departures and immigration raids between 1965 and 1985 normalized the deportation machine both at the border and in the interior, making the possibility of deportation an everyday reality for many, if not most, undocumented immigrants. Scholars have described the pattern of circular, undocumented Mexican migration that emerged during this period as a "relatively open and benign labor process with few negative consequences."[4] Although the prevailing system may have benefited employers, consumers, the INS, and even some migrants, it had serious punitive repercussions for both US citizen and noncitizen Latinos. I also seek here to reveal how, over the course of two decades, bureaucratic practices, changes in law, and a potent combination of political, economic, social, and cultural factors demonized ethnic Mexicans and solidified the stereotype of them as prototypical "illegal aliens."

## Creating a Crisis at the US–Mexico Border

From 1965 to 1985, changes in policy and the political economies of the United States and Mexico resulted in significant transformations to the deportation machine. The expiration of the Bracero Program at the end of 1964 had an immediate impact on immigration enforcement practices and migrants' lives. The following year, President Lyndon B. Johnson signed the Hart–Celler Act in a ceremony held at the base of the Statue of Liberty, ending the discriminatory national origins quota system that had been in place for more than four decades. But the act also implemented a 170,000-person quota on immigration from the Eastern Hemisphere (including a country cap of 20,000) and, for the first time ever, a 120,000-person quota on immigration from the Western Hemisphere. As INS Commissioner Raymond Farrell noted, "Mexican workers, cut off from the legal avenues of obtaining a livelihood which they had become accustomed to over the years, sought to enter illegally and thus obtain work."[5] Over the course of the next fiscal year, the number of Mexicans apprehended rose by more than 26 percent and total apprehensions topped 100,000 for the first time in a decade.[6]

Even though a 1966 INS intelligence report noted that "border pressures can be expected to continue heavy" for at least a decade, the service had no real sense of what was to come.[7] Population pressures, limited economic opportunities, and growing inequality in Mexico, combined with the need for labor in the United States, contributed to high levels of migration.[8] At the same time, efforts to regulate the movement of illicit drugs across the US–Mexico border led officials to ramp up enforcement. In September 1969, President Richard M. Nixon oversaw Operation Intercept, an unprecedented campaign during which US Customs officials from Texas to California stopped and searched all northbound vehicles for contraband marijuana. The short-lived initiative yielded few seizures, but had a lasting impact since it contributed to the criminalization of migrants. As a Mexican businessman observed, "Operation Intercept is just a spectacular stunt which gives the absurd idea that everyone in Mexico is a suspected drug trafficker."[9] As a result of these factors, while in 1968 the service projected 247,800 deportations for fiscal year 1974, the actual number eventually exceeded 738,000. Expulsions increased even more after Congress extended the 20,000-person country cap to the Western Hemisphere in 1976.[10]

The uptick in unauthorized migration coincided with a series of economic downturns in the United States. A recession in 1970–71, followed by the oil crisis and the subsequent drop in the value of the stock market a few years later, heightened feelings of economic and cultural instability across the country. Another recession in the late 1970s and early 1980s—during which the unemployment rate spiked to 10.8 percent, the highest it had been since the Great Depression—only reinforced such sentiments.[11]

Racist and xenophobic immigration coverage in the mainstream media scapegoated Mexicans for the country's economic woes. An analysis by Celestino Fernández and Lawrence R. Pedroza shows that news coverage of undocumented Mexican workers saw a nearly fourfold increase from 1972 to 1978. Some 80 percent of these articles used stigmatizing terms like "illegal aliens," and more than 40 percent had headlines that painted undocumented Mexicans in a negative light. "Aliens Reportedly Get $100 Million in Welfare," read a January 1973 headline in the *Los Angeles Times*. "Illegal Aliens Flooding Yuma, California Area," read another in the *Arizona Daily Star* a week later. The *New York Times* ran a December 1974 article under the headline "Unlawful Aliens Use Costly City Services, Thousands Compete for Jobs and Get School, Hospital and Welfare Benefits." A little over a year later, a *Washington Post* headline asked, "Can We Stop the Invasion of Illegal Aliens?" Moreover, 75 percent of the articles studied cited "unsympathetic" sources (Border Patrol and INS officers, politicians, police, and organized labor), while a mere 8 percent cited "sympathetic" sources (undocumented workers and Latino organizations). This type of coverage, Fernández and Pedroza conclude, gave readers "the image that the United States was being overrun by an 'influx' of 'illegal aliens'" who were "a tremendous drain on the American economy."[12]

The news media's sensationalism helped to create and foment the belief that Mexican immigration posed serious problems for the United States. It also led to mounting calls for immigration restriction, based in part on concerns about overpopulation, which had been growing since the publication of biologist Paul Ehrlich's *The Population Bomb* in 1968. That same year, Ehrlich and two colleagues founded Zero Population Growth (ZPG), an influential group that sought to reduce the birth rate and cut off immigration in hopes of avoiding what they believed to be an impending existential crisis. By the mid-1970s, fertility rates in the United States had dropped, but popular stereotypes of Mexican women who "bred like rabbits" persisted and spread. And ZPG increasingly focused its attention on immigration and what one *U.S. News & World Report* headline referred to as the "Time Bomb in Mexico."[13]

The person most responsible for ZPG's reorientation was John Tanton, an ophthalmologist from Michigan who became president of the group in 1975 and directed its energies toward fighting what he referred to as the "modern-day wetback" problem. Three years later, Tanton founded the Federation of American Immigration Reform (FAIR), the first of a number of spin-off organizations dedicated to restricting all types of immigration (and especially undocumented Mexican immigration) based on the belief that it posed a grave threat to the country's well-being and future existence. In 1980, in a clear effort to cause alarm in hopes of gaining support for their nativist agenda, FAIR estimated that there might be as many as 60 million "illegal immigrants" in the United States by the year 2000. Despite their modest membership rolls, ZPG and FAIR had considerable influence both in policy-making circles and in the public imagination, thanks to their extensive lobbying efforts, frequent appearances in the mainstream media, and close ties to prominent scholars and INS and Department of Justice officials.[14]

The INS, for its part, responded to the spike in unauthorized migration with force. In the fall of 1973, Richard Nixon appointed General Leonard F.

Chapman Jr. commissioner of the INS. Similar to his predecessor General Joseph Swing, who led the service during Operation Wetback in the 1950s, Chapman brought a military mentality to the agency, having fought in major battles in the Pacific during World War II before going on to serve as commandant of the marine corps during the war in Vietnam. An article introducing the new commissioner in the service's *I & N Reporter* highlighted his "extensive knowledge and experience in the field of management techniques as well as many years of troop leadership, both in combat and peacetime." In the eight years before Chapman took control the INS, the number of apprehensions had shot up from some 55,000 to more than 430,000 per year. In hopes of slowing down or reversing this trend, Chapman pushed Congress to allocate additional funds to put more Border Patrol agents on the line and investigators in immigrant communities, and he also supported New Jersey Democratic representative Peter Rodino's labor-backed H.R. 982 bill, which proposed implementing sanctions on employers who hired undocumented workers in hopes of "turning off the jobs magnet" that brought people to the United States in the first place.[15]

His efforts, however, were for naught. By 1975, apprehensions had increased another 50 percent to 680,000, leading the commissioner to declare that "the problem has grown rapidly to the point where it is now completely out of control."[16] Frustrated by the INS's inability to rein in unauthorized migration and concerned that its continued growth would thwart unionization efforts, labor organizations such as the United Farm Workers (UFW) attempted to take matters into their own hands. In 1974 and 1975, Cesar Chavez and the UFW launched their now infamous "Illegals Campaign," which called on the INS to enforce the border and "remove the hundreds of thousands of illegal aliens now working in the fields." However, UFW members and volunteers went even further, tracking down undocumented immigrants throughout California's Central Valley and reporting them to authorities. They also formed a "wet line," which consisted of 300 people wearing "UFW Border Patrol" armbands guarding the border near San Luis, Arizona. Led by Chavez's cousin Manuel and funded by the UFW central office until it was disbanded in early 1975, the "wet line" apprehended migrants crossing into the United States, in some cases administering severe beatings before forcing them back to Mexico. Despite public and private efforts to control the border, unauthorized migration only grew in the years to come, as apprehensions reached some 955,000 in 1977, Chapman's last year as commissioner, and ballooned to almost 1,270,000 by 1985.[17]

## Voluntary Departures and the "Revolving Door" Effect

In reality, the "border crisis" that emerged between 1965 and 1985 was, in part, a problem of the INS's own making. The pseudo-emergency was a product of continued US demand for Mexican labor in the Bracero Program's aftermath and the service's near-exclusive reliance on voluntary departures, which made up 97 percent of the 13,250,000 deportations during that two-decade period.[18] Voluntary departures continued to be, first and foremost, a cost-saving measure, as an internal 1968 agency document made clear: "In order to reduce costs, policy and procedural changes were made to utilize informal deportations in lieu of formal deportations in the rising number of Mexican cases."[19] As in the past, the service also pushed some of the cost of transportation onto the deportees. From fiscal year 1969 through the first half of fiscal year 1971, the US and Mexican governments removed 280,000 people into the Mexican interior via bus, plane, or train. More than two-thirds of those people covered 72 percent of the overall cost, with the US government making up the difference.[20] The service also forced some people to pay back taxes to the Internal Revenue Service (IRS) before they could voluntarily depart. Soon thereafter, in hopes of further minimizing expenses, an INS report recommended that "if a financially able alien refused to pay for his transportation, he could be held for a deportation hearing." However, this was little more than a threat, since the "INS [did] not have the authority to force aliens to pay," nor did it have the resources to cover hearings and the resultant increase in man-days in detention, which more than doubled between fiscal years 1965 and 1970.[21]

A few years later, a Government Accountability Office report found that the INS's dependence on voluntary departure and its inability to prosecute immigrants "diluted the deterrent effect of its enforcement efforts." But, as apprehensions spiked and pushed the service's resources to the limit, the INS's general counsel reiterated that "formal deportation proceedings are brought only in aggravated cases since they involve considerable expense and delay, and voluntary return is usually the most satisfactory way of dealing with this enormous volume of cases." An internal review also concluded that prosecuting additional people might not change much since judges granted voluntary departure to more than 70 percent of the people they saw in formal deportation proceedings.[22]

The service's reliance on voluntary departure and the border's porous nature created a "revolving door" effect in which deportation or the possibility of being deported became a normal part of many migrants' lives.[23] Even though the probability of being apprehended did not change, many Mexicans' increasingly binational existences and the realities of circular migration meant that migrants were likely to be caught, on average, around two out of every five times they crossed the border.[24] Alfonso, a twenty-seven-year-old man who migrated to the United States in 1968, was deported seven times during his first five years in the country.[25] In 1977 officers in El Paso apprehended Laura Mendarez-Pérez, who had forty-eight prior deportations. Officials in San Diego claimed to have detained another man twenty-five times.[26]

On some occasions, authorities deported migrants multiple times during a single attempt to cross into the United States.[27] Gustavo Ramírez recalled being deported ten times during a twenty-two-day period. "I went from [my pueblo in Jalisco] to Tijuana, and they caught me and threw me back to Tijuana. I tried to cross the next day and they caught me and back to Tijuana I went again. Ten times! . . . The next day I finally made it across." Though memory may have resulted in some creative authorship, Ramírez estimated that immigration officials deported him a total of seventy times between 1972 and 1982. Each time he gave a different name, a common strategy migrants employed to avoid problems if apprehended again.[28] As the commissioner of the INS put it during a television interview in the late 1970s, "We catch them in the morning, we deport them in the afternoon. We apprehend them. We deport them. We deported one guy five times in one day out of El Paso. It's just an unbelievable revolving door."[29] In exceptional cases, like that of one newlywed man from Jalisco who headed north in hopes of making enough money to build a house back home, migrants never succeeded in crossing the border. He tried and failed to reach Los Angeles on multiple occasions in the late 1970s and early 1980s, likening his many expulsions to the ocean repeatedly washing up garbage on the shore.[30] In all, the number of people deported who had at least one previous expulsion went from fewer than 14,000 in 1965 (13 percent of all deportees), to over 152,000 in 1973 (25 percent of all deportees), to more than 372,000 in 1985 (35 percent of all deportees).[31]

The INS's reliance on voluntary departures, combined with its stagnant budget and limited personnel, frustrated many Border Patrol agents working the line. While the number of deportations increased by a factor of ten between 1965 and 1985, the number of agents and linewatch hours only doubled, and the overall Border Patrol and INS budgets experienced a mere three-fold increase.[32] The year after the Bracero Program ended, an anonymous officer (or officers) expressed his (or their) frustration in a satirical memo on official INS stationery. The memo described "Operation RAPE" ("Re-assignment, Attrition and Personnel Elimination"), "Operation SCREW" ("Survey of Capabilities for Re-assignment of Eliminated Workers"), and "Operation SHAFT" ("Study by a High Authority Following Transfer"). It concluded by stating, "Employees who are RAPED may apply for only one additional SCREWING but may request the SHAFT as many times as they desire."[33] Morale remained low in the years ahead, as corruption and workforce shortages continued to plague the service.[34] As J. B. Hillard, the president of the INS Council, an organization that represented 5,300 service employees, put it in 1978, "As far as I'm concerned, we're drowning and have been for several years. I said a few years ago it's like trying to bail out the Queen Mary with a teacup. It's like it's down to a thimble now."[35] A couple of years later, the INS had a reputation, according to the *New York Times*, "as a bureaucratic stepchild beset by political interference and official indifference, an agency mired in mountains of unsorted paper and hampered by lost and misplaced files, and with a record of selective enforcement, brutality and other wrongdoing possibly unmatched by any other Federal agency."[36]

Misconduct within the service ranged from corruption, extortion, and smuggling, to the physical, psychological, and sexual abuse of migrants. "It's so bad we don't know how corrupt it is," a Department of Justice official lamented. "What we're frightened about at INS is what we don't know." What they did know—based on an internal investigation, media reports, and Border Patrol agents' firsthand accounts—was troubling enough: cases of officers administering severe beatings, separating children from their parents to extract confessions, raping women in their custody, and shooting and killing migrants who tried to avoid apprehension. One instructor told new

Figure 25. Commissioner Leonel Castillo speaking at the chief patrol agents conference in Alexandria, Virginia, spring 1979.
Courtesy of USCISHOL.

Border Patrol recruits that agents had even "push[ed] illegals off cliffs" and then tried to cover up the incident to make the deaths appear accidental. Even if only a small minority of officers committed the most egregious acts of violence against migrants, the larger problem according to Fred Drew, the lone black Border Patrol agent stationed at San Ysidro, "was that the rest of the patrolmen tolerated it." Most abuse went unreported and even when the agency handed down punishments, they tended to be administrative rather than criminal.[37]

During the late 1970s, the INS rank and file also directed their anger and frustration at INS Commissioner Leonel Castillo, the first Mexican American or Latino to lead the agency (see figure 25). Nominated by President Jimmy Carter and confirmed by the Senate in the spring of 1977, the thirty-seven-year-old former high school football star, Peace Corps volunteer, and Houston comptroller brought a public service rather than military background to the position.[38] Under the auspices of Carter's larger human rights agenda, Castillo tried to overhaul the service's image and approach to immigration enforcement. "We must reconsider our system of justice and not label as criminals those who enter the country illegally to look for work," he told a Mexican reporter. "As a government official I am obligated to enforce the law and this year we will deport more than a million people, but as a human being I believe that something has to change. . . . Above all, there should be respect for the undocumented worker."[39] The administration instructed INS offices across the country to refer to people as "undocumented workers" or "undocumented immigrants" instead of "illegal aliens."[40] Castillo rebranded the four INS detention facilities (El Centro, California; El Paso, Texas; Port Isabel, Texas; and Brooklyn, New York) as service processing centers and equipped them with libraries, televisions, and recreation areas.[41] Border Patrol officers chided the commissioner for being "soft on aliens," "build[ing] playgrounds for the 'wets' who [got] through," and turning the INS "into a service organization for the illegals." An agent near San Diego summed up the sentiment within the rank and file this way: "The border is leaking like a sieve and nobody gives a damn." At the same time, Chicano groups and immigrant rights activists criticized the administration for its ongoing enforcement efforts, including record-breaking deportations to Mexico. Getting slammed from both sides, Castillo, who saw service *and* enforcement as core elements of the INS's mission, lamented "The truth is, we don't have the budget for either."[42]

We must understand individual officers' criticisms of Castillo and his policies within the larger context of the long-standing, blatant anti-Mexican racism that defined the INS and its institutional mission. Castillo's subordinates responded to his attempts to reform the agency and its culture with "malignant compliance." Officials working under him frequently questioned every detail, no matter how small, of every order he gave as a way of stalling and pushing back from within the agency. Another report described agents "openly rebelling" against Castillo, who some referred to as "that wetback we have for a commissioner." An immigration official in the Washington, DC, office had a photo on his desk of the commissioner's face with a bull's-eye on it. The bulletin board of the El Paso Border Patrol station displayed a cartoon showing sombrero-wearing Mexicans crossing the Rio Grande above which someone scrawled "Castillo's cousins." It was not an uncommon belief within the service that Castillo "shows favoritism" to undocumented immigrants "because of his own ancestry." Responding to this claim, the commissioner stated, "I think that's a shade racist," as if bias existed in "every Anglo judge who deals with an Anglo client." Still, according to Philip Smith, head of INS investigations in Los Angeles, many people within the agency "didn't like the fact that he [Castillo] was Hispanic. They thought it was like putting Al Capone at the head of the FBI."[43] When Castillo's tumultuous tenure at the helm of the service came to an end in the fall of 1979, a Border Patrol agent (or small group of agents) penned a satirical memo on official INS stationery. Titled "My Departure from INS," laced with profanity, and bearing Castillo's name at the end, it read, in part:

> The past two years have been exciting and rewarding. Actually, they've been a royal pain in the ass. Every hair-brained scheme, every liberal, bleeding heart reform I tried to introduce was opposed all the way by you b——s. My choice of brown inspector's uniforms was laughed out of existence, our new automation system is all f——d up and even GS-4 clerk typists were making "wet" jokes about me behind my back.
>
> I especially want to extend my appreciation to you fascist p—s in the Border Patrol. When I proposed that we build a fence along the Mexican border, it was not, as many of you apparently assumed, there to inflict scars and marks for future identification purposes.
>
> Actually, I have no intention of going back to Houston. I am instead, purchasing a mud hut condominium in Chihuahua where I will spend the rest of my existence zonked on home-made tequila and translating the entire [Immigration and Naturalization] Act into one-syllable Spanish words.
>
> I do not wish you well. I hope you all end up on a midnight shift at Ft. Kent, Maine during the black fly season. A famous Chinese Philosopher once said, "You can lead a horse to water, but if you can teach him to do the back stroke, then you've got something." I have no idea what that means, but I've only recently learned English, and I can't be expected to understand Chinese. Good-bye and good riddance, you b—s.

At the bottom of the page was a drawing that juxtaposed a beat-up Border Patrol vehicle with an INS detention center that had a "Now Playing!" movie billboard out front, where a group of immigrants kicked around a soccer ball.[44]

## The Politics of Immigration Statistics

The prevailing border enforcement policies may have angered agents on the ground, but they actually served the bureaucratic interests of the INS. Immigration officials used the ever-rising number of apprehensions and deportations inherent to the voluntary departure–revolving door system to simultaneously celebrate their "accomplishments" and call attention to the dire need for additional funding, all while helping to fulfill the nation's ongoing labor demands.[45] "The pressure from the top people in the administration . . . is extreme," a former INS statistician explained in the mid-1970s. "We are told periodically that 'the heats [sic] on,' and we know that we had better get to work and make it look like we're after the 'devils' who are taking away the jobs from the little-man." To do so, he and his colleagues turned to the media, which he described as "one of our best tools in emphasizing the threat that the illegals pose to the stability of the economy."[46]

By the 1970s, this tactic was tried and true. As sociologist Gilberto Cárdenas has argued, throughout the service's history it strategically deployed statistics—and especially inflated expulsion numbers—as part of recurring propaganda campaigns based on fear and meant to scare people into leaving the country. "In what might be compared to a 'reign-of-terror,' the exaggeration of issues invariably involves the use of statistics," he notes. Authorities rely on statistics to create "a sense of alarm, urgency and a call for action," amplified by the media and followed by "the demand for the expansion and increased appropriations for the INS."[47]

Mexican authorities, for their part, also depended on voluntary departures and the revolving door that the border had become. Whether documented or undocumented, migration to the United States alleviated unemployment and economic underdevelopment in Mexico, especially in rural areas. By the early to mid-1970s the US ambassador to Mexico Joseph J. Jova told Mexican Ministry of Foreign Affairs official Rubén González Sosa that the situation had "almost reached 'mass population transfer'" and urged the Mexican government to "attempt to do its share to impede access of illegal migrants."[48] Mexico had supposedly "undertaken a permanent campaign along its northern frontier" to stop unauthorized migration and the smuggling of migrants, but this was little more than empty rhetoric; Mexican officials did little to stem migration to the United States.[49] In fact, they most

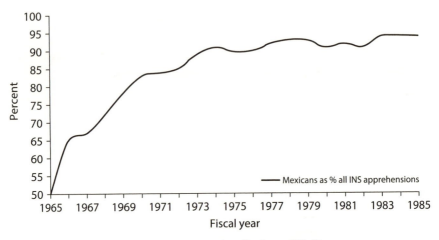

Figure 26. Mexicans as percentage of all INS apprehensions, fiscal years 1965–85.
1976 includes a fifteen-month period because the fiscal year changed. INS, "Deportable Aliens: Reports," USCISHOL. Calculations and graph by author.

feared the prospect of a mass deportation drive. As a columnist in a Mexican daily newspaper put it, "What would we do with this excess manpower, where would they live, where would they work, what would they eat? We cannot imagine the latent danger entailed in such a massive deportation."[50] Voluntary departures suited the needs of both countries in the sense that they allowed the United States to continue deporting people, while leaving open the possibility of future reentry to supply necessary labor north of the border and to ease economic and population pressures in Mexico.

The INS's dependence on voluntary departures may have benefited the agency, in addition to both the United States and Mexico, but it had devastating consequences for Mexican migrants. The criminalization of Mexicans was inherent to the constant cycle of unauthorized migration–apprehension–deportation–repeat unauthorized migration. Whereas the 55,000 Mexicans apprehended in 1965 represented 50 percent of all apprehensions, the 1.2 million Mexicans apprehended in 1985 made up 94 percent of all of that year's apprehensions (see figure 26).[51] The Border Patrol's obsession with stopping unauthorized Mexican migrants eventually led the agency to split their apprehension statistics into two categories: Mexicans and "Other Than Mexicans," or "OTMs." The fact that agents were tasked with stopping both immigrants in search of work as well as narcotics and drug smugglers sometimes led to the conflation of the two, which further criminal-ized Mexicans within the INS, in the media, and in the public's imagination. Ultimately, the mechanism officials used to deport people resulted in the disproportionate targeting of a single group and the reification of racialized stereotypes from earlier decades that treated all ethnic Mexicans as proto-typical "illegal aliens."[52]

## Immigration Raids and Internal Borders

The evening of Wednesday, October 30, 1974, Attorney General of the United States William B. Saxbe addressed the Cameron and Hidalgo County Bar Associations at the Valley Country Club in Brownsville, Texas, right along the Mexican border. An outspoken, tobacco-chewing fowl hunter, military veteran, and lawyer from Ohio, Saxbe was serving his first and only term as a US senator when President Richard Nixon appointed him to head the Department of Justice during the height of the Watergate scandal. Speaking fewer than three months after Nixon resigned, Saxbe warned the group gathered at the country club that "illegal immigrants do not consti-tute a trickle or a stream. They form a torrent that could inundate us unless effective action is taken soon."[53]

Saxbe estimated that between 4 million and 7 million—and perhaps as many as 12 million—people lived in the United States without authoriza-tion. "The impact of illegal aliens is sobering: They hold millions of jobs; they receive social services ranging from schools to welfare; large amounts of money they send out of the country drain funds from our troubled econ-omy; and they mock our system of legal immigration," he told the crowd of lawyers, without providing evidence to substantiate his claims. "The mas-sive number of illegal aliens constitutes a severe national crisis" since, ac-cording to Saxbe, immigrants were moving inland and settling in distant places and urban centers far away from the border. The situation was grave, he said, but it still could be fixed. Saxbe's proposed solution called for the de-portation of "one million persons now holding jobs—and then find[ing] those who have burrowed more deeply into our society." The attorney gen-eral had the support of the new president, Gerald Ford, who just a month after being sworn in wrote to a Republican congressional candidate in San Diego

Figure 27. INS agents apprehend workers during a raid on a Los Angeles garment factory circa mid-1970s.
Courtesy of the Department of Special Collections, Stanford University Libraries. Box 45, Folder 12, CASA Papers, m325, SCSUL.

that "the 'silent invasion'" from Mexico was "a matter of high national priority."[54]

Enforcement at the border continued to make up the vast majority of deportations from 1965 to 1985, but the INS also ramped up neighborhood and workplace raids, responding to the manufactured immigration crisis with force (see figures 27 and 28). Immigration officials had sporadically carried out raids since the agency's founding in the last decade of the nineteenth century, but it was during this period that large-scale roundups came to be a constant in many ethnic Mexican communities hundreds of miles from the geopolitical divide. While interior operations led to an increase in the number of people deported (almost all via voluntary departure) from across the country, the men and women apprehended were but a small portion of the number of people that the sweeps affected. During this period, heightened levels of INS surveillance effectively established internal borders that created a climate of terror in Mexican American and undocumented immigrant communities and made many people more aware of their "deportability."[55]

Figure 28. A Border Patrol raid interrupts a day's work at a McAllen, Texas ranch, circa mid-1970s.
Courtesy of USCISHOL.

Nowhere was this felt as much as in California, the destination of around 70 percent of all Mexican migrants at the time.[56]

From late May to late June of 1973, the INS set up staging areas at the Los Alamitos naval air station and carried out a series of raids in Los Angeles, which martyred Mexican American journalist Rubén Salazar had described as "the wetback capital of the world."[57] The service sent an additional fifty Border Patrol agents from across the country to assist twenty-five local investigators with the raids "because of a steady increase in the number of aliens in the Los Angeles area which 'normal INS operations simply could not handle.'"[58] The acting INS district director in Los Angeles justified the operation by pointing to undocumented Mexican immigrants' supposed negative economic impact on the country. "They attend schools at taxpayers' expense, they take jobs that normally would go to Americans, and many of them go on welfare and use other public social services." As a result, officials announced that "the mass crackdown [would] continue indefinitely."[59] On May 23 and 29, two "unusually large" garment factory raids alone resulted in the apprehension of 2,000 Mexicans, and a week or so later forty immigration officers apprehended 400 Mexicans, including twenty women, in a three-hour predawn raid on factories, bus stops, and city streets in Huntington Park. Over the course of a month (twenty working days) the raids resulted in the apprehension of 11,500 Mexicans.[60] Labor organizer and activist Bert Corona described them as "dragnets designed to stir up an antialien hysteria" and said that INS investigators were "harassing everybody with brown skin." Moreover, he pointed out that many of the people apprehended in the raids had families in the United States, and some had children who were US citizens.[61]

According to Salazar, by the early 1970s, undocumented Mexicans lived "in constant fear. Fear that [they] will be discovered. Fear of what might happen to [them] once la migra finds him. Fear that [they] will not be paid before being deported."[62] During the May–June 1973 raids, a twenty-two-year-old Mexican woman said, "Every time I see a man in a suit, I'm afraid."[63] A local migrant aid social agency "reported that its staff was besieged by phone calls and requests for assistance from aliens who have heard news reports of the raids."[64] Just three months earlier, Alicia, a thirty-two-year-old single mother who had lived in California for eight years and had two US-born children, told a *Los Angeles Times* reporter how her fear of deportation affected her life: "I sit at home a lot because I'm afraid to go out without my children for fear the authorities will pick me up and leave them at home alone. . . . Who would take care of them?" She also added, "I can't afford to make many friends because I'm afraid they would turn me in if they got angry with me." Her undocumented status even prevented her from receiving child support from the father of her one-year-old daughter. "He said just last week that if I took him to court, I would only get one week of child support because one way or another he'd get me across the border. I know he wants to take me out so he can keep on driving to Tijuana . . . and how would I get back?" Despite living in fear and barely being able to make ends meet most months, Alicia planned on staying in the United States to give her kids "the education I never had."[65] As another undocumented Mexican migrant put it a few years later, "Being here is like a

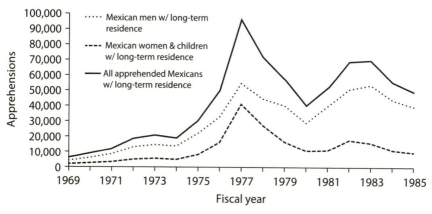

Figure 29. INS apprehensions of Mexicans with long-term residence, fiscal years 1969–85.
1976 includes a fifteen-month period because the fiscal year changed. INS, "Deportable Aliens: Reports," USCISHOL. Calculations and graph by author.

prison, a beautiful golden prison. You have everything, but at the same time you have nothing."[66]

Fear in the Mexican migrant community was understandable given the trends in immigration enforcement from 1969 to 1977. Even though Border Patrol agents accounted for the vast majority of total apprehensions, INS investigators apprehended more than 1.5 million Mexicans between 1969 and 1985. Investigators usually carried out workplace and neighborhood raids, which led to an increase in the apprehensions of Mexicans with long-term residency in the United States: In 1969 the service apprehended fewer than 6,500 Mexicans who had lived in the country for over a year; by 1973 that number grew to nearly 21,000, and in 1977 reached a high of more than 96,000 (see figure 29).[67] This was, in part, because thousands of undocumented Mexican migrants registered with the service after the courts ruled that US officials should not have counted Cuban refugees against the Western Hemisphere immigration quota, and ordered authorities to redistribute wrongfully denied visas. But the Silva program, named for a plaintiff in the lawsuit that resulted in the consequential decision, never gave migrants who turned themselves in a way to permanently regularize their status, thus leaving them vulnerable to deportation when it expired in 1981.[68]

Mexicans with long-term US residence as a percentage of total apprehensions by INS investigators increased over time as well (see figure 30).

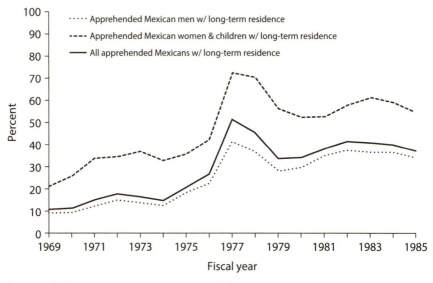

Figure 30. Mexicans with long-term residence in the United States as percentage of apprehensions by INS investigators, fiscal years 1969–85.

1976 includes a fifteen-month period because the fiscal year changed. INS, "Deportable Aliens: Reports," USCISHOL. Calculations and graph by author.

Whereas 11 percent of the Mexicans investigators apprehended in 1969 had lived in the United States for over a year, that number nearly quadrupled to an average of 41 percent from 1977 to 1985. During that same period, 63 percent of women and children arrested by investigators were long-term residents.[69]

Although it is important to highlight the different ways immigration enforcement policies affected men, women, and children, we cannot explain fear of deportation by supposed differences between the sexes. Rather, deportability tended to have a greater impact on people who had lived in the United States longer, whether man, woman, or child. During this period, Mexican women and children were generally two to three times more likely than men to be long-term residents at the time of apprehension.[70] This was, at least in part, a product of the fact that undocumented Mexican women were more likely than undocumented Mexican men to settle in the United States after arriving since crossing without authorization involved greater risks, including injury, robbery, and sexual assault.[71]

In addition to there being a higher probability that men would return to Mexico, the Border Patrol deported around six times as many men as women and children at entry or within a few days of entering the United States.[72] These two factors combined meant that men were less likely than women and children to be long-term residents and more likely to engage in circular migration patterns. But, as the following poem, "Al Estilo Americano" ("The American Way"), by community organizer Salvador Reza, made clear, raids and deportation affected all Mexicans with long-term residence, irrespective of sex, and including those left behind in the United States:

Immigration officials nabbed me, the American way
And although I'm not a criminal
That's the way they treated me.
And although I'm not a criminal, that's the way they treated me.

I worked in a factory in Los Angeles, hermano,
And right on payday they threw down a raid.
With pistol in hand to the wall they ordered me,
With pistol in hand to the wall they threw me.
Since I didn't know English they slapped handcuffs on me,
And with all of my friends on a plane they kicked us out
And with all of my friends on a plane they kicked us out.

I'm off to Mexico, to see what awaits me there.
I'm off to Mexico, to see what awaits me there.
Meanwhile, in Los Angeles, my family is alone.
God only knows how they'll survive.

I don't say goodbye because I have to come back,
To reunite with my family and collect my check.
I don't say goodbye, because I have to come back.[73]

For some Mexican migrants in the United States, deportability became so normalized that they prepared for expulsion as part of their daily routines, like getting dressed each morning. Alberto Hernández was five years old when he began working, bringing tortillas to his brothers who toiled in the fields of their pueblo in Jalisco. He migrated to the United States for the first time in 1972 when he was nineteen, without documents. For three years he worked cleaning horses and doing odd jobs on a ranch, and then he returned home, where he married his wife, Raquel. The couple then returned to California together. They later became citizens and have split their time between the United States and Mexico for the last four decades. But in the late 1970s and early 1980s, Alberto and his friends were well aware of the fact that when they left for work each morning there was always the possibility that they wouldn't return home. Fearing apprehension, every day they carried $20 with them, hidden somewhere on themselves, to ensure that they would have a little bit of money if immigration agents apprehended them and deported them to Tijuana. The precaution was not unreasonable: on many occasions *la migra* (a slang term for immigration enforcement officers) came to Alberto's work, forcing him and his friends to flee.[74]

## "Like Showing a Swastika in a Synagogue"

In August 1979, the INS increased the number of raids in residential neighborhoods and business districts in and around Los Angeles, "despite angry criticism from Hispanic leaders." As Joe Howerton, the service's new Los Angeles district director, told reporters, "We are trying to spread out and to touch everything. . . . We will work all kinds of business and will respond to whatever kind of information we receive that undocumented aliens are present." A 50 percent increase in apprehensions (to 865 per week) during a six-week trial period encouraged the INS, but also led to strong backlash from the Latino community. Louis Velasquez, the mayor of Fullerton, California, witnessed a September 14 raid and reported being "deeply concerned about sloppy enforcement of the law" by agents who violated the rights of both Mexican Americans and undocumented immigrants. David Lizárrga, president of the East Los Angeles Community Union and national director of Hispanic American Democrats, said, "I want to know why this is being done. It is not the policy in other parts of the Southwest. These indiscriminate sweeps are nothing more than a dragnet and I think those tactics are highly uncalled for."[75]

Although District Director Howerton claimed that the INS was "not merely sweeping everyone off the streets or kicking down doors," residential raids had a devastating effect on Mexican American and immigrant communities.[76] In the eyes of Rubén Bonilla Jr., national president of the League of

United Latin American Citizens (LULAC), the raids were "an act of reprisal and will result in deportation of illegal immigrants, the uprooting of legal resident aliens and discrimination against native-born Mexican-Americans." A US-born Latino Senate aide told a *Los Angeles Times* reporter, "You have no idea, unless you have brown skin, of how unsettling these raids can be. . . . It isn't a matter of the numbers of officers involved. . . . It is the whole idea. You only need to have one man in a green INS uniform walk through the mercado (market) and a shiver of fear runs through all of East Los Angeles."[77] An Eastside city councilman concurred, referring to raids as "haphazard and capricious methods of law enforcement that inflict cruel hardships, split families, violate rights, inconvenience the innocent and blanket the Hispanic community in a cloud of fear."[78]

Mexican Americans' fears were by no means unfounded. Since the mass expulsions during the Great Depression, neighborhood sweeps and expedited deportations had periodically resulted in the removal of US citizens and permanent residents. In 1975, after a raid on a Santa Monica house, the INS deported Salvador Sierra, a fifteen-year-old with permanent residency, along with Roberto, his thirteen-year-old US citizen brother. Authorities removed them to Tijuana, from where Mexican officials then transported them to Mexicali. The following day, 400 miles away from their home in Venice, California, the boys made a collect call to their parents, who had to borrow a car and some money so that they could go pick up their sons.[79] Nine years later, in February 1984, INS agents picked up fourteen-year-old Mario Moreno López and some thirty others from a street corner in Santa Ana, California, where people in search of work gathered. Moreno López, a permanent resident, informed officers about his legal status, but they did not believe him and coerced the boy into signing a voluntary departure form. His father spent the following days searching for his son in the streets of Tijuana with the help of Mexican officials and migrant aid organizations in the United States. The family eventually reunited in San Diego six days after Moreno López's deportation. The incident so disturbed a federal judge that he issued a short-lived temporary restraining order prohibiting the service from expelling juveniles. Moreno López later sued the INS and won a $110,000 settlement (see figure 31).[80]

In some cases, local police forces helped the INS carry out residential raids. At 8:00 a.m. on August 26, 1979, uniformed and plainclothes cops

Figure 31. Protestors march outside the INS office in Santa Ana, California, after authorities wrongfully deported fourteen-year-old legal resident Mario Moreno López.
The boy at center holds a sign reading "Reagan, Don't Separate Me from My Parents." February 1984. Paul Chinn, Los Angeles *Herald Examiner* Collection, Los Angeles Public Library.

surrounded two Huntington Park, California, apartment complexes and arrested eighty people. "Half-prepared morning meals were left on kitchen stoves; radios were still turned to Spanish language stations; beds were left unmade and bathtubs were still filled with water." After Fernando Artunez, a thirteen-year legal resident, showed police his documents they "shoved him aside and barged into [his] apartment," where they took both of his roommates away, including one in handcuffs. Artunez then watched as officers took one of his neighbors out wearing only his underwear, and another whom they "dragged out by the hair." "It's the first time I've ever seen anything like this," Artunez said. "It made me feel so bad that I got sick. . . . I love this country. It has been very good to me," he added. "And I understand the law is the law, but what happened that day was a gross trampling of people's dignity."[81]

Despite District Director Howerton's doubts about the revolving door theory, many of the people deported that morning returned to Los Angeles within days or weeks, at great financial cost—including paying smugglers and, in many cases, moving out of the building because they feared another raid. "But the worst part was the humiliation," according to twenty-nine-year-old Socorro Ramírez, who was allowed to stay to care for her three-year-old daughter. "You feel humiliated because you realize you have no security in your own home . . . because they step on all your rights and there's nothing you can do about it. . . . I don't understand," she said, as her voice rose. "Why do they do this? I don't feel I do any harm to anyone by working. We don't come here to take anything from anyone. On the contrary, we leave them all our taxes. And who else is going to work for $2.90 an hour?"[82]

Within the INS, some officers recognized that raids did "irreparable damage" to communities and thought of them as "a public relations disaster." In the opinion of Michael Harpold, a seventeen-year veteran of the Border Patrol, "The saddest part of an INS raid is that it often disrupts the lives of decent people and drives home the fact that the main activity of these aliens is not the illegal crossing of the border, which occurs within a relatively small time frame. The main activity is working, which is why some prefer the description 'undocumented workers to illegal alien.'" Another agent, who graduated from the University of California, Berkeley before joining the Border Patrol two years earlier, said, "You can't help but think you're arresting the wrong people. They're not the lawbreaker types. They're some of the best people you'll meet—hardworking, loyal to their families. Sometimes you think, 'Why don't we arrest the bums that don't work and just steal?' But these people have violated the immigration law and we have to arrest them."[83]

Many other immigration officers believed "that 'the home is not a sanctuary' if it is the home of illegals" and supported raids since they led to a bump in apprehensions. As one INS official put it, raids were "well within the law and our people are treating the aliens decently." However, he also acknowledged that the "symbolic content of the actions is very high, sort of like showing a swastika in a synagogue. And there is no way of countering that impact, for most people." Ultimately, he deflected any responsibility, stating that people should blame Congress for making the laws, rather than the INS and Border Patrol for enforcing them.[84]

In the coming years, immigration officials continued to deploy raids, including a nationwide ninety-city workplace campaign dubbed Operation Jobs, which generated considerable publicity and led to around 6,000 apprehensions in one week in the spring of 1982.[85] The Operation Jobs raids "created an atmosphere of terror in our communities," Bert Corona said, and often resulted in "extensive drops" in business and church and school attendance. A Huntington Park proprietor reported a 50 percent decline in business, adding that "the fear will hurt us for another couple of weeks. . . . The sweeps will continue and people are still afraid."[86] Two years later, after raids in March 1984, Mexican citizen María Martínez stated that she tried not to leave her Santa Ana apartment during the day and only shopped at night, since immigration agents were less likely to be around then. She was not the only one to do so, describing the places Mexicans usually gathered as being like "ghost towns."[87]

Álvaro Núñez Hernández and María Vela Morales had a similar experience. In 1981, these twenty-two- and eighteen-year-old newlyweds set out for California, leaving behind their small agricultural community in the migrant-sending state of Jalisco. Drawn by the promise of higher wages and family and friends already living there, Álvaro and María traveled to Tijuana, where they hoped to cross. On their first attempt, they walked for three hours through the desert before immigration authorities apprehended and deported them. They tried again the following evening and, despite rain and having to hide from a Border Patrol helicopter hovering ahead, they made it. But they spent the next week with thirty other people in a small, cramped garage of a safe house located between San Diego and Los Angeles. Desperate to leave, regardless of the risks involved, they made their way to Northern California, where Álvaro's older brother lived. Two weeks had passed since they had left home, two weeks since their worried families had heard from them.

Álvaro and María's first years in the United States were not easy. They found work and had their first child, but la migra's ubiquitous presence and increasing reliance on immigration raids forced them to live in a near-constant state of fear of being deported. "We were so hidden, so afraid . . . as if we really were two delinquents," Álvaro remembered. "But when it came down to it, we were in a foreign country and we had to try to survive." Once, while shopping, María, with her infant son in her arms, had to hide behind a clothing rack after an INS van parked in front of the store and an agent came in looking for undocumented immigrants. What she remembered most were his feet, visible from beneath the clothes, "going around and around" as he searched for them. Álvaro, María, and their son managed to avoid apprehension that day, but Álvaro's cousin was less fortunate: the agent found him, handcuffed him, and deported him without giving him a chance to collect his belongings.

Eventually, Álvaro and María stopped going to stores, restaurants, the movies, and other places where la migra carried out raids. When immigration agents started picking people up outside of churches, they stopped going to Sunday mass. Knowing that officers were out in force in the mornings and early afternoon, they scheduled doctors' appointments as late in the day as possible. "Since we suffered so much to cross, we didn't want to risk getting kicked out," María recalled. "We went out in the late afternoon or evening when we had to, but if we didn't have to leave the house, we didn't."[88]

Álvaro and María's story was not unique. The buildup of home and workplace raids—and the possibility of raids—over the course of two decades had the cumulative effect of creating visceral fear and internal borders in Mexican migrant and Mexican American communities throughout the country. During this period, as unauthorized migration increased to previously unknown levels, the INS became ever more dependent on voluntary departures and a number of publicity and scare tactics meant to cause people to self-deport.

Enhanced enforcement, both at the border and in the interior of the country, heightened ethnic Mexicans' sense of deportability and had a significant negative effect on people's everyday lives. But, as INS tactics normalized the deportation machine, people fought back, taking to the streets and the courts in increasing numbers, where they demanded civil and human rights for all and insisted on ethnic Mexicans' belonging.

# FIVE

# Fighting the Machine in the Streets and in the Courts

Javier García Bautista had not been working for long on Wednesday, May 17, 1978, when someone in the carpentry department of the Sbicca of California, Inc. shoe company in suburban South El Monte yelled out, "The migra is here!"[1] Early that morning, after a planning meeting in their downtown Los Angeles office, forty INS investigators piled into at least eight vans and one bus and headed east to their target.[2] They arrived a little before 8:00 a.m. and, after a company executive gave them permission to conduct a "survey," the agents blocked off all the exits: the front door leading out to the employee parking lot, the north-facing windows, and the loading dock near the gate around back.[3]

With the building secured, teams of three to four investigators entered the factory and fanned out. Hoping to avoid detection, the twenty-two-year-old García Bautista tucked himself out of sight. As he hid, the agents circulated throughout the massive 62,500-square-foot plant, indiscriminately questioning the workers and asking them if they had papers.[4] They arrested men and women, taking down their information, handcuffing some and pushing others. Soon after the raid started, two agents from Supervisor J. L. O'Bryant's crew approached seventeen-year-old Rosa Melchor López at her work station. When she didn't respond to their inquiry about whether she had papers they took ahold of her arms, one on either side of the five-foot two-inch woman. Once outside the factory an investigator searched Melchor López's bag and then shoved her onto the INS bus, which was already packed with her coworkers.[5] At 10:05 a.m., as the operation wound down, plainclothes investigator Rollie Clark shined his flashlight into a large container. "I see a body here," he called out, at which point he and another agent pulled Javier García Bautista from his hiding place, handcuffed him, and led him out to the waiting vehicles.[6]

The INS investigators returned to downtown Los Angeles that morning with 119 Sbicca employees in custody.[7] By midafternoon, they had coerced most of the people to sign voluntary departure forms. Around 5:00 p.m., no more than nine hours after the raid had started, half of the workers, some twenty-four men and all of the thirty-five women in the group, were aboard government buses headed to San Ysidro, where they would be deported to Mexico.[8]

But the buses never made it to the border that evening. What neither the immigration officials nor the Sbicca employees knew at the time was that as agents loaded the detainees onto the buses, a coalition of immigrants, labor organizers, and lawyer-activists had convinced a federal judge to sign a temporary restraining order stopping the workers' deportation. Nor could they have imagined that in the days, weeks, months, and years ahead, the case would provide a blueprint for how to bring the seemingly unstoppable deportation machine to a grinding halt.

This chapter documents the growing resistance to deportation at the dawn of the age of mass expulsion, focusing on metropolitan Los Angeles, ground zero of the INS's interior enforcement efforts in the 1970s. It argues that the tireless efforts of immigrants and activists helped to build solidarity and empower the undocumented community, in turn limiting the effectiveness of voluntary departures, INS raids, and fear campaigns meant to scare people into the shadows or out of the country altogether. They challenged the basic idea that being undocumented automatically implied deportability. And through their resistance, they helped determine the civil rights of noncitizens, while also defending immigrants' dignity and redefining belonging in ways that transcended legal status and citizenship.[9]

## The Immigrant Rights Movement of the 1970s

Although the response to the raid at Sbicca was not typical, it did not emerge out of a vacuum. The termination of the Bracero Program at the end of 1964 and the cap on immigration from the Western Hemisphere under the Immigration and Nationality Act of 1965 increased deportations at the border and in the interior. By the end of the 1970s, apprehensions reached more than one million per year, and the threat of being apprehended and expelled became an everyday reality for many immigrants. In the face of policies and tactics that disproportionately targeted and demonized Mexicans, generating fear in the documented and undocumented alike, immigrants and their allies fought back, identifying vulnerable points in the enforcement apparatus and applying pressure to them by taking to the streets and the courts. This surge in activism built on decades of organizing to defend immigrants and brought together the Chicano/a movement, the rights revolution, and the shifting priorities of labor unions and the Catholic Church. These new coalitions, engaged in a politics defined by "collective struggles for . . . socially meaningful power," helped to create the contemporary immigrant rights movement.[10]

In 1968, Latino leaders established two new organizations with financial backing from the Ford Foundation, the Mexican American Legal Defense and Education Fund (MALDEF), and the Southwest Council of La Raza (renamed the National Council for La Raza, or NCLR, in 1972). MALDEF sought to litigate to challenge discriminatory laws and empower Mexican Americans, just as the National Advancement for the Association of Colored People (NAACP) Legal Defense Fund had for African Americans. The NCLR aspired to achieve similar ends through lobbying. These organizations tallied major legal and policy victories for Mexican Americans and Latinos in the years ahead, even though the elite, white liberal leaders of large philanthropic foundations like Ford steered them to push for moderate, incremental change. None proved more consequential than *Plyler v. Doe*, a 1982 Supreme Court decision MALDEF had fought for that guaranteed the constitutional right to elementary and secondary school public education to all children, regardless of immigration status.[11]

But during the 1970s, a lesser-known, radical, grassroots organization led the fight for undocumented immigrants' rights. The same year the Ford Foundation funded MALDEF and NCLR, longtime labor organizers and community leaders Bert Corona and Soledad "Chole" Alatorre established El Centro de Acción Social Autónomo-Hermandad General de Trabajadores (the Center for Autonomous Social Action-General Brotherhood

Figure 32. One of CASA's mottos: "Chicano–Mexicano–Somos Un Pueblo" (Chicano–Mexican–We Are One People).

Courtesy of the Department of Special Collections, Stanford University Libraries. Box 54, Folder 3, CASA Papers, m325, SCSUL.

of Workers, or CASA). Formed in Los Angeles as a "voluntary, democratic mutual assistance social welfare organization," CASA expanded quickly, with local chapters in five states by 1970 and a membership of 2,000 to 4,000 a few years later. As historian David Gutiérrez has noted, unlike its more moderate and conservative counterparts, "CASA was unique . . . in building a political organization which strongly advocated both ethnic and working-class solidarity between Mexican Americans and Mexican immigrants to the United States." The group, which saw itself as building on the past efforts of immigrant defense organizations like the American Committee for Protection of Foreign Born, challenged racist tropes propagated by national media outlets that immigrants posed a security threat, stole jobs, and caused the nation's economic woes. Rather than Mexicans' supposed cultural inferiority, they blamed the exploitation inherent to the capitalist system for their marginalization. CASA's motto, "Somos Un Pueblo Sin Fronteras" (We Are One People without Borders), reflected its commitment to all workers and community members, regardless of race, ethnicity, religion, citizenship, or legal status (see figure 32).[12]

CASA deployed a multifaceted strategy to combat the deportation machine, but no tactic was more important than the organization and empowerment of undocumented people and their allies. Recognizing the integral role Mexican people had long played in the economy, society, and culture of the United States emboldened people to assert their belonging and lay claim to basic civil rights. This guiding principle of inclusion led the organization to forcefully push back against widespread racial profiling by INS agents who typically determined whether someone was an "illegal" based on the person's last name or how he or she looked or spoke. Such policies and practices had a devastating impact on all ethnic Mexicans, the group argued, since immigration officials placed "a whole people . . . the brown, Spanish-speaking people of this nation and of this entire hemisphere . . . in jeopardy, on the job, on the streets, in the schools, courts, hospitals . . . everywhere!"[13]

Throughout the 1970s, CASA and other organizations also fought against racial profiling by opposing numerous legislative proposals at the state and federal level, including the 1970 Dixon-Arnett Bill in the California State Assembly and the 1972 Rodino Bill in the US House of Representatives. These so-called employer sanctions bills, drafted by liberals like New Jersey Democrat Peter Rodino at the behest of the American Federation of Labor–Congress of Industrial Organizations (AFL-CIO) and in response to growing concerns about the recent spike in immigration, would have levied fines and imposed penalties on employers who knowingly hired undocumented workers. CASA members and other critics asserted that employer sanctions would only further racial stereotyping and discriminatory hiring practices that disproportionately affected Latinos. By the latter part of the decade, the INS and local police's ongoing targeting of Mexican immigrants and Mexican Americans alike helped to create a new consensus against employer sanctions among Latino rights organizations, including the more conservative ones like LULAC.[14]

Empowerment also stemmed from CASA's public protests against immigration raids and the abuses ethnic Mexicans suffered at the hands of federal authorities. After a series of INS sweeps in Los Angeles in the spring of 1973 resulted in the apprehension of more than 2,000 people in a single week, CASA organized a demonstration in which more than 200 Chicanos picketed the federal building in downtown Los Angeles."[15] Located at 300 N Los Angeles Street, between city hall and the 101 freeway, the federal building, as home to INS headquarters, was a symbolically important site for demonstrations. CASA continued to hold regular protests there in the years to come. After a May 1975 crackdown led to the deportation of a couple thousand workers (including some 500 people from one factory) in a single week, they started holding protests every Thursday at 4:00 p.m. The objective of these demonstrations was to "publicly expos[e] the INS, LAPD and FBI for violation of democratic rights and mistreatment of Mexicano and Latino workers and their families." Deportation, the press release asserted, was "not the solution to unemployment, high prices, low wages, intolerable working conditions, inadequate medical care, poor educations, drugs in our communities, etc. . . . JOBS FOR ALL, STOP DEPORTATIONS!!!!!!"[16]

Considered within the context of the INS's frequent mass deportation campaigns and the widespread fear that they engendered in the ethnic Mexican community, CASA's regular marches through city streets and claims to the public space in front of the INS office were bold acts of political defiance. In the mid-1970s, after years of "dragnet raids on the streets, outside the churches, in theaters and in factories . . . in every major industrial, agricultural and population center," the group called on undocumented immigrants and their allies to "unite and oppose such unjust and mercenary 'gestapo' tactics and inhuman exploitation." (Activists frequently compared the INS to Nazis, both in words and images, and described the agency's enforcement tactics and mentality as racist and fascist.)[17] As the local San José chapter explained in the lead up to CASA's "National Moratorium against Repression," which drew more than 5,000 people into the streets of Los Angeles on August 31, 1974, "Our people have come to realize that we have taken enough, that we must no longer hide in fear. For this reason CASA uses the tactic of public demonstrations to call out to the people that now is a time when we must all unite to defend ourselves."[18] Local and federal law enforcement officials took note, keeping tabs on CASA's activities, surveilling their demonstrations, arresting members, and even raiding the offices of the organization's legal team (see figure 33).[19]

Activists also turned to education campaigns as a way of guaranteeing the rights of all Latinos and slowing down summary deportations. Immigrant aid and defense organizations conducted know-your-rights workshops and distributed handouts in Spanish and English to inform people in the community about what to do if they encountered an INS investigator in their workplace or in the street. Over the course of the decade, activists' efforts

**Figure 33. Plainclothes officers monitor a CASA demonstration and express their displeasure with activists' countersurveillance efforts.**
Courtesy of the Department of Special Collections, Stanford University Libraries. Box 44, Folder 14, CASA Papers, m325, SCSUL.

increasingly centered on a simple, yet ingenious strategy of how people should respond: Don't say anything. Don't sign anything. Demand to see a lawyer. Demand a deportation hearing.[20] Although many undocumented immigrants might not have realized it, they possessed many of the same constitutional rights as other people in the country. Regardless of legal status, they still had the right to remain silent; the right to speak with a lawyer; the right not to sign anything; the right to a deportation hearing; and the right to be released on bond or on one's own recognizance and in the meantime remain free. People aware of these rights stood a much greater chance of fighting off any attempts to expel them.[21]

In order to deport someone, immigration officials first had to establish the individual's deportability, usually based on where a person was born and when and how he or she entered the country. With that information in hand, officials could then process the immigrant for deportation, which almost always occurred after an immigrant signed an I-214 voluntary departure form, stating that he or she would leave the country and forgo the right to a hearing.

Recognizing the INS's near-exclusive dependence on voluntary departures as a potential vulnerability within the machine, activists mobilized. The know-your-rights pamphlets informed migrants that invoking the right to remain silent could be a way to negate their deportability. "Remember: la Migra has to prove where you were born. If you tell them where you were born they will use those statements to deport you. If you don't tell them anything, they will not be able to prove where you were born and they will have to let you go."[22] Organizations also created handouts with marked-up copies of the Spanish-language version of the I-214 voluntary departure form warning, "Watch Out!" "Danger!" and "Don't Sign This Form!" So as to clear up any confusion created by legalese or euphemistic terminology, above the signature line they wrote: "This Is Deportation" (see figure 34).[23]

Activists were aware that in many cases basic knowledge of one's rights would not necessarily be enough to help someone in an actual encounter with an INS agent. In a 1972 handout titled "Loneliness and Helplessness When Facing the Immigration Interrogator," CASA walked people through the experience of apprehension, isolation, questioning, and sustained threat. Immigrants could expect to experience "psychological voids" in which they were "unable to remember [their] rights in front of the officials." The best defense against this was to keep "your mouth closed and your mind sharp" and to insist upon your basic rights.[24] For CASA and other activists, refusing to cooperate with immigration officers' requests was "an act of civil disobedience against la Migra and the Yankee state's racist and discriminatory attacks against the Mexican people and Latinos in general."[25] For the individuals who adopted these strategies, including some of the workers at the Sbicca shoe factory, they turned out to be among the most effective means of defense against deportation.

Social events, teach-ins, and local, regional, and national conferences offered other opportunities for Chicano groups to organize the community, contest discriminatory policies and legislative proposals, and raise awareness about the history, politics, and economics of immigration.[26] Binational meetings held in Mexico helped build solidarity across borders.[27] One of the largest events occurred in October 1977, when some 1,500–2,000 people,

**¡OJO! ¡PELIGRO!**  **NO FIRME ESTA FORMA!**

UNITED STATES DEPARTMENT OF JUSTICE
Immigration and Naturalization Service

### AVISO DE DERECHOS

Antes de que le hagamos cualquier pregunta, usted debe de comprender sus derechos:

Usted tiene el derecho de guardar silencio.

Cualquier cosa que usted diga puede ser usada en su contra en un juzgado de leyes, o en cualquier procedimiento administrativo o de inmigración.

Usted tiene el derecho de hablar con un abogado para que el lo aconseje antes d . que le hagamos alguna pregunta, y de tenerlo presente con usted durante las preguntas.

Si usted no tiene el dinero para emplear a un abogado, se le puede proporcionar uno antes de que le hagamos alguna pregunta, si usted lo desea.

Si usted decide contestar nuestras preguntas ahora, sin tener a un abogado presente, siempre tendrá usted el derecho de dejar de contestar cuando guste. Usted también tiene el derecho de dejar de contestar cuando guste, hasta que pueda hablar con un abogado.

**NO FIRME**          RENUNCIA          ← **ESTA ESTA ES DEPORTACION**

He leído esta declaración de mis derechos y comprendo lo que son mis derechos. Estoy dispuesto a dar una declaración y a contestar preguntas. Por ahora no deseo un abogado. Comprendo y sé lo que estoy haciendo. No me han hecho promezas ni me han amenazado, ni han usado presión o fuerza en mi contra.

_____
Firma

Fecha y hora: _____          Lugar: _____

### CERTIFICATION

I HEREBY CERTIFY that the foregoing Warning and Waiver were read by me to the above signatory, that he also read it and has affixed his signature hereto in my presence.

_____
Immigration Officer      Signature

_____
Witness' Signature

_____
Interpreter's Signature          Language

_____
Interpreter's Address

Form I-214 (Spanish)
(Rev. 11-24-67)

**Figure 34.** Marked-up copy of a Spanish-language I-214 voluntary departure form, meant for distribution as part of a know-your-rights campaign.

Courtesy of the Department of Special Collections, Stanford University Libraries. Box 11, Folder 1, BCP, m248, SCSUL.

representing Latino groups from across the political spectrum—including the AGIF, LULAC, MALDEF, NCLR, and CASA—gathered in San Antonio, Texas, for the First National Chicano/Latino Conference on Immigration and Public Policy.[28] Spearheaded by José Ángel Gutiérrez of La Raza Unida Party, the conference's diverse participants united around a single issue: their denunciation of the immigration plan President Jimmy Carter had submitted to Congress that summer, which included an employer sanctions provision and ramped-up border enforcement in exchange for offering legal status to undocumented immigrants who had been in the United States continuously since before 1970.[29] Speaking as part of a plenary session, Peter Camejo, the Socialist Worker Party's presidential candidate in 1976, called on attendees to set aside their political differences, "because when they come to deport us, we're all in the same boat." In making the case for "immediate, unconditional amnesty to stop all the raids and deportations, and to grant full civil and human rights," Camejo plainly put it, "All we're asking for is that Latinos and Chicanos be treated the same way the 40 million Anglos that came over here were treated."[30]

Grassroots Chicano organizations were not alone in struggling for immigrant rights. The Catholic Church became a leading proponent for migrants as well. During the Second Vatican Council, which brought about progressive change within the church in the mid-1960s, Pope Paul VI proclaimed that Catholics had a "special obligation . . . to make [them]selves the neighbor of every person without exception and of actively helping him when he comes across our path, whether he be an old person abandoned by all, a foreign laborer unjustly looked down upon, a refugee, . . ."[31] The pope and other leaders of the church continued to make migration a priority in the years to come. Although religious conviction and humanitarian obligation motivated the church, self-preservation also factored into its stance. At a northeast regional meeting of Latino clergy in 1974, Father José L. Alvarez asserted that the Catholic Church couldn't ignore the "grave and pressing problem" of "immigrants without documents, improperly called 'illegals,'" in part because "they are human beings in need of assistance," but also because "they are Latin Americans, [and] almost all (about 90%) are members of the Catholic Church."[32] The institution quickly became a leading advocate for undocumented immigrants, sponsoring conferences, joining in marches, and speaking out on behalf of undocumented immigrants and particularly against family separation. The church would remain a powerful ally in the decades ahead.[33]

As overall union membership declined during the 1970s, an increasing number of labor organizations broke from their long history of excluding undocumented workers from their ranks and took up the fight for immigrant rights.[34] None was more active in organizing the undocumented in Southern California than the International Ladies' Garment Workers' Union (ILGWU). In the words of the union's executive vice president, "We're trying to organize all unorganized workers. It's not of interest to us what their status is except their status as exploited workers." When the ILGWU shifted its policy in 1975 to include undocumented workers, the change arose largely from necessity. In the middle of the twentieth century the union had a membership around 20,000; a few decades later it hovered somewhere between 7,000 and 8,000. The $3 billion California garment industry (the equivalent of $11.7 billion today and second at the time only to New York City) employed around 100,000 workers, nearly 80 percent of whom worked for the more than 3,000 sweatshops in the Los Angeles area. Latinos and undocumented immigrants made up more than three-quarters of all California garment industry workers. (At the time, an INS spokesperson estimated that 40 percent of all undocumented workers labored in industry.) "The union [was] simply adapting to new conditions," ILGWU spokesman Mario Vásquez explained. "The ILG was built by immigrants and really could not get away from it. The only difference now is it's not legal to immigrate, but it's all the same thing."[35]

INS raids threatened undocumented workers and broader unionization efforts. The ILGWU claimed that many employers used the immigration service to combat labor organizing. "I first realized what was happening in 1975, when we had a strike with 20 people on the picket line and pretty soon an INS van appeared and took away 17 of our members," Philip Russo, the ILGWU's chief organizer said.[36] Their lack of unionization made it much easier for employers to exploit the majority of garment workers who lacked documentation. Whereas a union shop provided benefits, some protections, and an hourly wage rate of $3.00–$3.60 (roughly $11.75–$14.00 today), workers at nonunion shops oftentimes worked ten to twelve hours each day for only $1.00–$1.50 an hour ($3.90–$5.85 today). Moreover, the ILGWU received numerous complaints of people locked in the factory all night. Other documented abuses included "unsanitary conditions, lack of bathroom facilities and drinking water, overheating, sexual abuses of female workers, blackmail by employers of 'illegal aliens,' physical beatings, fake payroll deductions and lack of ventilation that results in a high concentration of cotton dust particles in the air." Being exposed to those particles could cause "byssinosis" (brown lung disease), which could "give rise to an asthma-like syndrome and over many years of exposure . . . chronically give rise to [irreversible] lung damage." A 1976 investigation by the California State Labor Commission found that 98.5 percent of all garment firms were "either in violation of the labor code or the industrial welfare commission orders." But the state only brought token criminal charges against fifteen firms, resulting in ten convictions over a two-year period.[37]

Organizations like the Comité Obrero en Defensa de los Indocumentados en Lucha (Defense Committee of Undocumented Workers in Struggle, or CODIL) pushed established unions to represent all workers, regardless of legal status. Inspired by the example of José "Pepe" Jacques Medina, a thirty-one-year-old CASA member, union organizer, and Mexican political exile who was fighting his own deportation at the time, undocumented immigrants in the Los Angeles area formed CODIL in April 1976 after a raid at a mattress factory resulted in the deportation of unionized workers demanding contractually obligated back pay. The group's twenty to thirty members, many of whom had been deported on numerous occasions while trying to unionize or claim benefits, challenged stereotypes of undocumented workers as passive or powerless and used organizing as a way to contest INS terror campaigns. Adopting slogans like "Fuera la migra de las fábricas" (Get la migra out of the factories) and "La lucha obrera no la detiene ninguna frontera" (No border can stop the working-class struggle), CODIL organized in workplaces and in the community, created defense committees, distributed educational materials, and pushed unions like the ILGWU, United Auto Workers, United Electrical Workers, and United Brotherhood of Carpenters to expand their membership to include the undocumented. "We have a right to a job, to a union, to the struggle," Jacques Medina told a group of trade unionists gathered in New York in April 1977 (see figure 35).[38]

But, in the 1970s, undocumented immigrants' rights before the law remained, in some cases, undefined. With interior expulsions topping 100,000 per year and total annual deportations exceeding one million, the fight for ethnic Mexicans' belonging—and against the repressive enforcement apparatus

Figure 35. José Jacques Medina speaking to a crowd of more than 200 people at the Embassy Auditorium in Los Angeles, March 1977.
Courtesy of the Department of Special Collections, Stanford University Libraries. Box 46, Folder 8, CASA Papers, m325, SCSUL.

that targeted them for removal—became more urgent than ever. At the same time as internal political divisions within CASA led to the group's decline, undocumented immigrants, union organizers, community groups, and young, activist lawyers (many with ties to the civil rights and Chicano movements) joined together in hopes that their collective power would be greater than the sum of their individual efforts. It usually was. And, in some cases, these broad coalitions sparked transformational change.

## A Family Business and Immigrant Workers in a Changing Global Economy

Sixty-one-year-old Arthur Sbicca had been in the family business for more than four decades when the immigration raid happened that May morning in 1978. His father, Francesco, a shoemaker by trade, founded the company in Philadelphia in 1920, seven years after leaving his town in the Umbria region of central Italy, crossing the Atlantic aboard a vessel named *America*, and passing through Ellis Island.[39] Sbicca specialized in making stylish footwear for young women and came up with innovative new manufacturing techniques.[40] In the 1940s, Francesco (who by then went by Frank) relocated the business to Los Angeles and changed its name to Sbicca of California, Inc. He explained the move by noting the increased national demand for "California-made merchandise" and "products which are manufactured with an eye to Hollywood styling." The factory, which employed seventy-five people and produced 500 pairs of shoes a day, was the first by an eastern company to open in the area. When Frank died a decade later, Arthur and his two brothers took over.[41]

Business boomed under the brothers' leadership. They bought a six-acre lot and built a larger factory in a part of eastern Los Angeles County, later incorporated as South El Monte, the "City of Achievement." Arthur, a graduate of the University of Pennsylvania and World War II veteran, assumed the executive responsibilities. A Republican and an active member of Italian American social organizations in Los Angeles, Arthur received a "Star of Solidarity" award from the Italian government in recognition of his success as a manufacturer and his contributions "to Italian welfare and progress." In 1967, the *Los Angeles Times* described the company as an industry leader, reporting that they were "fast building an outstanding fashion image with their young, up-to-the-minute Sbicca shoes." By the late 1970s Sbicca employed over 750 people who produced 4,000 pairs of shoes a day, from heels to sandals to clogs that ranged in price from $20–$26 ($106–$138 today).[42]

At the same time as the company expanded its production capacity, global economic forces were reshaping the shoe industry. A 50 percent reduction of tariff rates in 1968 resulted in an influx of foreign-made shoes into the country. Between 1969 and 1973 the number of pairs of women's nonrubber shoes imported from abroad spiked from 139 million to 212 million, going from one-third to more than one-half of all US consumption. During the same period, domestic production declined, dropping from 319 million in 1965 to just 190 million in 1973. Facing these changes, Sbicca experienced a decline in sales, even recording net losses in 1972 and 1973. The following year, in response to the company's application for the federal Trade Adjustment Assistance program to offset losses caused by imports, two members of the US Tariff Commission found that Sbicca was "experiencing serious injury" and was "threatened with serious injury." To compensate, Sbicca relied on its "good knowledge and expertise in manufacturing and design," making use of "four modern conveyor-belt systems to speed the flow of materials in the stitching room" and "several programmed conveyers [to] ensure that cut materials are readily available at proper assembly points."[43]

But the company still had "a difficult problem with the imports," Arthur Sbicca lamented. "The imports from Korea and Taiwan where they employ slave labor, and [pay] twenty cents an hour, is our competition." By contrast, he claimed that Sbicca paid "above minimum wage by quite a bit" and provided "lots of benefits."[44] In fact, wages and benefits varied considerably among the company's overwhelmingly Mexican workforce, and the conditions at the factory left much to be desired. Some received an hourly wage, while others worked for a piecemeal rate. María Guadalupe González was just nineteen years old when she started working at Sbicca in the fall of 1977 shortly after arriving from northern Mexico. She and around fifty other women in the cement department spent eight hours a day, five or six days a week affixing different leather uppers to a variety of specially molded single-piece polyurethane soles. They often talked, sang, or ate sweets to pass the time. The job was repetitive, but not particularly difficult. "What was difficult was enduring the smell of the cement," she said. "But we had to do it." Sbicca did not provide the workers with any safety equipment. "It was just, 'There's your container and your brush, go to work.' There weren't ear plugs for the noise or face masks" to protect workers from the fumes and dust. She earned around $3.50 an hour (around $13.50 an hour today) for her labor, more than many of her coworkers and a dollar above California's minimum wage, but received no benefits. By the end of her thirty-two-year career, mostly spent at another shoe company, it was not uncommon for González to get nose bleeds and headaches and experience symptoms of withdrawal.[45]

Sbicca workers also described a toxic work environment that included favoritism, verbal abuse, the sexual harassment of female employees, and the firing of people at will. While it's unclear whether this reached upper management, which at that time included Arthur (whom employees referred to as "Arturo") and his two sons Dominic ("Don") and Arthur Jr. ("Junior"), such abuses were a pervasive problem among middle management. For a while, no one said anything out of fear of being fired. But in early December 1977, Jesse Gonzales, a thirty-five-year-old Spanish-speaking organizer for the Retail Clerks Union Local 1428, started an organizing campaign at the factory with the help of former employee David Hernández. Workers soon began meeting weekly, sometimes in the house of Hernández's brother-in-law Arturo Vallejo, to strategize about how to win representation. Gonzales would go to the factory and speak with workers as they entered at the start of the day, came out for their lunch break, or left to go home. He told Sbicca employees about how the union could help them increase their pay and fight for benefits, and he educated them about the personal health risks and environmental impact of their work. That was enough to convince María Guadalupe González, who signed on in support of the drive.[46]

In April 1978 lawyers for the Retail Clerks Union and Sbicca reached an agreement, approved by the National Labor Relations Board (NLRB), to hold an election the following month. In the weeks leading up to the vote, Sbicca, which had a long antiunion history, tried to intimidate the workers by threatening to call the INS and have them deported. Supervisors encouraged their charges to vote no by handing out raffle tickets for a gift basket and promising that the benefits would improve. They also began giving days off without explanation to employees like González who supported the union. On May 11, the NLRB conducted the election at the factory, posting two polling stations on either end of the property. When the final tally was recorded the union had lost by nine votes: 208 in favor and 217 against, with 224 challenged ballots. Based on the challenged ballots and reports of intimidation and the lack of proper election monitoring, the Retail Clerks Union decided to contest the result with the NLRB. Six days later, with the election results still uncertified and the union in the process of filing an objection, the INS carried out its raid on the factory.[47] This was far from the first "survey" of the company. In fact, immigration investigators had carried out eighteen operations at Sbicca over the previous eleven years, resulting in the apprehension of more than 1,100 people.[48] But the response to the May 1978 "survey" was different. An excavation and analysis of the raid and its aftermath sheds light not only on the inner workings of the deportation machine in the 1970s, but also on how immigrants and their allies fought against it—and won.

## The Anatomy of Effective Resistance

María Guadalupe González never made it to work on Wednesday, May 17. She and her sister-in-law were running late that morning. When they pulled up to Sbicca and saw what was happening they kept on going. They weren't there when the forty immigration investigators arrived, but Jesse Gonzales was. He was handing out leaflets in front of the factory when all of a sudden "the INS c[a]me rolling in like gestapo." At some point during the raid Gonzales spoke with Philip H. Smith, assistant district director for investigations and the officer in charge, who denied having any prior knowledge of the contested union election and also denied that Sbicca management had contacted the service. Unsure of what to do, Gonzales returned to the office and called immigration attorney Peter Schey, whose number he had gotten from another lawyer. That phone call began a chain of events that would play out over the course of more than a decade.[49]

Schey, who was born in South Africa and spent his high school and college years in Northern California, was just thirty-one years old and five years out of law school when he received Gonzales's call.[50] At the time he was working for the Legal Services Aliens' Rights Program of the Legal Aid Foundation of Los Angeles and was also representing José Jacques Medina. He was part of a generation of young lawyers who came of age during the social movements of the 1960s and took up the fight for immigrant rights in the 1970s. Schey believed in organizing the unorganized and educating undocumented workers about their rights so that they could fight back against the INS. He was also part of a coalition of immigrants and allies developing legal strategies to stop factory raids and protect people from deportation. The Sbicca case gave them a chance to put their plan into action.[51]

Well aware that standard INS practice was to deport people via voluntary departure the same day they apprehended them, Schey moved quickly to block the imminent expulsion of the 119 Sbicca workers. Time was of the essence. He first reached out to a couple of colleagues who had institutional support.

Mark Rosenbaum was a brilliant, thirty-year-old Harvard-trained lawyer from Cincinnati who had worked on the Pentagon Papers case and taken a job with the American Civil Liberties Union while still in law school. Twenty-eight-year-old Bill Blum was an up-and-coming attorney with the People's College of Law who had received his degree from the University of San Diego and had only been practicing for around a year and a half. They both signed on. Later that afternoon they were joined by Antonio Rodríguez, a thirty-five-year-old University of California, Los Angeles School of Law graduate. Born in Torreón, Coahuila, Rodríguez later immigrated to the United States, naturalized, and became involved in the Chicano movement, eventually going on to lead CASA.[52]

While Schey worked on drafting the complaint that he would use to seek the temporary restraining order, Blum rushed downtown to INS headquarters in the basement of the federal building. Ever since returning to the office that morning, Assistant District Director Smith had been "inundated with telephone calls" from newspaper and television reporters, as well as people like the lawyer for the Retail Clerks Union, the Mexican consul Ernesto Acevedo, and Schey, who informed him that he was one of the attorneys representing the Sbicca workers. Blum arrived around noon (just an hour after the vans and bus full of the detained Sbicca workers), and presented Smith with a letter demanding that the INS "cease all questioning and cease all attempts to procure waivers of any and all legal rights." It also demanded the "right to interview them and appraise them of their legal rights prior to any interrogation by the Immigration Service." Such basic protections, hardly ever granted to people in INS custody, were essential if the team was to convince the Sbicca employees to reject voluntary departure and fight their cases. But Smith refused, telling Blum that he would advise the detainees about the possibility of speaking with a lawyer, but only "after [officials] completed the preliminary processing." Although Smith later allowed Consul Acevedo and Blum to speak with some of the workers, by then it was too late: most of them had already been processed and had signed voluntary departure forms.[53]

Meanwhile, after getting off the phone with Blum, Schey spent the next six hours assembling the materials needed to request a court injunction to stop the workers' deportation. The main legal grounds for the complaint were based on Smith and the INS's refusal to "grant adequate and available counsel" (which he argued violated 8 USC 1362 and the plaintiffs' Fifth and Sixth Amendment rights) and failure to stop interrogating the plaintiffs at the request of counsel (which he argued violated 8 CFR 287.3 and their Fifth and Sixth Amendment rights against self-incrimination, to counsel, and to due process of law).[54] Schey also asserted that the INS's "questioning of all Hispanic persons" at Sbicca "placed such persons in a custodial setting" in violation of the Fourth Amendment. But "even if the questioning was not custodial in nature," he continued, agents' indiscriminate questioning during the raid was illegal, citing a recent federal district court decision in New York that established that "INS officials may approach persons to inquire about their citizenship status only on a reasonable suspicion based on specific articulable facts, that the person may be an alien who is illegally in the country."[55] Schey also noted that many of the detained workers were material witnesses to the contested union election and sought class action certification for the case in hopes of protecting all Sbicca employees apprehended that day, including Arturo Vallejo and the other named plaintiffs, as well as other individuals who might find themselves in a similar situation in the future.[56] He warned that his clients would "suffer immediate and irreparable injury in that they will be wrongfully deported" within hours, which would result in them losing their right to appeal their case or challenge the constitutionality of the INS's practices. Schey urged the district court to act and Judge Robert Firth did. Just before 4:30 p.m., with two buses already en route to Mexico, he signed the temporary restraining order halting the Sbicca workers' deportation.[57]

Having staved off the Sbicca employees' immediate expulsion, the inchoate coalition of lawyers, organizers, and activists shifted their energies to the workers' fight to stay. Judge Firth had enjoined the INS from "all further questioning, interrogation, and processing including deporting and transporting for purposes of deportation of plaintiff employees . . . until they have been afforded direct access to adequate and available counsel." So the first step was to get access to the detainees and determine who among them wanted to challenge their removal. Some of the workers, including Arturo Vallejo, had refused to agree to voluntary departure since the beginning. Others, like Rosa Melchor López, had only done so because an INS agent had scared her by yelling and saying that she would be held in a jail for women for up to a year, at which point she would be returned to Mexico. Martín López Rocha declared that after refusing to sign the form an immigration agent forged an X and wrote "(His Mark)" next to it.[58]

Two days later, on May 19, the court authorized Mexican Consul Acevedo to read a statement in Spanish to the workers, with Schey, Rodríguez, Jesse Gonzales, two INS representatives, and a US Attorney's Office representative present. Acevedo informed the group of their rights to counsel, to a hearing, and to make phone calls, and told them that Schey, Rodríguez, Rosenbaum, and Blum were willing to represent them pro bono and speak with them about "whether you should sign a voluntary departure form, whether you should have a hearing before an Immigration Judge, whether you are entitled to bail, or any other problem that you may have." After finishing, he went around with a pad of paper, asking anyone interested in speaking with one of the lawyers to give their name. If they did, he told them, they had the right not to answer any INS questions in the meantime. More than sixty people added their names to the list.[59]

The Sbicca workers' decision to challenge their removal posed a serious threat to the INS. As a *Wall Street Journal* editorial later observed, immigration officials' "great nightmare" during this period was "that some part of a million aliens a year will suddenly stop agreeing to 'accept voluntary departure.'"[60] In a system that depended on these coercive deportations, low-level immigration officers served as judge, jury, and executioner and investigators frequently went to extreme lengths to push people out of the country. They applied psychological pressure, lied to people about their rights and potential relief, and singled out, segregated, and ridiculed "troublemakers" who insisted on consulting legal counsel and having a hearing. From the agency's perspective, such practices allowed authorities to make the most of their limited resources and avoid backlogs.[61]

In a study of enforcement practices at the time, based on extensive interviews with immigration agents and largely sympathetic to the government, Edwin Harwood concluded that noncitizens' decision to reject voluntary departure would "hamstring the INS because, if very many aliens decided to challenge their arrests, field officers would have been called to testify at hearings, and they would have that much less time to carry out apprehensions." Not to mention: "It would also have given aliens an incentive to demand hearings, which would have increased the burden on detention facilities and the immigration courts."[62] Senior immigration judge Jay Segal expressed a similar sentiment when testifying before the California Advisory Committee to the United States Commission on Civil Rights a couple of weeks after the Sbicca raid. In response to a question from committee member Jane Fonda about the impact of the shoe workers' insistence on hearings, Segal replied that they would "probably reduce our capability to handle other cases greatly."[63] Charles Gordon, the former INS general counsel, went even further, stating that exclusively relying on formal deportations "would cause a breakdown of the Immigration and Naturalization Service. . . . [If everyone] were subjected to a hearing, the administrative mechanism would collapse. It would never complete a case."[64] If apprehended immigrants started challenging their expulsions en masse they held the potential to stop the deportation machine in its tracks.[65] Whether or not they would be able to depended in part in how organized they were, and in part on what rights they had before the law. Going into the individual Sbicca hearings and class action case, both activists and the INS understood the high stakes.

The Sbicca team next sought to find legal representation for all of the workers who had decided to stay. They recruited other young attorneys to serve as counsel and energetic law students to provide research assistance, translate affidavits, and offer additional support in any way possible. More than a dozen people signed on.[66] The group first visited immigration headquarters downtown to speak with their clients and record their basic information, as well as the circumstances of their arrest. When they arrived, they entered into a hostile environment. Edward Ortega, a twenty-six-year-old lawyer with the Legal Aid Foundation of Los Angeles who had been on the job for just six months, remembered that the INS "really was very surprised to see us all there. They had never experienced anything like that before; having all of these legal workers come in." The environment was tense and at one point an immigration official locked Ortega in the large glass holding room with the Sbicca detainees, perhaps in an attempt to intimidate him.[67]

In addition to providing legal counsel to the Sbicca workers, the team also sought their immediate release, either by bond or on their own recognizance. This was an important piece of the larger strategy, since the prospect of an extended stay in a bare-bones desert detention camp like the one in El Centro, which was located near the border and far from family, friends, and legal help, was one of the most powerful weapons immigration authorities had when trying to coerce people into voluntary departure. To secure the workers' release, the group turned to Antonio Rodríguez's brother, Jacobo, a bail bondsman and CASA member who had worked with the Brown Berets (a Chicano community defense and empowerment organization) in the past and saw his job as a social justice and community education initiative, rather than a profit-making venture. He believed that if the battle against voluntary departure and the INS's repressive tactics was to be won, activists "must also be there to represent them and get them release[d]." In order to do so, people had to come up with 10 percent of the bond and put up some form of collateral that would guarantee their presence in immigration court. Jacobo helped secure bonds, ranging from $500–$3,000 (with most in the $1,000–$2,000 range), for all of the Sbicca employees. Nine people were also released on their own recognizance. Although a few workers ended up spending a week and a half in detention, most were out within two to five days of the raid. This "kind of broke the back of [the] INS, because they couldn't wear people down and keep them in indefinite detention," Mark Rosenbaum recounted. "Once they were out, that became the motivation for INS to get the hearings going, but otherwise it was the equivalent of locking them up and throwing away the key." Winning clients' freedom also helped to win the workers' trust and instill confidence in them for the fight ahead, not to mention the fact that it allowed them to stay in the country and to continue working.[68]

Activists and organizers also took immediate action in the wake of the May 17 raid. Jesse Gonzales went house to house, visiting the families of the detained workers, offering encouragement, and assuring them that the Retail Clerks Union would support them. Within a week, José Jacques Medina and representatives from at least a dozen different labor, rights, and community organizations had formed the Centro de Acción Laboral Contra "La Migra," known in English as the Labor and Immigration Action Center. The immediate and long-term goals of the center included supporting the Sbicca workers, developing a legal arm that could bring class action suits to combat factory raids, creating know-your-rights materials and promoting education campaigns, and fundraising to create a general bond fund for undocumented workers. The group, which served as a rapid response network, also organized demonstrations and created a twenty-four-hour phone hotline to collect and disseminate information about raids.[69]

While Jacques Medina organized and Schey, Rosenbaum, and Rodríguez strategized about how to tackle the federal class action suit against the INS's blanket targeting of ethnic Mexicans and Latinos during raids, everyone's first priority was to defend the Sbicca workers facing deportation.[70] Adopting the approach pioneered by groups like CASA and the National Lawyers Guild in the early 1970s, the team advised all of the Sbicca workers to exercise their Fifth Amendment right to remain silent. Under the law, the government had the burden of proof to present "clear, convincing, and unequivocal evidence" of a person's deportability, at which point the burden would then shift to the individual to show his or her lawful presence in the country. The INS usually had been able to meet its burden by interrogating people about where they were born and whether they had papers—all *before* advising them of their rights. As Rosenbaum put it, the Sbicca team's straightforward strategy was to tell the service, "You have to meet your burden by yourself. We're not going to help you." The tactic proved to be incredibly effective.[71]

In the days and weeks leading up to the hearings, the lawyers spent hours preparing each Sbicca worker. They translated the text of the Fifth Amendment into Spanish so that everyone had a clear understanding of their rights and the legal strategy they would be employing. Working in pairs, they role played simulations of the hearing so that people knew what to expect in hopes that they would be less intimidated during the proceedings. Since many of the lawyers were relatively inexperienced (for some it would be the first time they had ever appeared in court), the team deliberately scheduled the cases of the more seasoned attorneys first so that they could serve as prototypes for everyone else.[72]

When the deportation hearings began, the Sbicca workers refused to answer questions by invoking their rights under the Fifth Amendment and Section 291 of the Immigration and Nationality Act. At the same time, their attorneys argued that any prior statements their clients had made had been unconstitutionally obtained. It quickly became clear that the government was in trouble. "They panicked," Rosenbaum remembered. In some cases, the service's lawyers sought continuances in order to buy time. They sent investigators to migrants' supposed hometowns and reached out to State Department officials stationed in Mexico in hopes of turning up original birth certificates that would help them establish an individual's deportability.

"You might as well have been telling [the] INS to bring back moon rocks," Rosenbaum exclaimed. "They did not know how to do it. They absolutely did not know how to do it."[73]

Despite intense interrogations by government lawyers and repeated admonitions from immigration judges to respond to questions or risk that "adverse inferences" might be drawn from their silence, most of the Sbicca workers withstood the pressure. Before long, immigration judges had no option but to terminate their deportation proceedings. They dismissed at least five cases from early July to early September. Immigration judge Robert T. Griffin terminated eighteen-year-old Luis Manuel Cervantes Cervantes's removal after the "government decline[d] to produce any evidence of deportability at all, much less clear, convincing and unequivocal evidence." By November immigration judges had canceled the deportations of seventeen Sbicca employees, a number that would continue to rise in the months and years ahead. "The results indicate that when required to follow congressionally mandated procedures, I.N.S. cannot establish the deportability of approximately 50% of the persons whom they take into detention," Peter Schey reported. He made clear the landmark nature of the case: "This in turn reflects the possibility that approximately one half of the one million people forcefully deported each year by I.N.S. may not be deportable under current laws." As attention and energies shifted to the class action suit, activists and immigration officials alike took note, redoubling their energies for the struggle that lie ahead.[74]

## Fighting for the Future

During the 1970s immigrants and advocates filed a number of lawsuits attempting to rein in the INS.[75] As Felipe Aguirre, coordinator of the National Coalition for Fair Immigration Laws and Practices and a former CASA member, put it at the time, "Essentially we are dealing with an agency that has a fiefdom of its own, that handles people without any discretion [in] terms of their rights, and without any discretion in terms of what they are enforcing or what law they are breaking."[76] Rosenbaum described the environment as like "the wild, wild West," in which undocumented immigrants had no rights and the INS "did not recognize any sorts of limitations."[77] That was

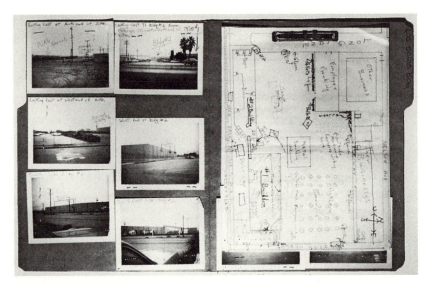

Figure 36. INS surveillance photographs and a hand-drawn map agents created in preparation for a raid on a Los Angeles factory, circa late 1970s.
Courtesy of USCISHOL.

certainly true when it came to immigration raids. In February 1978, the ILGWU had filed suit against the INS in the federal district court for its practice of raiding factories in Los Angeles's garment district "with or without search warrants" and questioning all people who appeared to be Latino. This practice, the ILGWU claimed, led to the harassment of US citizens and violated people's due process rights and "guarantees of privacy and protection against unreasonable search and seizure." The union's lawyer noted that the suit challenged immigration authorities' practice of "'barging in,' sealing off the exits of a factory, and 'holding them in what is essentially custody and questioning them when they haven't done anything wrong.'" He added that the service was "riding roughshod over the rights of these workers" and it "shouldn't be allowed to stop someone anywhere simply because they're Latino or Mexican."[78]

Some legal advocates questioned the constitutionality of the raids themselves, which most often took place without a warrant (see figure 36). Employers usually granted the immigration investigators permission to search factories, knowing that denying them access would end up hurting their bottom line. The Sbicca owners had learned this the hard way. During an area control operation in the late spring of 1974, they refused the service's request to search the premises. A couple of weeks later agents returned with a search warrant and, according to Arthur Sbicca, "took a lot longer to survey our place that day." For Sbicca and other employers, the INS's message was clear: "The idea is, if you are agreeable . . . it is better . . . it was our feeling we would be better off to cooperate."[79]

Some companies, though, did not cooperate, which slowed down the INS's work by forcing agents to seek out search warrants. However, the ILGWU suit and other immigration attorneys called into question the legality of such court orders since they authorized the service to search for property rather than people. Immigration authorities simply crossed out "property" and inserted "individuals, namely a large number of illegal aliens who are working and hiding at the above premises."[80] Robert L. Miller, the president of the board of directors of One-Stop Immigration Center, Inc. in Los Angeles, pointed out that in some instances the INS didn't even bother to make the modification. "Property, property, property. I counted it one time. I think there is something like at least 15 references to the word property, none to people anywhere on this."[81] The search warrants also raised questions about whether immigration enforcement was a strictly civil matter. Testifying before the California Advisory Committee to the US Commission on Civil Rights in June 1978, Bernard Karmiol, the regional counsel for the INS, tried to clarify: "The search warrant that we use is not a criminal proceeding. We just—unfortunately, we—for convenience we use a form . . . copied out of a form book . . . for a criminal proceeding, and we change it for our own purposes. . . . It is just to save time." The committee expressed skepticism about the INS's use of criminal search warrants for civil purposes. As one member responded: "That seems very Mickey Mouse to me if I might say so, that people can cross out certain things on legal documents and change them."[82] Regardless of whether or not the law allowed the service to appropriate criminal search warrants for civil purposes, the ILGWU lawyers and others argued that general factory raids and warrants' generic references to unspecified "illegal aliens" failed to meet the legal standard of having "articulable facts" about each person they interrogated.[83]

While the ILGWU's suit questioned the constitutionality of INS practices, the Sbicca class action case, *Vallejo, et al. v. Sureck*, sought to define and defend the rights of undocumented immigrants. The plaintiffs hoped that the class would include all people "who were on May 17, 1978, or have been or will be at any time thereafter, subject to custodial interrogation by INS agents without being advised of their right to representation and without being allowed immediate access to available counsel of their choice." As Schey and Rosenbaum noted in their initial filing the day of the raid, neither side disputed immigrants' right to counsel. "The only question that remains is <u>when</u> does this right attach, prior to, during, or subsequent to INS interrogation."[84] The issue of timing wasn't addressed by federal statue 8 CFR 287.3, which described immigration officers' interrogation power. The INS often used this ambiguity to its benefit and to immigrants' detriment, as Maurice Roberts, the former chairman of the Board of Immigration Appeals, made clear in an article published earlier that year:

> The statutory right to representation by counsel in deportation proceedings can also be meaningless unless counsel is present when his advice is really needed. . . . The INS often established its case, not on the basis of the alien's testimony at the deportation hearing, where he is represented by counsel, but on the basis of his admissions made to INS officers during the course of investigation, where he is usually unrepresented. Where an unsophisticated alien, anxious to please awesome officials, answers "yes" to the sometimes suggestive and leading questions of an overzealous INS investigator, he may unwittingly supply inaccurate information which would have been obviated or clarified if he had available the advice of counsel aware of the significance of the questions.[85]

In addition to the question of when did immigrants' rights attach, Federal District Court Judge William Matthew Byrne Jr. zeroed in on whether or not the Sbicca workers had been "arrested," since that was the language used in 8 CFR 287.3. Byrne considered this question important because the regulation provided that someone arrested by an immigration officer without a warrant had to be "advised of the reasons for his arrest and his right to be represented by council [*sic*] of his own choice, at no expense to the Government . . . [and] 'that any statement he makes may be used against him in a subsequent proceeding.'"[86]

Had the INS's interrogation and detention of the Sbicca workers constituted an arrest? Byrne concluded that it had. "The seizure of the Sbicca plaintiffs for more than four hours, their transportation to INS headquarters, and the reasonable inference that these persons understood themselves to be under arrest all weigh in favor of a finding that arrests had been effected."[87] As a result, per 8 CFR 287.3, the INS had an obligation to advise the Sbicca workers of their right to an attorney, and to grant them "some right of access" to legal counsel. On December 27, 1978, Byrne ruled that the plaintiffs' claims—based on 8 CFR 287.3 and their Fifth Amendment rights to due process and against self-incrimination—"must stand."[88]

As a commenter observed after the long-awaited decision, the Sbicca workers' "unprecedented action . . . is a very significant, organized form of resistance" with far-reaching implications "for all undocumented workers who are fighting for their rights."[89] The ILGWU and Sbicca cases, along with others and the continued protests and pressure from activists, organizers, and religious leaders, resulted in important victories for undocumented people. In the fall of 1978 the INS announced it was halting most factory raids because of the pending lawsuits against the agency and "a growing tendency of people seized by INS officers to fight deportation." The service also decided to stop requesting search warrants until the resolution of the ILGWU case. The policy change (along with cutting the number of area control investigators by half) caused apprehensions to drop 70 percent in Los Angeles and Orange Counties, in addition to "significant decrease[s]" in large cities across the country.[90] While the INS apprehended a record 96,000-plus Mexicans with long-term US residence in fiscal year 1977, the following year the number fell to just under 72,000, before dropping off even more to around 58,000 in 1979 and slightly over 40,000 in 1980. Overall apprehensions by investigators decreased by around half during that four-year period, going from around 162,000 to 83,000.[91]

The reduction in raids and gains made by immigrants and activists were difficult to enforce on the ground and were, in some cases, short lived. In March 1979, while the government's appeal of the Sbicca decision had yet to be decided, the INS altered 8 CFR 287.3, erasing the section stipulating that apprehended people must be advised of their rights at the time of a warrantless arrest. They did so in direct response to the Sbicca case and in order to legitimize the agency's long-standing practice of "interrogation first, rights, second."[92] Bruce Bowman, a student at the People's College of Law, noted that the changes to the regulation spoke to "the extreme flexibility INS has as the state's agent." The Sbicca team's victory, he continued, would "only give [them] a little room to breathe before people are put into a new chokehold."[93] The service's decision to go to great lengths to keep people in the dark about their rights is not surprising; the deportation machine depended on it. Both neighborhood and workplace raids continued in the months and years ahead, with the INS becoming even more emboldened after 1984, when the Supreme Court upheld the constitutionality of factory "surveys."[94]

It wasn't until the summer of 1992 that the Sbicca class action suit was finally settled.[95] The *New York Times* reported, "After a 14-year legal battle, the Immigration and Naturalization Service has agreed to inform people arrested as illegal aliens of their legal rights and to offer them the opportunity to consult a lawyer." As part of the settlement, which was agreed to by Schey and then–INS commissioner Gene McNary in June and approved by Judge Byrne in August, the service had to provide apprehended immigrants with a revised "Notice of Rights" form that advised them of their right to contact a lawyer, communicate with a consular official from their home country, and request a list of free or low-cost legal services. It also required officials to inform detainees about different legal avenues to becoming permanent residents. The second form, a "Request for Disposition," asked immigrants (excluding Mexicans and Canadians) if they believed they would face harm if deported to their home countries. If they responded yes, agents were then supposed to give them the chance to request political asylum before an immigration judge. Noting that the resolution would provide "the closest thing to a Miranda-type warning for immigrants facing deportation," Schey stated, "For the first time, people being arrested as suspected illegal immigrants will have the same rights as those arrested for suspicion of criminal behavior. For the first time they will be given the rights guaranteed to everyone in this country, Americans and non-Americans alike, guaranteed by the American Constitution."[96]

The historic, nationwide settlement affected more than one million people each year, but it had started with just over sixty undocumented immigrants who had fought against expulsion and stood up for their rights and belonging. The case forever changed all of the people involved, including the thirty-one individuals who had their deportations stayed. And the more cases the team won the more empowered the Sbicca workers, lawyers, and organizers felt. "When we first got there these people were scared, frightened, bewildered, and at the end you had people who were confident. . . . It changed them significantly," Edward Ortega recalled. For Mark Rosenbaum, it was "hard to describe the 'headiness' that people felt that they had defeated the government at its own game." The key, according to him, was the Sbicca employees' resolve, stamina, and insistence on asserting their constitutional rights. "You didn't have to be a smart lawyer to come up with the strategies, you had to be a courageous worker to execute them. . . . And we didn't lose because the workers were the strength of this." Writing in the *Los Angeles Times* six months after the raid, Bill Blum and Gina Lobaco pointed out that "When the Sbicca cases first arose, no one had ever heard of a suspected 'illegal alien' arrested in a factory raid winning a deportation hearing. . . . But history has a way of surprising the complacent."[97] By attacking the INS's near-exclusive reliance on coercive voluntary departures and raids meant to instill widespread fear, a coalition of undocumented immigrants and their allies had figured out a way to begin to dismantle the deportation machine, revealing that it was anything but invincible.

# SIX

# Deportation in an Era of Militarized Borders and Mass Incarceration

The truck was already packed and the refrigerator was empty when Mario and María Márquez's phone rang. It was their lawyer, calling with good news: immigration officials had granted them an extension, which meant that they and their four young sons wouldn't have to start the long drive back to Mexico that day in late November 1986. A couple of years before, the Márquezes had left their home in Los Mochis, in the northern Mexican state of Sinaloa, and entered the United States on six-month tourist visas to attend a Mormon conference in Salt Lake City, Utah. At the urging of a Mormon friend in Vermont, the family drove east, eventually settling in the 810-person town of Leicester, where Mario worked tending corn and alfalfa fields and fixing machinery on a dairy farm. María helped out as well, doing everything from washing machines to making piñatas for holiday parties and taking care of the kids. The family lived on the farm in a small two-bedroom trailer that had a television and tape player. Mario and María learned English through a home tutoring program, and the two eldest boys enrolled in the local elementary school. The Márquezes quickly became involved in the local church and community. And when their visas expired in the spring of 1985, they stayed. Everything was going well for the family until that fall when immigration agents showed up at their door.[1]

The Márquezes spent the next few years in deportation limbo as their cases moved through the labyrinthine immigration bureaucracy that was stretched well beyond capacity. In April 1986, an immigration judge ruled that the family had to leave the country via voluntary departure by the end of the summer or face formal deportation proceedings. But thanks in part to their lawyer's efforts, the INS granted the Márquezes multiple extensions. The town also rallied around the family, organizing a petition and letter-writing campaign, in addition to a couple of large public gatherings. Around 200 people—a quarter of Leicester's population—showed up to an October 1986 rally in support of the Márquezes. "They were always doing things for the community. They were good neighbors. We wanted people like that in Leicester," one resident told a reporter. A thirty-five-year-old woman described the town's support by saying, "Our attitude was these were hard-working people. To us, it took a lot of brass for the government to go chasing down people who weren't asking for food stamps or anything like that. Why not just let them alone?" In November 1986, in the days leading up to when the Márquezes thought they would finally have to leave, townspeople stopped by their trailer to wish the family well and give them chocolates, a card that said "they were glad to have known [them]," and $130 they had collected. Republican representative Langdon Smith's support also aided the family. "I think the public and political pressure had a bearing on this case," the congressman said. "It definitely helped slow it down."[2]

While immigration officials' decision to repeatedly put off the family's deportation allowed them to remain in the country for the short term, changes to the immigration law presented people like the Márquezes with new legal avenues to regularize their status. In the fall of 1986, Congress passed and President Ronald Reagan signed the Immigration Reform and Control Act (IRCA), which provided legal status to anyone who could prove continuous residency in the United States since January 1, 1982. It also included a Special Agricultural Workers (SAW) provision for people who had toiled over perishable crops for at least ninety days between May 1, 1985 and May 1, 1986. The family didn't meet the residency requirement, but the SAW program presented them with a possible opportunity to escape expulsion. On June 24, 1987, Mario applied to become a permanent resident; a week later he got into the family's old brown station wagon and drove two hours to St. Albans, Vermont, for his INS interview.[3]

The drawn-out and uncertain process took a toll on the family. As Mario noted after his interview, "It's hard again to wait and wait. . . . We have more than two years in this process. The boys sometimes [ask] what's going to happen. I don't know what to tell them." The low point came when they couldn't return to Mexico to see María's grandmother before she died.[4]

In February 1988, the INS approved Mario's application. "We were worried. We couldn't make any plans for the future. We didn't know if we were going to be able to stay or if we had to leave," Mario said after learning of the decision. "Now, we have hope and the security that we will be able to accomplish something." The family looked forward to visiting relatives in Mexico they had not seen in years. The local INS chief was also pleased with the outcome of the case, claiming that it was evidence that "the process works."[5]

However, as the Márquezes knew all too well, the immigration adjudication system was both complex and problematic, and IRCA's implementation was anything but smooth. Although the SAW provision covered Mario, they soon discovered that it did not apply to María or their children. Two and a half years after they had first been apprehended, the Márquezes found themselves in the precarious position of being a mixed-status family still in legal limbo.[6]

In many ways, the Márquezes' story offers insights into some of the core elements of immigration enforcement in the mid- to late 1980s and beyond. The INS targeted the vast majority of people for deportation because they entered the country without authorization or overstayed a visa. Most undocumented people could best be described as hard workers who formed an integral part of their communities. In some instances, widespread public support, legal representation, positive media coverage, and one or two powerful political allies could slow down or even halt a person's expulsion. Yet there was no guarantee of that and as cases worked their way through the immigration bureaucracy at a tortoise's pace, individuals and families were left to bear the ever-increasing psychological toll of knowing they might have to leave at any time. Moreover, because benefits weren't evenly distributed under IRCA, an increasing number of people in the country without authorization had immediate family members who were either US citizens or permanent residents. This in turn led to more division of families across borders whenever someone was deported or coerced into leaving, while others stayed behind.

Although much remained the same over the course of the next few decades, significant changes in immigration law combined with the militarization of the US–Mexico border and the events of September 11, 2001, drastically altered the deportation machine. Immigration officials and legislators implemented policies and passed measures that further criminalized unauthorized migration and treated migrants as dangerous lawbreakers at best and potential terrorists at worst. The new regime led to a bonanza in enforcement funding and spending.

Lawmakers and immigration authorities also developed streamlined mechanisms to formally deport noncitizens, limiting any type of relief or discretion previously available to people like the Márquezes. Contrary to popular and scholarly belief, the number of total deportations has actually declined in the twenty-first century, dropping from an all-time high of more than 1.86 million in 2000 during the final year of Bill Clinton's presidency to just over 446,000 in 2016 at the end of Barack Obama's second term. Expulsions decreased in part because immigration officials' mechanism of choice changed. Between fiscal years 1986 and 2013, the number of formal deportations (known in bureaucratic parlance as "removals") rose from around 24,600 to a historic high of around 433,000, while the number of voluntary departures (or "returns") dropped from more than 1.58 million to just under 179,000. By 2011, formal deportations outnumbered voluntary departures for the first time in seven decades; five years later, they made up three out of every four expulsions from the United States. During this period, formal removals came to resemble voluntary departures in their expedited nature and their restrictions on due process—but they carried much harsher consequences. This shift in how officials deported people represented a radical break from the past century of immigration enforcement policy and practice (see figure 37).[7]

The transformation in the way officials deported people coincided with a shift in whom they deported. Mexicans remained the largest group by far, but Central Americans increasingly found themselves in the crosshairs as well. After 9/11, authorities turned their attention to people from—or perceived to be from—Arab, Muslim, and Middle Eastern countries.

Regardless of whom immigration officials targeted, their growing reliance on formal deportations has been a central part of the carceral state's expansion over the last few decades. As the number of immigration hearings, people held in detention, and average time detained increased, the federal government came to rely more heavily on private, multibillion-dollar prison companies. In turn, these companies came to play an influential role in lobbying for stricter immigration policies. At the same time, restrictionist politicians and

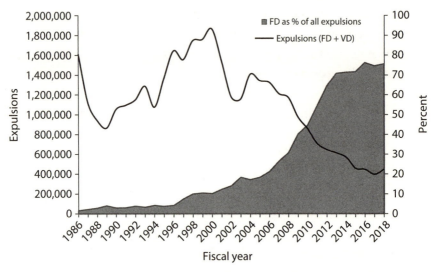

**Figure 37. Expulsions and formal deportations as a percentage of all expulsions, fiscal years 1986–2018.**
On the left Y-axis is the number of total expulsions (the sum of formal deportations and voluntary departures). On the right Y-axis are formal deportations as a percentage of total expulsions. While total expulsions dropped over time, formal deportations rose dramatically. DHS, *YOIS: 2018*, 103. Graph by author.

think tanks developed and propagated local- and state-level legislative proposals meant to demonize immigrants and provoke widespread fear in hopes that doing so would result in an uptick in self-deportations.

The criminalization of migrants, growth of immigration detention, and concurrent militarization of the border meant that deportation represented a more permanent separation than ever before. Immigrant activists, advocates, and allies employed an array of protest strategies in response, including mass marches, protests, direct action, civil disobedience, and sophisticated social media campaigns. They won important gains in many cases, stopping deportations for some and winning temporary legal status for hundreds of thousands of others. But the dramatic changes to the methods of deportation had an enduring influence on individuals, families, communities, and the nation. Only through a combination of quantitative and qualitative analyses, situated within the shifting domestic and geopolitical context of the time, can we understand the deportation machine's punitive turn in the late twentieth and early twenty-first centuries—a trend reinforced by the policies of both Republican and Democratic administrations.

## The Militarization of the Border and the Criminalization of Immigrants

A "new era of Mexican migration" began in November 1986 when President Reagan signed into law the most far-reaching immigration reform legislation in more than two decades. IRCA's enactment had been anything but certain since legislators, business interests, labor groups, and ethnic organizations had all repeatedly rejected previous bills that sought to overhaul the system. But public pressure to restrict immigration and the persistence of the bill's sponsors, Republican senator Alan Simpson of Wyoming and Democratic representative Romano Mazzoli from Kentucky, finally led lawmakers and the White House to strike a compromise. The act resulted in the legalization of approximately 3 million people—some 1.7 million who regularized their status by proving long-term residency, and another 1.3 million who did so through the SAW program meant to appease growers. In all, Mexicans made up 2.3 million, or 75 percent, of the total. As a result, IRCA is commonly thought of as a generous and liberal act, which one political scientist has described as "the largest amnesty program for undocumented aliens of any country to date."[8]

Obtaining legal status changed migrants' lives in consequential ways. People who became permanent residents not only could stay and work in the United States—they could also return to Mexico. Fernanda Camacho and her sister Claudia grew up in a small pueblo in Jalisco where most people made their living off the land and, starting in the middle of the twentieth century, many ventured off to the United States in search of better economic opportunities. The Camachos first went to California as teenagers in the 1970s. Though they returned to their town on occasion, their undocumented status meant that they ran the risk of apprehension each time they crossed back into the United States. After IRCA, Fernanda and Claudia visited a couple of times a year to celebrate holidays and to see their younger sister, Gabriela, the only one of the family's eight siblings who stayed in Mexico. However, not all of the Camacho siblings became legal residents or citizens under IRCA. "It has been fifteen years since I last saw my sister Conchita. And my youngest brother, three years," Gabriela said in 2013, as tears wetted her cheeks. "I want to see them."[9]

While IRCA provided a path to regularization for people like Mario Márquez and facilitated reunification for families like the Camachos, it also ramped up enforcement and guided the deportation machine in a more punitive direction. The law implemented long-proposed sanctions on employers who hired unauthorized workers, including fines of up to $10,000 and possible criminal prosecution, though they were not enforced evenly or with regularity, which rendered the policy ineffective. But employer sanctions were just one of a number of punitive stipulations contained in the new law. In the lead-up to IRCA's passage, and in the context of the Cold War, President Reagan scapegoated immigrants for the nation's economic woes and painted them as potential terrorists and threats to national security. Playing on such fears, Congress included provisions in IRCA to stop future unauthorized migration—or, the "invasion," in the parlance of many politicians and media outlets. The new law gave the Border Patrol $400 million to hire more agents in 1987 and 1988, provided the Department of Labor with new funds to carry out workplace inspections, and authorized the president to use $35 million for any future "immigration emergencies."[10] However, more than anything, an exhaustive study by two leading policy scholars concluded that IRCA "emphasizes the appearance of control while in fact failing to stop substantial undocumented flows," a reflection of the "curiously contradictory character" of US immigration policy toward unauthorized Mexican migration.[11]

In specific regard to deportation, beginning with IRCA the laws became, in the words of legal scholar Daniel Kanstroom, "harsher, less forgiving, and more insulated from judicial review." The result was the creation of "an exceptionally rigid legal regime . . . riven with discretionary executive authority, and increasingly immune from meaningful oversight." Internal pressure within the INS led to increased attention on deporting "criminal aliens," and a provision within IRCA called on the agency to do so "as expeditiously as possible." To facilitate this, the service used funds the law allocated to implement, and then expand, the Alien Criminal Apprehension Program.[12]

The INS's efforts to deport "criminals" became more intense in the years following IRCA. In 1988 the Anti-Drug Abuse Act created the legal category of "aggravated felony," under which a person convicted of such a crime would be formally deported and would face "severe criminal sanctions" if apprehended again after reentering the United States without authorization. While murder, drug trafficking, and illicit trafficking in firearms were the only offenses that counted as aggravated felonies at first, the category expanded over time, resulting in stiffer penal consequences for an increasing number of unauthorized migrants. The 1990 Immigration Act made money laundering and "(nonpolitical) 'crimes of violence'" aggravated felonies. Immigration authorities deemed people convicted of such crimes to be ineligible for asylum and lacking "good moral character," which meant they could not receive discretionary relief. The act also retroactively eliminated judges' ability to halt expulsions through "Judicial Recommendations against Deportation," thus further reducing the possibility of relief from removal. Moreover, anyone convicted of an aggravated felony and deported faced an automatic twenty-year bar to reentering the United States.[13]

Regardless of the measures Congress and the INS implemented, unauthorized migration from Mexico continued—and even increased—in the late 1980s and early 1990s. This trend affected few, if any, places more than Southern California, which remained the primary crossing point for most migrants. Between 1960 and 1990 California's foreign-born population increased from 1.3 million to 6.5 million, going from 9 percent to 22 percent of the state's population. Even though San Diego remained majority white until 2000, the rising number of immigrants, both documented and undocumented, and the growing ethnic Mexican population created heightened tensions in the city in the last decades of the twentieth century. To deflect blame and win votes, politicians adopted the time-tested tactic of scapegoating immigrants for the state's financial woes. Nobody did so more than Pete Wilson, the Republican governor and former San Diego mayor, who pinned California's $12.6 billion deficit on unauthorized migrants who supposedly drained the state's welfare coffers. Wilson and other local and state politicians also faulted the federal government for its inaction and inability to control the US–Mexico border.[14]

The expansion of liberal trade policies and integration of the North American economies fueled the growth in undocumented Mexican migration to the United States. Mexico's entrance into the General Agreement on Tariffs and Trade (GATT) in 1986 and the signing of the North American Free Trade Agreement (NAFTA) six years later had serious negative repercussions on ordinary Mexicans and the Mexican economy as a whole. NAFTA, which went into effect on January 1, 1994, allowed US companies to relocate factories south of the border and export corn and other staple crops to Mexico. The trilateral agreement between the United States, Mexico, and Canada integrated all economic factors but one: labor. As a comprehensive overview of Mexican migration noted, after NAFTA the United States "pursue[d] a politics of contradiction—simultaneously moving toward integration while insisting on separation."[15] Without protectionist agricultural policies, Mexicans who made their living from working the land could not compete with US-based companies receiving government subsidies. Soon they began emigrating north in large numbers in search of work. From 1994 to 2000 the number of Mexicans leaving for the United States increased by nearly 80 percent, going from 430,000 to 770,000. And between 1990 and 2000, Mexican-born residents living in the country more than doubled, going from 4.5 million to 9.4 million. NAFTA actually helped to halt Mexican economic growth. In December 1994, the value of the peso fell by almost half and Mexico lost nearly 10 percent of its gross domestic product over the course of the next six months. Moreover, on a smaller scale the adoption of free trade policies did nothing to improve individual Mexicans' economic well-being. In fact, poverty rates rose in the two years following NAFTA, and nearly two decades later had not changed from pre-NAFTA levels.[16]

Heightened levels of unauthorized Mexican migration, US domestic economic woes, and rising political conservatism contributed to anti-immigrant sentiment peaking in the lead-up to the 1994 midterm elections. In hopes of garnering more votes, Governor Wilson focused his campaign around Proposition 187. Drafted by a group of restrictionist activists and former INS officials at an Orange County country club in October 1993, Proposition 187 excluded unauthorized immigrants from social services and benefits, including nonemergency health care and education.[17] Ultimately, Wilson hoped that the proposal, known as the "Save Our State" initiative, would ease California's budget shortfall by reducing the number of unauthorized immigrants living in the state. "If it's clear to you that you cannot be employed, and that you and your family are ineligible for services, you will self-deport," the governor explained.[18] Though most people stayed, the widespread anti-immigrant rhetoric and climate of fear affected undocumented immigrants' everyday lives. And some indeed decided to leave the state or the country altogether. Silvia Alfaro, a twenty-year-old indigenous Mixtec woman living in Oxnard, California, with her fiancé and two infant US citizen sons, decided to return to her small, mountainous town in the southern Mexican state of Oaxaca. "I walk in fear. . . . I'm afraid to take my children to the doctor. I'm afraid to wait for the bus. I'm afraid to leave my house," she

Figure 38. El Paso Border Patrol Chief Silvestre Reyes briefs (right to left) President Bill Clinton, Vice President Al Gore, INS Commissioner Doris Meissner, Secretary of Labor Robert Reich, and Attorney General Janet Reno, February 1995.
Official White House Photo/USCISHOL.

told a *Los Angeles Times* reporter in November 1994. "My oldest son will soon be 4 years old, and I'm scared to put him in school," she continued. "They say they will use the children to find parents who are here illegally." Although she knew that her children wouldn't have the same educational opportunities or healthcare resources, Alfaro explained her decision to leave the United States in straightforward terms: "I was tired of hiding, of feeling unwanted in this country." Rather than returning to Mexico with them, her fiancé decided to move to Minnesota, where jobs were supposedly available and where no anti-immigration laws were on the books. After a follow-up article on Alfaro readjusting to life in Mexico ran, a reader asserted in a letter to the *Times*, "I guess in a small way Proposition 187 is starting to work."[19]

In addition to promoting legislation that would harm the quality of life of people in the country without authorization, Governor Wilson also demanded that the federal government act to control migration across the US–Mexico border. What he had in mind was something like Operation Hold the Line. Launched in the fall of 1993 by El Paso Border Patrol Chief Silvestre Reyes (and originally named Operation Blockade), the initiative was meant to stop migrants from crossing into the United States near the city (see figure 38). Some 400 Border Patrol agents patrolled a twenty-mile section of the border with Ciudad Juárez, resulting in a dramatic drop in apprehensions. Operation Hold the Line received national attention and, hoping that a similar strategy could be applied in other densely populated border areas, Southern Californian politicians, including Wilson, pushed the federal government to implement a version of it in the San Diego sector. In the summer of 1994, in large part in response to public pressure, the Border Patrol's strategic plan announced the new strategy of "prevention through deterrence," and stated that the agency would "control the borders of the United States between the ports of entry, restoring our Nation's confidence in the integrity of the border." It also stressed that "a well-managed border will enhance national security and safeguard our immigration heritage." A few months later, on October 1, 1994, immigration authorities implemented Operation Gatekeeper along the San Diego border.[20]

Under Operation Gatekeeper the federal government began an unprecedented militarization campaign of the US–Mexico border that continues to this day. Whereas the San Diego sector had only nineteen miles of border wall before the operation commenced, some five years later fifty-two miles of walls demarcated the divide, including fourteen miles of ten-foot-high primary walls (made from steel landing mats from the Vietnam War) and two fifteen-foot-tall backup walls—the first made of concrete pillars, the second of wire mesh and support beams, and both topped with barbed wire. The rapid erection of border walls in the post-NAFTA era was a response to the increased flow of consumer goods, capital, illegal drugs, and people, and the realization that the United States could not fully regulate these flows. Immigration authorities also installed high-intensity stadium lights, surveillance cameras, and high-tech motion sensors. And the number of Border Patrol agents stationed in the San Diego sector increased from 980 before Operation Gatekeeper to more than 2,250 in June 1998. The result, according to geographer Joseph Nevins, was that "a semblance of control and order . . . replaced the image of chaos that once seemed to reign in the urbanized border region of the San Diego sector."[21] But, as in the past, the INS's control of the border remained incomplete.

The policies and laws implemented in the 1980s and 1990s increased the INS's importance within the federal bureaucracy. Whereas the service's budget was around $474 million in 1986, a decade later it had shot up to nearly $2.6 billion (some $1.8 billion controlling for inflation), and $4.2 billion ($2.7 billion controlling for inflation) by the year 2000. Meanwhile, the Border Patrol went from "a backwater agency with a budget smaller than that of many municipal police departments . . . to a large and powerful organization with more officers licensed to carry weapons than any other branch of the federal government save the military." From 1986 to 2000 the Border Patrol's budget increased by a factor of seven, going from $151 million to more than $1 billion. During that same period, the number of Border Patrol officers spiked from under 3,700 to more than 9,200, and the number of linewatch hours more than tripled.[22]

The ramping up of border and immigration enforcement did not stop unauthorized migration to the United States. It did, however, make migrating costlier, in both physical and financial terms. Enhanced enforcement near urban centers forced migrants to cross the border in more desolate and dangerous areas. So while apprehensions dropped in the Chula Vista/San Diego (from around 532,000 in 1993 to 248,000 in 1998) and El Paso (from some 286,000 to 125,000) sectors, they rose sharply in the El Centro, California sector (30,000 to 227,000) and the Tucson (93,000 to 387,000) and Yuma (23,500 to 76,000), Arizona sectors.[23]

Instead of stopping undocumented migration, Operation Hold the Line and Operation Gatekeeper just moved it from public view. These policies had a devastating impact on migrants. First, they forced migrants to rely more heavily on coyotes, or migrant smugglers, who doubled or tripled their fees in accordance with the newfound demand. Second, they increased the amount of time it took to cross the border. While entering near San Diego might have only taken ten or fifteen minutes, traversing deserts, mountains, and canyons generally took at least twelve hours and up to four days. Ultimately, the United States government's prevention through deterrence strategy resulted in more migrant deaths than ever before. In 1994 officers recovered the remains of twenty-three people along the California–Mexico border. Two had died of hypothermia or heatstroke and nine of drowning. Just four years later authorities recorded 145 deaths—including sixty-eight of hypothermia or heatstroke and fifty-two of drowning—along that same stretch, although the actual number was certainly higher, since agents never found some of the dead.[24] Even after immigration officials realized that prevention through deterrence would make crossing more dangerous, but would not stop people from migrating, they chose to stay the course. "I will be absolutely frank with you," Doris Meissner, INS commissioner from 1993 to 2000, later told an interviewer. "The idea of abandoning any kind of strengthened border enforcement because of [the dangers of the desert] was not . . . a point of serious discussion."[25] The death toll rose dramatically in the decades ahead: More than 7,500 people died trying to cross the US–Mexico border in the quarter century after authorities started cracking down.[26]

The year 1994 also ended up marking an important shift in the history of US–Mexico relations, Mexican migration, and US immigration enforcement. Less than a year after NAFTA became law, Governor Pete Wilson handily won reelection in California and Proposition 187 passed with 59 percent of the vote. Even though a federal district court later struck down Proposition 187 on constitutional grounds, its passage and Wilson's victory foreshadowed local and state politicians' efforts to take federal immigration policy into their own hands in the years to come.[27] Furthermore, Operation Gatekeeper proved to be the beginning of what has become an intractable campaign to "secure" the US–Mexico border. These developments, combined with the passage of a series of draconian laws two years later, fundamentally changed how officials deported people, in addition to the consequences of being expelled.

## A New Harshness

The 1996 Illegal Immigration Reform and Immigrant Responsibility Act (IIRIRA) has done more to reshape the deportation machine than any other law over the last half-century. Signed by Democratic president Bill Clinton as part of his get-tough-on-crime reelection campaign, the law broadened the scope of who the United States could formally deport; made it easier for authorities to apprehend, detain, and expel people; and rolled back the rights of individuals facing deportation. IIRIRA expanded the number of "aggravated felonies" resulting in mandatory detention and formal deportation to twenty-eight, including any offense that carried at least a one-year prison sentence—even if it were as insignificant as shoplifting or low-level drug possession, or as vague as a crime of "moral turpitude" or any "crime of violence." IIRIRA applied retroactively, which meant that authorities could remove someone for a crime that was a deportable offense under the new law, but not at the time of conviction. As one legal scholar put it, the INS adopted a "take-no-prisoners approach with regard to the deportation of criminal aliens"—with "criminal aliens" now encompassing a much broader group of people.[28]

IIRIRA also established three new streamlined administrative procedures to formally expel people that fundamentally altered how the deportation machine worked. "Expedited removals" and "reinstatement of removal" gave immigration officers the power to arrest, charge, and formally deport people without bringing them before a judge or conducting any real investigation of their cases. The former applied to anyone authorities apprehended within one hundred miles of the border whom they deemed inadmissible at the time of entry, while the latter encompassed individuals with prior formal deportations or voluntary departures. Under "stipulated removal" noncitizens already in deportation proceedings could forgo their right to a hearing, which allowed an immigration judge to order their formal expulsion without ever seeing them face to face. By creating these three summary removal mechanisms and expanding the number and type of deportable classes, IIRIRA resulted in the ramping up of formal expulsions to previously unknown levels (see figure 39). After 1996, migrants whom officials would have once expelled via voluntary departure now found themselves subject to formal deportation, bans on reentry ranging from five years to life, and possible felony criminal charges for returning to the United States.[29]

Under IIRIRA, *all* noncitizens, including many long-term, legal permanent residents, found themselves subject to formal deportation. Standing in opposition to core values that undergirded US immigration policies, the law's elimination of relief hearings prevented immigration judges from considering personal or family circumstances, including the best interests of US citizen spouses and children.[30] Danny Kozuba moved to the United States from Canada with his parents and brother when he was five and became a permanent resident in 1958. He went on to serve in the US Army during the Vietnam War and later worked designing and installing custom kitchens in a suburb east of Dallas, Texas. After spending a few years in prison on drug possession charges in the early 1990s, an immigration judge granted him a waiver of deportation given his community ties, four decades in the country, and the fact that his wife was a US citizen. But the INS appealed this decision and, in 1997, Kozuba found himself in deportation

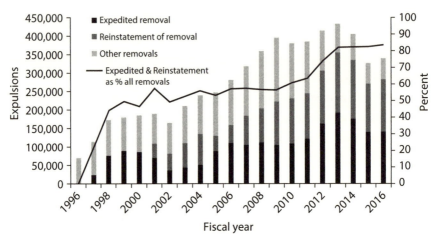

**Figure 39.** Formal deportations by type and "expedited removals" + "reinstatement of removal" as percentage of all formal deportations, fiscal years 1996–2016.
After IIRIRA, the number of fast-track formal deportations via "expedited removal" and "reinstatement of removal" steadily increased, making up more than half of all removals from fiscal year 1998 on, and more than 80 percent of all removals in fiscal years 2013–16. At the same time, voluntary departures decreased dramatically between fiscal years 2000 and 2016. Statistics for "reinstatement of removal" are unavailable prior to 2001; statistics on stipulated removal are unavailable. DHS, "Immigration Enforcement Actions," 2004, 2010, and 2016. Calculations and graph by author.

proceedings after IIRIRA made people like him ineligible for any kind of relief. Thirty-five-year-old Charlie Jaramillo found himself in a similar situation. He faced deportation to Colombia for pleading guilty to a minor drug charge in 1989, despite the fact that he had been in the United States since he was eight months old, didn't speak Spanish, and had a wife and two teenage sons, all US citizens.[31]

The immigration act of 1996 allocated more money for enforcement at the border and in the interior. In the six years after Congress passed the legislation, detention and deportation spending increased by more than 160 percent, reaching nearly $1.28 billion in fiscal year 2002. The law also implemented a web-based system (later renamed E-Verify) that allowed employers to instantaneously verify workers' employment eligibility. And it provided for the construction of border walls and the hiring of 1,000 Border Patrol agents a year over a five-year period, leading some to refer to it as the "Mexican Exclusion Act." Moreover, in 2000, officials started fingerprinting all adults apprehended in the Southwest. Entering migrants' biometric data into a central database made it easier to identify—and punish—people with previous expulsions. These new enforcement practices and the fortification of the US–Mexico border made it more expensive and dangerous for migrants to reenter the United States, increasing the human costs of deportation and making family separation more prevalent and more permanent.[32]

The same year Clinton signed IIRIRA, he also signed two other pieces of legislation into law as part of his centrist-Democrat agenda to reclaim law enforcement from Republicans. These acts magnified IIRIRA's severe impact on unauthorized migrants. Along with the Personal Responsibility and Work Opportunity Reconciliation Act—the "end welfare as we know it" act, which barred undocumented migrants from access to public services and most federal, state, and local benefits—IIRIRA effectively implemented Proposition 187 on a national scale. They required the INS to verify individuals' legal status before granting them federal benefits, and they gave states more power to determine eligibility rules. IIRIRA also included Section 287(g), which allowed local and state law enforcement officers to carry out immigration enforcement in collaboration with the INS. And IIRIRA combined with the Antiterrorism and Effective Death Penalty Act to eliminate undocumented migrants' due process rights and any chance of judicial review in expulsion cases. This led one scholar to describe 1996 as "the year in which the rule of deportation law died."[33]

The consequences of being deported became even harsher after the events of September 11, 2001. In the wake of the attacks that brought down the World Trade Center towers in New York City and damaged the Pentagon, Congress hastily passed and Republican president George W. Bush signed the Uniting and Strengthening America by Providing Appropriate Tools Required to Intercept and Obstruct Terrorism Act. The USA PATRIOT Act, as it is known, broadened the definition of what constituted "terrorist activity," limited the rights of foreigners already in the country, and authorized officials to indefinitely detain noncitizens. As anthropologist Nicholas De Genova has noted, in the aftermath of 9/11 "'terrorism' [came] to ubiquitously serve the same ideological role of pervasive and imminent external threat to the stability and security of the United States that 'communism' previously did during the Cold War." Less than two years later, the newly created Department of Homeland Security (DHS) absorbed the INS as part of what the White

House called "the most extensive reorganization of the federal government in the past fifty years."[34]

Immigration policies during the post-9/11 Bush administration became more restrictive and prioritized security over human rights and civil liberties. The rhetorical shift from the Immigration and Naturalization Service to the Department of Homeland Security made the bureaucracy's priorities clear. The restructuring further boosted the agency's prominence and resulted in a sharp spike in its enforcement budget.[35] In 2003, DHS announced Endgame, a ten-year strategic enforcement plan whose goal was "the removal of all removable aliens."[36] These changes had a profound effect on both border control and interior enforcement, which are inextricably linked. "Although homeland security may strive to cordon off the nation as a domestic space from external foreign threats," Amy Kaplan insightfully argues, "it is actually about breaking down the boundaries between inside and outside, about seeing the homeland in a state of constant emergency from threats within and without."[37] This in turn served to justify the racial profiling and persecution of Muslims, Arabs, South Asians, and unauthorized immigrants—regardless of whether they lived in the United States or not.

Although the people apprehended and deported to majority-Muslim countries remained small in real numbers, the existential threat members of Congress and DHS officials thought they posed exerted a tremendous influence over policy. Lawmakers relied on the conflation of immigrants as potential terrorists to rationalize the targeting of people perceived to be Arab, Muslim, or Middle Eastern.[38] The criminalization of migration and elevated fears about domestic terrorism produced a pervasive sense of insecurity that justified expanding DHS's influence and unchecked power, as well as a "specter of guilt" around unauthorized migrants that legitimized the violation of their rights and liberties. Nothing better represented this new enforcement context than the increased surveillance of Muslims. In 2002, the federal government created the National Security Entry-Exit Registration System, which required men from certain countries determined to be harboring terrorists to register and periodically check in with homeland security officials. Authorities detained an increasing number of Muslims as well, and held some indefinitely.[39]

Linking immigration and terrorism also allowed DHS to secure additional resources from Congress. The Customs and Border Protection (CBP) budget spiked from $5.9 billion in 2003 to $13.6 billion in 2016, and the number of Border Patrol agents more than doubled, going from 9,200 to more than 23,000 (some 90 percent of whom patrolled the southwestern border). During that same period, the Immigration and Customs Enforcement (ICE) budget grew by 50 percent, reaching an unprecedented $6.3 billion in 2016.[40] This funding boom facilitated the deportation machine's punitive turn because it enabled the INS/DHS to formally deport more people than ever before, just as the 1996 immigration act called for. It also furthered the agency's self-deportation efforts by contributing to what Nadine Naber has described as the "internment of the psyche," in which Arabs and Muslims in the post-9/11 United States experienced an "internal incarceration" based on "the sense that, at any moment, one may be picked up, locked up, or disappeared."[41]

Legislative proposals and new DHS policies contributed to the criminalization of migrants as well. In December 2005, the House passed the Border Protection, Antiterrorism, and Illegal Immigration Control Act (H.R. 4437), known as the Sensenbrenner Bill, which sought to make being in the United States without authorization a felony offense instead of a civil violation. That same month, DHS implemented Operation Streamline, which called for the criminal prosecution of unauthorized entry and reentry before placing people in removal proceedings and implemented a "zero tolerance" policy that reduced the number of voluntary departures. Eight years later, unauthorized border crossings made up around half of all federal criminal prosecutions, whether immigration-related or not. In 2006, after the Sensenbrenner Bill died in the Senate, Congress passed and George W. Bush signed the Secure Fence Act, providing funding for 700 miles of walls on the US–Mexico border and authorizing the purchase of new sensors, cameras, lighting, vehicle barriers, checkpoints, and drones.[42]

The following year, ICE launched the Secure Communities program. Similar to 287(g), Secure Communities called for the cooperation of law enforcement officials at every level to carry out immigration enforcement. It integrated local, state, and federal databases, which meant that any interaction an undocumented migrant had with a law enforcement official could result in that person's deportation. As a result, the number of ICE apprehensions in the interior of the country quadrupled between 2007 and 2011, going from around 84,000 to a high of more than 338,000. Whereas the Obama administration at first offered localities the option of participating in Secure

Communities, it later announced that the program would extend nationwide by 2013, with no choice of opting out. Some mayors and cities protested, citing the detrimental effects the program had on police–community relations and the reduced likelihood that undocumented people would report domestic violence and other crimes. The Obama administration justified the program by claiming that it targeted hard criminals. But during the first two years of Secure Communities more than three-quarters of all people identified by the program had no record at all or just a traffic violation or some other minor offense. The farming out of immigration enforcement to local law enforcement officials—including Sheriff Joe Arpaio in Maricopa County, Arizona—made it nearly impossible to implement a uniform, top-down policy. These new trends also led to further racial profiling, the criminalization of Latinos regardless of legal status, and ultimately an increase in interior apprehensions in established communities (both in real numbers and relative to border apprehensions). Programs like Secure Communities propagated fear in the undocumented community—ultimately making communities less secure.[43]

The criminalization of immigrants and growth of the homeland security state helped spur a resurgence of virulent nativism, as evidenced by the formation of "Minutemen" militias that began patrolling the US–Mexico border in the early 2000s and the rising power and influence of anti-immigration think tanks and lobby groups.[44] Right-wing restrictionist organizations like the Center for Immigration Studies (CIS) and Numbers USA—both of which could be traced back to John Tanton—and individuals like former Kansas secretary of state Kris Kobach drove through draconian state laws meant to coerce people into self-deporting from places like Arizona and Alabama. Large, attention-grabbing raids, like the apprehension of nearly 400 people at a meatpacking plant in Postville, Iowa, in 2008, further heightened anxiety levels in immigrant communities. Restrictionists pushed self-deportation as a "third way" between legalization and mass expulsion. Their goal, as a 2003 CIS report put it, was to do everything possible to make immigrants' lives miserable, in hopes of "squeezing the illegal population so that it declines over time, through attrition." Expanding on this in a 2008 article, Kobach asserted that "the twelve to twenty million illegal aliens in the United States need not be rounded up and forcibly removed through direct government action." Instead, he continued, "illegal aliens can be encouraged to depart the United States on their own, through a concerted strategy of attrition through enforcement. . . . If the risks of detention or involuntary removal go up, and the probability of being able to obtain unauthorized employment goes down, then at some point, the only rational decision is to return home." However, as had long been true, rather than returning people to their "homes," self-deportation campaigns in fact tore long-term undocumented residents from them.[45]

## Rejecting Refugees and Externalizing Migration Control

While self-deportation campaigns were meant to make the lives of people already in the United States miserable in hopes of coercing them into leaving, officials also implemented tactics aimed at preventing immigrants from arriving in the first place. The externalization of migration control especially targeted individuals who came from countries other than Mexico and Canada. Though the practice's roots go back to the nineteenth century, when transportation companies and later US officials stationed abroad began screening people before they left their countries of origin, it took on a new guise in the 1980s, when Central Americans started migrating in increasing numbers. The majority of Central Americans were refugees fleeing civil wars—funded by billions of dollars of US aid to right-wing governments in El Salvador and Guatemala—that left at least a quarter of a million people dead and three million more displaced throughout the region.[46] Overwhelmed by ongoing mass migration from Mexico and the spike in Central American asylum applications, US officials started pressuring and paying Mexico to carry out its dirty work. According to Larry Richardson, the US Border Patrol chief in McAllen, Texas, at the time, "the United States ha[d] quietly been paying Mexicans to deport Central Americans to Guatemala" since 1981. The INS also "organized a spy ring in Mexico to assist in intercepting Central Americans headed for the United States" and to offer immigration enforcement training to Mexican officials. For at least three years in the early 1990s, the US Congress appropriated $350,000 a year to pay Mexico to deport transit migrants. In 2001, as part of Mexican President Vicente Fox's "Plan Frontera Sur," the United States offered its southern neighbor as much as $2 million per year to deport Central Americans to their home countries instead of just across the border to Guatemala.[47]

The Mexican government, to be sure, was not just a puppet for the United States. Mexican officials had their own reasons and motivations for cracking down on Central American refugees, including unemployment and general economic hardship in the wake of the 1982 debt crisis. As Bill Frelick, a senior policy analyst with the US Committee for Refugees, put it, in the years leading up to NAFTA, there existed "an unspoken, but clearly understood, quid pro quo: You stop these Central Americans, says the United States, and we will be sympathetic toward you on matters like trade barriers and debt."[48] This confluence of US and Mexican interests—clearly shaped by the United States' pressure on its southern neighbor—altered the dynamics of immigration enforcement in consequential ways. As a representative of the Catholic Church observed, by the 1990s the border had "moved south. It [was] no longer between Mexico and the United States but between Guatemala and Mexico."[49]

The United States' outsourcing of deportation to Mexico was part of a larger strategy of preventing all refugees from reaching US soil, effectively denying people their human right to seek asylum. In 1981, the same year that the Reagan administration started paying Mexico to crack down on Central Americans headed north, it also authorized the Coast Guard to intercept boats thought to be carrying Haitians, and then return anyone they found to Port au Prince. The Clinton administration continued this policy of interdiction and redirected boats of refugees to other countries in order to skirt the asylum process. Then, in 1997, the INS launched Operation Global Reach, an $8.2-million initiative based on "combating illegal immigration through emphasis on overseas deterrence." Between 1997 and 2001 the service established forty overseas offices, staffed by 150 US government employees who focused on intelligence gathering, reducing migrant smuggling, and training foreign law enforcement and airline officials to identify fraudulent documents. During the operation's first four years, the INS trained more than 45,000 foreign officials around the globe, from West Africa to Western Europe, from East and South Asia to Latin America—including San Salvador, Tegucigalpa, Guatemala City, Mexico City, Ciudad Juárez, and Tijuana. Reporting on the inauguration of Operation Global Reach, two *Los Angeles Times* journalists zeroed in on the impetus behind it (and outsourcing deportation in general): "It is much cheaper to deter people from migrating illegally from abroad rather than attempt to find, detain and deport them once they are here." By 2016, DHS spent $123 million a year to station some 300 officials in sixty-three different offices in forty-nine countries around the world.[50]

The externalization of immigration control came at a high physical, psychological, and financial cost to Central American refugees. Despite a reputation as a country that welcomed exiles, Mexico was not a signatory to the 1951 United Nations Convention Relating to the Status of Refugees, nor the subsequent 1967 protocol. Moreover, under Article 33 of the Mexican Constitution the government had the right to deport foreigners without due process. As a result, migrants faced abuse from Mexican migration officials, police, and criminals alike. As a migrant advocate in Mexico's religious community noted in the mid-1990s, "The government of Mexico was always complaining about the treatment of Mexicans in the US. But they don't look here. . . . There are more human-rights violations here in one day than there are in a year in the United States."[51] Drug cartels' increasing control over the migration routes and illicit border crossing only upped the stakes. By the 2010s, Central Americans paid up to $7,000 to traverse Mexico and reach the United States. Between 60 and 80 percent of women were raped or sexually assaulted while en route. As many as 20,000 migrants were kidnapped in Mexico in a single year alone. Cartel killings, like the Zetas' 2010 massacre of seventy-two migrants in San Fernando, Tamaulipas, were not uncommon and almost always went unpunished. Well aware that many Mexican officials robbed migrants, or worse, few Central Americans turned to Mexican authorities for help. According to Salvadoran journalist Óscar Martínez, doing so would have been like "a soldier asking for a sip of water at enemy headquarters."[52]

Those who managed to make it through Mexico and successfully cross into the United States faced additional challenges upon arriving. US officials denied the asylum claims of nearly all of the people from El Salvador, Guatemala, and Honduras. Recognizing the legitimacy of such claims would have amounted to the United States admitting its own culpability in funding the repressive regimes that forced Central Americans to flee. The United States approved just 3 percent of Salvadoran and Guatemalan asylum applications in the 1980s. Moreover, most Central Americans did not qualify for legalization under IRCA since the January 1, 1982 cutoff date was before the vast majority had arrived. The best Salvadorans could hope for was Temporary Protected Status (TPS), a provision of the 1990 Immigration Act signed by President George H. W. Bush that granted short-term relief from the threat of deportation to people the government determined were unable to return to their home countries because of political unrest or natural disaster. Some 187,000 Salvadorans received TPS for an initial period of eighteen months, which the US government extended multiple times in the years and decades ahead. Although the status provided some security, it also left recipients in what sociologist Cecilia Menjívar has referred to as a state of "liminal legality" characterized by inherent ambiguity. People with TPS fell into a gray area of being neither documented nor undocumented and constantly faced with the possibility that their temporary status might soon come to an end. Living with a tenuous legal status had a significant impact on a person's educational and employment opportunities, access to health care and housing, and personal safety since many undocumented immigrants and TPS recipients were hesitant to call the police. Many people who had come to the United States as adults experienced a visceral fear of being apprehended, while individuals who had arrived as children felt stigma and shame because of their uncertain legal status.[53]

US immigration officials' increased targeting of Central Americans in the 2000s both coincided with and was a product of shifting patterns of Mexican migration. Starting around 2008, the economic recession in the United States, combined with lower birth rates in Mexico and the elevated costs and heightened risks of unauthorized migration, resulted in a significant drop in the number of Mexicans going north. "The largest wave of immigration in history from a single country to the United States has come to a standstill," a leading research center reported.[54] Mexicans as a percent of overall apprehensions declined considerably: Whereas they represented 90 percent or more of all apprehensions from the mid-1970s to the mid-2000s, they made up just half of all apprehensions by fiscal year 2016. During Barack Obama's presidency, immigration officials apprehended record numbers of non-Mexicans, referred to as "Other Than Mexicans," or OTMs, in agency lingo. The vast majority were Central American men. Whereas people from El Salvador, Guatemala, and Honduras represented just 9 percent of all apprehensions in 2008, they made up more than 42 percent by 2016, while people from the rest of the world comprised just 6 to 9 percent (see figure 40). Enhanced enforcement affected all undocumented immigrants, but it singled out some groups more than others.[55]

Heightened levels of violence in the region during Obama's second term led hundreds of thousands of people to flee. Sensational media coverage de-

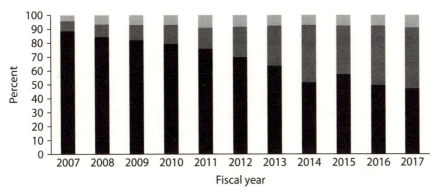

Figure 40. DHS apprehensions by nationality, fiscal years 2007–17.
DHS, *YOIS: 2017*, 92. Calculations and graph by author.

scribing brutal killings carried out by tattoo-covered gang members helped create inaccurate yet pervasive stereotypes equating Central Americans and dangerous criminals. In reality, the emergence of transnational gangs was, in part, a problem of the United States' own making. The roots of the ongoing political and economic instability go back to the US-backed civil wars of the 1970s to 1990s, and the rise of transnational gangs began in 1980s Los Angeles. In fact, gangs like La Mara Salvatrucha, or MS-13, only gained a foothold in Central America after US officials started deporting its members.[56] Yet rather than offering humanitarian solutions to a crisis that the United States helped create, the Obama administration slashed refugee admissions, increased detention capacity, expedited deportations, and expanded efforts to stop people from reaching the United States altogether—as if continuing to push the problem out of sight and out of mind might solve it. In fiscal year 2014 alone, US Border Patrol officers apprehended more than 237,000 Salvadorans, Guatemalans, and Hondurans, including nearly 52,000 unaccompanied children and over 61,000 people who arrived with their families. They also formally deported more than 121,000 people from these three countries, 70 percent of whom the government classified as "non-criminals."[57] The following year, the US Border Patrol apprehended half as many Central Americans, leading some people to declare that the "surge" had ended. In reality, however, the decline in apprehensions was a product of the US government outsourcing to Mexico the deportation of asylum seekers. From 2014 to 2015, the number of people Mexico deported to Central America shot up from 91,000 to more than 165,000, more than making up for the nearly 40 percent drop in US deportations to the region. When considered together, the number of people the United States and Mexico deported to El Salvador, Guatemala, and Honduras actually increased, from 213,000 to more than 251,000. The difference was whereas the United States accounted for more than half of all deportations in fiscal year 2014, Mexico was responsible for two-thirds of the deportations in 2015.[58]

## Punishment and Profits over People's Well-Being Redux

Another key component of the deportation machine's post-1986 punitive turn was the dramatic expansion of immigration detention. The imprisonment of immigrants is part of the longer, broader history of human caging and settler colonialism in the United States. Along with expulsion, incarceration has served as a tool to eliminate from society—if not the country altogether—anyone deemed to be a racial, economic, or cultural outsider.[59] Despite its deep roots, the incarceration boom did not occur until the last decades of the twentieth century. Up until the 1970s, the United States had an incarceration rate on par with other liberal democracies. That changed when Democrats and Republicans alike began implementing a series of get-tough policies cracking down on crime.[60] Between 1972 and 1997, the country's general incarceration rate increased by a factor of five.[61] More than 3 percent of all adults in the United States "were under some form of correctional custody" by the end of that period. As legal scholar Jonathan Simon observed, "No other society in history ha[d] ever tried to govern such a large proportion of its population through prisons or their specter."[62] The statistics support this assertion. The United States has imprisoned more people since 1970 than any other country in the world.[63] By the mid-2010s, the country warehoused nearly one out of every four prisoners on the planet even though just 5 percent of the global population lived there.[64]

The immigration detention system also underwent significant transformations around the same time.[65] In fact, the growth of immigration detention also stemmed from the sharp increase in the number of incarcerated US citizens. In order to free up bed space for the mostly black and Latino men targeted by the rapidly expanding war on drugs, officials sped up the deportation of immigrants held in overcrowded local jails and state and federal prisons. However, rather than reducing the number of immigrants held in detention, the 1980s and 1990s laws' criminalization of unauthorized reentry after expulsion turned deportation into what sociologist Patrisia Macías-Rojas has referred to as a "pipeline to prison."[66] Whereas the service detained an average of just under 6,800 people each day in 1994, that number grew to more than 37,000 by 2006. Between 1980 and 2011, immigrants went from representing less than 4 percent of the federal inmate population to constituting more than one out of every three federal convictions— around 75 percent of them for immigration violations. By 2016, the United States detained around 360,000 immigrants each year in more than 600 facilities in all fifty states, in addition to Puerto Rico, Guam, the Virgin Islands, and the Northern Mariana Islands. The average length of detention was thirty-five days, at a daily rate of $126.[67]

The growth of immigration detention also had to do with its shifting geography and the Cold War politics of the time. While INS detention camps had historically been concentrated on the US–Mexico border in places like in El Centro, California, and Port Isabel, Texas, the arrival of as many as 125,000 Cubans to South Florida during the 1980 Mariel boatlift, combined with thousands of Haitian asylum seekers in years prior, led the agency to shift its attention and enforcement resources east to the Caribbean. The US government and media racialized Cubans and Haitians, depicting them as criminals, homosexuals, and undeserving economic migrants, rather than refugees fleeing repressive regimes deserving of humanitarian assistance. US officials developed an onshore–offshore system of interdiction and migrant detention in hopes of deterring future asylum seekers. The INS held Cubans and Haitians at military bases like Fort Chaffee in Arkansas and at abysmal detention centers like Krome in Miami. At the end of July 1981, the Reagan administration announced that it would stop releasing Haitians while they awaited their exclusion hearings. The growing detention population that resulted from the new policy, combined with the closing of Fort Chaffee around the same time, led officials to propose dozens of other possible sites, including Ellis Island in New York, Alcatraz Island in California, Fort Allen in Puerto Rico, and a number of military sites in the Rocky Mountain states and along the Canadian border. The majority were never used, though, and officials ended up transferring Cubans and Haitians to federal prisons across the country. In the years ahead, the number of permanent INS facilities multiplied and new detention centers popped up in remote places like Oakdale, Louisiana, whose representatives and community members lobbied hard to be chosen. The deportation machine provided small, struggling cities like Oakdale, which had an unemployment rate of close to 30 percent, with an opportunity to revitalize their economies. "Our unemployed are in critical need of this facility," a group of local and state politicians wrote to Associate Attorney General Rudolph Giuliani in April 1982 before a final decision had been made about the location. Over time, the US government came to rely on offshore detention sites. By September 1994, nearly 48,000 Cubans and Haitians were being held at the US naval base at Guantánamo Bay. As the geography of migrant detention became decentralized, Mexican, Cuban, Haitian, and Central American detainees found themselves farther away from family, friends, and legal aid, which put them in increasingly precarious positions.[68]

Despite the expansion of federal facilities, insufficient detention space forced US officials to subcontract immigrant imprisonment to local governments and private third parties. By 1998 the INS had detention agreements with more than 1,000 county jails across the country. For-profit companies also sought out these contracts and spent tens of millions of dollars on political lobbying to influence DHS policy and state-level immigration laws. Large international detention conglomerates with immigrant and nonimmigrant facilities across the country and around the world—and their shareholders—have financially benefited from detaining more migrants for longer periods of time. The two largest such companies, CoreCivic (formerly known as the Corrections Corporation of America) and the GEO Group, first opened immigrant detention facilities in 1984 and expanded their portfolios in the years to come.[69] Thirty years later these two corporations operated eight of the ten largest immigrant detention centers in the country, and accounted for 45 percent of all ICE detention beds and almost three-quarters of all privately contracted detention beds.[70] In 2016, CoreCivic and the GEO Group operated 113 correctional facilities and immigration detention centers in total and reported annual revenues of $1.85 billion and $2.18 billion, respectively, a 200 percent increase from a decade earlier.[71]

Public policies propelled the boom in immigration detention and the growth of the enforcement bureaucracy, helping to make the system more profitable than ever. In 2009, Congress implemented a quota that eventually required as many as 34,000 immigration detention beds to be available on a daily basis, irrespective of need. Bed mandates created an artificial floor on detentions. They also incentivized harsher enforcement policies by limiting the government's ability to rely on less costly, more humane alternatives to detention that could have saved up to $1.44 billion a year. Instead, CoreCivic and GEO Group's shareholders have lined their pockets while taxpayers have footed the bill. By the last year of Barack Obama's presidency, DHS's detention and deportation operations cost some $3.3 billion, or more than $9 million per day.[72]

Immigrants have of course paid the steepest price of all. People held in immigration detention have limited rights and little means of recourse. Noncitizens have frequently been transferred to remote facilities across the country that are far from their loved ones and lawyers. The map of internal and international airlifts is so extensive that some have described it as "look[ing] like a page from a commercial carrier's in-flight magazine." (In fiscal year 2016 alone, US officials deported more than 110,000 people on chartered planes and 6,100 on commercial flights.)[73]

Many immigrants have also been held in local jails, which have not always had to meet federal detention standards. Immigration officials have been willing to accept or overlook this. As the service's senior counsel for field operations explained in May 1998, "It's not in the INS's interest to force the jails to meet certain standards because we need the space."[74] Private detention centers have not proven any better and have become notorious for their treacherous conditions, systematic cover-ups of negligent medical care, and widespread abuse at the hands of guards. At least 180 people have died in immigration custody since October 2003.[75]

## Mobilizing against the Machine

Building on the strategies and struggles of the past, migrants and their allies mobilized in the face of increasing militarization of the border and criminalization, detention, and formal deportation of people in the country without authorization. In the summer of 1981, Jim Corbett, a Quaker from Tucson, Arizona, launched what would soon become known as the sanctuary movement. Disturbed by Central Americans' plight and the US government's involvement in creating and perpetuating the crisis, Corbett began taking people in on his ranch, in addition to organizing other safe houses and support networks for people seeking refuge. The following spring, Tucson's social justice–minded Southside Presbyterian Church and five churches in Berkeley, California, declared themselves sanctuaries after criticizing the US policy of deporting Salvadorans and Guatemalans to their deaths, rather than granting them asylum. The movement spread quickly in the years to come: by the end of 1987 there were 450 places of sanctuary and some 70,000 active participants spanning the country. Beyond providing physical sanctuary, the movement's symbolic importance raised public awareness and support that contributed to far-reaching legal victories in the courts. In January 1991, the US District Court for the Northern District of California approved a settlement agreement in *American Baptist Churches v. Thornburgh*, a lawsuit originally brought by eighty religious groups and refugee aid organizations six years earlier that claimed the government had discriminated against Salvadorans and Guatemalans who had requested asylum. The agreement stayed the deportation of eligible class members and granted them new asylum hearings. Some 240,000 people eventually benefited from the settlement.[76]

In 1994, grassroots activists in California and national Latino and immigrant rights groups organized against Proposition 187. However, tensions existed within the campaign and the strategies of how to fight the measure sharply diverged. Although they ultimately failed to convince enough people to vote against the proposition, a broad coalition of rights, labor, religious, educational, and medical groups immediately filed legal challenges (consolidated as the *League of United Latin American Citizens, et al. v. Wilson*) that prevented it from ever being implemented.[77]

Both before and after the midterm elections artists offered biting critiques of the ballot initiative and the anti-Mexican and anti-immigrant fear mongering that propelled it. In the months leading up to the vote satirists Lalo Alcaraz and Esteban Zul created the character "Dr. Daniel Portado," whose first initial and last name, "D. Portado," sounded like the Spanish word for deportee when said together. Portado was supposedly a representative of the made-up "Hispanics for Wilson" advisory committee of the National Pochisimo Institute. A September 1994 press release Alcaraz and Zul sent to media outlets announced a "reverse-immigration" border run and rally to "Get Out the Vote and Get Out the Immigrants" in support of the governor's reelection campaign. In addition, the group proposed to create "Self Deportation Centers" that would "encourage all Hispanics regardless of citizenship status, especially their elderly relatives, to return to their countries of origin." (The announcement stated that all of the committee's members would also leave voluntarily after Wilson won the election.) The act fooled some mainstream outlets and the duo appeared—Alcaraz as D. Portado and Zul as his bodyguard—on Spanish-language television station Telemundo the week of the election.[78]

Performance artist Guillermo Gómez-Peña also tackled self-deportation, but through a dystopian rather than comical lens. In 1995, he penned a short essay imagining an "angry white man" who witnesses the aftermath of "an epic self-deportation program" in which Latinos departed the United States en masse, leaving the service, construction, taxi, and tourist industries in disarray, crops rotting in the fields, cities bankrupt, and the country paralyzed. "A nervous President Clinton is pleading for all unemployed Anglos and African-Americans to show up immediately to the closest emergency labor recruitment center." But they don't. "The unemployed 'citizens' were clearly not inspired by the idea of working for minimum wage and no benefits," Gómez-Peña wrote. Clinton, in a last-ditch act of desperation, begs the remaining Mexicans to stay in broken Spanglish. The piece concludes with a question to the nativist politicians and citizens groups who used immigrants as scapegoats to stoke people's fears about crime, the economy, and the "uncertain future": "Are you guys truly, truly aware of the logical consequences of your anti-immigrant politics?"[79]

A decade later, immigrants and activists protested en masse against policies that sought to ramp up border and interior enforcement. In the spring of 2006, after the Sensenbrenner Bill passed the House, as many as 5 million people—including hundreds of thousands during single marches—took to the streets of more than 160 cities across the country. These mass marches demanded justice and equal rights for migrants and proved key to preventing the Senate from passing the draconian measure.[80] In the years that followed, immigrants and their allies directed their energies against

Figure 41.   Young people march through the streets of Chicago during a 2010 "Coming Out of the Shadows" rally.
Photo: Peter Holderness.

Figure 42.   Chicagoans and members of Undocumented Illinois participate in a November 2013 direct action blocking a DHS bus from transporting immigrants to O'Hare Airport for deportation.
Photo: Stephen Pavey/Hope In Focus.

policies and programs like 287(g) and Secure Communities that generated fear and resulted in family separation. Youth immigrant activists were at the forefront of this movement. After Congress repeatedly failed to pass the Development, Relief, and Education for Alien Minors Act (first introduced in 2001 and known as the DREAM Act), which would have granted legal status and the possibility of citizenship to some young people, undocumented teenagers and twenty-somethings organized. This diverse group, some of whom referred to themselves as Dreamers, formed organizations like United We Dream, DreamActivist, the National Immigrant Youth Alliance, and the Immigrant Youth Justice League, which deployed an array of sophisticated political tactics. Taking inspiration from the civil rights and LGBTQ movements, they staged sit-ins in senators' offices, undertook hunger strikes, engaged in acts of nonviolent civil disobedience in front of ICE offices and state capitols, orchestrated a "Trail of Dreams" march from Florida to Washington, DC, and a cross-country Freedom Dream Ride bus trip, and held "coming out of the shadows" events in which they publicly identified as undocumented and unafraid. Many of the groups used social media as a mobilizing tool to gain support for their cause and, in some cases, stop the deportation of their friends and family members (see figures 41 and 42).[81]

Although youth immigrant activists did not succeed in pushing Congress to pass the DREAM Act or comprehensive immigration reform, they pressured the Obama administration into implementing broad prosecutorial discretion in June 2011 (which offered some protection to people not considered to be enforcement priorities) and Deferred Action for Childhood Arrivals (DACA) the following summer. DACA provided young undocumented people who were brought to the United States as children with the opportunity to remain in the country and work without the threat of deportation, albeit temporarily, if they met certain requirements. More than 800,000 people applied for DACA over the course of the next four years, and officials approved 87 percent of those applications. (In November 2014, Obama also tried to roll out Deferred Action for Parents of US Citizens and Lawful Permanent Residents [DAPA], but more than twenty-five states filed a lawsuit blocking it.) Rifts between organizations about where to focus attention or how to most effectively push for change existed, but didn't impede the movement from winning impressive victories that expanded the rights and improved the lives of undocumented people, their families, and their communities.[82]

Despite renewed activism and enhanced efforts in defense of the undocumented community, federal officials expelled millions of people and deportation became harsher than ever between 1986 and 2016. Ironically, the fortification of the border meant that more migrants stayed in the United States since it became more expensive and more dangerous to reenter the country after expulsion. The result was more permanent family separation and a growing deportee population living in dire conditions along the Mexican side of the border. Some deportees, including fifty deported veterans in Tijuana who had served in the US military and whose families still lived north of the border, organized in hopes on drawing attention to their cause and winning a reprieve. Children bore a considerable burden when they or one of their family members were removed or faced the prospect of being removed.[83] Between 2005 and 2010, some 1.4 million people—half of them children born in the United States—returned to Mexico either by choice, coercion, or force. Deportees who grew up in the United States faced a variety of challenges when trying to find their place in countries they had only lived in as infants. The best many could do was use their English language skills to get a job in a call center that a US company had relocated for economic reasons. Many struggled, despite the efforts of a growing number of Mexican civil society organizations geared toward assisting returned and deported migrants.[84]

In his second term, some migrant activists and advocates took to calling Barack Obama the "Deporter-in-Chief." The moniker stemmed from the fact that formal deportations reached unprecedented levels during his presidency.[85] But total expulsions dropped. Assigning responsibility to a particular president or solely focusing on how many people he expelled does not explain immigration enforcement's punitive turn. It is only by examining the cumulative policy changes under both Republican and Democratic administrations since 1986—from the unprecedented spending on enforcement, militarization of the border, and increased reliance on expedited formal deportations to the criminalization of migration, externalization of migration control, and expansion of immigration detention—that we can begin to understand the recent transformation of the deportation machine.

# Epilogue

## Reckoning with the Machine

The deportation machine has been running on all cylinders in recent years. But, as this book has shown, it did not just come into being during the presidency of Donald J. Trump. Nor did it first emerge during the administrations of Barack Obama, George W. Bush, or Bill Clinton. The machine's roots are much deeper, dating back to the late nineteenth century, when Congress gave the federal government exclusive authority over immigration. Since then, both Democratic and Republican politicians and private third parties have contributed to its growth, implementing punitive policies and pouring the equivalent of hundreds of billions of dollars into enforcement efforts that have resulted in tens of millions of expulsions by whatever means necessary. The machine's mechanisms have largely remained the same over time and have functioned in unison, though at different levels at distinct moments. Persistent political economic realities, racial prejudices, and cultural concerns have been a driving force behind anti-immigrant sentiment and restrictive measures, and economic crises and wars have often led to rising xenophobia and dramatic, even if temporary, spikes in deportations. Aside from these external factors, it is tempting to say that the machine has operated autonomously given the immigration bureaucracy's mission and prerogative. And to an extent it has. Throughout the last 140-plus years, regardless of which party has been in the White House or controlled Congress, immigration officials have relied on a combination of force and coercion to maximize deportations and minimize costs, all in hopes of bolstering the agency's legitimacy and reaffirming the United States' sovereignty.

Yet although institutional inertia matters, who is in power does, too—as the current administration has made clear. Donald Trump has waged an all-out war against immigrants and immigration. His brazen anti-black, anti-Latino, and anti-Muslim nativism has played a significant role at every stage of his political career. Trump's popularity among conservatives dates back at least to 2011, when he began repeatedly questioning the validity of then-president Barack Obama's birth certificate. He continued to cast doubt in the years ahead on where the nation's first black president was born, and his virulent dog-whistle politics helped him gain support on the right. Trump doubled down on these tactics during the 2016 campaign. In a June 2015 speech announcing his candidacy, he referred to Mexican immigrants as criminals, drug smugglers, and rapists, and promised to "build a great, great wall on our southern border" for which Mexico would supposedly pay. In the lead-up to the election, Trump also pushed for more interior enforcement, mandatory detention after apprehension, and an end to sanctuary cities that offered certain protections to undocumented immigrants. Such a position helped him gain endorsements from the two largest unions representing Border Patrol and ICE agents.[1] A former ICE official told *The Atlantic* that after Trump's surprise victory, some officers "thumped their chest as if they had just won the Super Bowl."[2]

Following his inauguration in January 2017, Trump set out to make good on the draconian campaign promises that had rallied the Republican base around him. During his first week in office he signed a series of executive orders calling for the construction of a nearly 2,000-mile wall along the US–Mexico border, the hiring of an additional 10,000 ICE officers and 5,000 Border Patrol agents, and a ban on immigration from seven majority-Muslim countries. The orders also threatened to publish weekly lists of crimes immigrants committed and to fine and penalize not only undocumented people but also "those who facilitate their presence in the United States."[3]

Such dramatic policy changes and proclamations further emboldened immigration officers, whose morale skyrocketed in the weeks and months ahead. In a marked departure from Obama-era policies of prosecutorial discretion and preferential categories that offered some semblance of protection in name if not always in practice, officials made clear that all undocumented people were now deportation priorities. Trump, his then–press secretary Sean Spicer explained, "wanted to take the shackles off" immigration agents.[4] In early February, ICE deported Guadalupe García de Rayos, the mother of two US citizen children who had been in the country for more than two decades, after a routine immigration check-in. Around the same time, officials apprehended Daniel Ramírez Medina, a young man with DACA status living in the Seattle area. Ramírez Medina spent six weeks in detention before authorities released him. On February 17, Border Patrol agents deported Juan Manuel Montes, a twenty-three-year-old two-time DACA recipient who had lived in the United States since age nine. During the first eight months of Trump's presidency apprehensions of immigrants with no criminal record increased, as ICE arrests spiked 42 percent. In the years thereafter, the crackdown on interior enforcement continued as arrests, workplace raids, and neighborhood sweeps spread throughout the nation and DHS reinitiated and expanded federal partnerships with local law enforcement agencies through programs such as 287(g) and Secure Communities.[5]

Private prison companies capitalized on the Trump administration's anti-immigrant rhetoric and enforcement-first mentality. GEO Group and Core-Civic each contributed $250,000 to Donald Trump's inauguration festivities. Between the November 2016 election and late February 2017, their stock prices had increased 140 and 98 percent, respectively. By the end of that year GEO Group's revenue reached an all-time high of $2.3 billion, up more than 250 percent from a decade earlier. During the president's first eighteen months in office, GEO Group and CoreCivic combined to spend more than $3 million on federal lobbying—and DHS granted them a total of $800 million in contracts. In June 2019, the number of migrants detained in public and private facilities—including a makeshift, outdoor camp in El Paso an observer described as "a human dog pound"—reached an all-time high of more than 54,000.[6]

In addition to ratcheting up enforcement the Trump administration rolled out radical policies meant to curtail legal immigration. The president sought to end family-based "chain migration" from Latin America, Asia, Africa, and the Caribbean by eliminating key provisions of the 1965 Immigration and Nationality Act. The White House attempted to terminate DACA, for young people brought to the United States as children, and Temporary

Protected Status, for people from war-torn or natural-disaster-stricken countries like El Salvador, Haiti, and South Sudan. The programs' futures remain uncertain as legal challenges work their way through the courts, but if authorities succeed in ending them as many as 1 million people—many of them long-term residents with US citizen relatives—will find themselves in legal limbo and potentially subject to deportation. Meanwhile, DHS set up a "denaturalization task force" to ferret out people who supposedly made false statements on their immigration petitions and strip them of citizenship. Agents arrested people who showed up for regular immigration check-ins and marriage interviews, and they denied passports to ethnic Mexicans born in the United States along the southwestern border. Officials proposed restricting immigrants' eligibility for visas and green cards if they had ever used public benefits such as food stamps or Medicaid, calling to mind restrictions on people "likely to become public charges" going back to the founding of the nation. And, in hopes of speeding up deportations, the Department of Justice hired more than one hundred new immigration judges to handle the backlog of cases, which had ballooned to more than 1 million by the end of August 2019. The president, for his part, has taken to Twitter to call for denying due process rights to immigrants in order to streamline expulsions: "We cannot allow all of these people to invade our Country. When somebody comes in, we must immediately, with no Judges or Court Cases, bring them back from where they came. Our system is a mockery to good immigration policy and Law and Order."[7]

The administration also drastically reduced the annual refugee quota, from 110,000 during Obama's last year in office to 30,000 in fiscal year 2019 and 18,000 in fiscal year 2020. To cut admissions even further, officials turned people away at the border before they could even request asylum, gummed up the vetting process, suspended the federal refugee resettlement program, and rewrote the rules to exclude victims of gang violence and domestic violence. In fiscal year 2018, the United States only admitted 22,491 refugees, fewer than half of the allotted quota. To justify such actions, Trump has demonized black and brown migrants and refugees as "animals," potential terrorists, "thieves and murderers," "snakes," and people from "shithole countries" who pose an existential threat to the United States and Europe.[8]

However, no policy change garnered more public attention or condemnation than President Trump's "zero tolerance" strategy. In April 2018, in response to an increase in migration across the southwest border, then–attorney general Jeff Sessions declared that anyone entering the country without authorization would be criminally charged and ineligible to apply for asylum. Prosecutors charged migrants with no prior record with a misdemeanor and judges in South Texas carried out mass hearings of up to eighty people at once and 200 people per day, which was as many as the overwhelmed government lawyers could handle. Judges usually handed down sentences of time served to first-time offenders, which meant formal deportation was imminent. But people with prior offenses, including those who had been previously apprehended, faced felony convictions that resulted in stiffer prison sentences followed by expulsion and a twenty-year or even lifetime ban from the United States. Zero tolerance's crackdown on all unauthorized entries turned an increasing number of migrants and refugees into criminals in the eyes of the law. By the end of July 2018, the Department of Justice had convicted more than 30,000 migrants.[9]

The month after zero tolerance went into effect, officials announced a second facet of the policy: the forced separation of detained parents and children, most of them Central American refugees, in hopes of deterring future unauthorized migration. The idea of separating families was not new. US Citizenship and Immigration Services officer John Lafferty had first floated it in February 2017, just two weeks after Trump's inauguration and more than a year before it gained national notoriety. Between October 2017 and May 2018, the Trump administration separated more than 1,350 children from their parents, "including more than 100 children under the age of four." DHS took another 2,300-plus kids from their parents between then and June 20, 2018, when widespread protests and public pressure forced Trump to sign an executive order supposedly ending family separation.[10]

By then, however, considerable, lasting damage had already occurred. The American Academy of Pediatrics warned that the family separation policy could "cause irreparable harm." Although a top ICE official described the detention facilities housing children—more than one hundred of them privately run—as "like a summer camp," photographs showed kids in cages and leaked audio revealed their desperate, inconsolable cries for "Mami" and "Papá." Detained children's days were regimented. At one facility near the Mexican border in South Texas, kids woke up at dawn and proceeded to clean the bathroom, including scrubbing the toilet, before eating breakfast and going on to have some schooling. The rules included no running, no sitting on the floor, no sharing food, and no touching other children, "even if that child is your hermanito or hermanita—your little brother or sister." DHS held some 250 kids and teens at a remote Border Patrol station in Clint, Texas, without adequate food, water, or sanitation. Some of the children had been there for weeks, without showering or changing clothes, even though government regulations require immigration officials to transfer them to the Department of Health and Human Services (HHS) within seventy-two hours. And at federally funded immigrant shelters in Chicago where authorities held minors for months, some tried to escape, undertook hunger strikes, and even contemplated suicide. Between fall 2018 and spring 2019, six children died in federal custody.[11]

Even though a federal court ordered authorities to reunite separated families by set dates, DHS and HHS authorities had no mechanism in place to easily do so since they had purposefully scattered them across the country. More challenging still was reconnecting kids with already-deported parents. Officials coerced some people into dropping their asylum claims and agreeing to deportation under the false pretense that it would expedite their family reunion. Instead, the opposite was true: some of these parents and children may never be reunited. While the Trump administration's zero tolerance policy tore apart families, it did not stop people from coming to the United States. Similar to other prevention through deterrence measures, from the boatlift of the 1950s to the militarization of the border during the last quarter century, family separation represented an extreme form of state-sponsored violence that traumatized thousands of migrants and refugees.[12]

In some ways, Trump's immigration enforcement policies represent a continuation of rather than a break from those of his predecessors: formal deportations have remained high, officials' dependence on private immigration detention has only increased, and voluntary departures have steadily declined.[13] But the administration's heavy reliance on self-deportations, the machine's third mechanism, represents an important break from the recent past, even if it is not entirely unprecedented.[14]

Since taking office, Trump has deployed concerted fear campaigns, along with nativist policies and virulent anti-immigrant rhetoric, to push people further into the shadows or out of the country altogether. "Real power is . . . fear," he told two *Washington Post* reporters in the lead-up to the 2016 election.[15] And, to be sure, the administration's scare tactics have had a considerable impact on immigrant communities. As Juanita Molina, the executive director of the Tucson-based Border Action Network, told *The Guardian* a month after Trump's inauguration, "It's almost like it's psychological warfare that's being waged against people of color to create a constant feeling of fear and uncertainty."[16] Testifying before Congress a few months later, then-acting director of ICE Thomas D. Homan essentially confirmed Molina's assessment. "If you're in this country illegally and you committed a crime by being in this country, you should be uncomfortable, you should look over your shoulder. You need to be worried."[17]

In response, dozens of people sought sanctuary in churches across the country. Jeanette Vizguerra, a forty-five-year-old undocumented immigrant from Mexico, took refuge in the basement of the First Unitarian Church in Denver for nearly three months before receiving a temporary stay of deportation. Forty-year-old Javier Flores García, an undocumented Mexican immigrant with three US citizen children, spent nearly eleven months at the Arch Street United Methodist Church in downtown Philadelphia. He only left after receiving a special U visa for victims of crimes who agree to cooperate with the police.[18]

Other people self-deported. Thirty-six-year-old Miguel Hernández had lived and worked on the same Wisconsin dairy farm for sixteen years when, in June 2017, he, his wife, Luisa, and their two US-born sons, five and four, decided it was time to leave. While Luisa and the kids flew back to Mexico from Chicago, Hernández and four coworkers who also chose to return after years in the United States made the 2,300-mile trip to their mountainous town in the state of Veracruz in a Honda pickup truck packed with their possessions—"bags of clothes and shoes, TV sets in boxes and a bucket of children's toys." Explaining the reasoning behind their decision, one of the men told a Wisconsin Public Radio reporter, "It's better to go back home because of the laws—they're coming after us. It's better to go willingly and be with the family rather than getting deported."[19]

But the vast majority of the estimated 10 million to 12 million undocumented immigrants in the United States stayed. And, for many of them, living in constant fear became commonplace. "There is a dreadful sense of fear," Fred Morris, a United Methodist pastor in a mostly Latino neighborhood in Los Angeles told the Associated Press a few weeks after Trump's inauguration. "It's more than palpable. It's radiating. People are terrified." Some undocumented immigrants stopped going to the grocery store and no longer sought out medical care or public nutrition services. Worried that a run-in with the police might lead to their deportation, the number of immigrant street vendors in New York City plummeted and Latina women made fewer domestic violence reports in cities such as Los Angeles, San Diego, Denver, and Houston.[20]

The threat of deportation and family separation weighed heavily on both parents and children. Fear led some people to pull their kids from schools across the country. During the first month of Trump's presidency, enrollments dropped by 43 percent at some Head Start preschool programs in Florida that used to have long waiting lists. The following year, the day after a large ICE raid at a meatpacking plant in eastern Tennessee, 500 kids stayed out of school. A study of fifty-five counties with active 287(g) partnerships between DHS and local law enforcement agencies found that the agreements reduced the Latino student population by 10 percent in two years. Many children experienced heightened levels of stress and anxiety, had difficulty concentrating, and needed more frequent referrals to specialists. They also struggled with tardiness, absences, and sleep problems, and some got into fights. "The fear is affecting every part of their lives," a counselor with Catholic Charities Archdiocese of New Orleans told *The Atlantic* in March 2017. A Southern California pediatrician elaborated: "Kids are suffering from anxiety about not wanting to leave their parents or being worried [about if] they'll still be there when they get home." As a result, many families put action plans into place, instructing their kids—some of them still in elementary school—what they should do if they ever returned home to an empty house. Still, youths could not help but play out, in great detail, nightmare scenarios in their heads of immigration agents arresting, detaining, and deporting their parents.[21]

The pitched battles over immigration during the last four years have left many to wonder about the question that began this book: What kind of nation is the United States? Is it a white Anglo-Saxon Protestant, English-speaking nation, as some people imagine it, or a multiracial, multicultural, multilingual nation? Is it a nation of immigrants, a deportation nation, or some combination of the two?

The Trump administration has made its views on these questions clear, from the president's sympathetic statements about Nazis and white supremacists, to the US Citizenship and Immigration Service's decision to remove the phrase "nation of immigrants" from its mission statement.[22] Authorities have drawn hard lines around inclusion and exclusion, both at the border and in the interior, and they have relied on the machine's coercive mechanisms to enforce them. Today, as in the past, streamlining expulsions and promoting self-deportation continues to serve as a way to augment state power while sidestepping legal and financial constraints without regard to individuals, families, and communities' well-being.

At the same time, immigrants and their allies have put forth a very different vision of the country, forming nothing less than a mass solidarity movement in the process. They have taken to the streets, filed lawsuits, descended on airports to protest the Muslim ban, organized know-your-rights workshops and antideportation trainings, and pushed religious institutions, towns, and cities to declare themselves sanctuaries for undocumented people. They have also called for the abolition of ICE and for an end to inhumane policies both fueled by and meant to instill fear. Recognizing the many personal and familial connections between citizens and noncitizens and the impossibility of neatly dividing "us" from "them," activists have insisted that all people are deserving of basic rights, respect, and dignity.

Their struggle will not end when Donald Trump leaves office. Although racist, fear-mongering politicians share the blame, they are hardly the only ones responsible for creating and perpetuating inhumane immigration policies and enforcement practices during the last century and a half. Numerous others have also propelled and profited from the deportation machine, from employers seeking a steady supply of exploitable labor and consumers only willing to pay rock-bottom prices, to bureaucrats trying to justify annual budgets and investors in private firms eager to make millions of dollars at noncitizens' expense. The diverse stakeholders that benefit from expulsion mean that the relentless targeting and scapegoating of immigrants will likely continue—regardless of which politician or party is in power.

# NOTE ON SOURCES AND LANGUAGE

This book is based on nearly a decade of research in more than twenty archives spread across the United States and Mexico. I also conducted more than thirty in-depth English- and Spanish-language interviews and oral histories with migrants and their family members, activists, lawyers, union organizers, and immigration officials. Most names of migrants and deportees are pseudonyms. I make extensive use of more than fifty English- and Spanish-language US and Mexican newspapers and periodicals, in addition to dozens of government reports, hearings, previously unreported quantitative data, and sources obtained through the Freedom of Information Act.

Most scholars and journalists equate expulsion with "formal deportations." According to the Department of Homeland Security (DHS), formal deportations, also known in bureaucratic parlance as "removals," are "the compulsory and confirmed movement of an inadmissible or deportable alien out of the United States based on an order of removal." Anyone formally deported "has administrative or criminal consequences placed on subsequent reentry owing to the fact of the removal." Until the end of the twentieth century, most formal deportations occurred by order of an immigration judge. However, since Congress passed the Illegal Immigration Reform and Immigrant Responsibility Act of 1996, the majority have occurred via a few different fast-track methods, as discussed in chapter six. According to DHS's 2018 *Yearbook of Immigration Statistics*, federal officials have formally deported some 8,350,000 people since 1892.[1]

My approach and perspective differ in that I adopt an expansive definition of deportation that also includes "voluntary departures" and "self deportations." I argue that we must account for any time state actors have forced or coerced someone into leaving the country, regardless of whether by judicial or administrative order or in response to concerted campaigns to push people out.

Voluntary departures, also known as "informal deportations" or "returns," are "the confirmed movement of an inadmissible or deportable alien out of the United States not based on an order of removal."[2] They have typically occurred by administrative order of an immigration official after apprehension, whether near the border or in the interior of the country. Authorities have used voluntary departure to deport both recent arrivals and long-term residents. DHS describes them as a privilege or "a form of relief from formal removal," but we must keep in mind what the agency itself noted in 2003: "Although such departures are called 'voluntary departures,' they are required and verified."[3] From 1978 to 1994, the INS *Statistical Yearbook* referred to voluntary departures as "aliens required to depart" or simply "required to depart."[4] And if further proof is needed that there's nothing voluntary about them, DHS's United States Citizenship and Immigration Services History Office and Library created a subject guide that classifies voluntary departures under the broader category of "Deportation."[5] Immigration authorities have carried out more than 48,360,000 voluntary departures since 1892.[6]

Considering the fact that voluntary departures account for 85 percent of the nearly 57 million total expulsions during the last 125 years, any definition of deportation that excludes them is both inaccurate and misleading. The same is true for fear campaigns, vigilante violence, and other measures meant to induce self-deportation. As a group of international legal scholars noted in 1983, "the concept of expulsion encompasses indirect measures including ill-treatment, racial and other forms of discriminatory practices, harassment and other means of coercion designed to force people to leave." In addition to "the direct exercise of State power," expulsion can also result from a variety of "indirect measures ... sometimes of a subtle kind," including those "of a psychological, as well as of an economic or social nature."[7] Yet few scholarly or popular works on deportation include a substantive discussion of these informal expulsions.[8] Perhaps some authors accepted the narrow definition of deportation out of hand. Others may have found voluntary departures and self-deportations difficult to track, or may have failed to recognize their punitive nature.

As the book's first endnote explains, the 57 million deportations figure refers to expulsion "events," rather than the number of unique individuals removed. Officials have deported many people on more than one occasion. In fact, a close examination of more than half a century of the Immigration and Naturalization Service's annual reports and statistical yearbooks reveals that "previously expelled aliens" represent around 13 percent of all apprehensions between 1937 and 1964, and nearly 25 percent of all apprehensions between 1965 and 1989.[9] (Chapter 4 describes why this increase occurred.) Although immigration officials recorded whether apprehended migrants had prior deportations, they did not systematically track how many times people had been deported, making it impossible to know whether someone had two, five, or ten or more expulsions. (A Freedom of Information Act request and inquiries to nonpartisan immigration policy think tanks and the Department of Homeland Security's Office of Immigration Statistics confirmed that no such data exist.) While I hoped to obtain this information, doing so was of secondary importance since my primary interests are the state's capacity to deport people (again, "events" rather than unique individuals); how authorities have expelled people and how immigrants have fought against expulsion; and the cumulative effect repeated deportations have had on individuals, families, communities, and the nation.

Throughout the book I use deportation interchangeably with expulsion, treating them as umbrella terms that encapsulate the machine's three mechanisms: formal deportation, voluntary departure, and self-deportation. This does not mean that we should conflate different types of expulsion; rather, we should recognize the important distinctions between them, while also seeking to understand how they have functioned together and changed over time.

# ACKNOWLEDGMENTS

Generous financial support for this book came from the Fulbright-García Robles Scholar program; the Miller Center National Fellowship program; a National Endowment for the Humanities Summer Seminar on "Rethinking International Migration"; the Immigration and Ethnic History Society's George E. Pozzetta Dissertation Award; the Department of History at the University of Pennsylvania; the Provost's Postdoctoral Scholars Program in the Humanities at the University of Southern California; and the University of Illinois at Chicago's Latin American and Latino Studies program, Department of History, Global Migration Cluster, and faculty fellowship program at the Institute for the Humanities.

Archivists, demographers, historians, lawyers, and librarians provided invaluable assistance navigating the collections and identifying the sources that enabled me to write this book. In the United States, thanks to Zack Wilske, Marian Smith, Char Cook, and Leanna Feinleib of the United States Citizenship and Immigration Services; Bill Creech, Lynn Goodsell, Jessie Kratz, Rebecca Sharp, and Alexandra Villaseran at the National Archives and Records Administration; Tim Noakes and Ignacio Ornelas at Stanford University Libraries' Department of Special Collections; Peter Schey of the Center for Human Rights and Constitutional Law; Dan Kesselbrenner of the National Lawyers Guild National Immigration Project; Annette Hekking of the National Border Patrol Museum; Randy Capps of the Migration Policy Institute; Marc Rosenblum of the Department of Homeland Security's Office of Immigration Statistics; Nick Okrent and Mitch Fraas at the

University of Pennsylvania; and Steve Wiberley and Paula Dempsey at the University of Illinois at Chicago. In México, thanks to Laura Ivette González Cortés of the Archivo Histórico del Instituto Nacional de Migración; Laura Beatriz Moreno Rodríguez of the Archivo Histórico Genaro Estrada, Acervo Histórico Diplomático de la Secretaría de Relaciones Exteriores; and Jesús García at the Centro de Estudios Migratorios. Special thanks as well to Bill Blum, Richard Boswell, Jesse Gonzales, María Guadalupe González, José Jacques Medina, Edward Ortega, Antonio Rodríguez, Mark Rosenbaum, Leo Soto, Robert Warren, Peter Williamson, and the migrants and their families on both sides of the border (unnamed here to protect their anonymity) who shared their stories with me.

At Princeton University Press, Eric Crahan understood my vision for the project and adeptly guided the book from proposal to publication. Thalia Leaf and Pamela Weidman provided sound advice at every stage and helped me navigate the ins and outs of the publishing process. Chris Ferrante designed the striking jacket. Karen Carter of PUP and Erin Davis and the team at Westchester Publishing Services ably managed the production phase. Julia Kurtz's expert copyediting improved the manuscript. Fred Kameny created the index. Thanks also to the editors of the Politics and Society in Modern America series, and to Gary Gerstle in particular. He believed in this book long before it existed, patiently waited as it came into being, and offered constructive feedback on the complete manuscript.

Part of this book first appeared in Adam Goodman, "The Long History of Self-Deportation," *NACLA Report on the Americas* 49, no. 2 (2017): 152–58; and Adam Goodman, "The Human Costs of Outsourcing Deportation," *Humanity* 8, no. 3 (Winter 2017): 527–29. The epigraph comes from Adrienne Rich's poem "Deportations" in her collection *Dark Fields of the Republic: Poems 1991–1995* (New York: W. W. Norton, 1995), 30.

The kernel of the idea for this book first came to me a decade ago at the University of Pennsylvania, where I benefited from the incomparable mentorship of the late Michael B. Katz. The example Michael set showed me the impact historians could have on public policy and people beyond the academy. I feel his absence every day. Tom Sugrue offered encouragement and intellectual inspiration. His politically engaged work continues to serve as a model. Ann Farnsworth-Alvear schooled me in oral history and pushed me to ask smart questions I never would have considered. Eiichiro Azuma imparted his expertise in migration history and entertained my then-half-baked ideas. Steve Hahn, Kathy Peiss, Amy Offner, Stephanie McCurry, Kathy Brown, and Walter Licht taught me to read widely and think big. Antonio Feros and Ben Nathans supported me at crucial moments. Joan Plonski was always quick to lend a helping hand.

At the University of Southern California, Bill Deverell, Alice Echols, Josh Kun, Nathan Perl-Rosenthal, George Sanchez, and Dan Carino took an interest in my work and made me feel welcome during my year as a postdoctoral fellow in Los Angeles.

I wrote most of this book while teaching at the University of Illinois at Chicago. I feel fortunate to be part of such a collaborative, dynamic community, and I have learned much from friends, colleagues, and students across the university. Special thanks to Marta Ayala, Xóchitl Bada, Chris Boyer, Andreas Feldmann, Anna Guevarra, Michael Jin, Robert Johnston, Amalia Pallares, Gayatri Reddy, Jeff Sklansky, Nena Torres, and Bruce Tyler. Thanks also to Cynthia Blair, Jennie Brier, Rosa Cabrera, Tanya Cabrera, Mark Canuel, Joaquín Chávez, Ralph Cintrón, Teresa Córdova, Jonathan Daly, Gosia Fidelis, Leon Fink, Lorena García, Elena Gutiérrez, Laura Hostetler, Lynn Hudson, Joel Huerta, Cedric Johnson, Nicole Jordan, Ronak Kapadia, Sue Levine, Patrisia Macías-Rojas, Rama Mantena, Ellen McClure, Marina Mogilner, Nadine Naber, Akemi Nishida, Helena Olea Rodríguez, Junaid Quadri, Cristián Roa, Atef Said, Kevin Schultz, Keely Stauter-Halsted, Elizabeth Todd-Breland, Linda Vavra, and the past and present members of the Fearless Undocumented Alliance. I'm grateful to Janet Smith, Jeff Edwards, and the UIC United Faculty Local 6456 staff for all they do on behalf of the membership and the university. I appreciate Amanda Lewis and Iván Arenas of the Institute for Research on Race and Public Policy for connecting people across the institution and for organizing faculty writing retreats, which is where this book took form under the guidance of Jill Petty. I'm also indebted to Brad Hunt and Keelin Burke for providing me with a place to research and write through the Newberry Library's scholar-in-residence program. Thanks as well to Jesús Osorio.

A large number of incredibly generous friends and colleagues shaped this book through our conversations, through their own work, and through the feedback and advice they provided over the years. Thanks to C. J. Alvarez, Brian Balogh, Shana Bernstein, Jen Boles, Gerry Cadava, Merlin

Chowkwanyun, Deborah Cohen, Sarah Coleman, N. D. B. Connolly, Sean Dempsey, Dan Denvir, Greg Downs, Jorge Durand, Max Felker-Kantor, Delia Fernández, Patricia Fernández-Kelly, Anne Fleming, Vanessa Freije, Josh Frens-String, Donna Gabaccia, Matt García, Tanya Golash-Boza, Frank Goldman, Ruth Gomberg-Muñoz, Fredy González, Carly Goodman, Julia Gunn, Cindy Hahamovitch, Torrie Hester, Hidetaka Hirota, Madeline Hsu, Sarah Igo, Daniel Immerwahr, Mike Innis-Jiménez, Debbie Kang, Ceyda Karamursel, Matt Karp, Erika Kitzmiller, Paul Kramer, Freddie LaFemina, Nancy Landa, Beth Lew-Williams, Julian Lim, Sarah Lopez, Rosina Lozano, Kelly Lytle Hernández, Maddalena Marinari, Cecilia Márquez, Doug Massey, Ana Minian, Natalia Molina, Hiroshi Motomura, Monika Navarro, Gabriella Navarro-Busch, Mae Ngai, Becky Nicolaides, Bruno H. Piché, Yuridia Ramírez, Nadiah Rivera Fellah, Roberto Saba, Gema Santamaría, Ragini Shah, Justin Simard, Evan Taparata, Lorrin Thomas, Catherine Vézina, Patrick Weil, Julie Weise, Elliott Young, Verónica Zapata Rivera, and the colleagues who read and commented on chapter drafts I presented at Vanderbilt University's Legal History Colloquium and the Huntington-USC Institute on California & the West's LA History & Metro Studies Group.

The following people deserve special mention. Dan Amsterdam's and Peter Pihos's unwavering personal and professional support has meant more than they know. Their incisive feedback on the entire manuscript helped me sharpen the analysis and the writing. I'm fortunate to count them as family. Special thanks as well to Shane Dillingham, Carribean Fragoza, Romeo Guzmán, Stefania Heim, Miriam Pawel, Stuart Schrader, and Christy Thornton for their friendship and for inspiring me to do meaningful work with real historical and political stakes. María Cristina García and Roger Waldinger have long been two of my biggest champions, for which I'm grateful. Erika Lee, David Gutiérrez, Xóchitl Bada, Andreas Feldmann, Angela García, Ramón Gutiérrez, Michael Jin, Ben Johnson, Juan Mora-Torres, and Allison Brownell Tirres all went above and beyond, offering thoughtful critiques on a near-complete draft of the manuscript. Ben also shared much appreciated advice during our regular lunches at the Newberry. Robert Johnston's generosity knows no limits. He line edited every chapter, pushed me to make bold arguments, and fielded all questions no matter how insignificant. The late Gerald R. Gill always had my back. He introduced me to archival research and taught me to use history to shed light on past injustices in hopes of creating a more just future. I do my best each day to carry his legacy forward. Thanks also to Lee Coffin, Steve Cohen, Dave Patterson, Jeanne Penvenne, the late Anna Serafini, Marty Sherwin, and Darryl Tiggle—all influential teachers and mentors.

For their years of friendship and for opening their homes to me while I researched and wrote this book, special thanks to Tim Brown, Barbara Glaser and Paul Zachos, Leo Hernández López, Philippe Jacquart, Dan Kalik, Steve Krubiner, Angelo Malfatti, Lina Martínez Hernández, James Nicholson, Andria Pihos and John Vatianou, the Rotheim family, Eric Ruben, Vanessa Salcido Ibáñez, Patrick Tuck, Oliver Wise, and Lizbeth Zavala Mondragón.

None of this would have been possible without my family. In México, thanks to don Andrés, doña Hilda, Claudia, Valentina, Leszek, Beto, Lucia, and the rest of the Medina Jiménez family for embracing me. I so admire my sister Alyssa Goodman and my brother-in-law Jake Lappi, whose selflessness and dedication to creating a better world inspire me. My nephew Jakobe brings me joy. I cannot repay my debts to Margie Ingram and Joel Goodman, incredible people, partners, and parents. Their boundless love has been a constant source of strength. Hilda Vázquez Medina has celebrated the highs with me and sustained me during the lows—siempre a mi lado. Qué suerte tengo yo de tenerla como mi pareja de la vida.

# NOTES

## Archives Consulted and Abbreviations

American Friends Service Committee Archives, Philadelphia, PA (AFSC)

Archivo General de la Nación, Mexico City, México (AGN)

Archivo Histórico del Instituto Nacional de Migración, Mexico City, México (AHINM)

Archivo Histórico Genero Estrada, Acervo Histórico Diplomático, Secretaría de Relaciones Exteriores, Mexico City, México (AHSRE)

C. L. Sonnichsen Special Collections Department, University of Texas at El Paso, El Paso, TX (UTEP)

Chicago History Museum, Chicago, IL (CHM)

Chicano Studies Library Serial Collection, University of Southern California Library, Los Angeles, CA (CSLSC)

Chicano Studies Research Center, University of California, Los Angeles, Los Angeles, CA (CSRC)

Department of Special Collections, Stanford University Libraries, Palo Alto, CA (SCSUL)

Lyndon B. Johnson Presidential Library, Austin, TX (LBJ)

National Archives and Records Administration I, Washington, DC (NARA1)

National Archives and Records Administration II, College Park, MD (NARA2)

National Border Patrol Museum, El Paso, TX (NBPM)

Nettie Lee Benson Latin American Collection, University of Texas at Austin, Austin, TX (Benson)

Personal Papers of José Jacques Medina, Mexico City, México (JJM)

Records of the Center for Human Rights & Constitutional Law, Los Angeles, CA (CHRCL)

Records of the National Lawyers Guild National Immigration Project, Boston, MA (NLG-NIP)

Records of the United States District Court, Central District of California, Los Angeles, CA (CDC)

Special Collections & Archives, University of California, San Diego, San Diego, CA (SCA-UCSD)

Special Collections & Archives, University of Texas Rio Grande Valley, Edinburg, TX (UTRGV)

Special Collections & University Archives, University of Illinois at Chicago, Chicago, IL (UIC)

United States Citizenship and Immigration Services History Office and Library, Washington, DC (USCISHOL)

US Army Heritage and Education Center, Carlisle, PA (USAHEC)

## Introduction

1. Deportation here, and subsequently, refers to the sum of formal deportations and voluntary departures. Self-deportations are not included since they are unquantifiable. This statistic refers to the number of times the federal government has expelled someone (deportation "events"), rather than the number of unique individuals expelled. From 1920 to 2018, the most recent year for which statistics are available at the time of writing, expulsions totaled more than 56,300,000, while the number of times the federal government granted someone lawful permanent resident status (immigration "events") came to just over 51,700,000. I first made such a comparison in 2011. United States Department of Homeland Security (hereafter DHS), *Yearbook of Immigration Statistics* (hereafter *YOIS*): *2018* (Washington, DC: DHS, Office of Immigration Statistics, 2020), 5, 103; Adam Goodman, "A Nation of (Deported) Immigrants," *Dissent* 58, no. 2 (2011): 64–68; Jeremy Diamond, "Trump's Immigration Plan: Deport the Undocumented, 'Legal Status' for Some," *CNN*, Jul. 30, 2015, http://www.cnn.com/2015/07/29/politics/donald-trump-immigration-plan-healthcare-flip-flop.index.html.

Scholars have critically examined the United States' reputation as a nation of immigrants. See, for example, Donna R. Gabaccia, "Is Everywhere Nowhere? Nomads, Nations, and the Immigrant Paradigm of United States History," *Journal of American History* 86, no. 3 (Dec. 1999): 1115–34; Matthew Frye Jacobson, *Roots Too: White Ethnic Revival in Post-Civil Rights America* (Cambridge, MA: Harvard University Press, 2006), 312–88; Mae M. Ngai, *Nation of Immigrants: A Short History of an Idea* (under contract with Princeton University Press). Some have offered alternative monikers: Erika Lee has referred to the United States as a "gatekeeping nation"; Aristide Zolberg has described it as "a nation by design"; and Daniel Kanstroom has called it a "deportation nation." Erika Lee, *At America's Gates: Chinese Immigration during the Exclusion Era, 1882–1943* (Chapel Hill: University of North Carolina Press, 2003); Aristide R. Zolberg, *A Nation by Design: Immigration Policy in the Fashioning of America* (New York and

Cambridge, MA: Russell Sage Foundation and Harvard University Press, 2006); Daniel Kanstroom, *Deportation Nation: Outsiders in American History* (Cambridge, MA: Harvard University Press, 2007). Others have argued that competing ideals have been in tension throughout US history: Gary Gerstle has shown how both "civic nationalism" and "racial nationalism" shaped twentieth-century America; Madeline Hsu has examined both "gates" and "gateways," framing immigration as both restrictive and selective; and in her latest book, Erika Lee argues that the United States has been both "a nation of immigrants" and "a nation of xenophobia." Gary Gerstle, *American Crucible: Race and Nation in the Twentieth Century* (Princeton, NJ: Princeton University Press, 2001); Madeline Y. Hsu, *The Good Immigrants: How the Yellow Peril Became the Model Minority* (Princeton, NJ: Princeton University Press, 2015); Erika Lee, *America for Americans: A History of Xenophobia in the United States* (New York: Basic Books, 2019).

2. For more on my definition of deportation and the different mechanisms of expulsion, see the Note on Sources and Language.

3. William Walters, "Deportation, Expulsion, and the International Police of Aliens," *Citizenship Studies* 6, no. 3 (2002): 265–92; Dirk Hoerder, *Cultures in Contact: World Migrations in the Second Millennium* (Durham, NC: Duke University Press, 2002); Richard Bessel and Claudia B. Haake, eds., *Removing Peoples: Forced Removal in the Modern World* (New York: Oxford University Press, 2009); Nicholas De Genova and Nathalie Peutz, eds., *The Deportation Regime: Sovereignty, Space, and the Freedom of Movement* (Durham, NC: Duke University Press, 2010).

4. Kanstroom, *Deportation Nation*, 21–90; Kunal Parker, *Making Foreigners: Immigration and Citizenship Law in America, 1600–2000* (New York: Cambridge University Press, 2015), 22–80; Hidetaka Hirota, *Expelling the Poor: Atlantic Seaboard States and the 19th-Century Origins of American Immigration Policy* (New York: Oxford University Press, 2017), 100–128.

5. Kanstroom, *Deportation Nation*, 21–90; Parker, *Making Foreigners*, 81–115; K-Sue Park, "Self-Deportation Nation," *Harvard Law Review* 132 (2019): 1878–1941; Eric Foner, *The Fiery Trial: Abraham Lincoln and American Slavery* (New York: W. W. Norton, 2011), 17–20, 221, 259–61. On expulsion from contemporary economic, environmental, social, and political life, see Saskia Sassen, *Expulsions: Brutality and Complexity in the Global Economy* (Cambridge, MA: Harvard University Press, 2014).

6. The federal government's power to deport Chinese immigrants was established in 1882. It was not until nine years later, in 1891, that Congress granted the new immigration bureaucracy the authority to expel any immigrant that had entered the country without authorization. See Kanstroom, *Deportation Nation*, 91–130; Marian Smith, "Overview of INS History," in *A Historical Guide to the U.S. Government*, ed. George Kurian (New York: Oxford University Press, 1998); Torrie Hester, *Deportation: The Origins of US Policy* (Philadelphia: University of Pennsylvania Press, 2017). On the rise of nation-states and hardening of borders around the world in the late nineteenth and early twentieth centuries, see John Torpey, *The Invention of the Passport:*

*Surveillance, Citizenship and the State* (New York: Cambridge University Press, 2000); Adam M. McKeown, *Melancholy Order: Asian Migration and the Globalization of Borders* (New York: Columbia University Press, 2008).

7. DHS, *YOIS: 2018*, 103; Smith, "Overview of INS History."

8. The state has long used the threat of penalties and punishments—ranging from fines and imprisonment to the loss of fundamental rights and, in some cases, death—to influence people's decisions and shape their behavior. The coercive nature of the law, which hinges on the state's perceived monopoly on legitimate force and ability to implement sanctions, helps to explain why people pay taxes, drive at or around the speed limit, and refrain from committing any number of other offenses. Just as we cannot understand the law without considering its compulsory character, we cannot understand the history of deportation without grappling with voluntary departure and self-deportation, expulsion mechanisms considered to be both more palatable to the public and more feasible based on the immigration bureaucracy's limited funds. On coercion and "the creativity of a constrained central state in circumventing the formal limits of its power" throughout US history, see Gary Gerstle, *Liberty and Coercion: The Paradox of American Government from the Founding to the Present* (Princeton, NJ: Princeton University Press, 2015). On coercion and the law, see Frederick Schauer, *The Force of Law* (Cambridge, MA: Harvard University Press, 2015). On the coercive nature of plea bargains and the essential role they play in the criminal justice system and the growth of mass incarceration, see John H. Langbein, "Torture and Plea Bargaining," *University of Chicago Law Review* 46, no. 3 (1978): 3–22; Robert E. Scott and William J. Stuntz, "Plea Bargaining as Contract," *Yale Law Journal* 101, no. 8 (1992): 1909–68; Mary E. Vogel, *Coercion to Compromise: Plea Bargaining, the Courts, and the Making of Political Authority* (Oxford: Oxford University Press, 2007); Michelle Alexander, *The New Jim Crow: Mass Incarceration in the Age of Colorblindness* (New York: The New Press, 2010), 87–89; Emily Bazelon, *Charged: The New Movement to Transform American Prosecution and End Mass Incarceration* (New York: Random House, 2019), 122–46. On coercive social regulation and contemporary migration control, see Antje Ellermann, *States against Migrants: Deportation in Germany and the United States* (New York: Cambridge University Press, 2009). While Ellermann's insightful comparative study examines the legislation, implementation, and contestation of formal deportations in Germany and the United States, it ignores both voluntary departures and self-deportation campaigns.

9. An exception is S. Deborah Kang, who states that voluntary departures date back to 1918. See S. Deborah Kang, *The INS on the Line: Making Immigration Law on the US-Mexico Border, 1917–1954* (New York: Oxford University Press, 2017), 66. I discovered numerous examples of voluntary departures and a similar process referred to as "foreign reshipment" from the first years of the twentieth century. See chapter 1.

10. I document this history in the chapters that follow. This book represents the first in-depth study of voluntary departures.

11. As quoted in Leander W. Cogswell, *History of the Town of Henniker, Merrimack County, New Hampshire, from the Date of the Canada Grant by the Province of Massachusetts, in 1735, to 1880; with a Genealogical Register of the Families of Henniker* (Concord, NH: Republican Press Association, 1880), 342–43. On warning out, see Josiah Henry Benton, *Warning Out in New England* (Boston: W. B. Clarke, 1911); Gerald L. Neuman, *Strangers to the Constitution: Immigrants, Borders, and Fundamental Law* (Princeton, NJ: Princeton University Press, 1996); Kanstroom, *Deportation Nation*; Hirota, *Expelling the Poor.*

12. On political fear and its multiple forms, see Corey Robin, *Fear: The History of a Political Idea* (New York: Oxford University Press, 2004); John Hollander, "Fear Itself," *Social Research* 71, no. 4 (Winter 2004): 865–86. On fear in twentieth-century US history, see Ira Katznelson, *Fear Itself: The New Deal and the Origins of Our Time* (New York: Liveright, 2013). On the history of nativism and xenophobia, see John Higham, *Strangers in the Land: Patterns of American Nativism, 1860–1925* (New Brunswick, NJ: Rutgers University Press, 1955); Juan F. Perea, ed., *Immigrants Out! The New Nativism and the Anti-Immigrant Impulse in the United States* (New York: New York University Press, 1997); Gary Gerstle, "The Immigrant as Threat to American Security: A Historical Perspective," in *From Arrival to Incorporation: Migrants to the U.S. in a Global Era*, ed. Elliott R. Barkan, Hasia Diner, and Alan M. Kraut (New York: New York University Press, 2007), 217–45; Peter Schrag, *Not Fit for Our Society: Immigration and Nativism in America* (Berkeley: University of California Press, 2010); Lee, *America for Americans.* On racial violence against African Americans, see Ida B. Wells, *Southern Horrors: Lynch Law in All Its Phases* (New York: The New York Age Print, 1892); Ida B. Wells, *The Red Record: Tabulated Statistics and Alleged Causes of Lynching in the United States* (pamphlet, 1895), http://www.gutenberg.org/ebooks/14977; Philip Dray, *At the Hands of Persons Unknown: The Lynching of Black America* (New York: Modern Library, 2002); Kidada E. Williams, *They Left Great Marks on Me: African American Testimonies of Racial Violence from Emancipation to World War I* (New York: New York University Press, 2012). On racial violence against Mexicans, see Benjamin H. Johnson, *Revolution in Texas: How a Forgotten Rebellion and Its Bloody Suppression Turned Mexicans into Americans* (New Haven, CT: Yale University Press, 2003); William D. Carrigan and Clive Webb, *Forgotten Dead: Mob Violence against Mexicans in the United States, 1848–1928* (New York: Oxford University Press, 2013); Monica Muñoz Martinez, *The Injustice Never Leaves You: Anti-Mexican Violence in Texas* (Cambridge, MA: Harvard University Press, 2018). On racial violence against Chinese people, see Jean Pfaelzer, *Driven Out: The Forgotten War against Chinese Americans* (New York: Random House, 2007); Beth Lew-Williams, *The Chinese Must Go: Violence, Exclusion, and the Making of the Alien in America* (Cambridge, MA: Harvard University Press, 2018). On how the threat of deportation affected undocumented immigrants in the United States, see Nicholas De Genova, "Migrant 'Illegality' and Deportability in Everyday Life," *Annual Review of Anthropology* 31 (2002): 419–47.

13. A notable exception is Daniel Kanstroom, whose book *Deportation Nation* is the only major study that traces deportation throughout US history, from the days of the

founding fathers to the early twenty-first century. Although my book overlaps with Kanstroom's in terms of its broad chronological and topical coverage, it also differs in important ways. Whereas Kanstroom provides a top-down study of expulsion's ideological and legal origins, *The Deportation Machine* combines a top-down institutional history along with a bottom-up social history of deportation from the perspective of both immigration officials and immigrants. Moreover, Kanstroom pays little attention to the targeting of Mexicans and the post-1965 period. Kanstroom, *Deportation Nation*. On the history of deportation prior to federal control, see Neuman, *Strangers to the Constitution*; Hirota, *Expelling the Poor*. On deportation's legal and policy origins at the turn of the twentieth century, see Lucy Salyer, *Laws Harsh as Tigers: Chinese Immigrants and the Shaping of Modern Immigration Law* (Chapel Hill: University of North Carolina Press, 1995); Hester, *Deportation*; Deirdre Moloney, *National Insecurities: Immigrants and US Deportation Policy since 1882* (Chapel Hill: University of North Carolina Press, 2012); Dorothee Schneider, *Crossing Borders: Migration and Citizenship in the Twentieth Century United States* (Cambridge, MA: Harvard University Press, 2011), 113–49. For a multiscalar history of deportation during the 1920s, see Emily Pope-Obeda, "'When in Doubt, Deport!' U.S. Deportation and the Local Policing of Global Migration during the 1920s" (Ph.D. diss., University of Illinois at Urbana-Champaign, 2016). For an influential history of immigration restriction, deportation, and the creation of the category of the "illegal alien" from 1924–65, see Mae M. Ngai, *Impossible Subjects: Illegal Aliens and the Making of Modern America* (Princeton, NJ: Princeton University Press, 2004). On the relationship between deportability and labor exploitation in postwar America, see Cindy Hahamovitch, *No Man's Land: Jamaican Guestworkers in America and the Global History of Deportable Labor* (Princeton, NJ: Princeton University Press, 2011). A recent edited volume on the history of deportation in the Western Hemisphere is Kenyon Zimmer and Cristina Salinas, eds., *Deportation in the Americas: Histories of Exclusion and Resistance* (College Station: Texas A&M University Press, 2018). On the expulsion of Chinese during the exclusion era, see the numerous secondary sources cited in chapter 1. On the targeting of Mexicans at different points throughout the twentieth century, see the numerous secondary sources cited in chapters 2, 4, 5, and 6.

Social scientists, legal scholars, and journalists have done excellent work on contemporary expulsion, but some of it might lead us to believe that serious immigration enforcement only emerged in the mid-1980s or later. See, for example, Douglas Massey, Jorge Durand, and Nolan Malone, *Beyond Smoke and Mirrors: Mexican Immigration in an Era of Economic Integration* (New York: Russell Sage Foundation, 2003); Bill Ong Hing, *Deporting Our Souls: Values, Morality, and Immigration Policy* (New York: Cambridge University Press, 2006); Ellermann, *States against Migrants*; De Genova and Peutz, *The Deportation Regime*; David C. Brotherton and Luis Barrios, *Banished to the Homeland: Dominican Deportees and Their Stories of Exile* (New York: Columbia University Press, 2011); David C. Brotherton and Philip Kretsedemas, eds., *Immigration Policy in the Age of Punishment: Detention, Deportation, and Border Control* (New York: Columbia

University Press, 2018); Hiroshi Motomura, *Immigration Outside the Law* (New York: Oxford University Press, 2014); Todd Miller, *Border Patrol Nation: Dispatches from the Front Lines of Homeland Security* (San Francisco: City Lights, 2014); Tanya Maria Golash-Boza, *Deported: Immigrant Policing, Disposable Labor and Global Capitalism* (New York: New York University Press, 2015); Jason De León, *The Land of Open Graves: Living and Dying on the Migrant Trail* (Berkeley: University of California Press, 2015); Tom K. Wong, *Rights, Deportation, and Detention in the Age of Immigration Control* (Palo Alto, CA: Stanford University Press, 2015); Margaret Regan, *Detained and Deported: Stories of Immigrant Families Under Fire* (Boston: Beacon Press, 2015); Deborah Boehm, *Returned: Going and Coming in an Age of Deportation* (Berkeley: University of California Press, 2016); Bill Ong Hing, *American Presidents, Deportations, and Human Rights Violations: From Carter to Trump* (New York: Cambridge University Press, 2018).

14. Other groups the government has targeted include Chinese laborers, and eventually all Asians, during the exclusion era; southern and eastern European political radicals in the 1910s and 1920s; people deemed to be immoral or a threat to public health, including women working or suspected to be working as prostitutes and individuals officials considered gay or lesbian; Filipinos pressured to repatriate in the 1930s; Japanese immigrants and Japanese Americans forcibly moved to internment camps during World War II; and, more recently, Central American asylum seekers accused of being gang members and Muslims, Arabs, and Middle Easterners stereotyped as potential terrorists.

15. These statistics refer to Mexican people officials deported, not people (of any nationality) deported to Mexico. Immigration service annual reports and *YOIS*, 1892–2017. On immigration officials targeting Mexicans, see Ngai, *Impossible Subjects*, 50–75, 127–66; Kelly Lytle Hernández, *Migra! A History of the U.S. Border Patrol* (Berkeley: University of California Press, 2010); Natalia Molina, *How Race Is Made in America: Immigration, Citizenship, and the Historical Power of Racial Scripts* (Berkeley: University of California Press, 2014). On Mexican American history during the twentieth century, see George Sánchez, *Becoming Mexican American: Ethnicity, Culture, and Identity in Chicano Los Angeles, 1900–1945* (New York: Oxford University Press, 1993); David Gutiérrez, *Walls and Mirrors: Mexican Americans, Mexican Immigrants, and the Politics of Ethnicity* (Berkeley: University of California Press, 1995); Vicki L. Ruiz, *From out of the Shadows: Mexican Women in Twentieth-Century America* (New York: Oxford University Press, 2008).

16. Immigration service annual reports and *YOIS*, 1892–2017. See also chapters 2 and 4.

17. Meeting with Marian Smith, Washington, DC, Jun. 25, 2010.

18. Marian Smith, "Vast INS Archival Resources Move to National Archives," *Immigration History Newsletter* 28, no. 2 (Nov. 1996): 1, 8; US Citizenship and Immigration Services, "INS Case, Correspondence, Policy and Administrative Records Overview," accessed Jun. 6, 2018, https://www.uscis.gov/history-and-genealogy/research/topics-and-events/ins-case-correspondence-policy-and-administrative-records-overview.

## Chapter 1: Creating the Mechanisms of Expulsion at the Turn of the Twentieth Century

1. M. Nona McGlashan, *Give Me a Mountain Meadow: A Biographical Account of a Remarkable Man* (Fresno, CA: Valley Publishers, 1977), 15–57, 245; Census of 1850, cxxvi; M. Nona McGlashan and Betty H. McGlashan, eds., *From the Desk of Truckee's C. F. McGlashan* (Truckee, CA: Truckee-Donner Historical Society, 1986), x.

2. Adam McKeown makes a convincing case for why this was a period of mass global migration. He shows that while US historians have paid much attention to trans-Atlantic migration, migration within Asia far exceeded European migration. He estimates global long-distance migration totaled 149 million to 161 million between 1846 and 1940. The approximation of 100 million global migrants between 1880 and 1920 comes from figure 1, page 165 of Adam McKeown, "Global Migration, 1846–1940," *Journal of World History* 15, no. 2 (Jun. 2004): 155–89. See also David A. Gerber, *American Immigration: A Very Short Introduction* (New York: Oxford University Press, 2011), 35; Walter Nugent, *Crossings: The Great Transatlantic Migrations, 1870–1914* (Bloomington: Indiana University Press, 1992), 14–18, 150.

3. McKeown, *Melancholy Order*; Torpey, *The Invention of the Passport*. Though the transition from state to federal control over immigration marked an important shift, historians have dispelled the myth that the United States had open borders prior to the last decades of the nineteenth century. See Neuman, *Strangers to the Constitution*; Zolberg, *A Nation by Design*; Parker, *Making Foreigners*; Hirota, *Expelling the Poor*; Anna O. Law, "Lunatics, Idiots, Paupers and Negro Seamen: Immigration Federalism in the Early American State," *Studies in American Political Development* 28 (Oct. 2014): 107–28. On the use of photography in immigration enforcement, see Anna Pegler-Gordon, *In Sight of America: Photography and the Development of US Immigration Policy* (Berkeley: University of California Press, 2009). On "remote control," see Aristide R. Zolberg, "The Archeology of Remote Control," in *Migration Control in the North Atlantic World: The Evolution of State Practices in Europe and the United States from the French Revolution to the Inter-War Period*, ed. Andreas Fahrmeir, Olivier Faron, and Patrick Weil (New York: Berghahn Books, 2003), 195–222.

4. Ideas about race, class, gender, politics, religion, and physical and mental ability had long shaped notions of belonging and determined eligibility for citizenship. See, for example, Barbara Young Welke, *Law and the Borders of Belonging in the Long Nineteenth Century United States* (New York: Cambridge University Press, 2010); Parker, *Making Foreigners*.

5. Salyer, *Laws Harsh as Tigers*, 7–18; Ching Chao Wu, "Chinatowns: A Study of Symbiosis and Assimilation" (Ph.D. diss., University of Chicago, 1928), 82; Census of 1880, Table Ia & Ib, pp. 3–4. On transnational Chinese migration to the United States and throughout the Americas during this period, see Madeline Y. Hsu, *Dreaming of Gold, Dreaming of Home: Transnationalism and Migration between the United States and South China, 1882–1943* (Palo Alto, CA: Stanford University Press, 2000); Adam McKe-

own, *Chinese Migrant Networks and Cultural Change: Peru, Chicago, Hawaii, 1900–1936* (Chicago: University of Chicago Press, 2001); Elliott Young, *Alien Nation: Chinese Migration in the Americas from the Coolie Era through World War II* (Chapel Hill: University of North Carolina Press, 2014). On Chinese laborers and the construction of the transcontinental railroad, see Gordon H. Chang, *The Ghosts of Gold Mountain: The Epic Story of the Chinese Who Built the Transcontinental Railroad* (Boston: Houghton Mifflin Harcourt, 2019); Gordon H. Chang and Shelley Fisher Fishkin, eds., *The Chinese and the Iron Road: Building the Transcontinental Railroad* (Palo Alto, CA: Stanford University Press, 2019); Manu Karuka, *Empire's Tracks: Indigenous Nations, Chinese Workers, and the Transcontinental Railroad* (Oakland: University of California Press, 2019).

6. Stuart Creighton Miller, *The Unwelcome Immigrant: The American Image of the Chinese, 1785–1882* (Berkeley: University of California Press, 1969), 83–190; "Chinese Immigration to California," *New-York Daily Tribune*, Sep. 29, 1854, 4; Moon-Ho Jung, *Coolies and Cane: Race, Labor, and Sugar in the Age of Emancipation* (Baltimore: Johns Hopkins University Press, 2006). Anti-Irish and anti-Catholic sentiments also swelled in the 1850s, culminating in the formation of the nativist Know-Nothing Party, which won governorships and controlled state legislatures throughout the northeast during the second half of the decade. See, for example, Hirota, *Expelling the Poor*, 100–128.

7. Lee, *At America's Gates*, 23–46; Lew-Williams, *The Chinese Must Go*, 8–9, 17–52; Alexander Saxton, *The Indispensable Enemy: Labor and the Anti-Chinese Movement in California* (Berkeley: University of California Press, 1971), 70–75, 104–9; Salyer, *Laws Harsh as Tigers*, 8–18; Andrew Gyory, *Closing the Gate: Race, Politics, and the Chinese Exclusion Act* (Chapel Hill: University of North Carolina Press, 1998); Gunther Peck, *Reinventing Free Labor: Padrones and Immigrant Workers in the North American West, 1880–1930* (New York: Cambridge University Press, 2000).

8. Saxton, *The Indispensable Enemy*, 116–21; Lee, *At America's Gates*, 34.

9. Lee, *At America's Gates*, 40–45. Beth Lew-Williams argues that the 1882 act aimed to restrict, rather than exclude, and we should refer to the legislation as such. Lew-Williams, *The Chinese Must Go*. On class-based exemptions to restriction and ongoing Chinese migration during the exclusion era, see Paul A. Kramer, "Imperial Openings: Civilization, Exemption, and the Geopolitics of Mobility in the History of Chinese Exclusion, 1868–1910," *Journal of the Gilded Age and Progressive Era* 14 (2015): 317–47.

10. Lew-Williams, *The Chinese Must Go*, 1–2, 247–51. According to Jean Pfaelzer, some 200 communities attempted to purge their Chinese residents during the 1880s. For a list of incidents of anti-Chinese violence during the 1880s, see Pfaelzer, *Driven Out*, 252–90. Communities in the Pacific Northwest organized their own border patrols, which sometimes deported people without first consulting federal officials. See Lew-Williams, *The Chinese Must Go*, 73–79. On local anti-Chinese violence and expulsion tactics, see also Wu, "Chinatowns," 74–80.

11. Pfaelzer, *Driven Out*, 121–66; Lew-Williams, *The Chinese Must Go*, 113–16.

12. Pfaelzer, *Driven Out*, 209–15; Lew-Williams, *The Chinese Must Go*, 115–18.

13. Pfaelzer, *Driven Out*, 209–29; Lew-Williams, *The Chinese Must Go*, 91–165.

14. Men represented nine out of every ten Chinese in Truckee in the 1860s. W. F. Edwards, publisher, and Chas. D. Irons, editor and compiler, *W. F. Edwards' Tourists' Guide and Directory of the Truckee Basin* (Truckee, CA: "Republican" Job Print, 1883), 13–15, 108; Saxton, *The Indispensable Enemy*, 60–66; Michael Andrew Goldstein, "Truckee's Chinese Community: From Coexistence to Disintegration, 1870–1890" (M.A. thesis, University of California, Los Angeles, 1988), 10–16.

15. Gordon Richards, "1860s Reports Reveal Wild West Ruckus," *Sierra Sun*, Aug. 2, 2004, https://www.sierrasun.com/news/1860s-reports-reveal-wild-west-ruckus/.

16. "The Fire. Lucky Truckee. Chinatown Holocausted," *Truckee Republican* (hereafter *TR*), May 29, 1875, 3.

17. Pfaelzer, *Driven Out*, 171–74; Guy Coates, "The Trout Creek Outrage," Truckee-Donner Historical Society, accessed Nov. 16, 2018, https://www.truckeehistory.org /the-trout-creek-outrage.html.

18. Silver production continued to decline in the years ahead, plummeting to just $1 million by 1881. Goldstein, "Truckee's Chinese Community," 33–38.

19. After the deadline passed and the Chinese still had not left, Fong Lee, a well-off property-owning merchant, addressed a group of white residents that had gathered to decide what action to take. Lee described the discriminatory treatment the town's Chinese residents had endured and insisted that Chinese and white people were equals. He concluded his comments in frustration and resignation. Edwards and Irons, *W. F. Edwards' Tourists' Guide*, 118.

20. Despite the violence against them, Chinese people remained in the Truckee area because the transcontinental railroad and related industries provided ample economic opportunities. "The Chinese Must Go!," *TR*, Nov. 20, 1878; Pfaelzer, *Driven Out*, 175–77.

21. "If the Chinese Don't Go," *TR*, Nov. 21, 1885, 2; McGlashan, *Give Me a Mountain Meadow*, 142–5; Pfaelzer, *Driven Out*, 178–97.

22. "If the Chinese Don't Go," 2.

23. "The Cue Klux Klan," *TR*, Nov. 25, 1885, 2; "Cue Cutting," *TR*, Jan. 6, 1886, 3.

24. "The Chinese Must Go," *TR*, Dec. 2, 1885, 3; "Truckee vs. the Chinese," *TR*, Dec. 5, 1885, 3; "How It Was Done," *TR*, Jan. 30, 1886, 3.

25. "Boycotting," *TR*, Jan. 13, 1886, 2; "The Good Work: Minutes of Saturday's Anti-Chinese Mass Meeting," *TR*, Jan. 20, 1886, 3; "Circular Number One," *TR*, Feb. 10, 1886, 3; "Truckee vs. the Chinese," 3.

26. "The Anti-Chinese Meeting," *TR*, Dec. 9, 1885, 3; "How It Was Done," 3; "California: The Leading Question," *Sacramento Daily Record-Union*, Feb. 12, 1886, 1; Pfaelzer, *Driven Out*, 178–97. On Chinese resistance to racial violence and expulsion campaigns across the US West, see Lew-Williams, *The Chinese Must Go*, 91–112.

27. "Joy to the World, Truckee Celebrates in Torchlight and Illumination To-Night," *TR*, Feb. 13, 1886, 3; "The Illumination," *TR*, Feb. 17, 1886, 3.

28. "Anti-Chinese Convention," *Daily Alta California*, Feb. 5, 1886, 8; "Circular Number One," 3; "Vox Populi," *TR*, Feb. 20, 1886, 2; "Moving On," *TR*, Jan. 27, 1886, 2; Pfaelzer, *Driven Out*, 178–97; Lew-Williams, *The Chinese Must Go*, 223.

29. Pfaelzer, *Driven Out*, 189–91; Lew-Williams, *The Chinese Must Go*, 169–93.

30. The 1882 Chinese Exclusion Act allowed for officials to provide Chinese migrants with return certificates. In 1888, US lawmakers hoped that exclusion would limit white mob violence and anti-Chinese expulsion campaigns on the Pacific coast. Congress approved a $276,619.75 payment to the Chinese government in recognition of past wrongs, but also to placate officials outraged by the United States' unilateral action. Salyer, *Laws Harsh as Tigers*, 21–23; Lew-Williams, *The Chinese Must Go*, 169–93.

31. *Chae Chan Ping v. United States*, 130 U.S. 581 (1889); Hiroshi Motomura, *Americans in Waiting: The Lost Story of Immigration and Citizenship in the United States* (New York: Oxford University Press, 2006), 26–36; Salyer, *Laws Harsh as Tigers*, 21–23; Lew-Williams, *The Chinese Must Go*, 169–93. On plenary power's roots in federal Indian law, see Parker, *Making Foreigners*, 119, 131–35; Maggie Blackhawk, "Federal Indian Law as Paradigm within Public Law," *Harvard Law Review* 132, no. 7 (May 2019): 1787–1877.

32. Higham, *Strangers in the Land*, 35–105; Salyer, *Laws Harsh as Tigers*, 23–26, 159–60; Kanstroom, *Deportation Nation*, 97–115. In the first years of the twentieth century, Grinnell College professor Edward Steiner, himself an immigrant from what was then the Austro-Hungarian Empire, asserted: "Let no one believe that landing on the shores of 'The land of the free, and the home of the brave' is a pleasant experience; it is a hard, harsh fact, surrounded by the grinding machinery of the law, which sifts, picks, and chooses; admitting the fit and excluding the weak and helpless." Edward A. Steiner, *On the Trail of the Immigrant* (New York: Fleming H. Revell, 1906), 72. Thanks to Lucy Salyer for bringing this quote to my attention. On the Castle Garden immigration station, see Brendan P. O'Malley, "Protecting the Stranger: The Origins of US Immigration Regulation in Nineteenth-Century New York" (Ph.D. diss., City University of New York, 2015).

33. Immigration Act of 1891, 26 Stat. 1084; Salyer, *Laws Harsh as Tigers*, 26; Kanstroom, *Deportation Nation*, 94, 115.

34. Hidetaka Hirota, "The Moment of Transition: State Officials, the Federal Government, and the Formation of American Immigration Policy," *Journal of American History* 99, no. 4 (Mar. 2013): 1092–1108.

35. Ironically, Chinese laborers could still turn to the courts for relief after 1891 since the Chinese exclusion laws, rather than general immigration laws, continued to dictate their status and rights. Congress finally merged the two systems in 1903. Salyer, *Laws Harsh as Tigers*, 26–32; *Nishimura Ekiu v. United States*, 142 U.S. 651, 660 (1892).

36. Geary Act of May 5, 1892, 27 Stat. 25; Salyer, *Laws Harsh as Tigers*, 45–64; Motomura, *Americans in Waiting*, 34.

37. Quoted in Julian Lim, *Porous Borders: Multiracial Migrations and the Law in the U.S.-Mexico Borderlands* (Chapel Hill: University of North Carolina Press, 2017), 109. On how Chinese migrants strategically used deportation for their own ends, see Lim, *Porous Borders*, 109–12; Hester, *Deportation*, 51–54.

38. Justice Stephen Field joined Brewer in dissent, writing that deportation represented a "cruel and unusual" punishment "beyond all reason in its severity." *Fong Yue Ting v. United States*, 149 U.S. 698 (1893); Salyer, *Laws Harsh as Tigers*, 46–58; Motomura, *Americans in Waiting*, 34–36; Kanstroom, *Deportation Nation*, 116–19; Hester, *Deportation*, 7–23.

39. Salyer, *Laws Harsh as Tigers*, 55; Kanstroom, *Deportation Nation*, 120; Mary Roberts Coolidge, *Chinese Immigration* (New York: Henry Holt, 1909), 219n21; Saxton, *Indispensable Enemy*, 229.

40. Some immigration authorities tried to make the case for restriction by describing it as an American tradition that dated back to the Plymouth and Massachusetts Bay colonies. Although officials rejected and removed just a small percentage of the millions of people who arrived at the nation's sea and land borders from the 1890s to the 1920s, the threat of exclusion and expulsion was real. W. W. Husband, "Immigration Restriction," address to the Fifth Congress of the National Federation of Religious Liberals, Philadelphia, Feb. 23, 1915, Folder 1891–1920, Box 1, W. W. Husband Papers, CHM; Schneider, *Crossing Borders*, 114–16. On the growth of the federal bureaucracy at the turn of the twentieth century, see Daniel P. Carpenter, *The Forging of Bureaucratic Autonomy: Reputations, Networks, and Policy Innovation in Executive Agencies, 1862–1928* (Princeton, NJ: Princeton University Press, 2001). On the history of Ellis Island, see Vincent J. Cannato, *American Passage: The History of Ellis Island* (New York: HarperCollins, 2009). On the history of Angel Island, see Erika Lee and Judy Yung, *Angel Island: Immigrant Gateway to America* (New York: Oxford University Press, 2010). On the rise of restriction and nativism from the 1880s to the 1920s, see Higham, *Strangers in the Land*; Alan M. Kraut, *The Huddled Masses: The Immigrant in American Society, 1880–1921* (Arlington Heights, IL: Harlan Davidson, 1982), 147–78; Roger Daniels, *Guarding the Golden Door: American Immigration Policy and Immigrants since 1882* (New York: Hill and Wang, 2004), 3–58. On the history of xenophobia more broadly, see Schrag, *Not Fit for Our Society*; Lee, *America for Americans*.

41. Higham, *Strangers in the Land*, 68–105; Kitty Calavita, *U.S. Immigration Law and the Control of Labor: 1820–1924* (New York: Academic Press, 1984); Salyer, *Laws Harsh as Tigers*, 122; Moloney, *National Insecurities*, 28–50, 79–104; US Citizenship and Immigration Services (hereafter USCIS), "Commissioners and Directors," USCIS History Office and Library (hereafter USCISHOL), accessed Dec. 22, 2018, https://www.uscis.gov/history-and-genealogy/our-history/commissioners-and-directors. Terence V. Powderly led the Knights of Labor before acting as commissioner general from 1897 to 1902. Frank P. Sargent, commissioner general from 1902 to 1908, was the former president of the Brotherhood of Locomotive Firemen. And Daniel J. Keefe was

president of the National Longshoreman's Association and a member of the American Federation of Labor's executive committee before serving as commissioner general from 1909 to 1913. On local and national immigration officials during the late nineteenth and early twentieth centuries, see Lee, *At America's Gates*, 47–74.

42. Daniel Tichenor, *Dividing Lines: The Politics of Immigration Control in America* (Princeton, NJ: Princeton University Press), 75–85, 115–28; Matthew Frye Jacobson, *Barbarian Virtues: The United States Encounters Foreign Peoples at Home and Abroad, 1876–1917* (New York: Hill and Wang, 2000), 139–72; "Facts concerning the Immigration Restriction League," 1910, The Immigration Restriction League Papers, Immigration Collection of Prescott Farnsworth Hall, Widener Library, Harvard University, Cambridge, MA, https://id.lib.harvard.edu/curiosity/immigration-to-the-united-states-1789-1930/39-990100070950203941. On immigration, disability, and eugenics, see Douglas C. Baynton, *Defectives in the Land: Disability and Immigration in the Age of Eugenics* (Chicago: University of Chicago Press, 2016). On immigrants as public health threats, see Alan M. Kraut, *Silent Travelers: Germs, Genes, and the "Immigrant Menace"* (New York: Basic Books, 1994); Nayan Shah, *Contagious Divides: Epidemics and Race in San Francisco's Chinatown* (Berkeley: University of California Press, 2001); Emily K. Abel, "From Exclusion to Expulsion: Mexicans and Tuberculosis in Los Angeles, 1914–1940," *Bulletin of the History of Medicine* 77, no. 4 (Winter 2003): 823–49; Alexandra Minna Stern, *Eugenic Nation: Faults and Frontiers of Better Breeding in Modern America* (Berkeley: University of California Press, 2005); Natalia Molina, *Fit to Be Citizens? Public Health and Race in Los Angeles, 1879–1939* (Berkeley: University of California Press, 2006); Moloney, *National Insecurities*, 105–33. On the United States as a leader among liberal democracies in creating racist immigration policies, see David Scott FitzGerald and David Cook-Martín, *Culling the Masses: The Democratic Origins of Racist Immigration Policy in the Americas* (Cambridge, MA: Harvard University Press, 2014). On the Dillingham Commission, see Katherine Benton-Cohen, *Inventing the Immigration Problem: The Dillingham Commission and Its Legacy* (Cambridge, MA: Harvard University Press, 2018). Some of the commission's members had close ties to nativist organizations and at least one, Massachusetts Republican senator Henry Cabot Lodge, was himself an IRL member. For more on the connections between nativism and racism during this period, see Higham, *Strangers in the Land*, 131–93, 264–330; Gerstle, *American Crucible*, 1–122.

43. On "perversion" and immigration officials' attempts to regulate homosexuality throughout the twentieth century, see Margot Canaday, *The Straight State: Sexuality and Citizenship in Twentieth-Century America* (Princeton, NJ: Princeton University Press, 2009), 11, 19–54, 214–54; Eithne Luibhéid, *Entry Denied: Controlling Sexuality at the Border* (Minneapolis: University of Minnesota Press, 2002).

44. In 1907, legislators passed a law ordering the expulsion of women determined to be prostitutes within three years of having entered the country. The 1910 law removed this time limit. Canaday, *The Straight State*, 19–54; Martha Gardner, *The Qualities of a*

*Citizen: Women, Immigration, and Citizenship, 1870–1965* (Princeton, NJ: Princeton University Press, 2005), 13–117; Moloney, *National Insecurities*, 28–78; Hester, *Deportation*, 82–111; The Mann Act, June 25, 1910, 36 Stat. 825. On different racial and national groups' supposed proclivity to crime, see Khalil Gibran Muhammad, *The Condemnation of Blackness: Race, Crime, and the Making of Modern Urban America* (Cambridge, MA: Harvard University Press, 2010). Daniel Kanstroom makes the useful distinction between "extended border control" and "post-entry social control." E. P. Hutchinson and Lucy Salyer draw a similar distinction. Kanstroom, *Deportation Nation*, 5–6, 125–26, 133–36; E. P. Hutchinson, *Legislative History of American Immigration Policy, 1798–1965* (Philadelphia: University of Pennsylvania Press, 1981), 457–58; Salyer, *Laws Harsh as Tigers*, 131–32.

45. The statute of limitations on deportation for most offenses gradually increased from one year in 1891, to two years in 1903, to three years in 1907, and five years in 1917. By 1917, in addition to anarchists and people convicted of "a crime of moral turpitude," the list of deportable categories included people likely to become public charges, prostitutes and procurers, "imbeciles" and the "insane," individuals with "loathsome or dangerous contagious diseases," and migrants who entered the country without inspection, among others. Immigration Act of February 5, 1917, 39 Stat. 874; Higham, *Strangers in the Land*, 194–263; Salyer, *Laws Harsh as Tigers*, 131–35; Kanstroom, *Deportation Nation*, 132–46; Ngai, *Impossible Subjects*, 59; Parker, *Making Foreigners*, 168–69; Christopher Capozzola, *Uncle Sam Wants You: World War I and the Making of the Modern American Citizen* (New York: Oxford University Press, 2008), 117–43. On the targeting of radicals and anarchists, see William Preston Jr., *Aliens and Dissenters: Federal Suppression of Radicals, 1903–1933* (Cambridge, MA: Harvard University Press, 1963); Kenyon Zimmer, *Immigrants against the State: Yiddish and Italian Anarchism in America* (Urbana: University of Illinois Press, 2015); Julia Rose Kraut, *Threat of Dissent: A History of Ideological Exclusion and Deportation in the United States* (Cambridge, MA: Harvard University Press, July 2020).

46. The secretary of treasury had the final say on deportation decisions until 1903, when control of the Bureau of Immigration shifted to the Department of Commerce and Labor. (In 1913, the department split in two and the Department of Labor retained control over a combined Bureau of Immigration and Naturalization. Twenty years later, the bureau became the Immigration and Naturalization Service [hereafter INS].) Also, a separate deportation procedure existed for Chinese immigrants authorities charged under the exclusion act. These individuals benefited from judicial review and basic procedural protections unavailable to other groups. Chinese immigrants' success in using the federal courts to beat their exclusion and deportation cases eventually led authorities to increasingly arrest them under general immigration law. But officials continued to use the Chinese exclusion laws to deport some people until Congress finally repealed them in 1943. William C. Van Vleck, *The Administrative Control of Aliens: A Study in Administrative Law and Procedure* (New York: The Commonwealth Fund, 1932), 83–148,

219–37; Salyer, *Laws Harsh as Tigers*, 136–56; Kanstroom, *Deportation Nation*, 152–54; Schneider, *Crossing Borders*, 116–19; Hester, *Deportation*, 16–34; George T. Kurian, ed., *A Historical Guide to the U.S. Government* (New York: Oxford University Press, 1998), 305–8; Report of the Commissioner General of Immigration, 1924, Table XVI-A, 129; Annual Report of the INS (hereafter AR), 1942, Table 10, USCISHOL.

47. Van Vleck, *The Administrative Control of Aliens*, 227–28; Salyer, *Laws Harsh as Tigers*, 140–52. Members of the boards of special inquiry regularly abused their power and rendered arbitrary decisions. In 1911, the Dillingham Commission estimated that the secretary of commerce and labor overturned close to half of the board of special inquiry decisions sent to him on appeal. Salyer, *Laws Harsh as Tigers*, 156, 288 fn76. On discretion in immigration enforcement, past and present, see Motomura, *Immigration Outside the Law*, 113–44; Kang, *The INS on the Line*; Hidetaka Hirota, "Exclusion on the Ground: Racism, Official Discretion, and the Quotidian Enforcement of General Immigration Law in the Pacific Northwest Borderland," *American Quarterly* 69, no. 2 (Jun. 2017): 347–70.

48. This description specifically referred to officials at Ellis Island after 1909. Max J. Kohler, *Immigration and Aliens in the United States* (New York: Bloch, 1936), 169. Also quoted in Salyer, *Laws Harsh as Tigers*, 154.

49. "Would Not Set Woman Free," *New York Times* (hereafter *NYT*), Dec. 4, 1898, 13.

50. Legal scholar William Van Vleck drew this conclusion in 1932: "we have devised a system of administrative procedure, of executive justice, with a maximum of powers in the administrative officers, a minimum of checks and safeguards against error and prejudice, and with certainty, care, and due deliberation sacrificed to the desire for speed." Van Vleck, *The Administrative Control of Aliens*, 224.

51. Louis F. Post, *The Deportation Deliriums of Nineteen-Twenty: A Personal Narrative of an Historic Official Experience* (Chicago: Charles H. Kerr, 1923), 34, 185–91, 203–22; Salyer, *Laws Harsh as Tigers*, 218–44; Hester, *Deportation*, 130–32; Matthew Guariglia, "Wrench in the Deportation Machine: Louis F. Post's Objection to Mechanized Red Scare Bureaucracy," *Journal of American Ethnic History* 38, no. 1 (Fall 2018): 62–77.

52. R. J. McLauchlin, "Violent Reds Turned Loose Here by Decisions of Post," quoted in Guariglia, "Wrench in the Deportation Machine," 63.

53. Formal deportations under general immigration law and Chinese exclusion laws totaled 487 per year between 1892 and 1907. This figure increased to 2,951 per year from 1908 to 1920, and 4,756 per year between 1921 and 1924. AR 1924, 129; Ngai, *Impossible Subjects*, 59. Between fiscal years 1909 and 1921, Congress's appropriation for the enforcement of immigration laws increased from $200,000 "or so much thereof that may be necessary" to $2.6 million. Sixtieth Congress, Session I, Chapter 200, 329; Sixty-Sixth Congress, Session II, Chapter 235, 935–37.

54. Salyer, *Laws Harsh as Tigers*, 136–38; Schneider, *Crossing Borders*, 123–28.

55. Hester, *Deportation*, 35–60, 112–40; Schneider, *Crossing Borders*, 117–19; "Deportation: Hearings before the Committee on Immigration and Naturalization, House of

Representatives," Sixty-Ninth Congress, Session I, 19–20. On the SS *Buford* and the deportations of Emma Goldman and Alexander Berkman, see also Alexander Berkman and Emma Goldman, "Deportation: Its Meaning and Menace" (Ellis Island, 1919), https://catalog.hathitrust.org/Record/002917032; Post, *The Deportation Deliriums of Nineteen-Twenty*, 1–35; Patrick Weil, *The Sovereign Citizen: Denaturalization and the Origins of the American Republic* (Philadelphia: University of Pennsylvania Press, 2013), 55–64; Hester, *Deportation*, 113–24; Kenyon Zimmer, "The Voyage of the *Buford*: Political Deportations and the Making and Unmaking of America's First Red Scare," in *Deportation in the Americas: Histories of Exclusion and Resistance*, ed. Kenyon Zimmer and Cristina Salinas (College Station: Texas A&M University Press, 2018), 132–63. On immigration and deportation as matters of foreign relations and global politics, see Donna R. Gabaccia, *Foreign Relations: American Immigration in Global Perspective* (Princeton, NJ: Princeton University Press, 2012); Hester, *Deportation*; Emily Pope-Obeda, "National Expulsions in a Transnational World: The Global Dimensions of American Deportation Practice, 1920–1935," in *Deportation in the Americas*, ed. Zimmer and Salinas, 18–49; Paul A. Kramer, "The Geopolitics of Mobility: Immigration Policy and American Global Power in the Long Twentieth Century," *American Historical Review* 123, no. 2 (Apr. 2018): 393–438; Jane H. Hong, *Opening the Gates to Asia: A Transpacific History of How America Repealed Asian Exclusion* (Chapel Hill: University of North Carolina Press, 2019).

56. On immigration law and policy and the policing of Asians and Europeans during the late nineteenth and early twentieth centuries, see, among many others, Salyer, *Laws Harsh as Tigers*; Lee, *At America's Gates*; Kanstroom, *Deportation Nation*; Moloney, *National Insecurities*; Hester, *Deportation*.

57. AR 1907, 144; AR 1916, 227. Streamlined, discretionary expulsions were not unprecedented. In 1859, prior to federal control over immigration, Massachusetts legislators gave "Alien Commissioners" the power "to deport foreign inmates in state charitable institutions . . . *without* putting them on trial first." Hirota, *Expelling the Poor*, 126–29.

58. AR 1907, 144. For examples of early voluntary departures of immigrants from China, Japan, Italy, Russia, Poland, France, Newfoundland, and the Ukraine, see 53108/71-L, 54646/190, 54646/290, 54646/350, 54860/22, 55225/303, 55483/424, 55612/367, 55715/822, and 55759/882, INS, NARA1.

59. As early as 1923, immigration officials also developed a mechanism to deport people across the Atlantic and Pacific Oceans on the cheap. They used "foreign reshipment" in lieu of deportation (also known as "reshipment foreign," "one-way shipping," or simply "reshipment") primarily to expel seamen. Though reshipment foreign and voluntary departures both served as economical ways to expel immigrants, they also differed in an important sense. As Jane Perry Clark explained in 1931, "Aliens who leave the United States by 'reshipment foreign' are technically considered deported and are in no better position as regards return to this country than other deportees,

unless they have been allowed to 'reship foreign' as voluntary departure before the issuances of warrants of arrest. . . . The advantage of 'reshipment foreign' to the alien lies in being paid the wages of a member of the crew during the trip; the advantage to the United States consists in considerable financial saving. Assuming the cost of deportation to Europe to be $100 per deportee, the savings during 1930 to the appropriation were $55,500." Jane Perry Clark, *Deportation of Aliens from the United States to Europe* (New York: Columbia University Press, 1931), 406n2. For examples of cases of foreign reshipment, see 53244/1D; 54933/351E; 54933/351G; 54933/351H; 55231/127; 55608/134, Entry 9, Record Group 85 (hereafter RG 85), INS, NARA1. See also annual reports of the commissioner general of immigration (CGI) from the mid- to late 1920s.

60. Harris indicated that, at the time, the Bureau of Immigration criticized his decision. George J. Harris, Acting Supervising Inspector, El Paso, Texas, to Commissioner General of Immigration, Washington, DC, Aug. 10, 1921, 53244/1C, INS, RG 85, NARA1. Although this case did not technically involve voluntary departure, in 1903 two immigration inspectors apprehended and "summarily hurried out of the United States" a group of eight Mexicans who had been living and working in Texas for a few months without a deportation warrant. See Files 33698 and 33452, Box 134, Entry 7, RG 85, INS, NARA1.

61. Juan Mora-Torres, "'Los de casa se van, los de afuera no vienen': The First Mexican Immigrants, 1848–1900," in *Beyond la Frontera: The History of Mexico-U.S. Migration*, ed. Mark Overmyer-Velázquez (New York: Oxford University Press, 2011), 3–27; Susan Lee Johnson, *Roaring Camp: The Social World of the California Gold Rush* (New York: W. W. Norton, 2000). On the relationship between Mexico and its diaspora in the United States and the expulsion of Mexican Americans during the nineteenth century, see José Angel Hernández, *Mexican American Colonization during the Nineteenth Century: A History of the U.S.-Mexico Borderlands* (New York: Cambridge University Press, 2012).

62. AR 1921, 104–5. As part of the Gentlemen's Agreement of 1907, US officials agreed to end the segregation of Japanese students in schools and the Japanese government agreed to restrict labor migration to the United States. Tichenor, *Dividing Lines*, 127.

63. AR 1921, 104–5; Mark Reisler, *By the Sweat of Their Brow: Mexican Immigrant Labor in the United States, 1900–1940* (Westport, CT: Greenwood Press, 1976); Lawrence A. Cardoso, *Mexican Emigration to the United States, 1897–1931: Socio-Economic Patterns* (Tucson: University of Arizona Press, 1980); Sánchez, *Becoming Mexican American*; Neil Foley, *The White Scourge: Mexicans, Blacks, and Poor Whites in Texas Cotton Culture* (Berkeley: University of California Press, 1999). On the United States' demand for Mexican labor and active recruitment of immigrant workers throughout the twentieth century, see Gutiérrez, *Walls and Mirrors*.

64. Section 36 of the Immigration Act of 1907 explicitly included such a provision: "That all aliens who shall enter the United States except at the seaports thereof, or at such place or places as the Secretary of Commerce and Labor may from time to time designate, shall be adjudged to have entered the country unlawfully and shall be deported

as provided by sections twenty and twenty-one of this Act: Provided, That nothing contained in this section shall affect the power conferred by section thirty-two of this Act upon the Commissioner-General of Immigration to prescribe rules for the entry and inspection of aliens along the borders of Canada and Mexico." The exception mentioned in section 32 reflected the intent behind the law: to crack down on Europeans and Asians entering the United States via Canada and Mexico, while not disturbing "ordinary travel" in border communities for personal and business reasons. It is unclear how the commissioner general of immigration implemented the law on the ground. Hutchinson, *Legislative History of American Immigration Policy*, 127–33, 459–60; Immigration Act of 1907, 34 Stat. 898; AR 1904, 89, 148.

65. The supervising inspector of the border region made a similar report in 1917: "The practice of permitting voluntary return to Mexico of those aliens whose sole offense has been the technical one of entry without inspection has been continued, with substantial financial and other advantages. Of course care is exercised to the end that those aliens of the immoral classes for whose return following formal deportation on such ground the statute provides criminal prosecution shall not be accorded this privilege." AR 1915, 264–65; AR 1916, 227; AR 1917, 227.

66. Some 200 Mexican women and a few men protested the quarantine the week it went into effect, temporarily shutting down traffic across the Santa Fe international bridge in what became known as the "bath riots." Alexandra Minna Stern, "Buildings, Boundaries, and Blood: Medicalization and Nation-Building on the US-Mexico Border, 1910–1930," *Hispanic American Historical Review* 79, no. 1 (Feb. 1999): 41–81; John McKiernan-González, *Fevered Measures: Public Health and Race at the Texas-Mexico Border, 1848–1942* (Austin: University of Texas Press, 2012), 165–97.

67. Reisler, *By the Sweat of Their Brow*, 3–76; Cardoso, *Mexican Emigration to the United States, 1897–1931*, 18–95; Sánchez, *Becoming Mexican American*, 15–62; Kang, *The INS on the Line*, 11–35.

68. AR 1919, 403; Kang, *The INS on the Line*, 11–35.

69. In addition to providing the US government with "enormous saving" (at least $60,000 during fiscal year 1919, the equivalent of some $900,000 today), authorities stated that voluntary departures allowed them "to devote their attention to more important official duties." AR 1917, 227; AR 1918, 317; AR 1919, 402–3; Kang, *The INS on the Line*, 11–35.

70. Harris to Commissioner General of Immigration, Washington, DC, Aug. 10, 1921, 53244/1C, Entry 9, RG 85, INS, NARA1; John Martínez, "Mexican Emigration to the U.S. 1910–1930" (M.A. thesis, University of California, Berkeley, 1957), 52–57.

71. Inspector in Charge, Douglas, Ariz., to Supervisor, Immigration Service, El Paso, Texas, Oct. 3, 1923, 54951/General, Entry 9, RG 85, INS, NARA1. Officials in Nogales reported a similar policy. "In the vast majority of cases such aliens [held in jails] are accorded the privilege of voluntarily returning to Mexico in lieu of being made the subject of warrant proceedings if they are subject to deportation." Inspector in Charge,

Nogales, Ariz., to Supervisor, Immigration Service, El Paso, Texas, Oct. 3, 1923, Entry 9, RG 85, INS, NARA1.

72. Borderland historians have documented officials' increased policing of Mexican migrants during the 1910s, in large part because of the Mexican Revolution. See, for example, Minna Stern, "Buildings, Boundaries, and Blood," 41–81; Patrick Ettinger, *Imaginary Lines: Border Enforcement and the Origins of Undocumented Immigration, 1882–1930* (Austin: University of Texas Press, 2009), 123–44; Lim, *Porous Borders*, 124–57. On the Johnson-Reed Act of 1924 (named for its sponsors, Republican representative Albert Johnson of Washington and Republican senator David Reed of Pennsylvania), the making of "illegal aliens," and the shift toward policing and deporting undocumented Mexican migrants, see Ngai, *Impossible Subjects*, 56–90. On the history of the Border Patrol, see Lytle Hernández, *Migra!*

73. Scholars had not reported voluntary departure statistics prior to 1927, the year the federal immigration bureaucracy in Washington, DC, began recording them. I managed to piece together the figures from 1918–21 after painstakingly digging through the annual reports and files of the immigration inspector in charge of the US–Mexico border region. CGI, AR 1918, 152–55; CGI, AR 1919, 184–87; CGI, AR 1920, 200–203; CGI, AR 1921, 120–23; Harris to Commissioner General of Immigration, Aug. 10, 1921, 53244/1C, Entry 9, RG 85, INS, NARA1.

74. On the policing of Asian and European migrants in the US–Canada and US–Mexico borderlands, see Lee, *At America's Gates*, 147–220; Ettinger, *Imaginary Lines*; Kornel Chang, *Pacific Connections: The Making of the U.S.-Canadian Borderlands* (Berkeley: University of California Press, 2012), 147–78; Ashley Johnson Bavery, "Crashing America's Back Gate: Illegal Europeans, Policing, and Welfare in Detroit, 1921–1939," *Journal of Urban History* 44, no. 2 (2018): 239–61; Hirota, "Exclusion on the Ground," 347–70.

75. Post, *The Deportation Deliriums of Nineteen-Twenty*, 51–147; Preston, *Aliens and Dissenters*, 208–37; Paul C. P. Siu, *The Chinese Laundryman: A Study of Social Isolation*, ed. John Kuo Wei Tchen (New York: New York University Press, 1987), 198–99; Lee, *At America's Gates*, 237–40; Hester, *Deportation*, 42–43.

76. In July 1917, for example, local law enforcement officers and 2,000-plus deputized citizens went through the town of Bisbee, Arizona, rounding up copper miners suspected of participating in a strike organized by the Industrial Workers of the World (IWW). Acting at the behest of the Phelps Dodge Corporation, the largest mining company in town, the mob loaded a multiracial, multiethnic group of 1,186 miners into train boxcars and left them in the middle of the New Mexico desert. The Bisbee Deportation quickly became front-page news across the nation and drew the attention of the president, but it was hardly the only vigilante expulsion campaign of its time. In fact, during the first two decades of the twentieth century, local deportations were "a relatively conventional and well-practiced method of getting rid of undesirables." The following is an incomplete list of local, vigilante expulsions in the early twentieth century, both before and after the Bisbee Deportation. 1904: The "Mine Owners'

Association and the local Citizens Alliance" in Cripple Creek, Colorado, drove out members of the Western Federation of Miners; more than one hundred men deported from Telluride, Colorado. 1913: On June 25, IWW members deported from Marshfield, Oregon; on December 26, a union president was deported from Hancock, Michigan. 1917: On July 10, more than 200 armed men in Jerome, Arizona, identified and deported 104 members of the IWW; the Bisbee Deportation of July 12; mobs near lead mines around Flat River, Missouri, drove out hundreds of Italian, Russian, Polish, and other immigrant workers; similar vigilante removals reported in Bemidji, Minnesota; Gallup, New Mexico; and Fairbury, Nebraska. 1919: Vigilantes in Pomona Valley, California, drove out a group of orange grove workers, citing Bisbee as inspiration. James W. Byrkit, *Forging the Copper Collar: Arizona's Labor-Management War of 1901–1921* (Tucson: University of Arizona Press, 1982), 144–214; Katherine Benton-Cohen, *Borderline Americans: Racial Division and Labor War in the Arizona Borderlands* (Cambridge, MA: Harvard University Press, 2009); Kanstroom, *Deportation Nation*, 141–45.

77. AR 1925, 19.

78. Two months later, the assistant secretary of labor issued a memorandum allowing voluntary departure, at individuals' own expense, to "all aliens now in the United States who entered surreptitiously from contiguous foreign territory and for whom warrants of deportation have been issued . . . and are to be deported solely because of unlawful entry from contiguous foreign territory." However, the order, which gave eligible individuals thirty days to accept voluntary departure, did not apply to people who had entered the country after October 1, 1921. Harris to Commissioner General, Aug. 10, 1921, 53244/1C, Entry 9, RG 85, INS, NARA1; E. J. Henning, Assistant Secretary of Labor, Memorandum for the Commissioner General, Oct. 19, 1921, 55063/548, Entry 9, RG 85, INS, NARA1.

79. John P. Johnson, Commissioner of Immigration, Boston, to W. W. Husband, Commissioner General of Immigration, Washington, DC, Feb. 7, 1925, 54933/351D, Entry 9, RG 85, INS, NARA1.

80. Johnson to Husband, Feb. 7, 1925; Husband to Johnson, Feb. 25, 1925, 54933/351D, Entry 9, RG 85, INS, NARA1. On the ad hoc nature of voluntary departure in 1925 and 1926, see various memos in 53244/1E, 54933/351D, 54933/351F, Entry 9, RG 85, INS, NARA1. The official, central office policy remained in flux until 1940, when the federal immigration bureaucracy received the statutory authority to expel people via voluntary departure. See chapter 2.

81. Johnson to Husband, Feb. 7, 1925, 54933/351D, Entry 9, RG 85, INS, NARA1.

## Chapter 2: Coerced Removal from the Great Depression through Operation Wetback

1. "Wilmoth, Grover Cleveland," Department of Justice, Official Personnel Folders, National Archives and Records Administration, St. Louis, MO; "Grover C. Wilmoth

Dies Suddenly," *El Paso Herald-Post*, Feb. 1, 1951, 1, 19. For more on Wilmoth, see Lytle Hernández, *Migra!*, 65–67; Kang, *The INS on the Line,* especially pp. 114–38. Debbie Kang shows how agents like Wilmoth not only enforced immigration law, but also shaped it during the first half of the twentieth century. Wilmoth helped the United States negotiate multiple bracero temporary guestworker agreements with Mexico during the latter part of his career. In January 1951, he was part of a twelve-man US delegation in Mexico City for bilateral discussion when he died of a heart attack at age sixty-six. I would like to thank Kang for pointing me to Wilmoth's civilian personnel record at the National Archives in St. Louis.

2. George J. Harris to Inspector in Charge, Immigration Service, Jan. 6, 1926; Grover C. Wilmoth to US Immigration Service, Mar. 16, 1927, both found in 55494/25, Entry 9, RG 85, INS, NARA1.

3. Statistics from the annual reports of the Bureau of Immigration (1924–33) and INS (1934–64), compiled and calculated by author.

4. Statistics from the annual reports of the Bureau of Immigration (1924–33) and INS (1934–64), compiled and calculated by author.

5. For a parallel argument about how state actors strategically used the drug war for their own ends, rather than to stop the trade in illicit narcotics, see Kathleen J. Frydl, *The Drug Wars in America, 1940–1973* (New York: Cambridge University Press, 2013).

6. Act of May 26, 1924, 43 Stat. 153; Act of March 4, 1929, 45 Stat. 1551; Ngai, *Impossible Subjects*, 59–60; Kelly Lytle Hernández, *City of Inmates: Conquest, Rebellion, and the Rise of Human Caging in Los Angeles, 1771–1965* (Chapel Hill: University of North Carolina Press, 2017), 131–57.

7. Grover C. Wilmoth to Inspector in Charge, US Immigration Service, Presidio, Texas, Mar. 30, 1929; Wilmoth to Commissioner General of Immigration, Mar. 28, 1931, both found in 55639/731, Entry 9, RG 85, INS, NARA1.

8. Under the 1929 act, officials considered anyone facing expulsion who left the country on his or her own (i.e., via voluntary departure or self-deportation) to have been deported. Wilmoth to Commissioner General, Mar. 28, 1931, 55639/731, Entry 9, RG 85, INS, NARA1; Act of March 4, 1929, 45 Stat. 1551. On formal deportations as a matter of international law, see chapter 1.

9. Robert N. McLean, "Goodbye, Vicente!," *The Survey*, May 1, 1931, 183; Robert N. McLean, "Tightening the Mexican Border," *The Survey*, Apr. 1, 1930, 29, 54; "Mexican Exodus Held Groundless by Quota Backer," *San Antonio Light*, Jul. 2, 1929, 1; "Aliens Seeking to Be Deported Swamp Immigration Men," *San Antonio Express*, Oct. 22, 1930, 1.

10. "United States Should Clean House," *San Antonio Light*, Aug. 2, 1930, 6. On Hearst newspapers' editorial line on immigration during the Great Depression, see Melita M. Garza, *They Came to Toil: Newspaper Representations of Mexicans and Immigrants in the Great Depression* (Austin: University of Texas Press, 2018). On Mexicans as supposed threats to public health, see Minna Stern, "Buildings, Boundaries, and Blood," 41–81; Molina, *Fit to Be Citizens?*; McKiernan-González, *Fevered Measures*.

11. J. C. Brodie to Mr. Ashurst (Senator, Arizona), n.d.; J. C. Brodie to Mr. Wright, Immigration Inspector, Tucson, Ariz., Mar. 18, 1934; G. C. Wilmoth to Commissioner of INS, Dec. 22, 1933; G. C. Wilmoth to Commissioner of INS, Apr. 24, 1934, all found in 55739/674A, Entry 9, RG 85, INS, NARA1. For more letters expressing broad anti-immigrant sentiment and public support of federal deportation efforts, see Cybelle Fox, *Three Worlds of Relief: Race, Immigration, and the American Welfare State from the Progressive Era to the New Deal* (Princeton, NJ: Princeton University Press, 2012), 126–27. On the resurgence of the Ku Klux Klan in the 1920s, see Linda Gordon, *The Second Coming of the KKK: The Ku Klux Klan of the 1920s and the American Political Tradition* (New York: Liveright, 2017).

12. "Says 400,000 Aliens Are Here Illegally," *NYT*, Jan. 6, 1931, 5; "1,100 Deported Here since Mid-January," *NYT*, Apr. 11, 1931, 14; Robert S. Allen, "One of Mr. Hoover's Friends," *The American Mercury*, Jan. 1932, 58–59; "Attacks Raids on Aliens as Illegal," *NYT*, Feb. 18, 1931, 6; "Wagner Protests Alien Raid Methods," *NYT*, Feb. 24, 1931, 14; W. N. Doak, "United States Gradually Closing Gates against Immigration," *San Antonio Light*, Jun. 21, 1931, 31. For critiques of deportation policies at the time, see US National Commission on Law Observance and Enforcement, *Report on the Enforcement of the Deportation Laws of the United States* (Washington, DC: Government Printing Office, 1931) (commonly referred to as the Wickersham Report); Perry Clark, *Deportation of Aliens from the United States to Europe*; Van Vleck, *The Administrative Control of Aliens*. For an overview of these works, see Moloney, *National Insecurities*, 203–10.

13. Abraham Hoffman, *Unwanted Mexican Americans in the Great Depression: Repatriation Pressures, 1929–1939* (Tucson: University of Arizona Press, 1974), 42–45.

14. Hoffman, *Unwanted Mexican Americans in the Great Depression*, 45–49; Rafael de la Colina to Ambassador to Mexico, Washington, DC, Jan. 29, 1931; "Próxima Razzia de Mexicanos," *La Opinión*, Jan. 29, 1931, both found in File IV-343-19, AHSRE. On the role newspapers played in spreading fear, sometimes based on distorted or misleading information, see McLean, "Goodbye, Vicente!," 182–83, 195–97; Robert N. McLean, "Hard Times Oust the Mexican," *Mexican Life*, Sep. 1931, 19–21.

15. Hoffman, *Unwanted Mexican Americans in the Great Depression*, 53–66; "La junta de anoche con el Cónsul," *La Opinión*, Feb. 14, 1931; "Mexicans' Fear Allayed," *Los Angeles Times* (hereafter *LAT*), Feb. 19, 1931; Rafael de la Colina, Cónsul de México, Los Angeles, to Secretario de Relaciones Exteriores, Feb. 23, 1931, File IV-343-19, Acervo Histórico de la Secretaría de Relaciones Exteriores, Ciudad de México, México.

16. Hoffman, *Unwanted Mexican Americans in the Great Depression*, 56. The following day and 3,000 miles across the country, twenty immigration agents and ten New York City police officers burst into a Harlem building where the Finnish Workers' Education Association was hosting a dance. After the officials blocked the exits and ordered the musicians to stop playing, they demanded that all 1,000 attendees show documents proving their legal status, which created "an atmosphere of hysteria tinged with in-

dignation." In the end, though, they only apprehended sixteen men and two women, whom they took to Ellis Island for deportation. "18 Aliens Seized at Finnish Dance," *NYT*, Feb. 16, 1931, 17.

17. "11 Mexicanos Presos en un Aparatoso Raid a la Placita," *La Opinión*, Feb. 27, 1931, 1, 6; Hoffman, *Unwanted Mexican Americans in the Great Depression*, 59–65.

18. On the repatriation campaigns of the Great Depression, see, among others, Emory S. Bogardus, "Mexican Repatriates," *Sociology and Social Research*, Nov./Dec. 1933, 169–76; Ralph Guzmán, *Roots without Rights: A Study of the Loss of United States Citizenship by Native-Born Americans of Mexican Ancestry* (Los Angeles: East Los Angeles Chapter of the American Civil Liberties Union, 1958); Hoffman, *Unwanted Mexican Americans in the Great Depression*, 83–132, 174–75; Sánchez, *Becoming Mexican American*, 209–26; Camille Guérin-Gonzales, *Mexican Workers & American Dreams: Immigration, Repatriation, and California Farm Labor, 1900–1939* (New Brunswick, NJ: Rutgers University Press, 1994), 77–94; Francisco E. Balderrama and Raymond Rodríguez, *Decade of Betrayal: Mexican Repatriation in the 1930s*, rev. ed. (Albuquerque: University of New Mexico Press, 2006), 119–51; Fox, *Three Worlds of Relief*; Kang, *The INS on the Line*, 62–86. On the history of repatriation and deportation from the Mexican perspective, see Mercedes Carreras de Velasco, *Los Mexicanos que Devolvió La Crisis, 1929–1932* (México, DF: Secretaría de Relaciones Exteriores, 1974); Fernando Saúl Alanís Enciso, *Que se queden allá: El gobierno de México y la repatriación de mexicanos en Estados Unidos (1934–1940)* (Tijuana y San Luis Potosí, México: El Colegio de la Frontera Norte y El Colegio de San Luis, 2007); Fernando Saúl Alanís Enciso, *Voces de la repatriación: La sociedad mexicana y la repatriación de mexicanos de Estados Unidos 1930–1933* (San Luis Potosí y Tijuana, Mexico: El Colegio de San Luis y El Colegio de la Frontera Norte, 2015); Laura D. Gutiérrez, "A Constant Threat: Deportation and Return Migration to Northern Mexico, 1918–1965" (Ph.D. diss., University of California, San Diego, 2016); Romeo Guzmán, "Migrant Parents, Mexican-Americans, and Transnational Citizenship, 1920s–1940s" (Ph.D. diss., Columbia University, 2017). On repatriation campaigns in the Midwest, see Norman D. Humphrey, "Mexican Repatriation from Michigan Public Assistance in Historical Perspective," *Social Service Review* 15, no. 3 (1941): 497–513; Neil Better and Raymond A. Mohl, "From Discrimination to Repatriation: Mexican Life in Gary, Indiana, during the Great Depression," *Pacific Historical Review* 42, no. 3 (Aug. 1973): 370–88; Dennis Nodín Valdés, "Mexican Revolutionary Nationalism and Repatriation during the Great Depression," *Mexican Studies/Estudios Mexicanos* 4, no. 1 (Winter 1988): 1–23; Zaragosa Vargas, *Proletarians of the North: A History of Mexican Industrial Workers in Detroit and the Midwest, 1917–1933* (Berkeley: University of California Press, 1999).

19. Bogardus, "Mexican Repatriates," 174.

20. McWilliams offered the comment as a criticism, rather than compliment. Carey McWilliams, "Getting Rid of the Mexican," *American Mercury* 28 (Mar. 1933): 323; Sánchez, *Becoming Mexican American*, 210.

21. On the repatriation campaign against Filipinos, see Ngai, *Impossible Subjects*, 120–26; Lee and Yung, *Angel Island*, 290–97. On the repatriation of Europeans, see Fox, *Three Worlds of Relief*, 176–77.

22. As Fernando Saúl Alanís Enciso has shown, while the Mexican government and some citizens supported repatriation, not all people welcomed migrants back. Alanís Enciso, *Voces de la repatriación*. Leo Grebler, "Mexican Immigration to the United States: The Record and Its Implications," *Mexican-American Study Project*, Advance Report 2 (Los Angeles: Division of Research, Graduate School of Business Administration, University of California, Los Angeles, 1966), 25. For more on the murky terminology of repatriation and deportation, see McLean, "Goodbye, Vicente!"; Robert N. McLean, "The Mexican Return," *The Nation*, Aug. 24, 1932, 165–66; Hoffman, *Unwanted Mexican Americans in the Great Depression*, 166–69.

23. These statistics come from the Mexican Migration Service and the US Immigration and Naturalization Service. Hoffman, *Unwanted Mexican Americans in the Great Depression*, 2; Alanís Enciso, *Voces de la repatriación*, 348; Statistics from the annual reports of the Bureau of Immigration (1929–33) and INS (1934–39), compiled and calculated by author. For a much higher estimate of how many Mexicans left the United States during the 1930s, see Balderrama and Rodríguez, *Decade of Betrayal*. For a lower estimate, see Brian Gratton and Emily Merchant, "Immigration, Repatriation, and Deportation: The Mexican Origin Population in the United States, 1920–1950," *International Migration Review* 47, no. 4 (Winter 2013): 944–75.

24. According to Mae Ngai, "rough estimation suggests that between 1925 and 1965 some 200,000 illegal European immigrants who were construed as deserving successfully legalized their status." Ngai, *Impossible Subjects*, 75–90.

25. Section 20(c) of the act reads: "In the case of any alien . . . who is deportable under any law of the United States and who has proved good moral character for the preceding five years, the Attorney General may (1) permit such alien to depart the United States to any country of his choice at his own expense, in lieu of deportation, or (2) suspend deportation of such alien if not racially inadmissible or ineligible to naturalization in the United States if he finds that such deportation would result in serious economic detriment to a citizen or legally resident alien who is the spouse, parent, or minor child of such deportable alien." Alien Registration Act of 1940, 54 Stat. 670.

26. For classic accounts of the Bracero Program, most of which are place-specific, see Ernesto Galarza, *Merchants of Labor: The Mexican Bracero Story: An Account of Managed Migration of Mexican Farm Worker in California 1942–1960* (San José: Rosicrucian Press, 1964); Erasmo Gamboa, *Mexican Labor & World War II: Braceros in the Pacific Northwest, 1942–1947* (Seattle: University of Washington Press, 2000); Barbara A. Driscoll, *The Tracks North: The Railroad Bracero Program of World War II* (Austin: CMAS Books, University of Texas Press, 1999). For accounts that argue against seeing the program as entirely exploitative, see Jorge Durand, "¿Un acuerdo bilateral o un convenio obrero patronal?," in *Braceros: Las miradas mexicanas y estadounidense*, ed.

Jorge Durand (Zacatecas, México: Universidad de Zacatecas, 2007), 11–29; Michael Snodgrass, "The Bracero Program, 1942–1964," in *Beyond La Frontera: The History of Mexico-U.S. Migration*, ed. Mark Overmyer-Velázquez (New York: Oxford University Press, 2011), 79–102. On the politics of the Bracero Program and the role of the state, see Kitty Calavita, *Inside the State: The Bracero Program, Immigration and the I.N.S.* (New York: Routledge, 1992); Manuel García y Griego, "The Importation of Mexican Contract Laborers to the United States, 1942–1964," in *Between Two Worlds: Mexican Immigrants in the United States*, ed. David G. Gutiérrez (Wilmington, DE: Jaguar Books, 1996), 45–85; Ngai, *Impossible Subjects*, 127–66; Gutiérrez, *Walls and Mirrors*, 117–51; Catherine Vézina, *Diplomacia Migratoria: Una Historia Transnacional del Programa Bracero, 1947–1952* (Ciudad de México: Secretaría de Relaciones Exteriores, 2017). On gender, sexuality, and the Bracero Program, see Matthew Garcia, *A World of Its Own: Race, Labor, and Citrus in the Making of Greater Los Angeles, 1900–1970* (Chapel Hill: University of North Carolina Press, 2001), 157–88; Deborah Cohen, *Braceros: Migrant Citizens and Transnational Subjects in the Postwar United States and Mexico* (Chapel Hill: University of North Carolina Press, 2011); Ana E. Rosas, *Abrazando el Espíritu: Bracero Families Confront the US-Mexico Border* (Berkeley: University of California Press, 2014); Mireya Loza, *Defiant Braceros: How Migrant Workers Fought for Racial, Sexual, and Political Freedom* (Chapel Hill: University of North Carolina Press, 2016). Additional works that expand our understanding of the Bracero Program include Julie Weise, *Corazón de Dixie: Mexico and Mexicans in the U.S. South since 1910* (Chapel Hill: University of North Carolina Press, 2015); Lori A. Flores, *Grounds for Dreaming: Mexican Americans, Mexican Immigrants, and the California Farmworker Movement* (New Haven, CT: Yale University Press, 2016); Mario Jimenez Sifuentez, *Of Forests and Fields: Mexican Labor in the Pacific Northwest* (New Brunswick, NJ: Rutgers University Press, 2016); Chantel Rodríguez, "Health on the Line: The Politics of Citizenship and the Railroad Bracero Program of World War II" (Ph.D. diss., University of Minnesota, 2013).

27. A bureaucratic reshuffling shifted control of the INS from the Department of Labor to the Department of Justice in 1940. AR 1954, 2.

28. "Wetbacks Swarm In," *LIFE*, May 21, 1951, Trabajadores Migratorios (hereafter TM), "Trabajadores ilegales-CA," AHSRE.

29. Garcia to Brownell, Aug. 15, 1953, 56364/45.7, Entry 9, RG 85, INS, NARA1. For a definitive account of Mexican immigrant–Mexican American relations and intraethnic tensions during the twentieth century, see Gutiérrez, *Walls and Mirrors*.

30. Albert B. Colby to Brownell, Aug. 20, 1953, 56364/45.7, Entry 9, RG 85, INS, NARA1.

31. Rutledge was valedictorian of his high school class, a graduate of the University of Illinois, and a World War I veteran. Although the origins of his interest in contraception are unknown, he admired international birth control advocate Margaret Sanger and maintained a somewhat regular correspondence with her in the early 1950s. During the first decades of the century, Sanger promoted both eugenics

and immigration restriction, in part to advance her own cause. B. I. Rutledge to Attorney General Herbert Brownell Jr., Aug. 20, 1953, 56364/45.7, Entry 9, RG 85, INS, NARA1; "Burtch I. Rutledge," World War II Draft Cards (Fourth Registration) for the State of Iowa, Records of the Selective Service System, 1926–1975, Box or Roll 198, RG 147, National Archives and Records Administration, St. Louis, MO, Ancestry.com; "U.S., World War II Draft Registration Cards, 1942," Ancestry.com; Burtch I. Rutledge to Margaret Sanger, Dec. 15, 1952, Reel S40:0480, Margaret Sanger Papers Microfilm Edition (Bethesda, MD: University Publications of America, 1995); Sherman W. Needham, ed., "State of Iowa: Official Register, 1953–1954" (Des Moines: State of Iowa, 1953), 248, 282, 311–29, 394. On Margaret Sanger and eugenics, see Daniel Okrent, *The Guarded Gate: Bigotry, Eugenics, and the Law That Kept Two Generations of Jews, Italians, and Other European Immigrants out of America* (New York: Simon & Schuster, 2019), 7, 244–46, 353.

32. Even though men constitute the vast majority of Mexican deportees, scholars must go beyond the gendered history that paints deportation as being limited to one-dimensional, temporary male laborers. Instead, we must examine deportation's impact on men, women, and children on both sides of the border, each of whom belonged to familial, local, national, and transnational networks. Scholars like Ana Rosas have already done this. She frames the Bracero Program as a "transnational immigrant family experience," highlighting its impact on Mexican women and children. Rosas and historians such as Deborah Cohen have argued that traditional gender roles and Mexican societal norms dictated that while men could migrate in search of work in order to provide for their family, husbands and communities expected women to stay at home and care for their children. Women's migration was discouraged, treated with suspicion, and viewed as a personal, familial, and communal failure. Instead of pointing out the Mexican government's and men's failure to provide for families, many people used unaccompanied female migrants as scapegoats, and believed them to be prostitutes and criminal in nature. General suspicion that female migrants were prostitutes led Mexican government officials to conduct humiliating physical examinations and venereal disease tests on all women working in the general vicinity of bracero selection centers near the border. Rosas, *Abrazando el Espíritu*; Cohen, *Braceros*, 67–86; Ana Elizabeth Rosas, "Flexible Families: Bracero Families' Lives across Cultures, Communities, and Countries, 1942–1964" (Ph.D. diss., University of Southern California, 2006), 180–84, 213–17, 221–26. For examples of the deportation of unaccompanied children, see 4-356-1947-4952; 4-356-1948-4986; 4-356-1949-5042, AHINM. All names from AHINM are pseudonyms.

33. Celestino Aleman Carvajal, Jefe de Servicio Int., Matamoros, Tamalipas, to C. Presidente de la H. Junta de Admin. Civil, Aug. 20, 1948, 4-356-1948-5010, AHINM.

34. The archive offers no indication of the outcomes of Prieto's and Gómez's cases. At the end of Prieto's letter she indicated that she was separated from her husband and in the process of finalizing their divorce. She also claimed that he had taken their daughter

from her ten months prior. It is unclear whether her strained domestic relationship played any role in her expulsion. María Fernanda Prieto, Matamoros, Tamaulipas, to Sr. Jefe de Migración, Ciudad Matamoros, Tamaulipas, Mar. 20, 1942; Andrés Guerra G. to C. Consul de México, McAllen, Tex., Mar. 21, 1942, both found in 4-356-1942-4150, AHINM.

35. Andrés Guerra G. to H. Consul de México, McAllen, Tex., Oct. 6, 1949; Sworn statement by Gómez, in Reynosa, Tamaulipas, Oct. 5, 1949; Lazaro Izaguierre, Consul de McAllen, to C. Jefe de la Oficina de Población, Reynosa, Tamaulipas, Oct. 20, 1949, all found in 4-356-1949-5051, AHINM. In 1953, another woman who found herself in a similar situation wrote to authorities in hopes of receiving permission to cross the border and recover "what is legitimately hers and what she acquired only with great effort." See Andrés Guerra G. to Cónsul de México, McAllen, Texas, Jun. 3, 1953, 4-356-1953-5242, AHINM. For another case of a parent's deportation leaving a child in limbo and subject to both countries' inefficient migration bureaucracies, see 4-356-1960-5377, AHINM. In other instances, parents successfully reunited with their children or arranged for their return to Mexico. See 4-356-1956-5308, AHINM.

36. The letter writer also believed that such policies proved counterproductive since they led to further unauthorized migration. He or she described the area as being in a state of anarchy, with a constant influx of migrants. J. Jones to Attorney General Brownell, Aug. 19, 1953, 56364/45.7, Entry 9, RG 85, INS, NARA1.

37. Andrés Guerra G., El Jefe de Servício de Población, C. Reynosa, Tamaulipas, to Consul de México, McAllen, Texas, Apr. 14, 1953; Guerra G. to Consul de México, McAllen, Texas, Apr. 16, 1953, both found in 4-356-1953-5214, AHINM. For examples of other cases, see 4-356-1953-5226, 4-356-1953-5227, and 4-356-1953-5228, AHINM. Mexican women turned to a form of what Jocelyn Olcott has dubbed revolutionary citizenship, less a collection of laws than "a set of social, cultural, and political processes that both shaped and refracted contemporary political discourses and practices." Olcott argues that men and women exercised their citizenship in collective, public, and deliberative ways, and emphasizes that women activists insisted on being recognized as political, "public" actors. Moreover, by fulfilling their obligations as revolutionary citizens—in this case as braceros and braceros' family members—men and women expected the Mexican state to fulfill its revolutionary commitments of ensuring citizens' well-being. See Jocelyn Olcott, *Revolutionary Women in Post-Revolutionary Mexico* (Durham, NC: Duke University Press, 2005); see also Cohen, *Braceros*.

38. Andres Guerra G., Jefe de Servicio de Población, Reynosa, Tamaulipas, to Consul de México, McAllen, Texas, Sep. 6, 1948; Juana Estévez de Llano to Jefe de Aduana, n.d., both found in 4-356-1948-5013, AHINM. For other examples of women calling for their husbands' deportation, see 4-356-1947-4939, 4-356-1953-5216, and 4-356-1953-5211, AHINM. For an example of a woman in the United States calling for the deportation of her husband's girlfriend, see Oral History with Bertha A. Martínez, Apr. 14, 1996, Louise Kerr Papers, UIC.

39. Carl J. Bon Tempo, *Americans at the Gate: The United States and Refugees during the Cold War* (Princeton, NJ: Princeton University Press, 2008), 8, 30–32. On the 1952 act, see Maddalena Marinari, "Divided and Conquered: Immigration Reform Advocates and the Passage of the 1952 Immigration and Nationality Act," *Journal of American Ethnic History* 35, no. 3 (Spring 2016): 9–40. On immigration policy and deportation during the McCarthy era, see Ellen Schrecker, "Immigration and Internal Security: Political Deportation during the McCarthy Era," *Science and Society* 60, no. 4 (Winter 1996–1997): 393–426.

40. Declassified Memo, "Operation Cloud Burst," Jul. 29, 1953; Declassified Draft Press Release, 1953, "Operation Cloud Burst," both found in 56363/299, Entry 9, RG 85, INS, NARA1; Lytle Hernández, *Migra!*, 183; Manuel García y Griego, "The Bracero Policy Experiment: U.S.-Mexican Responses to Mexican Labor Migration, 1942–1955" (Ph.D. diss., University of California, Los Angeles, 1988), 524–25.

41. Interview with General Joseph Swing, by Ed Edwin, Jun. 21, 1967, 1–2, 55, Columbia University, Oral History Research Office, Eisenhower Administration Project, copy held at USAHEC; "Dear General: World War II Letters, 1944–1945," 8, USAHEC; "Ike Classmate Is Named Chief of Immigration," *Chicago Tribune* (hereafter *ChiTrib*), Apr. 29, 1954, 3; J. Lee Rankin, Assistant Attorney General, Office of Legal Counsel, to Swing, May 24, 1954, 56363/299, Entry 9, RG 85, INS, NARA1.

42. The Border Patrol, as Kelly Lytle Hernández has noted, organized "Special Mexican Deportation Parties" as early as 1944. Concerns about how such actions might affect US–Mexico and US–Latin American relations led Congress and the president to reject the proposal, known as Operation Cloud Burst, to send army troops to the border in the summer of 1953. On these earlier operations, see Kelly Lytle Hernández, "The Crimes and Consequences of Illegal Immigration: A Cross-Border Examination of Operation Wetback, 1943 to 1954," *Western Historical Quarterly* 37, no. 4 (Winter 2006): 428, 441; Wm. A. Whalen, District Director, San Antonio, Texas, to Commissioner, Washington, DC, Mar. 2, 1950, 56364/43 SW pt2, Entry 9, RG 85, INS, NARA1; J. A. Cushman, District Enforcement Officer, Chicago, to Commissioner, Mar. 21, 1952, 56364/43 NW, Entry 9, RG 85, INS, NARA1; Lytle Hernández, *Migra!*, 125–50, 183; Declassified Memo, "Operation Cloud Burst," Jul. 29, 1953; Declassified Draft Press Release, 1953, "Operation Cloud Burst," both found in 56363/299, Entry 9, RG 85, INS, NARA1; García y Griego, "The Bracero Policy Experiment," 524–25.

43. Considerable digging through Mexican archives turned up the previously unreported information that the INS's original plan for Operation Wetback consisted of deporting 25,000 people over the course of four to six weeks. Lic. Pablo Campos Ortíz to C. Secretario de Gobernación, May 22, 1954; Lic. Miguel G. Calderón, Opinion, May 21, 1954; Gustavo Díaz Ordaz to C. Oficial Mayor de la Secretaria de Relaciones Exteriores, May 31, 1954, all found in TM-94-1, AHSRE; Calavita, *Inside the State*, 55, 145; Gutiérrez, *Walls and Mirrors*, 163–65; García y Griego, "The Importation of Mexican Contract Laborers to the United States," 58–59; Grebler, "Mexican Immigration

to the United States," 33–34. See also Juan Ramón García, *Operation Wetback: The Mass Deportation of Mexican Undocumented Workers in 1954* (Westport, CT: Greenwood Press, 1980).

44. DHS, *YOIS: 2012*, 91, 103. The exact numbers for fiscal year 1954 were 1,074,277 voluntary departures and 30,264 formal deportations.

45. García, *Operation Wetback*, 227–32. See also García y Griego, "The Bracero Policy Experiment," 794–96; Lytle Hernández, *Migra!*, 171–73; Calavita, *Inside the State*.

46. INS Press Release on Operation Wetback, Jul. 29, 1954, 56364/45.6, Vol 9, Entry 9, RG 85, INS, NARA1. The INS continued to rely on voluntary departures after Operation Wetback ended. As the 1956 annual report noted, "The policy of granting voluntary departure whenever possible prior to an issuance of an order to show cause or subsequent thereto but prior to an administrative hearing, will be continued during the coming year. Formal deportation cases will be held to a minimum, with resultant savings in time and effort." AR 1956, 15. Immigration authorities recognized detention costs and deportation hearings as costs it could not bear. As early as 1951, the INS noted that "if the Service is forced to go through deportation proceedings in the case of every Mexican who has entered the country illegally, the procedure will take 'some time!'" As a result, the federal government agreed to pay the way for people offered voluntary departure who could not pay their own way. It saw this as "an expense that is 'necessary for the administration and enforcement of the laws relating to immigration.'" Albert E. Reitzel, Acting General Counsel, to Argyle R. Mackey, Commissioner, INS, and L. Paul Winings, General Counsel INS, Jul. 12, 1951, "MxAirlift 1951," NBPM.

47. On weak bureaucracies not necessarily reflecting the real power of the federal state, see Quinn Mulroy, "Public Regulation through Private Litigation: The Regulatory Power of Private Lawsuits and the American Bureaucracy" (Ph.D. diss., Columbia University, 2012); Robert C. Lieberman, *Shifting the Color Line: Race and the American Welfare State* (Cambridge, MA: Harvard University Press, 2001).

48. "Outline for Discussion: Special Patrol Force," May 19, 1954, 56364/45.6, Vol 7, Entry 9, RG 85, INS, NARA1.

49. H. R. Landon, District Director, Los Angeles, to J. M. Swing, Commissioner, Jun. 11, 1954, 56364/45.6, Vol 1, Entry 9, RG 85, INS, NARA1.

50. Gordon B. Greb, Director, News & Public Affairs, KSJO, San José, to Attorney General Herbert Brownell, Jun. 21, 1954, 56364/45.6, Vol 1, Entry 9, RG 85, INS, NARA1.

51. Marcus T. Neely, District Director, El Paso, Texas, to the Commissioner, Jun. 1, 1954, 56364/45.6, Vol 1, Entry 9, RG 85, INS, NARA1.

52. Stressing the differences between "braceros" and "wetbacks" was also key to Operation Wetback's success since, in addition to being a mass deportation campaign, its other primary goal was to convince—or force—employers to hire workers through the Bracero Program. When Attorney General Brownell first announced the drive, he described braceros as "a welcome and appreciated addition to our work force," and

"wetbacks" as causing "serious social and economic problems for the United States." The Department of Justice pushed Congress to enact legislation preventing employers from hiring unauthorized migrants and allowing the INS to seize "any vehicle or vessel used to transport aliens in violation of the immigration laws"—thus providing "much needed weapons to assist in bringing to a halt the increasing illegal crossings of the borders by the so-called 'wetbacks.'" At the same time, to put US growers at ease, the Department of Labor promised it "would cooperate to the fullest extent in giving the program considerable advanced publicity in order that employers of wet labor would have ample opportunity to recruit legal labor" and "continue to have legal Mexican laborers available to meet all requests." See A. C. Devaney, Memorandum for File, May 20,1954; Department of Justice Press Release, Jun. 9, 1954, both found in 56364/45.6, Vol 1, Entry 9, RG 85, INS, NARA1.

53. Dulles to American Embassy, México, DF, May 20, 1954, 56364/45.6, Vol 6, Entry 9, RG 85, INS, NARA1.

54. A. C. Devaney, Assistant Commissioner, Inspections & Examinations Division, Memorandum for File, May 20, 1954, 56364/45.6, Vol 1, Entry 9, RG 85, INS, NARA1.

55. US Embassy, Mexico City, to US Information Agency, May 28, 1954, 56364/45.6, Vol 6, Entry 9, RG 85, INS, NARA1.

56. Joint US Information Agency-State Message (Confidential), Jun. 8, 1954, 56364/45.6, Vol 6, Entry 9, RG 85, INS, NARA1. Two months into the campaign, US officials continued to pressure their Mexican counterparts to impede northbound migration to the border. E. DeWitt Marshall, deputy chief of the Border Patrol and, for a time, an INS attaché in Mexico City, suggested "that the Mexican Government's cooperation be solicited in use of moral persuasion, appeals to patriotism, warnings of hardships and dangers suffered by illegal emigrants, etc." He added: "Such warnings and appeals should be made in person by agents of the Mexican Government at reference interior transportation focal points" since "past similar appeals made through Mexican Government press releases have not been effective." Little, if anything, came of these efforts, since the Mexican constitution prevented officials from restricting travel within the country. Marshall to A. C. Devaney, Assistant Commissioner, Inspections & Examinations Division, Aug. 18, 1954, 56321/448f, Entry 9, RG 85, INS, NARA1.

57. On the dilemma of writing international or transnational histories that decenter the United States while still accounting for "the centrality of American power" in shaping the post-1945 world, see Marilyn B. Young, "The Age of Global Power," in *Rethinking American History in a Global Age*, ed. Thomas Bender (Berkeley: University of California Press, 2002), 274–94.

58. The start date was delayed because of upcoming California primary elections and the fact that the Mexican government needed more time to prepare to receive the deportees. Department of Justice Press Release, Jun. 9, 1954; A. C. Devaney, Memorandum for File, May 27, 1954, both found in 56364/45.6, Vol 1, Entry 9, RG 85, INS,

NARA1; "Outline for Discussion: Special Patrol Force," May 19, 1954, 56364/45.6, Vol 7, Entry 9, RG 85, INS, NARA1; District Director, Los Angeles, to Commissioner, Washington, DC, Aug. 26, 1954, 56321/448f, Entry 9, RG 85, INS, NARA1; "7,280 Wetbacks Deported at Nogales Past Week," *Nogales International* (AZ), Jun. 18, 1954, TM-94-1, AHSRE.

59. The INS contracted a local catering company to supply packaged lunches consisting of one meat sandwich, one cheese sandwich, and one hard-boiled egg, at a cost of $0.40 per lunch. District Director, Los Angeles, to Commissioner, accepted bid and contract with Los Angeles Department of Recreation and Parks attached, Jun. 18, 1954; Correspondence between the INS and Fisher Catering, Inc., Jun. 8–23, 1954, both found in 56310/918, Entry 9, RG 85, INS, NARA1. For firsthand accounts of people apprehended during Operation Wetback, see Ralph Guzmán, "La repatriación forzosa como solución política concluyente al problema de la emigración ilegal. Una perspectiva histórica," in *Indocumentados: Mitos y realidades* (México, DF: El Colegio de México, 1979), 137–63. For context, it should be noted that the day after the INS launched Operation Wetback, the CIA-orchestrated Guatemalan coup d'état commenced, marking an important turning point in US–Latin American relations. On Operation Wetback in Los Angeles and Southern California, see Molina, *How Race Is Made in America*, 112–38. On Operation Wetback in agriculture-centered communities in California's Salinas Valley, see Flores, *Grounds for Dreaming*, 75–107.

60. Harlon B. Carter to Bruce G. Barber, Jun. 11, 1954, 56364/45.6, Vol 7, Entry 9, RG 85, INS, NARA1; E. B. Topmiller, Chief Patrol Inspector, Sacramento, Calif., to All Officers, Task Force "A," Jun. 30, 1954, 56364/45.6, Vol 4, Entry 9, RG 85, INS, NARA1.

61. Swing, Memo, Jul. 2, 1954, 56364/45.6, Vol 4, Entry 9, RG 85, INS, NARA1.

62. Department of Justice Press Release, Jun. 9, 1954; Brownell to Senator Thomas H. Kuchel, Calif., Jun. 9, 1954, both found in 56364/45.6, Vol 1, Entry 9, RG 85, INS, NARA1.

63. What happened once deportees arrived back in Mexico is less clear, as discussed in chapter 3. Carter to All Stations in Los Angeles District, Jun. 10, 1954; INS Appropriation Request, Jun. 14, 1954; Pacific Greyhound Lines—INS Charter Agreement, San Francisco, Jun. 5, 1954, all found in 56310/918, Entry 9, RG 85, INS, NARA1; Statistics of Special Border Patrol Task Force Operations, 56364/45.2, Entry 9, RG 85, INS, NARA1.

64. Carter had a history of violence prior to joining the Border Patrol and later led the National Rifle Association. Carter to Partridge, Jun. 16, 1954, 56364/45.6, Vol 1, Entry 9, RG 85, INS, NARA1. On Carter, see Lytle Hernández, *Migra!*, 68–69.

65. B. D. Diaz, Inventor, to Edmund H. Gies, Officer in Charge, US INS, El Centro, California, Jun. 17, 1954, 56364/45.6, Vol 4, Entry 9, RG 85, INS, NARA1. The full metaphor read, "I used to live in the State of Ohio and in Winter we hunt rabbits. It was very easy and very sporty. We always see the rabbits at the end of the trails in snow. So Mr. and/or Mrs. Rabbit sitting pretty looking at us. We can not shoot them as they are (it is like murder) so we throw clods and if one is to [sic] lazy to stay so we shouts [sic] or stump [sic] our feet on the ground so the creatures have a chance to run. So there we are as 'the

Omnipotent Judge.' 'Shoot or not to shoot?' These are the conclusion [*sic*]: You scared [them] and they did run to save yourselves the trouble of enforcing and the cash for our Government."

66. "Report on the New 'Wetback' Program," *INS Information Bulletin* IV, 25, Jun. 30, 1954, USCISHOL.

67. "New Phase of 'Wetback' Drive to Begin This Week," *INS Information Bulletin* IV, 26, Jul. 7, 1954, USCISHOL. A little over a month later, the Los Angeles district director made a similar assertion. "The operation, heralded by a wide publicity program, caused thousands of 'wetbacks' to flee to Mexico and elsewhere to escape apprehension." District Director, Los Angeles, to Commissioner, Washington, DC, Aug. 26, 1954, 56321/448f, Entry 9, RG 85, INS, NARA1.

68. Gus O. Krausse, Brownsville Chief of Police, to Fletcher Rawls, Jul. 16, 1954; John L. Guseman, Chief of Police, Harlingen, to Rawls, Jul. 13, 1954; Tom Mayfield, Constable, San Juan, to Rawls, July 1954; Assistant Commissioner, Border Patrol, Detention and Deportation Division, to Harlon B. Carter, Jul. 26, 1954, all found in 56364/45.6, Vol 5, Entry 9, RG 85, INS, NARA1.

69. Press Release, Department of Justice, Jul. 2, 1954, 56364/45.6, Vol 5, Entry 9, RG 85, INS, NARA1.

70. Memo to D. R. Kelley for presentation by him to General Swing, Jul. 1954, 56364/45.6, Vol 3, Entry 9, RG 85, INS, NARA1.

71. J. W. Holland to Chris Aldrete, President, AGIF, Del Rio, Texas, Jul. 7, 1954, 56364/45.6, Vol 3, Entry 9, RG 85, INS, NARA1.

72. Holland to Swing, Jul. 22, 1954; Holland to Swing, Jul. 13, 1954, both found in 56364/45.6, Vol 5, Entry 9, RG 85, INS, NARA1.

73. Press Release on Operation Wetback, Jul. 29, 1954, 56364/45.6, Vol 9, 7/54–9/54, Entry 9, RG 85, INS, NARA1; Illegible title, *San Antonio Express*, Jul. 7, 1954; Holland to Swing, Jul. 4, 1954, 56364/45.6, Vol 5, Entry 9, RG 85, INS, NARA1.

74. Untitled, *San Benito News*, Jul. 8, 1954, 56364/45.6, Vol 5, Entry 9, RG 85, INS, NARA1.

75. E. R. Decker to Carter, Jul. 21, 1954, 56364/45.6, Vol 5, Entry 9, RG 85, INS, NARA1.

76. James Mulkey Jr., Past President of Area X Future Farmers, Mercedes, Texas, to President Eisenhower, Aug. 3, 1954, 56364/45, Entry 9, RG 85, INS, NARA1.

77. Geo. W. Hackney, Weslaco, Texas, to the President of the United States, Aug. 4, 1954, 56364/45, Entry 9, RG 85, INS, NARA1.

78. On a similar note, a Brownsville woman stated that the "bracero thing" would not help the thousands of small farmers in the Rio Grande Valley, and ended her letter asking Eisenhower, "Did you ever try to pick cotton? Well, I have since you have taken my labor and it is quite hopeless!" Mrs. Cecil (illegible), Harlingen, Texas, to President Eisenhower, Jul. 20, 1954; Mrs. J. B. Kee, Brownsville, Texas, to President Eisenhower, Jul. 1954, both found in 56364/45, Entry 9, RG 85, INS, NARA1. On race relations and rights during the Cold War, see Thomas Borstelmann, *The Cold War and the Color Line: American Race Relations in the Global Arena* (Cambridge, MA:

Harvard University Press, 2001); Mary Dudziak, *Cold War Civil Rights: Race and the Image of American Democracy* (Princeton, NJ: Princeton University Press, 2002).

79. Lowell C. Martindale and Harold W. Lauver, Investigators, to Chief Patrol Inspector Charles E. Kirk, Aug. 31, 1954, 56364/45.6, Vol 9, Entry 9, RG 85, INS, NARA1.

80. Press Release, Department of Justice, Jul. 29, 1954, 56364/45.6, Vol 9, Entry 9, RG 85, INS, NARA1; "New Definition," *Valley Evening Monitor*, Aug. 16, 1954, 4; Holland to A. C. Devaney, Assistant Commissioner, Inspections & Examinations Division, Central Office, Aug. 6, 1954, 56321/448f, Entry 9, RG 85, INS, NARA1.

81. Partridge to Swing, Jul. 9, 1954, 56364/45.6, Vol 5, Entry 9, RG 85, INS, NARA1; "No se Comprueban Malos Tratos a Nuestros Braceros," *Excélsior*, Jul. 21, 1954, 1, Headquarters History Publicity, NBPM.

82. AR 1955, 14–15. The exact figure was 60,456.

83. "Wetback Roundup Termed Greatest Modern Migration," *San Antonio Express*, Jul. 30, 1954, Headquarters History Publicity, NBPM.

84. Swing, "Report to the American Section of Joint Commission on Mexican Migrant Labor," Sep. 3, 1954, 56321/448f, Entry 9, RG 85, INS, NARA1. Swing also falsely stated that "Opportunity was given to all to collect wages due and gather personal belongings and other property before being returned to Mexico."

85. Most historians who have written about Operation Wetback mention the INS's Chicago and Midwest campaign briefly, if at all. See, for example, Lytle Hernández, *Migra!*; García y Griego, "The Bracero Policy Experiment"; García, *Operation Wetback*; Calavita, *Inside the State*. For scholarship that examines Mexicans in Chicago in the postwar period, see Lilia Fernández, *Brown in the Windy City: Mexicans and Puerto Ricans in Postwar Chicago* (Chicago: University of Chicago Press, 2012); Mike Amezcua, "The Second City Anew: Mexicans, Urban Culture, and Migration in the Transformation of Chicago, 1940–1965" (Ph.D. diss., Yale University, 2011).

86. On the politics of immigration statistics and the INS's strategic use of data to push for stricter enforcement, see chapter 4. John P. Swanson, Chief Patrol Inspector, Grand Forks, North Dakota, to District Director, Chicago, Mar. 18, 1954, 56364/45.6, Vol 8, Entry 9, RG 85, INS, NARA1; Interview with General Joseph Swing by Ed Edwin, 15–16. For examples of Mexicans hiring smugglers to transport them to Chicago, see "Gets 4 Year Term for Harboring of Mexican Aliens," *ChiTrib*, Mar. 4, 1954, B9; "Convicted Aid of 'Wetbacks' on Probation," *ChiTrib*, Nov. 18, 1955, B5.

87. Robinson to District Director, Chicago, Jun. 14, 1954, 56364/45.6, Vol 8, Entry 9, RG 85, INS, NARA1.

88. Ralph W. Dusha, Investigator, to Irving I. Freedman, Chief, Investigations Branch, Chicago, Jul. 13, 1954, 56364/45.6, Vol 8, Entry 9, RG 85, INS, NARA1. This quote is Dusha's recounting of what Swing said.

89. Walter A. Sahli, "Delayed Birth Certificate," Commonwealth of Pennsylvania, Department of Health, Bureau of Vital Statistics," Feb. 10, 1949, Box 63, Certificate Number: D-180546-06, Pennsylvania Historical and Museum Commission,

Harrisburg, PA, Ancestry.com; "Pennsylvania, Birth Certificates, 1906–1910," Ancestry.com; "New Immigration Chief Takes Charge of Office," *ChiTrib*, Feb. 19, 1954, 2.

90. Congress and the public criticized Swing's appointment of Partridge on the grounds of nepotism and questioned the legality of filling the civilian immigration agency with former military officers. Frank H. Partridge to District Director, Chicago, Jul. 27, 1954, 56364/45.6, Vol 8, Entry 9, RG 85, INS, NARA1; Wolfgang Saxon, "Frank H. Partridge, Immigration Official and General, 100," *NYT*, Jul. 2, 1994, 46. Partridge's memo is mostly based on D. R. Kelley's recommendations to him. Kelley stated that if the INS implemented such measures, he felt "certain that many hundreds of the Mexicans would choose to return to Mexico on their own, thereby saving the Government many thousands of dollars." D. R. Kelley, Memorandum for General Partridge, Jul. 14, 1954, 56364/45.6, Vol 8, Entry 9, RG 85, INS, NARA1. Swing later faced public scrutiny for his alleged use of public funds to pay for personal hunting trips to Mexico and to recruit a Mexican maid to work in his Washington, DC, home. See "LBJA Subject File / [Immigration] [Investigation of General Swing and the Immigration and Naturalization Service, 1956]," Box 70, LBJ.

91. "Federal Drive on 'Wetbacks' to Center Here," *ChiTrib*, Jul. 31, 1954, 12.

92. Press Release, INS, Chicago, Aug. 2, 1954; Sahli to Partridge, Aug. 3, 1954, 56364/45.6, Vol 8, Entry 9, RG 85, INS, NARA1. As of early August, it seems as if the INS had not decided whether the drive would actually happen. Sahli told Partridge that if it did they would have to give "serious consideration . . . to the handling of aliens" since many were well established in Chicago and could not be processed as quickly as people on the southwestern border.

93. "Wetbacks Get Help in Returning," *Chicago Daily News*, Aug. 2, 1954, Midwest Committee for Protection of Foreign Born (hereafter MCPFB) 10.8, CHM; "Illegal Aliens Who Surrender Will Benefit," *ChiTrib*, Aug. 3, 1954, 14; Press Release, INS, Chicago, Aug. 2, 1954, 56364/45.6, Vol 8, Entry 9, RG 85, INS, NARA1. The INS believed that the advanced publicity in the lead-up to the Chicago operation may have led other Mexicans to relocate within the Midwest. Based on the belief that some people may have settled in surrounding suburban communities and smaller industrial centers, the service sent officers to St. Louis, Kansas City, Omaha, Milwaukee, Duluth, and the St. Paul–Minneapolis area "to prevent the wetbacks finding a haven anywhere in this section of the country." But investigations turned up "no evidence of any significant movement of Mexican aliens from Chicago to other communities." From Sep. 23 to Oct. 6, two officers in Minnesota and Wisconsin checked "celery and cauliflower farms, packing companies, food processing plants, county agents, employment offices, mining companies, Sheriff's offices, canning factories and cheese factories," but were "unable to apprehend any Mexican aliens who were illegally in the United States." Officials described apprehensions outside of Chicago as being "extremely low," and noted that Omaha's eighty-one apprehensions by the last week of November was more than two times as many as any other suboffice. Sahli

to Partridge, Oct. 22, 1954; Harry Gordon to Sahli, Oct. 11, 1954; Cushman to Commissioner, Nov. 24, 1954, all found in 56364/45.3, Entry 9, RG 85, INS, NARA1.

94. John P. Boyd, Seattle District Director, to All Officers in Charge, District No. 12, Chief Patrol Inspectors at Blaine, Spokane, and Havre, Oct. 8, 1954, 56364/43 NW, Entry 9, RG 85, INS, NARA1. In hopes of minimizing overall expenses, Boyd added that the INS could grant people voluntary departure even if they could not pay, or were unwilling to pay, for their own transportation. This contradicted statements Sahli made less than two weeks earlier, although it is unclear whether the policy changed or whether it simply differed by district or region. See Sahli to Carter, Sep. 27, 1954, 56364/45.6, Vol 8, Entry 9, RG 85, NARA1.

95. Sahli to R. H. Robinson, Acting Assistant Commissioner, Border Patrol, Detention & Deportation Branch, Jun. 21, 1954, 56364/45.6, Vol 8, Entry 9, RG 85, INS, NARA1. A month later Sahli suggested that holding hearings in Chicago might be more practical, since it was "a well known fact that all unlawful entry cases cannot be presented to the Courts in the districts where such entries occur." Sahli to E. A. Loughran, Assistant Commissioner, Administrative Division, Central Office, Jul. 26, 1954, 56364/43 NW, Entry 9, RG 85, INS, NARA1. Contemporary research shows that the certainty of apprehension serves as more of a deterrent than the severity of punishment. See, for example, Daniel S. Nagin, "Deterrence in the Twenty-First Century," *Crime and Justice* 42, no. 11 (2013): 199–263.

96. Sahli to R. H. Robinson, Acting Assistant Commissioner, Border Patrol, Detention & Deportation Branch, Jun. 21, 1954, 56364/45.6, Vol 8, Entry 9, RG 85, INS, NARA1.

97. Kelley to Partridge, Jun. 28, 1954, 56364/45.6, Vol 8, Entry 9, RG 85, INS, NARA1.

98. Robert C. L. George to Sahli, Jul. 6, 1954; Partridge to District Director, Chicago, Jul. 27, 1954, both found in 56364/45.6, Vol 8, Entry 9, RG 85, INS, NARA1.

99. Sahli to Partridge, Aug. 3, 1954; "Latin Americans and the Immigration Service," pamphlet published by ACLU, Chicago; Press Release, ACLU, Illinois Division, to All Illinois Newspapers, Aug. 3, 1954, all found in 56364/45.6, Vol 8, Entry 9, RG 85, INS, NARA1.

100. Henry Heineman, Chairman, Committee on Nationality and Loyalty Matters, ACLU, to General J. M. Swing, Jul. 30, 1954, 56364/45.6, Vol 8, Entry 9, RG 85, INS, NARA1.

101. Emmett D. Helliher, Investigator, Chicago, to Harold E. Hulsing, Chief, Inspections and Examinations Branch, Chicago, Oct. 7, 1954, 56364/45.3, Entry 9, RG 85, INS, NARA1.

102. Notes on Meeting about "Mexican Laborers," Aug. 13, 1954, 56321/448f, Entry 9, RG 85, INS, NARA1.

103. John P. Swanson, Chief Patrol Inspector, Grand Forks, North Dakota, to District Director, Chicago, Mar. 18, 1954, 56364/45.6, Vol 8, Entry 9, RG 85, INS, NARA1.

104. Mary M. Oddson to Sahli, Sep. 22, 1954, 56364/45.3, Entry 9, RG 85, INS, NARA1; Ralph W. Dusha, Investigator, to Irving I. Freedman, Chief, Investigations Branch, Chicago, Jul. 13, 1954, 56364/45.6, Vol 8, Entry 9, RG 85, INS, NARA1.

105. Joseph A. Cushman, Acting District Director, Chicago, to Commissioner, Nov. 24, 1954; Sahli to Commissioner, Oct. 7, 1954, 56364/45.3, Entry 9, RG 85, INS, NARA1.

106. Sahli to Loughran, Jul. 26, 1954, 56364/43 NW, Entry 9, RG 85, INS, NARA1.
107. Edwin B. Topmiller, Chief Patrol Inspector, to H. B. Carter, Chief, Border Patrol Branch, Aug. 10, 1954, 56364/45.6, Vol 9, Entry 9, RG 85, INS, NARA1.
108. Sahli to Loughran, Jul. 26, 1954, 56364/43, NW, Entry 9, RG 85, INS, NARA1.
109. Partridge to District Directors, San Antonio and Los Angeles, Sep. 7, 1954, 56364/45.6, Vol 6, Entry 9, RG 85, INS, NARA1; Sahli, District Director, Chicago, to All Officers, Sep. 17, 1954, 56364/45.6, Vol 8, Entry 9, RG 85, INS, NARA1.
110. "Chicago Operation," Sep. 9, 1954, 56364/45.6, Vol 8, Entry 9, RG 85, INS, NARA1.
111. "'Wetback' Roundup in High Gear," *Chicago Daily News*, Sep. 20, 1954, MCPFB 10.8, CHM.
112. Before the drive started, officials had decided, largely for budgetary reasons, not to patrol on weekends. Fewer than 2 percent of people authorities apprehended gave "housewife" as an occupation. Although this led the INS to conclude that few Mexican men brought their families to Chicago, it also simply could have reflected the service's targeting of male laborers. Sahli to James L. Hennessy, Executive Assistant to the Commissioner, Sep. 27, 1954; Harold E. Hulsing, Chief, Inspections and Examinations Branch, Chicago, to Sahli, Sep. 30, 1954, 56364/45.6, Vol 8, Entry 9, RG 85, INS, NARA1; Harold E. Hulsing, Chief, Inspections and Examinations Branch, Chicago, to Sahli, Dec. 3, 1954, 56364/45.3, Entry 9, RG 85, INS, NARA1.
113. "Drive on Aliens by U.S. Brings 320 Detentions," *ChiTrib*, Sep. 28, 1954, 23; Nathan Caldwell Jr., Executive Secretary, to Rose Chernin, Los Angeles Committee for Protection of Foreign Born, Sep. 20, 1954; Caldwell to Josefina Yanez, Oct. 5, 1954, MCPFB 10.8, CHM. On the American Committee for Protection of Foreign Born's immigrant advocacy and deportation defense work, see Rachel Ida Buff, *Against the Deportation Terror: Organizing for Immigrant Rights in the Twentieth Century* (Philadelphia: Temple University Press, 2017).
114. Apprehensions rose to 921 in October, but then dropped down to 445 in November. During the first three months of the campaign the INS found that around one-third of all Mexicans apprehended in Chicago had entered as braceros or nonimmigrants. Two months into the Chicago operation, Cushman reported that "the program of voluntary surrenders and departure unescorted has produced excellent results. Through November 17, 1954, a total of 1427 letters granting voluntary departure unescorted were issued in the Chicago office. Through the same date a total of 1216 such departures had been verified." An investigation found seventy-three others—fifty of whom had left for Mexico without turning in their voluntary departure letter; sixteen that could not be located; and seven that had not departed but moved to new residences. Sahli to Commissioner, Oct. 7, 1954; Sahli to Partridge, Oct. 22, 1954; Cushman, Acting District Director, Chicago, to Commissioner, Nov. 24, 1954; Harold E. Hulsing, Chief, Inspections and Examinations Branch, Chicago, to Sahli, Dec. 3, 1954, all found in 56364/45.3, Entry 9, RG 85, INS, NARA1.

115. Sahli to Partridge, Dec. 6, 1954, 56364/45.3, Entry 9, RG 85, INS, NARA1; Ralph H. Holton, Chicago District Director, to Commissioner, May 17, 1955, 56364/43 NW, Entry 9, RG 85, INS, NARA1; "End Campaign for Deporting Wetbacks Here," *ChiTrib*, Jul. 23, 1955, 16.

116. On Operation Wetback as a publicity campaign, see García, *Operation Wetback*; Calavita, *Inside the State*; Lytle Hernández, *Migra!*

117. Swing stated that by early October some 163,000 had been deported to Mexico, adding "I feel we are over the hump in mass apprehensions." Swing to William R. Sabin, Senior Patrol Inspector, McAllen, Texas, Nov. 30, 1954, Border Patrol file, NBPM.

118. AR 1955, 15.

119. It is impossible to say how many undocumented migrants evaded INS detection or if the probability of being caught might have changed over time. Calavita, *Inside the State*; García y Griego, "The Bracero Policy Experiment"; DHS, *YOIS: 2012*, 91.

120. Operation Wetback cannot be entirely credited for the increasing number of braceros. The number of labor contracts started rising in the early 1950s, going from 67,500 in 1950 to 192,000 in 1951, before reaching 309,033 in 1954 and 445,197 in 1956. Unsurprisingly, after Operation Wetback, the largest increases in contracts occurred in Texas and California, the two states with the highest demand for agricultural labor, and the two states Operation Wetback had targeted above all others. Calavita, *Inside the State*, Appendix B, 218; García y Griego, "The Bracero Policy Experiment," 846–48.

## Chapter 3: The Human Costs of the Business of Deportation

1. I. M. Adler, Steamship & Tourist Agency, to Senator George P. McLean, Jan. 13, 1928; Commissioner of Immigration, Ellis Island, to Senator George B. McLean, Jan. 30, 1928, both found in 55608/133, Entry 9, RG 85, INS, NARA1.

2. On the history of the government's reliance on private third parties for public purposes, in matters ranging from the construction of the transcontinental railroad to the funding of political parties, schools, hospitals, and other institutions, see Michael B. Katz, *In the Shadow of the Poorhouse: A Social History of Welfare in America*, Tenth Anniversary Edition, Revised and Updated (New York: Basic Books, 1996); Brian Balogh, *The Associational State: American Governance in the Twentieth Century* (Philadelphia: University of Pennsylvania, 2015); Gerstle, *Liberty and Coercion*.

3. On the political and social exclusion, racialization, and economic exploitation of people of African descent, representative works include Cedrick J. Robinson, *Black Marxism: The Making of the Black Radical Tradition* (London: Zed Press, 1983); Douglas A. Blackmon, *Slavery by Another Name: The Re-Enslavement of Black Americans from the Civil War to World War II* (New York: Random House, 2008); Edward E. Baptist, *The Half Has Never Been Told: Slavery and the Making of American Capitalism* (New York:

Basic Books, 2014). On political and social exclusion, racialization, and economic exploitation of immigrants, and especially Mexicans, see, among many others, Sánchez, *Becoming Mexican American*; Gutiérrez, *Walls and Mirrors*; Peck, *Reinventing Free Labor*; Lee, *At America's Gates*; Ngai, *Impossible Subjects*; Kanstroom, *Deportation Nation*; Lytle Hernández, *Migra!*; Hahamovitch, *No Man's Land*; Leo Chávez, *The Latino Threat: Constructing Immigrants, Citizens, and the Nation*, 2nd ed. (Palo Alto, CA: Stanford University Press, 2013); Molina, *How Race Is Made in America*; Parker, *Making Foreigners*; Hirota, *Expelling the Poor*; Kang, *The INS on the Line*.

4. On the business of transoceanic migration and immigration control, see Robert Eric Barde, *Immigration at the Golden Gate: Passenger Ships, Exclusion, and Angel Island* (Westport, CT: Praeger, 2008); Ethan Blue, "Finding Margins on Borders: Shipping Firms and Immigration Control across Settler Space," *Occasion: Interdisciplinary Studies in the Humanities* 5 (Mar. 1, 2013): 1–20; Torsten Feys, *The Battle for the Migrants: The Introduction of Steamshipping on the North Atlantic and Its Impact on the European Exodus* (St. John's, NL: International Maritime Economic History Association, 2013); Yukari Takai, "Navigating Transpacific Passages: Steamship Companies, State Regulators, and Transshipment of Japanese in the Early-Twentieth-Century Pacific Northwest," *Journal of American Ethnic History* 30, no. 3 (Spring 2011): 7–34. On the transportation of Mexican and Jamaican guestworkers and the precarious conditions they faced, see Cohen, *Braceros*, 89–115; Hahamovitch, *No Man's Land*, 56–61; Flores, *Grounds for Dreaming*, 135–62. On the contemporary "migration industry" and "immigration industrial complex," see Stephen Castles and Mark J. Miller, *The Age of Migration: International Population Movements in the Modern World*, 2nd ed. (London: Macmillian Press, 1998); Deepa Fernandes, *Targeted: Homeland Security and the Business of Immigration* (New York: Seven Stories Press, 2007); Rubén Hernández-León, *Metropolitan Migrants: The Migration of Urban Mexicans to the United States* (Berkeley: University of California Press, 2008), 154–83; Tanya Golash-Boza, *Immigration Nation: Raids, Detentions, and Deportations in Post-9/11 America* (Boulder, CO: Paradigm Publishers, 2012); Thomas Gammeltoft-Hansen and Ninna Nyberg Sørensen, eds., *Migration Industry and the Commercialization of International Migration* (New York: Routledge, 2013); Ruben Andersson, *Illegality, Inc.: Clandestine Migration and the Business of Bordering Europe* (Berkeley: University of California Press, 2014).

5. *Fong Yue Ting v. United States*, 149 U.S. 698 (1893). On US immigration enforcement, punishment, and the carceral state, see chapter 6. On the key role bureaucratization and institutional inertia play in proliferating inhumane—even deadly—policies, see, among others, Debórah Dwork and Robert Jan van Pelt, *Auschwitz: 1270 to the Present* (New York: W. W. Norton, 1996); Nancy Hiemstra and Deirdre Conlon, "Beyond Privatization: Bureaucratization and the Spatialities of Immigration Detention Expansion," *Territory, Politics, Governance* 5, no. 3 (2017): 252–68.

6. Raymond L. Cohn, *Mass Migration under Sail: European Immigration to the Antebellum United States* (New York: Cambridge University Press, 2009), 1–2, 223–24; Barde,

*Immigration at the Golden Gate,* 89; Takai, "Navigating Transpacific Passages," 7–34; Feys, *The Battle for the Migrants*; Blue, "Finding Margins on Borders," 1–20.

7. Barde, *Immigration at the Golden Gate,* 63.

8. Barde, *Immigration at the Golden Gate,* 61–71; Lee and Yung, *Angel Island.*

9. J. F. Masters, New England Superintendent, Dominion Atlantic Railway, to Colonel Geo. G. Billings, Dec. 19, 1906; Sargent to Hurley, Dec. 27, 1906, both found in 51466/90, Entry 9, RG 85, INS, NARA1.

10. Inspector in Charge, Tucson, Arizona, to Commissioner General, Washington, DC, Jan. 7, 1907, 51466/104, Entry 9, RG 85, INS, NARA1.

11. John H. Clark, Commissioner, Montreal, to Mr. Parker, Feb. 19, 1919; Clark to Commissioner General of Immigration, Washington, DC, Apr. 10, 1919, both found in 54646/132, Entry 9, RG 85, INS, NARA1.

12. Walter E. Carr, District Director, Los Angeles, to Commissioner General, Washington, DC, May 3, 1926; Harry E. Hull, Commissioner General, to District Director, Los Angeles, May 13, 1926, both found in 55608/126, Entry 9, RG 85, INS, NARA1.

13. Leo B. Russell, "Report of Officer in Charge of Deportation and Transportation," AR 1920, 307–10.

14. AR 1931, 37. For more on these deportation trains, see Ethan Blue, "Strange Passages: Carceral Mobility and the Liminal in the Catastrophic History of American Deportation," *National Identities* 17, no. 2 (2015): 175–94. For a fictional account of what it was like aboard the trains, see Theodore D. Irwin, *Strange Passage* (New York: H. Smith and R. Haas, 1935).

15. F. S. McGinnis, Passenger Traffic Manager, Southern Pacific Company, to A. J. Poston, General Agent, Southern Pacific Company, Dec. 3, 1925, 55608/131, Entry 9, RG 85, INS, NARA1.

16. A. J. Poston, General Agent, Southern Pacific Company, to Bureau of Immigration, Mar. 10, 1926; Harry E. Hull, Commissioner General of Immigration, to A. J. Poston, General Agent, Southern Pacific Company, Mar. 10, 1926; R. D. Beard, Chief, Deportation Division, to Commissioner General, Mar. 4, 1926, all found in 55608/131, Entry 9, RG 85, INS, NARA1.

17. For example, officials contracted a mixture of US- and foreign-based shipping companies to execute deportations, including the Pacific Mail Company and Panama Mail Steamship Company, Toyo Kisen Kaisha Steamship Company of Japan, Spanish Royal Mail Line, Navigazione Libera Triestina of Italy, International Mercantile Marine Company, Pacific Railroad Company, Southern Banana Corporation, and Cuyamel Fruit Company. W. W. Husband, Commissioner General, Memorandum for the Assistant Secretary, Sep. 23, 1921, 55608/128, Entry 9, RG 85, INS, NARA1; R. A. Scott, Inspector in Charge, Tucson, Arizona, to Supervisor of Immigration Service, El Paso, Texas, Nov. 9, 1923, 54933/351B, Entry 9, RG 85, INS, NARA1; A. E. Burnett, Inspector in Charge, Los Angeles, to Supervising Inspector, El Paso, Texas, Oct. 14, 1921; District Director, Galveston, Texas, to Commissioner General, Washington, DC, Jul. 21,

1927; Commissioner, New Orleans, to Commissioner General, Washington, DC, Apr. 25, 1928; Memo by James B. Bryan, District Director, Galveston, Texas, Jan. 28, 1929, all found in 55608/129, Entry 9, RG 85, INS, NARA1.

18. W. A. Young, Panama Mail Steamship Company, to Commissioner General, Washington, DC, May 24, 1928; Harry E. Hull, Commissioner General, to Panama Mail Steamship Company, Jun. 26, 1928, both found in 55608/129, Entry 9, RG 85, INS, NARA1.

19. R. B. Sims, Superintendent, Arizona State Prison, to Governor Hunt, Aug. 16, 1923, 54933/351C, Entry 9, RG 85, INS, NARA1.

20. Sterling Robertson, Inspector in Charge, Phoenix, to Inspector in Charge, Tucson, Oct. 29, 1923; R. A. Scott, Inspector in Charge, Tucson, to Supervisor of Immigration Service, El Paso, Nov. 9, 1923, both found in 54933/351B, Entry 9, RG 85, INS, NARA1; G. Wilmoth, Immigrant Inspector, Acting in Charge, El Paso, to Commissioner General of Immigration, Nov. 13, 1923, 55608/126, Entry 9, RG 85, INS, NARA1.

21. Robe Carl White, Assistant Secretary of Labor, to Rep. Carl Hayden, May 21, 1925, 55608/126, Entry 9, RG 85, INS, NARA1.

22. Craig K. Moltzen, Flight Operations Officer, Brownsville, Texas, "Wings over the Southwest," *I & N Reporter*, Jan. 1965, 37–41.

23. Tim Z. Hernandez, *All They Will Call You: The Telling of the Plane Wreck at Los Gatos Canyon* (Tucson: University of Arizona Press, 2017).

24. Hugh E. Ramsell, La Mesa Helicopter Service, to US Immigration Service Headquarters San Francisco, Jun. 15, 1954, 56364/45.6, Vol 7, Entry 9, RG 85, INS, NARA1; Ramsay D. Potts Jr., President, Independent Military Air Transport Association, to Major General Frank H. Partridge, Special Assistant to the Commissioner, INS, Oct. 1, 1954, 56364/45.3, Entry 9, RG 85, INS, NARA1; Memo from H. B. Carter, Chief Border Patrol Branch, Nov. 8, 1954, Alien Airlift, NBPM.

25. Alva L. Pilliod, handwritten note, Mar. 1955, Alien Airlift, NBPM. Pilliod's wife sometimes accompanied him on board as the stewardess.

26. Andrea Adelson, "Federal Express to Buy Flying Tiger," NYT, Dec. 17, 1988, http://www.nytimes.com/1988/12/17/business/federal-express-to-buy-flying-tiger.html.

27. Unsigned memo, Jun. 26, 1952, Airlift, NBPM; "Observations of Investigator at Guadalajara, Jalisco, Mexico Concerning 'Airlift' of Mexicans Illegally in the United States"; Report of Chief Patrol Inspector, El Centro, Calif., Jun. 15, 1951, both found in Mexican Airlift (1951), NBPM; "Wetbacks Landed Here Total 1419," *El Sol de Durango*, Jun. 25, 1951, 56364/43 SW pt2, Entry 9, RG 85, INS, NARA1; "Wetback Lift Resumes," *San Antonio Light*, Jun. 10, 1952; "U.S. to Renew 'Wetback' Airlift for Deporting of Alien Workers," Associated Press, Jun. 10, 1952, TM-94-1, AHSRE.

28. Jack Yeaman, "Wetback Trek May Become Death March," *The Laredo Times*, Jun. 5, 1953, TM-27-29, AHSRE; "'Hot Foot' Desert Trek Continues," *The Laredo Times*, Jun. 7, 1953; Hilo Direcoto, "Arrojan Tierra al Maltrato a los Mojados," *El Mañana de Reynosa*, Jun. 12, 1953; Ernesto Zorrilla Herrera, Cónsul, Laredo, Texas, to C. Secretario de Relaciones Exteriores, Jun. 11, 1953, TM-27-29, AHSRE.

29. Yeaman, "Wetback Trek May Become Death March."

30. Sr. Director de Asuntos de Trabajadores Migratorios to Sr. Presidente de la República, Jun. 18, 1953, TM-94-1, AHSRE. Even when US officials deported people to populated parts of the border, the journey from there to their homes proved trying. Around 1953, a woman selling food twelve miles south of Reynosa along the Monterrey highway reported four families—three mothers carrying babies and the fourth pregnant—stopping at her stand two days into their trip, "with many more ahead." In another instance, Frank Ferree, a South Texas resident who operated a makeshift medical clinic out of a bus on both sides of the border, found "a nine-year-old girl lying prostrate beside the highway." Her parents told Ferree that the family had not eaten for three days. In addition to running his makeshift medical clinic, Ferree, known by residents on both sides of the border as "the Samaritan of Texas," also distributed candy and nuts to children at Christmas time, and donated food, clothing, and blankets to families. "It is obvious," Ferree wrote, "that much of the need for aid of those families occurs along the Mexican border after they are deported," and Ferree argued that "it takes us all, including the American and Mexican governments to provide a chance to live for these neglected families." Frank Ferree to Border Patrol/INS, Aug. 29, 1953, 56364/45.7, Entry 9, RG 85, INS, NARA1; Frank Ferree, Letter to the Editor, "Need for Aid," *Valley Morning Star* (hereafter *VMS*), undated, TM-94-1, AHSRE.

31. Carter to All Stations in Los Angeles District, Jun. 10, 1954; INS Appropriation Request, Jun. 14, 1954; Charter Agreement between Pacific Greyhound Lines and INS, San Francisco, Jun. 5, 1954, all found in 56310/918, Entry 9, RG 85, INS, NARA1. The INS solicited bids from a handful of companies and also considered offers from Allen Transportation and Orange Belt bus company, but neither had interstate licenses to remove deportees to Arizona, so the service decided to go with Greyhound, which charged a rate of $0.56–$0.64 per mile ($5.00–$6.00 today), plus an additional $35–$40 ($318–$363 today) to provide at least one guard to "maintain the aliens in custody while enroute [*sic*]." US officials also buslifted a small percentage of deportees locally through Calexico. Carter to Barber, Jun. 11, 1954, 56364/45.6, Vol 7, Entry 9, RG 85, INS, NARA1; Barber to Commissioner, Jun. 2, 1954, 56310/918, Entry 9, RG 85, INS, NARA1.

32. C. D. Sprigg, Senior Patrol Officer, Chula Vista, Calif., to Chief Patrol Inspector, Chula Vista, Calif. (Memo 1), Jul. 28, 1954; Sprigg to Chief Patrol Inspector, Chula Vista (Memo 2), Jul. 28, 1954, both found in 56321/448f, Entry 9, RG 85, INS, NARA1; Gilbert P. Trujillo, Immigration Patrol Inspector, El Paso, Texas, to A. S. Hudson, Chief, Border Patrol Branch, El Paso, Texas, Nov. 17, 1954, 56364/43 SW pt4, Entry 9, RG 85, INS, NARA1.

33. J. A. Hockaday, "Dr. J. A. Hockaday Collection—Operation Wetback (1954)," home movie, 5:40, Texas Archive of the Moving Image, http://www.texasarchive.org/library/index.php?title=2012_00583.

34. Brownell to Secretary of the Navy, Jul. 13, 1954; Rogers to Mollohan, Aug. 23, 1956, both found in 56364/36 pt1, Boatlift7, Entry 9, RG 85, INS, NARA1.

35. It is possible that TMF grounded the *Emancipación* on purpose in order to get an additional contract for the *Veracruz*. The Mexican government agreed to collaborate in response to US pressure to discourage undocumented migration and promote the Bracero Program. Commissioner to Rep. Kilgore, Mar. 31, 1955; E. DeWitt Marshall to General Partridge, Mar. 30, 1955; Commander Military Sea Transportation Service to Marshall, Mar. 9 and 11, 1955; Note for File, Marshall, Apr. 15, 1955; Commander Military Sea Transportation Service to INS, Mar. 17, 1955; Commander Military Sea Transportation Service to Transportes Marítimos y Fluviales, Mar. 18, 1955, all found in 56364/43.36 pt1, Boatlift3, Entry 9, RG 85, INS, NARA1; Marshall to E. A. Loughran, Jun. 10, 1955; Commissioner Swing to Secretary of State, Jun. 21, 1955, both found in 56364/43.36 pt1, Boatlift2, Entry 9, RG 85, INS, NARA1.

36. "Rep. Mollohan Orders Probe of 'Hell Ship,'" *Washington Daily News*, Aug. 28, 1956, 2; Stan Redding, "Deported Wetbacks Call Mercurio 'Black Slaver,'" *Houston Chronicle*, Sep. 14, 1956, 24, 56364/43.36 pt1, Boatlift5, Entry 9, RG 85, INS, NARA1.

37. Díaz Ordaz became infamous in 1968 when, as president of Mexico, he ordered a military crackdown on student protestors that resulted in the massacre of hundreds of people. Swing to Secretary of State, Jun. 21, 1955; Swing to Holland, Sep. 30, 1955; Mexican Ambassador to Secretary of State, Jun. 9, 1955, all found in 56364/43.36 pt1, Boatlift2, Entry 9, RG 85, INS, NARA1; Marshall to Carter, Jan. 3, 1955, 56364/43.36 pt1, Boatlift3, Entry 9, RG 85, INS, NARA1.

38. "Tremendous Tragedy of 800 Braceros," *La Prensa*, Jul. 25, 1955, 2 (govt. translation), 56364/43.36 pt1, Boatlift2, Entry 9, RG 85, INS, NARA1.

39. Owens to Sahli, Oct. 18, 1955, 56364/43.36 pt1, Boatlift1, Entry 9, RG 85, INS, NARA1.

40. Underline in original. Marshall for File, Jul. 26, 1955; Swing to Holland, Sep. 30, 1955; Beechie to Assistant Commissioner, Enforcement Division, Aug. 3, 1955; Swing to Holland, Sep. 30, 1955, all found in 56364/43.36 pt1, Boatlift2, Entry 9, RG 85, INS, NARA1.

41. Swing to Neil K. Dietrich, Oct. 25, 1955, 56364/43.36 pt1, Boatlift1, Entry 9, RG 85, INS, NARA1; Harlon B. Carter, Memo for File, Sep. 8, 1955, 56364/43.36 pt1, Boatlift2, Entry 9, RG 85, INS, NARA1.

42. Officials discussed a West Coast boatlift with another Mexican company, Transportes Marítimos Mexicanos, but it never materialized. Gonzalo Montalvo Salazar to Transportes Marítimos Refrigerados, Dec. 22, 1955; Marshall to File, Dec. 23, 1955; Beechie to Carter, Dec. 30, 1955; Boatlift-Port Isabel to Veracruz, fiscal years 1955 and 1956; Contract, US Department of the Navy–Transportes Marítimos Refrigerados, Dec. 23, 1955; Franco Ledesma to Military Sea Transportation Service, Jan. 3, 1956, all found in 56364/43.36, Boatlift pt2, Entry 9, RG 85, INS, NARA1; Edgardo Rodríguez L. to Alfonso Poire Ruelas, Oct. 28, 1955, 56364/43.36 pt1, Boatlift7, Entry 9, RG 85, INS, NARA1; *Tiempo*, Sep. 3, 1956, 17, 56364/43.36 pt1, Boatlift6, Entry 9, RG 85,

INS, NARA1; "Immigration, Navy Men Arrive to Start Probe of Wetback 'Hell Ship,'" *VMS*, Aug. 24, 1956, 1, 56364/43.36 pt1, Boatlift4, Entry 9, RG 85, INS, NARA1; Swing to Holland, Sep. 8 and 30, 1955; Holland to Swing, Sep. 23, 1955; Marshall to File, Sep. 27, 1955, all found in 56364/43.36 pt1, Boatlift2, Entry 9, RG 85, INS, NARA1.

43. Immigration officials usually met and often exceeded this monthly quota. Contract, US Department of Navy–Transportes Marítimos Refrigerados, Dec. 23, 1955; Ledesma to Military Sea Transportation Service, Jan. 3, 1956, both found in 56364/43.36, Boatlift pt2, Entry 9, RG 85, INS, NARA1.

44. Rodríguez L. to Poire Ruelas, Oct. 28, 1955, 56364/43.36 pt1, Boatlift7, Entry 9, RG 85, INS, NARA1. On banana production in Latin America and banana consumption in the United States, see John Soluri, *Banana Cultures: Agriculture, Consumption, & Environmental Change in Honduras & the United States* (Austin: University of Texas Press, 2005).

45. Beechie to Acting Assistant Commissioner, Enforcement Division, Jan. 10 and 29, 1956; Report, Patrol Inspector Moskolenko, Apr. 29, 1956; Ledesma to INS, January 1956, all found in 56364/43.36, Boatlift pt2, Entry 9, RG 85, INS, NARA1.

46. Officials never used the *Frida* because it failed inspection. "Conditions 'Good' on Wetback Ship," *VMS*, Aug. 25, 1956, 1–2, 56364/43.36 pt1, Boatlift4, Entry 9, RG 85, INS, NARA1; Beechie to Marshall, Aug. 16, 1956; Commissioner to Attorney General, Aug./Sep. 1956, both found in 56364/43.36, Boatlift pt2, Entry 9, RG 85, INS, NARA1.

47. A Veracruz newspaper reported that the Mexican government paid 80 pesos per boatlifted deportee, but internal US immigration records make no mention of this arrangement. US Naval Attaché, Mexico City, to Commander Military Sea Transportation Service, Apr. 4, 1955; Report, Patrol Inspector Conway, Dec. 22, 1954; "15 'Wetbacks' Are Detained for Re-Entering the U.S." (govt. translation), unspecified Veracruz newspaper, Sep. or Oct. 1954, all found in 56364/43.36 pt1, Boatlift3, Entry 9, RG 85, INS, NARA1; "Boatlift Protest Costs Five Lives," *VMS*, Aug. 28, 1956, 1, 56364/43.36 pt1, Boatlift5, Entry 9, RG 85, INS, NARA1; Boatlift-Port Isabel to Veracruz, fiscal years 1955 and 1956; Telegrams re: payments on the *Mercurio*, 56364/43.36, Boatlift pt2, Entry 9, RG 85, INS, NARA1.

48. William Walters, "Migration, Vehicles, and Politics: Three Theses on Viapolitics," *European Journal of Social Theory* 18, no. 4 (2015): 469–88.

49. Mollohan to Brownell, Aug. 10, 1956, 56364/43.36 pt1, Boatlift7, Entry 9, RG 85, INS, NARA1.

50. Sahli to R. H. Robinson, Acting Assistant Commissioner, Jun. 30, 1954; E. F. McWilliams, Missouri-Kansas-Texas Lines, S. W. Chilton, Frisco Lines, W. R. Godley, GM&O RR, C. T. McEvilly, I. C. RR, and G. G. Kottenstette, Wabash Railroad, to Sahli, Jun. 28, 1954, both found in 56364/45.6, Vol 8, Entry 9, RG 85, INS, NARA1.

51. Bus Bergen, "Wetbacks Shrug, Relax for Long Trip Home," *The Cleveland Press*, Jul. 21, 1954, found in 56364/45.6, Vol 8, Entry 9, RG 85, INS, NARA1.

52. The service estimated each flight using Air Force planes to cost around $1,125, whereas the lowest commercial bid it received was $1,750, and most were closer to

$4,000. Roger Lewis, Assistant Secretary of the Air Force, to Swing, Sep. 2, 1954; Partridge to District Director, Chicago, Sep. 14, 1954, both found in 56364/43.19, Entry 9, RG 85, INS, NARA1; "Commercial Airlift Fares"; Burwell to Brownell, Sep. 22, 1954; Sahli to All Officers, Sep. 17, 1954; "Spanish Language INS Document Informing/Advising Deportees of Customs Agents in Laredo, Texas"; Partridge to Swing, Sep. 27, 1954, all found in 56364/45.6, Vol 8, Entry 9, RG 85, INS, NARA1; S. G. Tipton, General Counsel, Air Transport Association of America, to Attorney General Herbert Brownell, Oct. 15, 1954, 56354/45.3, Entry 9, RG 85, INS, NARA1.

53. Six detainees escaped from McAllen on Dec. 10, 1954, and a demonstration took place ten days later. Carter to Kelley, Jan. 30, 1953, HQ History Border Patrol Story File, NBPM; Einar A. Wahl, Chief, Border Patrol, Detention and Deportation Branch, San Antonio, Texas, to Frank H. Partridge, Special Assistant to the Commissioner, Central Office, Jan. 3, 1955, 56364/43.39, Entry 9, RG 85, INS, NARA1; A. D. Brandon, Acting Officer in Charge, Alien Detention Facility, McAllen, Texas, to Wahl, Mar. 3, 1955, 56364/43.45, Entry 9, RG 85, INS, NARA1.

54. Report by Patrol Inspector Mix, Jun. 21, 1956; Report by Captain Reese, US Navy, to Commander, Military Sea Transportation Service, Aug. 31, 1956; Report by Patrol Inspector Young, Jul. 22, 1956, all found in 56364/43.36, Boatlift pt2, Entry 9, RG 85, INS, NARA1; Carter to Kelly, Feb. 26, 1953, HQ History Border Patrol Story File, NBPM.

55. On some boatlifts, Mexicans expelled via voluntary departure represented 100 percent of the deportees. Report, Patrol Inspector Conway, Jan. 2, 1955, 56364/43.36 pt1, Boatlift3, Entry 9, RG 85, INS, NARA1; Report, Patrol Inspector Hjelle, May 21, 1956, 56364/43.36, Boatlift pt2, Entry 9, RG 85, INS, NARA1; DHS, *YOIS: 2016*, 103.

56. Report, Reese, Aug. 31, 1956, 56364/43.36, Boatlift pt2, Entry 9, RG 85, INS, NARA1; "Two Wetbacks 'Jump' Patrol's Veracruz Trip," *Valley Morning Star*, Sep. 11, 1954, 1, Headquarters History Publicity, NBPM.

57. Report, Patrol Inspector Leach, Jun. 21, 1955, 56364/43.36 pt1, Boatlift2, Entry 9, RG 85, INS, NARA1; Report, Patrol Inspector Hjelle, May 21, 1956, 56364/43.36, Boatlift pt2, Entry 9, RG 85, INS, NARA1; "Conditions 'Good' on Wetback Ship," 1–2, 56364/43.36 pt1, Boatlift4, Entry 9, RG 85, INS, NARA1.

58. "Border Patrol's Initial Co-Educational Cruise Pulls Out for Veracruz," unspecified US newspaper, Sep. 9, 1954, Headquarters History Publicity, NBPM.

59. Marshall to Partridge, Oct. 8, 1954, Headquarters History Publicity, NBPM.

60. Swing to Secretary of State, Jun. 21, 1955; Report, Patrol Inspector Lacy, Aug. 19, 1955, both found in 56364/43.36, pt1, Boatlift2, Entry 9, RG 85, INS, NARA1; Report, Patrol Inspector Leach, Feb. 19, 1955; Report, Patrol Inspector Sutehall, Nov. 30, 1954; Report, Patrol Inspector Pugh, Oct. 27, 1954, all found in 56364/43.36 pt1, Boatlift3, Entry 9, RG 85, INS, NARA1.

61. Wahl to Partridge, Jan. 14, 1955; Report, Patrol Inspector Fortner, Jan. 10, 1955, both found in 56364/43.36 pt1, Boatlift3, Entry 9, RG 85, INS, NARA1.

62. Report, Patrol Inspector Butler, Jan. 21, 1955, 56364/43.36, pt1, Boatlift 3, Entry 9, RG 85, INS, NARA1; Report, Patrol Inspector Journ, Mar. 25, 1956, 56364/43.36, Boatlift pt2, Entry 9, RG 85, INS, NARA1.

63. Report, Patrol Inspector Journ, Mar. 25, 1956; Contract, US Department of Navy-Transportes Marítimos Refrigerados, Dec. 23, 1955, both found in 56364/43.36, Boat-lift pt2, Entry 9, RG 85, INS, NARA1; Report, Patrol Inspector Lacy, Aug. 19, 1955, 56364/43.36 pt1, Boatlift2, Entry 9, RG 85, INS, NARA1; "Conditions 'Good' on Wet-back Ship," 1–2, 56364/43.36, pt1, Boatlift 4, Entry 9, RG 85, INS, NARA1; Mollohan to Brownell, Aug. 10, 1956, 56364/43.36 pt1, Boatlift7, Entry 9, RG 85, INS, NARA1.

64. See, for example, Molina, *Fit to Be Citizens?*; Shah, *Contagious Divides.*

65. Report, Patrol Inspector Lacy, Aug. 19, 1955, 56364/43.36 pt1, Boatlift7, Entry 9, RG 85, INS, NARA1; Report, Patrol Inspector Leach, Feb. 19, 1955; Report, Patrol Inspector Sutehall, Nov. 30, 1954, both found in 56364/43.36 pt1, Boatlift3, Entry 9, RG 85, INS, NARA1; "Typical Menu of Food Provided the Crew and Passengers–MV MERCU-RIO," Mar. 31, 1956; Report, Patrol Inspector Zizik, Jan. 22, 1956, both found in 56364/43.36, Boatlift pt2, Entry 9, RG 85, INS, NARA1; Captain Jorge Noval E., Menu for *Mercurio*, Aug. 24–26, 1956, 56364/43.36 pt1, Boatlift6, Entry 9, RG 85, INS, NARA1; Meals and Menus from the *Mercurio*, Mar.–Aug. 1956, 56364/43.36 pt1, Boatlift7, Entry 9, RG 85, INS, NARA1; Report, Patrol Inspector Leach, Jun. 21, 1955, 56364/43.36 pt1, Boatlift2, Entry 9, RG 85, INS, NARA1; Author interview with Gabriel Esquivel (pseudonym), Mexico City, Apr. 30, 2013.

66. "Relata un Deportado el Infierno Vivido," *Ultimas Noticias*, Aug. 28, 1956, 7, 56364/43.36 pt1, Boatlift5, Entry 9, RG 85, INS, NARA1; Beechie to Marshall, Aug. 16, 1956; Report, Patrol Inspector Lewis, May 11, 1956, both found in 56364/43.36, Boatlift pt2, Entry 9, RG 85, INS, NARA1.

67. Report, Patrol Inspector Sutehall, Nov. 30, 1954 , 56364/43.36 pt1, Boatlift3, Entry 9, RG 85, INS, NARA1; Report, Patrol Inspector Lewis, May 11, 1956; Report, Patrol Inspector Zizik, Jan. 27, 1956; Report, Patrol Inspector Hjelle, May 21, 1956; Affidavit, Jesús Arana Bernal, Sep. 23, 1956, all found in 56364/43.36, Boatlift pt2, Entry 9, RG 85, INS, NARA1; Meals and menus from the *Mercurio*, Mar.–Aug. 1956; Report, Patrol Inspector Lacy, Aug. 19, 1955, both found in 56364/43.36 pt1, Boatlift7, Entry 9, RG 85, INS, NARA1.

68. Contract, US Department of Navy-Transportes Marítimos y Fluviales, June 1955, 56364/43.36 pt1, Boatlift1, Entry 9, RG 85, INS, NARA1; Poiré R. to Transportes Maríti-mos Refrigerados, Nov. 9, 1955, 56364/43.36 pt1, Boatlift7, Entry 9, RG 85, INS, NARA1; Gonzalo Montalvo Salazar to Transportes Marítimos Refrigerados, Dec. 22, 1955; Con-tract, US Department of Navy-Transportes Marítimos Refrigerados, Dec. 23, 1955; Reese to Commander, Military Sea Transportation Service, Aug. 31, 1956; Report, Patrol Inspector Lacy, Apr. 20, 1956, all found in 56364/43.36, Boatlift pt2, Entry 9, RG 85, INS, NARA1.

69. Marshall, Memo for File, Jan. 9, 1956, 56364/43.36, Boatlift pt2, Entry 9, RG 85, INS, NARA1; Carter for File, Sep. 17, 1956; Unsigned Letter to Mollohan, Sep. 14, 1956;

Unsigned Letter Draft, Sep. 1956, all found in 56364/43.36, Boatlift pt3, Entry 9, RG 85, INS, NARA1.

70. Source limitations prevent me from naming the first deportee who died aboard the ship. Sahli to Assistant Commissioner, Border Patrol, Detention and Deportation Division, Jan. 31, 1955, 56364/43.36 pt1, Boatlift3, Entry 9, RG 85, INS, NARA1; Beechie to Marshall, Aug. 23, 1955, 56364/43.36 pt1, Boatlift2, Entry 9, RG 85, INS, NARA1.

71. Report, Patrol Inspector Hjelle, May 21, 1956; Report, Patrol Inspector Zizik, Jan. 27, 1956; Swanson to Carter, Feb. 24, 1956; Beechie to Swanson, Feb. 21, 1956, all found in 56364/43.36, Boatlift pt2, Entry 9, RG 85, INS, NARA1; Report, Patrol Inspector Brady, Mar. 15, 1955; Report, Patrol Inspector Goff, Oct. 8, 1954; Report, Patrol Inspector Hensley, Dec. 5, 1954; Report, Patrol Inspector Sutehall, Nov. 30, 1954; Report, Patrol Inspector Butler, Jan. 21, 1955; Report, Patrol Inspector Pugh, Oct. 27, 1954, all found in 56364/43.36 pt1, Boatlift3, Entry 9, RG 85, INS, NARA1; Report, Patrol Inspector Leach, Jun. 21, 1955; Report, Patrol Inspector Lacy, Aug. 19, 1955, both found in 56364/43.36 pt1, Boatlift2, Entry 9, RG 85, INS, NARA1.

72. Deportees often censored their comments to immigration officials. Affidavit, Alejandro Salazar Sánchez, Sep. 28, 1956; Affidavit, David Flores Samorra, Sep. 25, 1956; Report, Patrol Inspector Fortner, Jan. 10, 1955; Affidavit, Maldonado Martinez, Sep. 21, 1956; Affidavit, Belmontes Ramos, Sep. 28, 1956, all found in 56364/43.36, Boatlift pt3, Entry 9, RG 85, INS, NARA1; Report, Patrol Inspector Moskolenko, Apr. 29, 1956; Report, Patrol Inspector Journ, Mar. 25, 1956; Report, Patrol Inspector Young, Jul. 22, 1956, all found in 56364/43.36, Boatlift pt2, Entry 9, RG 85, INS, NARA1; Report, Patrol Inspector Fortner, Jan. 10, 1955; Untitled article, *El Dictamen*, Dec. 10, 1954 (translation), both found in 56364/43.36 pt1, Boatlift3, Entry 9, RG 85, INS, NARA1; Report, Patrol Inspector Lacy, Aug. 19, 1955, 56364/43.36 pt1, Boatlift2, Entry 9, RG 85, INS, NARA1.

73. "Mexican Aliens Apprehended since the Establishment of the Boatlift Operation," 56364/43.36, Boatlift pt2, Entry 9, RG 85, INS, NARA1.

74. Mollohan to Brownell, Aug. 10, 1956; Mollohan to Richmond, Aug. 10, 1956, both found in 56364/43.36 pt1, Boatlift7, Entry 9, RG 85, INS, NARA1; "Immigration, Navy Men Arrive to Start Probe of Wetback 'Hell Ship,'" 1, 56364/43.36 pt1, Boatlift4, Entry 9, RG 85, INS, NARA1.

75. Reese to Commander Military Sea Transportation Service, Aug. 31, 1956, 56364/43.36, Boatlift pt2, Entry 9, RG 85, INS, NARA1; "Conditions 'Good' on Wetback Ship," 1–2, 56364/43.36 pt1, Boatlift4, Entry 9, RG 85, INS, NARA1.

76. Reese to Commander Military Sea Transportation Service, Aug. 31, 1956, 56364/43.36, Boatlift pt2, Entry 9, RG 85, INS, NARA1.

77. Report, Patrol Inspector Conway, Jan. 2, 1955, 56364/43.36 pt1, Boatlift3, Entry 9, RG 85, INS, NARA1.

78. "Conditions 'Good' on Wetback Ship," *VMS*, Aug. 25, 1956, 1–2, 56364/43.36 pt1, Boatlift4, Entry 9, RG 85, INS, NARA1.

79. "Llegó el 'Mercurio' sin Trabajadores a Veracruz," *Excélsior*, Aug. 28, 1956, 56364/ 43.36 pt1, Boatlift5, Entry 9, RG 85, INS, NARA1; "El Caso del 'Mercurio I," *Tiempo*, Sep. 3, 1956, 17; Affidavit, Jorge Rodríguez García, Sep. 5, 1956; Affidavit, Pedro Garcia-Velazquez, Sep. 7, 1956; Affidavit, Jorge Rodríguez García, Sep. 6, 1956, all found in 56364/43.36 pt1, Boatlift6, Entry 9, RG 85, INS, NARA1; "Mexico to Probe Ship Riot," *VMS*, Aug. 28, 1956, 1; "Boatlift Protest Costs Five Lives," *VMS*, Aug. 28, 1956, 1; "Mexico: Mutiny on the *Mercurio*," *Time*, Sep. 10, 1956, all found in 56364/43.36 pt1, Boatlift5, Entry 9, RG 85, INS, NARA1.

80. "Mexico to Probe Ship Riot," *VMS*, Aug. 28, 1956, 1; "Boatlift Protest Costs Five Lives," *VMS*, Aug. 28, 1956, 1; "Llegó el 'Mercurio' sin Trabajadores a Veracruz," *Excélsior*, Aug. 28, 1956; "EP Immigration Chief Discounts Reports of Wetback Boat Mishap," unspecified US newspaper, Aug. or Sep. 1956; "Very Shocking," unspecified US newspaper, Aug. or Sep. 1956; "Deported Wetbacks Call Mercurio 'Black Slaver,'" *Houston Chronicle*, Sep. 14, 1956, 24, all found in 56364/43.36 pt1, Boatlift5, Entry 9, RG 85, INS, NARA1; Affidavit, Felix Gudino Quevas, Aug. 31, 1956, 56364/43.36 pt1, Boatlift7, Entry 9, RG 85, INS, NARA1.

81. Whittinghill to Officer in Charge, Brownsville, Aug. 29, 1956, 56364/43.36 pt1, Boatlift7, Entry 9, RG 85, INS, NARA1; "5 Braceros Ahogados en Aguas del Pánuco," *Noticias de Tampico*, Aug. 28, 1956, 1, 56364/43.36 pt1, Boatlift5, Entry 9, RG 85, INS, NARA1; Whittinghill to Secretary of State, Aug. 29, 1956, 56364/43.36, Boatlift pt3, Entry 9, RG 85, INS, NARA1.

82. "Very Shocking," unspecified US newspaper, Aug. or Sep. 1956; "Vil Patrioterismo En La Alharaca Por el 'Mercurio,'" *Zócalo*, Aug. 28, 1956 (translated by author); "La Tragedia del 'Mercurio,'" *Excélsior*, Aug. 28, 1956; Carlos Denegri, title illegible, *Excélsior*, Aug. 28, 1956 (translated by author), all found in 56364/43.36 pt1, Boatlift5, Entry 9, RG 85, INS, NARA1.

83. "Gómez Maqueo Fue a Inspeccionar el 'Mercurio I,'" *Excélsior*, Aug. 28, 1956, 15, 56364/43.36 pt1, Boatlift5, Entry 9, RG 85, INS, NARA1; "Hell Ship," United Press, Aug. 28, 1956, 56364/43.36, Boatlift pt3, Entry 9, RG 85, INS, NARA1.

84. Cervantes to Beechie, Aug. 15, 1956; Schleske to Ball, Aug. 17, 1956, both found in 56364/43.36 pt1, Boatlift7, Entry 9, RG 85, INS, NARA1; "Deported Wetbacks Call Mercurio 'Black Slaver,'" 24.

85. Handwritten note by unidentified immigration official, Aug. 1956, 56364/43.36 pt1, Boatlift7, Entry 9, RG 85, INS, NARA1; "Culpan al Gobierno de la Tragedia de los Braceros del Barco Mercurio," *El Norte*, Aug. 28, 1956, 1, 56364/43.36 pt1, Boatlift5, Entry 9, RG 85, INS, NARA1.

86. Untitled article, *El Heraldo*, Aug. 30, 1956, 1 (govt. translation), 56364/43.36 pt1, Boatlift7, Entry 9, RG 85, INS, NARA1; "El Caso del 'Mercurio I,'" *Tiempo*, Sep. 3, 1956, 17, 56364/43.36 pt1, Boatlift6, Entry 9, RG 85, INS, NARA1; "Llegó el 'Mercurio' sin Trabajadores a Veracruz," *Excélsior*, Aug. 28, 1956, 56364/43.36 pt1, Boatlift5, Entry 9, RG 85, INS, NARA1.

87. Officials recorded only seventy-nine prior arrests for criminal offenses, some 95 percent of them for minor crimes. At most, 16.1 percent of the 500 men on board had prior arrests. Statistics from 1955–1956 also show that boatlifted deportees generally had no criminal record. "SS *MERCURIO*, Data Concerning Alien Passengers Sailing from Port Isabel on August 24, 1956," Aug. 24, 1956, 56364/43.36, Boatlift pt2, Entry 9, RG 85, INS, NARA1; Regional Commissioner, SW Region, to Commissioner, Aug. 31, 1956, 56364/43.36 pt1, Boatlift7, Entry 9, RG 85, INS, NARA1.

88. "El Siniestro 'Mercurio' no Transportará más Mojados," *El Fronterizo*, Aug. 31, 1956, 1; "The Braceros Will Be Repatriated by Other Means in the Future," *Noticias*, Sep. 7, 1956 (govt. translation); Ledesma to Beechie, Sep. 10, 1956, 56364/43.36 pt1, Boatlift6, Entry 9, RG 85, INS, NARA1; Veracruz Port Captain Bidart to Ruiz y Garcia, Aug. 31, 1956, 56364/43.36 pt1, Boatlift7, Entry 9, RG 85, INS, NARA1.

89. Rogers to Mollohan, Aug. 23, 1956, 56364/43.36 pt1, Boatlift7, Entry 9, RG 85, INS, NARA1.

90. Swing to Robert Murphy, Sep. 14, 1956, 56364/43.36, Boatlift pt2, Entry 9, RG 85, INS, NARA1.

91. "Air Transport Operations Portfolio," last revised Aug. 30, 1968, Air Operations, NBPM; Robert L. Stewart, "Cooperation with Mexican Government in Reducing Illegal Entry of Mexican Nationals," NBPM.

92. US Embassy in Mexico to Secretary of State, May 11 and 20, 1976, "Central Foreign Policy Files, created, 7/1/1973–12/31/1979," RG 59, Department of State (hereafter DoS), NARA2. Digital copies of the DoS "Central Foreign Policy Files, created, 7/1/1973–12/31/1979" records cited in chapters 3 and 4 are available here: https://aad.archives.gov/aad/series-list.jsp?cat=WR43.

93. US Embassy in Mexico to Secretary of State, July 5, 1974, "Central Foreign Policy Files, created, 7/1/1973–12/31/1979," RG 59, DoS, NARA2; Denny Walsh, "Ousted Mexicans Pay Off to Stay Close to U.S. Jobs," *NYT*, Apr. 15, 1973, 1; John Crewdson, *The Tarnished Door: The New Immigrants and the Transformation of America* (New York: Times Books, 1983), 151–52.

94. "An Evaluation of the Cost Effectiveness of Repatriating Aliens to the Interior of Mexico," 1977, USCISHOL; "Service Accomplishments in CY 1976," *I & N Reporter*, Summer 1977, 11; US Embassy in Mexico to Secretary of State, Jul. 23, 1976, "Central Foreign Policy Files, created, 7/1/1973–12/31/1979," RG 59, DoS, NARA2; Raúl Sánchez Carrillo and Conrado de la Torre, "Llegaron a México los 150 Deportados de Estados Unidos," *El Universal*, Aug. 5, 1976, 12; Frank del Olmo, "Illegal Aliens Go Home in Style, U.S. Pays Tab," *LAT*, Jul. 27, 1976, A3; Everett R. Holles, "U.S. Airlifting Mexican Aliens Home," *NYT*, Jul. 25, 1976, 20. On the 1970s airlifts from the Mexican perspective and the challenges deportees confronted upon returning to Mexico, see Expediente 10, Caja 1676c, Investigaciones Políticas y Sociales, Secretaría de Gobernación Siglo XX, AGN.

## Chapter 4: Manufacturing Crisis and Fomenting Fear at the Dawn of the Age of Mass Expulsion

1. Oral history with Juan Olivarez (pseudonym), Jalisco, México, Oct. 12, 2012 (translation by author).

2. Deportations hovered around one million per year from the late 1970s to the early 2000s. Nearly 90 percent of all expulsions throughout US history have occurred since 1970, during what I call the age of mass expulsion. DHS, *YOIS: 2018*, 103.

3. On "moral panic," see Stuart Hall, Chas Critcher, Tony Jefferson, John Clarke, and Brian Roberts, *Policing the Crisis: Mugging, the State and Law and Order*, 2nd ed. (London: Palgrave Macmillan, 2013).

4. Massey, Durand, and Malone, *Beyond Smoke and Mirrors*, 5.

5. The 1965 act's hemispheric quotas went into effect in 1968. AR 1966, 1; Ngai, *Impossible Subjects*, 258–64; Maddalena Marinari, "'Americans Must Show Justice in Immigration Policies Too': The Passage of the 1965 Immigration Act," *Journal of Policy History* 26, no. 2 (2014): 219–45.

6. AR, 1965, 8. Some Mexicans migrated to, but never crossed, the northern border. Instead, they stayed and labored in the transnational companies' factories, known as maquiladoras, that expanded as part of the Mexican government's Border Industrialization Program to provide jobs for migrants after the Bracero Program ended. On how maquiladoras have affected Mexican workers, and especially women, in the years since, see Alicia Schmidt Camacho, *Migrant Imaginaries: Latino Cultural Politics in the US-Mexico Borderlands* (New York: New York University Press, 2008), 237–82.

7. Program Memorandum, Immigration and Naturalization Service, Sep. 1966, 23–25, USCISHOL.

8. Ana Raquel Minian, *Undocumented Lives: The Untold Story of Mexican Migration* (Cambridge, MA: Harvard University Press, 2018), 14–76.

9. Juan de Onis, "Storm over 'Operation Intercept,'" NYT, Oct. 5, 1969, 5; Frydl, *The Drug Wars in America, 1940–1973*, 376–80.

10. INS Program Memos, 1966–68, USCISHOL; DHS, *YOIS: 2016*; Robert Scheer, "Law Part of Problem," *LAT*, Nov. 12, 1979, B1.

11. Judith Stein, *Pivotal Decade: How the United States Traded Factories for Finance in the Seventies* (New Haven, CT: Yale University Press, 2010); Meg Jacobs, *Panic at the Pump: The Energy Crisis and the Transformation of American Politics in the 1970s* (New York: Farrar, Straus and Giroux, 2016); "Week in Business; U.S. Unemployment Shoots up to 10.8%," *NYT*, Dec. 5, 1982.

12. Celestino Fernández and Lawrence R. Pedroza, "The Border Patrol and News Media Coverage of Undocumented Mexican Immigration During the 1970s: A Quantitative Content Analysis in the Sociology of Knowledge," *California Sociologist* 5, no. 2 (1982): 1–26. In February 1977, veteran reporter Susan Jacoby gave a talk at a conference at New York University explaining why the media presented biased coverage of

undocumented migrants. Jacoby attributed this, in large part, to the fact that "it is a lot easier [for a journalist] to go down to the INS, to the Labor Department, or to some other agency than to go out into the neighborhoods and spend months finding out what the lives of people are like." News outlets, she concluded, were "unwilling to commit money and manpower for this purpose," which distorted both public opinion and public policy. Susan Jacoby, "The Media and The Undocumented Migrants," National Consultation on Undocumented Migrants and Public Policies, New York University, Feb. 25, 1977, Box 32, Folder 12, CASA Papers, m325, SCSUL. On Mexicans and Latinos as outsiders and threats, see Chavez, *The Latino Threat*; Leo R. Chavez, *Covering Immigration: Popular Images and the Politics of the Nation* (Berkeley: University of California Press, 2001); Douglas S. Massey and Karen A. Pren, "Unintended Consequences of US Immigration Policy: Explaining the Post-1965 Surge from Latin America," *Population and Development Review* 38, no. 1 (Mar. 2012): 1–29, esp. 5–8.

13. Elena R. Gutiérrez, *Fertile Matters: The Politics of Mexican-Origin Women's Reproduction* (Austin: University of Texas Press, 2008), esp. 1–54, 73–93. On immigration and reproductive politics, see also Laura Briggs, *How All Politics Became Reproductive Politics: From Welfare Reform to Foreclosure to Trump* (Berkeley: University of California Press, 2017), 75–100.

14. Tanton also founded the Center for Immigration Studies and Numbers USA, which, along with FAIR, are the most powerful immigration restrictionist lobby groups in the country today. Gutiérrez, *Fertile Matters*, 73–93.

15. H.R. 982 passed the House, but died in the Senate. Employer sanctions would later become an integral part of the 1986 Immigration Reform and Control Act. "Introducing Leonard F. Chapman, Jr., Our New Commissioner," *I & N Reporter* 22, no. 4 (Spring 1974): 43; "How Millions of Illegal Aliens Sneak into U.S.: Interview with Leonard F. Chapman, Jr., Commissioner, Immigration and Naturalization Service," *U.S. News & World Report*, Jul. 22, 1974, 27–30; DHS, *YOIS: 2012*, 91. On Chapman's tenure as INS commissioner and efforts to raise public awareness of the supposed immigration crisis, see Jensen Elise Branscombe, "Clamping the Lid on the Melting Pot: Immigration Policy and the U.S.-Mexico Border, 1965–1986" (Ph.D. diss., Texas Christian University, 2013), 105–48, 164–68, 192.

16. Leonard F. Chapman Jr., "Illegal Aliens—A Growing Population," *I & N Reporter*, Fall 1975, 15–18; DHS, *YOIS: 2012*, 91.

17. Miriam Pawel, *The Crusades of Cesar Chavez: A Biography* (New York: Bloomsbury, 2014), 288–95; Frank Bardacke, "The UFW and the Undocumented," *International Labor and Working-Class History* No. 83 (Spring 2013): 162–69; DHS, *YOIS: 2017*, 103.

18. DHS, *YOIS: 2017*, 103.

19. "Program Justification, Immigration and Naturalization," Dec. 1968, 16, USCISHOL.

20. From fiscal year 1969 to the first half of fiscal year 1971, 190,612 of 280,250 deportees removed into the Mexican interior paid $1,715,329 of the $2,368,177 total cost of deportation. INS Budget, Fiscal Year 1972, USCISHOL.

21. From fiscal year 1965–70 the total number of man-days in detention increased from 430,120 to 914,117. The service's reliance on contract detention facilities increased as well, going from 30 percent to 44 percent of the total number of man-days in detention. The INS had a limited collaboration with the IRS, which had a presence, albeit an inconsistent one, with the El Paso detention facility and five district offices, including Los Angeles. Officials also questioned whether trying to collect taxes from people awaiting deportation made fiscal sense, since it would also require additional days in detention. "Opportunities for the Immigration and Naturalization Service to Reduce Costs of Returning Aliens to Mexico," Aug. 1971, "Airlift" folder, NBPM; INS Budget, Fiscal Year 1972, USCISHOL; "More Needs to Be Done to Reduce the Number and Adverse Impact of Illegal Aliens in the United States," Report of Comptroller General of the United States to the Congress, Jul. 31, 1973, 37–44, 62.

22. "More Needs to Be Done to Reduce the Number and Adverse Impact of Illegal Aliens in the United States," 1–29; Charles Gordon, "The Problem of Illegal Entries from Mexico," *I & N Reporter*, Spring 1973, 43–48.

23. Report by the Domestic Council's Committee on Illegal Aliens, Dec. 1976, quoted in Report by the Comptroller General of the United States to Congress, "Illegal Entry at United States-Mexico Border—Multiagency Enforcement Efforts Have Not Been Effective in Stemming the Flow of Drugs and People," Dec. 2, 1977, 17.

24. During this period the probability of being apprehended hovered between .35 and .45. Massey, Durand, and Malone, *Beyond Smoke and Mirrors*, 55–58. For a comparative, contemporary example of deportation's quotidian nature, see Treasa M. Galvin, "'We Deport Them but They Keep Coming Back': The Normalcy of Deportation in the Daily Life of 'Undocumented' Zimbabwean Migrant Workers in Botswana," *Journal of Ethnic and Migration Studies* 41, no. 4 (2015): 617–34.

25. Jane Leek, "Hopes for New Life Outweigh Aliens' Fears," *LAT*, Jan. 8, 1973, D1.

26. The outcome of Mendarez-Pérez's case is unclear, but it is likely that she was given a short prison sentence since the INS had formally deported her in the past. I should also note that I have no way of confirming the number of times authorities apprehended Mendarez-Pérez. Even if forty-eight is not a precise count, there is no reason to doubt that officials had expelled her on many occasions. Clarence H. Russell, "Even Chicanos Want to Halt Tide of Illegal Aliens," *Christian Science Monitor*, Aug. 15, 1977, 16; A. Garza Morales, "U.S. Immigration Chief Says Illegals Have the Right to Seek Work," *Excélsior*, Nov. 22, 1977.

27. Thomas J. Espenshade refers to this as the "repeated trials model." See Thomas J. Espenshade, "Undocumented Migration into the United States: Evidence from a Repeated Trials Model," in *Undocumented Migration to the United States: IRCA and the Experience of the 1980s*, ed. Frank D. Bean, Barry Edmonson, and Jeffrey S. Passel (Santa Monica, CA, and Washington, DC: Rand Corporation and The Urban Institute, 1990), 159–81.

28. Oral history with Gustavo Ramírez (pseudonym), Jalisco, México, Jan. 20, 2013 (translation by author). This tactic proved effective since the INS did not have the

institutional capacity to fingerprint the vast majority of apprehended Mexican migrants after 1970. During the previous decade, the service claimed that "nearly all adult Mexican male aliens apprehended were fingerprinted and held in detention until fingerprint returns were received." "More Needs to Be Done to Reduce the Number and Adverse Impact of Illegal Aliens in the United States," 30.

29. Barbara Matusow, "Leonel Castillo: INS' Man in the Middle," *Oakland Post*, Jul. 17, 1979. The head of the local National Border Patrol Council in San Ysidro, California, which represented two-thirds of the office's 300 agents, described a similar situation: "We are just recycling aliens. We send them back into Mexico. They return and we pick them up and ship them back again. We don't have any idea of the numbers of aliens we are actually fighting because so many of them keep coming back across the border." "Border Patrolmen Fighting 'Helpless' Battle," *Desert Sun* (Palm Springs, CA), Jul. 22, 1977, A12.

30. Jorge Durand, ed., *El Norte Es Como El Mar: Entrevistas a Trabajadores Migrantes en Estados Unidos* (Guadalajara, México: Universidad de Guadalara, 1996), 19–30.

31. AR and *YOIS*, 1965–85. Calculations by author.

32. Massey and Pren, "Unintended Consequences of US Immigration Policy," 27.

33. Satirical Memo, Dec. 1, 1965, "Airlift" folder, NBPM.

34. Lee Dye, "Corruption Plagues U.S. along Mexican Border," *LAT*, Dec. 17, 1972; Denny Walsh, "G.A.O. Finds Illegal-Aliens Problem Worsened by Lax Enforcement," *NYT*, Jun. 25, 1973, 28.

35. Christopher Dickey, "U.S. Shelves Illegal Alien Search Policy," *Washington Post* (hereafter *WaPo*), Nov. 5, 1978, A1. INS officers' organizing efforts occurred around the same time as other law enforcement officials unionized and pushed "law and order" politics. See, for example, William J. Bopp, *The Police Rebellion: A Quest for Blue Power* (Springfield, IL: Charles C. Thomas, 1971); Stuart Schrader, "To Protect and Serve Themselves: Police in US Politics since the 1960s" *Public Culture* 31, no. 3 (2019): 601–23.

36. John M. Crewdson, "U.S. Immigration Service Hampered by Corruption," *NYT*, Jan. 13, 1980, 1.

37. The internal investigation Operation Clean Sweep opened 300 potential criminal cases, but resulted in just seven indictments and five convictions. Explaining why he ended Clean Sweep soon after becoming commissioner, Leonard Chapman explained that he believed that "virtually all of the employees of the INS are honest, dedicated, hard-working and loyal public servants." Crewdson, *The Tarnished Door*, 143–217, esp. 160, 165, and 202. On the INS's abusive practices in the early 1970s, see also Trudy Hayden, "The Immigration and Naturalization Service and Civil Liberties: A Report on the Abuse of Discretion" (New York: ACLU, 1974); Files found in box 17, folders 8 and 9, Herman Baca Papers, MSS 0649, SCA-UCSD (also available online through the University of California, San Diego's Library Digital Collections). On private citizens' violence against migrants in the 1970s, see Geraldo L. Cadava, *Standing on Common Ground: The Making of a Sunbelt Borderland* (Cambridge, MA: Harvard University

Press, 2013), 188–98. On Chicana/o and Mexicana/o resistance to Border Patrol violence in the 1970s, see Jimmy Patiño, *Raza Sí, Migra No: Chicano Movement Struggles for Immigrant Rights in San Diego* (Chapel Hill: University of North Carolina Press, 2017), 47–66.

38. "Meet Leonel J. Castillo, Our New Commissioner," *I & N Reporter*, Summer 1977, 1; Crewdson, *The Tarnished Door*, 128.

39. Garza Morales, "U.S. Immigration Chief Says Illegals Have the Right to Seek Work."

40. Bob Williams, "Illegal Aliens Win a Beachhead for the Third World," *LAT*, Jun. 4, 1978, CS1.

41. Grace Halsell, *The Illegals* (New York: Stein and Day, 1978), 146–47.

42. Williams, "Illegal Aliens Win a Beachhead for the Third World"; Robert Lindsey, "Immigration Chief Called 'Soft' on Illegal Mexican Aliens," *NYT*, Nov. 19, 1978; Matusow, "Leonel Castillo: INS' Man in the Middle"; Dickey, "U.S. Shelves Illegal Alien Search Policy."

43. Dickey, "U.S. Shelves Illegal Alien Search Policy"; Lindsey, "Immigration Chief Called 'Soft' on Illegal Mexican Aliens"; Matusow, "Leonel Castillo: INS' Man in the Middle"; phone conversation between author and immigration lawyer Peter Williamson, Sep. 27, 2018; email correspondence between author and immigration lawyer Richard A. Boswell, Sep. 27, 2018; Crewdson, *The Tarnished Door*, 131; Bill Grinder, "Reagan Policies on Immigration Shift into Full Swing," *Los Angeles Daily Journal*, Jan. 28, 1982, 15.

44. Satirical draft memo, supposedly from Leonel Castillo, Commissioner, to All INS Employees, "My Departure from INS," Sep. 15, 1979, NBPM.

45. Anthropologist Josiah Heyman has described this system as "the voluntary departure complex." See Josiah McC. Heyman, "Putting Power in the Anthropology of Bureaucracy: The Immigration and Naturalization Service at the Mexico-United States Border," *Current Anthropology* 36, no. 2 (Apr. 1995): 261–87. On the "double problem" rule enforcers face in justifying their position by "demonstrat[ing] to others that the problem still exists," while also "show[ing] that [their] attempts at enforcement are effective and worthwhile," see Howard S. Becker, *Outsiders: Studies in the Sociology of Deviance* (New York: The Free Press, 1963), 157.

46. "Illegal Alien Survey," 1975, Chicano Studies Microfilm Collection, I.-H 10,251, University of Southern California Library, Los Angeles, CA. Robert Warren started working as an INS statistician in 1975 and later headed the division. He described the agency's leaders as espousing an attitude of "benign neglect" toward him and his colleagues, and he rarely got the sense that top immigration bureaucrats used statistics to inform policy. Instead, they treated the division's handful of statisticians and more than twenty clerical workers as the "compilers of whatever they chose to make available." Author phone interview with Robert Warren, Aug. 2, 2019. See also Daniel B. Levine, Kenneth Hill, and Robert Warren, eds., *Immigration Statistics: A Story of Neglect* (Washington, DC: National Academy Press, 1985).

47. Gilberto Cárdenas, "Critical Issues in Using Government Data Collected Primarily for Non-Research Purposes," in *Quantitative Data and Immigration Research*, ed. Stephen R. Crouch and Roy Simón Bryce-Laporte (Washington, DC: Research Institute on Immigration and Ethnic Studies, Smithsonian Institution, 1979), 55–98, esp. 80–82. See also Arthur Corwin, "The Numbers Game: Estimates of Illegal Aliens in the United States, 1970–1981," *Law and Contemporary Problems* 45, no. 2 (1982): 223–97.

48. US Embassy in Mexico to Secretary of State, Washington, DC, Jul. 26, 1974, "Central Foreign Policy Files, created, 7/1/1973–12/31/1979," RG59, DoS, NARA2.

49. US Embassy in Mexico to Secretary of State, Washington, DC, Jul. 11, 1973, "Central Foreign Policy Files, created, 7/1/1973–12/31/1979," RG 59, DoS, NARA2. Although the Mexican government publicly pushed for a new bracero program (until the end of 1974), Foreign Relations Secretary Emilio Rabasa confided that it "was personally embarrassing for him as a Mexican to have to plead that [the United States] accept Mexican laborers who were eager to leave their own country." But, because of domestic political pressures (including organized labor's staunch opposition), US officials had no intention of reinitiating a guest worker program. Speaking confidentially, Rabasa admitted that the "illegal immigration" problem "had been studied to death and he questioned whether it was solvable," and Mexican President Luis Echeverría allowed that "he really had no idea on a solution except the long-term one . . . of raising the standard of living in Mexico to decrease the temptation for illegal immigration." US Embassy in Mexico to Secretary of State, Washington, DC, Aug. 3, 1974; US Embassy in Mexico to Secretary of State, Washington, DC, Nov. 2, 1974; US Consul in Rio de Janeiro to Secretary of State, Washington, DC, May 19, 1973; US Embassy in Mexico to Secretary of State, Washington, DC, Oct. 5, 1973; US Embassy in Mexico to Secretary of State, Washington, DC, Jun. 18, 1973, all found in "Central Foreign Policy Files, created, 7/1/1973–12/31/1979," RG 59, DoS, NARA2. On Mexican emigration policy since 1965, see David FitzGerald, *A Nation of Emigrants: How Mexico Manages Its Migration* (Berkeley: University of California Press, 2009), 55–69; Natasha Iskander, *Creative State: Forty Years of Migration and Development Policy in Morocco and Mexico* (Ithaca, NY: Cornell University Press, 2010), 192–235; Alexandra Délano, *Mexico and Its Diaspora in the United States: Policies of Emigration since 1848* (New York: Cambridge University Press, 2011), 105–252; Minian, *Undocumented Lives*, 14–46.

50. US Embassy in Mexico to Secretary of State, Washington, DC, Jul. 25, 1974, "Central Foreign Policy Files, created, 7/1/1973–12/31/1979," RG 59, DoS, NARA2.

51. As Cárdenas warns, all INS data should be taken with a grain of salt, if not entirely discarded. But by recognizing statistics as social artifacts with performative elements meant to serve institutional purposes, I believe they can provide important insights into the service's strategies and tactics during a time of tremendous change within the bureaucracy. The graphs in this chapter come from a close analysis of twenty-two years of previously unreported apprehension data I discovered in the archives and carefully analyzed. The detailed, disaggregated data are broken down by a variety of

factors, including the sex of apprehended migrants, how long someone had been in the United States at the time of apprehension, city or region where apprehended, type of INS official responsible for apprehension, apprehensions of Mexicans relative to total apprehensions, type of employment (if any) at time of apprehension, etc. INS, "Deportable Aliens: Reports," USCISHOL.

52. Program Justification, Immigration and Naturalization, Dec. 1968, 11; INS, "Deportable Aliens: Reports," USCISHOL; DHS, *YOIS: 2012*. On the laws and policies from the early to mid-twentieth century that created the notion of Mexicans as "illegal aliens," see Ngai, *Impossible Subjects*, 56–90, 127–66; Lytle Hernández, *Migra!*; Molina, *How Race Is Made in America*, 43–67, 91–111. For a comparative example about the racial formation and production of difference of Chinese immigrants, see Shah, *Contagious Divides*. On Progressive Era authorities' use of statistics to criminalize blackness, see Muhammad, *Condemnation of Blackness*.

53. Address by the Honorable William B. Saxbe, Attorney General of the United States, before Cameron County and Hidalgo County Bar Associations, Oct. 30, 1974, accessed November 2, 2017, https://www.justice.gov/sites/default/files/ag/legacy/2011/08/23/10-30-1974.pdf; "Attorney General: William Bart Saxbe," US Department of Justice, accessed November 2, 2017, https://www.justice.gov/ag/bio/saxbe-william-bart; Anahad O'Connor, "William Saxbe, 94, Dies; Attorney General during Watergate Inquiry," *NYT*, Aug. 25, 2010, B9.

54. Address by the Honorable William B. Saxbe, Oct. 30, 1974; "Attorney General: William Bart Saxbe"; Gerald Ford to Wes Marden, Sep. 16, 1974, quoted in Secretary of State to US Embassy in Mexico, Oct. 1, 1974, "Central Foreign Policy Files, created, 7/1/1973–12/31/1979," RG 59, DoS, NARA2.

55. Nicholas De Genova defines "deportability" as "the possibility of deportation, the possibility of being removed from the space of the nation-state." By examining deportability, as opposed to the act of deportation, we can gain insight into how the threat of deportation affected undocumented migrants' lives in the United States. See De Genova, "Migrant 'Illegality' and Deportability in Everyday Life," 419–47. Although many undocumented migrants lived in fear, they also forged binational communities and organized to defend their civil rights and human rights. See Minian, *Undocumented Lives*, 104–82; See also chapter 5.

56. Massey, Durand, and Malone, *Beyond Smoke and Mirrors*, 59–60. As an agency report noted, the geography of crossing shifted during the 1960s. While only 19 percent of Mexicans crossed the California–Arizona border in calendar year 1963, more than half (52 percent) did in 1967. Robert L. Stewart, "Cooperation with Mexican Government in Reducing Illegal Entry of Mexican Nationals," NBPM.

57. In August 1970, a Los Angeles County sheriff's deputy shot a tear gas canister into a bar that struck and killed Salazar during the Chicano Moratorium protest march against the Vietnam War. "Review of the Administration of the Immigration and Nationality Act," Hearings before the Subcommittee on Immigration, Citizenship, and

International Law of the Committee on the Judiciary, House of Representatives, Ninety-Third Congress, Jul. 26, Sep. 13, 18, and 20, 1973 (Washington, DC: US Government Printing Office, 1973), 3–4; Ruben Salazar, "The 'Wetback' Problem Has More Than Just One Side," *LAT*, Apr. 24, 1970, 7; "Review of the Los Angeles County Sheriff's Department's Investigation into the Homicide of Ruben Salazar: A Special Report by the Los Angeles County Office of Independent Review," Feb. 2011, http://documents.latimes.com/salazar-independent-office-review/.

58. James F. Greene, the acting commissioner of the INS, also told Congress that they conducted the roundups because they had to use or lose leftover funds before the fiscal year expired. Frank Del Olmo, "600 More Aliens Rounded Up in Continuing L.A.-Area Raids," *LAT*, May 30, 1973, D1; "Review of the Administration of the Immigration and Nationality Act," 3–4.

59. Associated Press, "Raids Grab Mexican Illegal Aliens," *Christian Science Monitor*, Jun. 6, 1973, 11.

60. Betty Liddick, "A Critical Game of Hide and Seek," *LAT*, Jun. 8, 1973, I1; "400 Illegal Aliens Seized as Coast Roundup Goes On," *NYT*, Jun. 10, 1973, 21; "Review of the Administration of the Immigration and Nationality Act," 4, 44, 138–43. These raids were supposedly the largest since 1970, when the INS apprehended some 10,000 people over a six-week period. See Del Olmo, "600 More Aliens Rounded Up in Continuing L.A.-Area Raids."

61. Del Olmo, "600 More Aliens Rounded Up in Continuing L.A.-Area Raids." Acting Commissioner Greene expressed doubts about mass sweeps after the drive ended: "I have grave reservations whether I would ever do it again, because I think it stirs up more trouble in the community than the good of the 11,000 [sic] aliens being removed. It would be better to set up an orderly day-in and day-out control of this thing." "Review of the Administration of the Immigration and Nationality Act," 45.

62. Salazar, "The 'Wetback' Problem Has More Than Just One Side."

63. I recognize that the politics of representation and an individual journalist or particular publication's politics shape what is reported. But the consistency across sources—newspaper articles, oral histories, archival materials, and secondary literature—is striking and led me to conclude that the quotes in this chapter are representative of the impact immigration raids had on migrants and migrant communities. Liddick, "A Critical Game of Hide and Seek."

64. Del Olmo, "600 More Aliens Rounded Up in Continuing L.A.-Area Raids."

65. As quoted in Leek, "Hopes for New Life Outweigh Aliens' Fears."

66. As quoted in Patt Morrison, "Good Wages, Bad Jobs, Constant Fear," *LAT*, Jan. 22, 1977, 3.

67. The quantitative information in this section comes from previously unreported disaggregated apprehension data. The INS recorded how long people had been "illegally in the US" at the time of apprehension and broke down the data into six categories: "At entry," "Within 72 hours," "4–30 days," "1–6 months," "7 months–1 year," and

"Over 1 year." Although I recognize the limitations of the open-ended "Over 1 year" category, it serves as a valuable, if imperfect, estimate of people with long-term US residence at the time of apprehension. INS, "Deportable Aliens: Reports," USCISHOL. Calculations by author.

68. Secretary of State Cyrus Vance to Santiago Roel García, Secretary of Foreign Relations, Mexico, Feb. 26, 1979, III-6350-1 3(a), AHSRE; Massey, Durand, and Malone, *Beyond Smoke and Mirrors*, 43. Jody Agius Vallejo argues that although the Silva protections expired in 1981, the case "provided pressure for a pathway to legalization, eventually granted under the 1986 Immigration Reform and Control Act (IRCA)." Jody Agius Vallejo, "Silva Letters and the Mexican-American Middle Class," *Contexts* 14, no. 2 (Spring 2015): 17–18. On IRCA, see chapter 6.

69. In some years, such as 1977, long-term residents constituted more than half of all apprehensions by investigators. INS, "Deportable Aliens: Reports," USCISHOL. Calculations by author.

70. INS, "Deportable Aliens: Reports," USCISHOL. Calculations by author.

71. According to the Mexican Migration Project, from 1965 to 1985 the probability that an undocumented man would return to Mexico within two years of entering the United States was generally between .55 and .60, while the probability that a woman would do so was generally between .30 and .40. Massey, Durand, and Malone, *Beyond Smoke and Mirrors*, 62–64.

72. INS, "Deportable Aliens: Reports," USCISHOL. Calculations by author.

73. Salvador Reza, "Al Estilo Americano," *Voz Fronteriza*, Nov. 1976, 13, UTRGV (original in Spanish, translation by author). Original:

> "Al Estilo Americano," por Salvador Reza
>
> Me agarró la immigración [*sic*], al estilo Americano
> Y aunque no soy criminal
> De ese modo me han tratado.
> Y aunque no soy criminal, de ese modo me han tratado.
>
> Trabajaba en una fábrica de Los Angeles, hermano,
> Y en el mero día de pago una redada tiraron.
> Con la pistola en la mano a la pared me ordenaron,
> Con la pistola en la mano a la pared me aventaron.
> Como no sabía el inglés las esposas me ajustaron,
> Y con todos mis amigos en un avión nos echaron
> Y con todos mis amigos en un avión nos echaron.
>
> Rumbo a México ya voy, a ver que me espera allá.
> Rumbo a México ya voy, a ver que me espera allá.
> Mientras tanto, allá en Los Angeles, queda mi familia sola.
> ¿Sabe Dios como le harán?

Despedida no les doy porque tengo que volver,

A mi familia reunirme y una cuenta cobraré.

Despedida no les doy, porque tengo que volver.

The *Voz Fronteriza* was founded at the University of California, San Diego in 1975. Reza and his parents came to the United States as undocumented immigrants in 1961, when he was still a child. He later served in the air force and became a citizen. Today he continues to work as an activist and organizer in Phoenix, Arizona. See Ted Robbins, "Community Organizer Fights for Immigrants," *NPR*, Mar. 11, 2008, http://www.npr.org/templates/story/story.php?storyId=88083529.

74. Oral history with Alberto Hernández (pseudonym), Jalisco, México, Jan. 20, 2013. Oral histories are crucial to understanding the history of deportation. Just like any other source, they do not provide a complete, or more accurate, record of the past. They depend on the interview setting and how well the interviewer and interviewee know each other. Additionally, the stories included in oral histories always pass through the filter of memory, while others are sometimes consciously withheld or altered. We should use the oral history not as the only source or as a better or more reliable source, but as a source that complements what we find in the archives. On oral history methodology, see Daniel James, *Doña María's Story: Life History, Memory, and Political Identity* (Durham, NC: Duke University Press, 2000); Alessandro Portelli, *The Death of Luigi Trastulli and Other Stories: Form and Meaning in Oral History* (Albany: State University of New York Press, 1991); Luisa Passerini, *Fascism in Popular Memory: The Cultural Experience of the Turin Working Class*, trans. Robert Lumley and Jude Bloomfield (Cambridge: Cambridge University Press, 1987); Peter Winn, "Oral History and the Factory Study: New Approaches to Labor History," *Latin American Research Review* 14, no. 2 (1979): 130–40; Michael H. Frisch, *A Shared Authority: Essays on the Craft and Meaning of Oral and Public History* (Albany: State University of New York Press, 1990); Ann Farnsworth-Alvear, *Dulcinea in the Factory: Myths, Morals, Men, and Women in Colombia's Industrial Experiment, 1905–1960* (Durham, NC: Duke University Press, 2000).

75. Evan Maxwell, "Neighborhood Raids for Illegal Aliens Resumed," *LAT*, Oct. 10, 1979, A18.

76. Maxwell, "Neighborhood Raids for Illegal Aliens Resumed."

77. Evan Maxwell, "INS Reexamines Plan for Raids," *LAT*, Oct. 26, 1979. On how the blanket targeting of ethnic Mexicans after 1965 changed the politics of groups like LULAC and the relationship between Mexican immigrants and Mexican Americans, see Gutiérrez, *Walls and Mirrors*, 179–205.

78. "The Raids Are Wrong," *LAT*, Oct. 30, 1979, C4.

79. Jack Jones, "Deported as Illegal Aliens, 2 U.S. Youths Claim," *LAT*, Jun. 7, 1975, A25; Gerald Faris, "$2.1 Million Sought in Deportation Case," *LAT*, Sep. 2, 1975, WS1.

80. H. G. Reza, "U.S. Deports Youth, 14, by 'Mistake,'" *LAT*, Feb. 19, 1984, A3; Josh Getlin, "Resident Alien Illegally Deported to Tijuana by INS Is Asking $1 Million," *LAT*, Mar. 7,

1987, OCB3; Henry Weinstein, "$110,000 Paid in Settlement for Boy's Mistaken INS Deportation," *LAT*, Sep. 23, 1989, OCA1. The INS deported many other US citizens and permanent residents as well. See, for example, Evan Maxwell, "U.S. Citizen Mistakenly Deported as Illegal Alien," *LAT*, Mar. 10, 1981, A7.

81. Marita Hernandez, "Deportation Didn't Last Long," *LAT*, Oct. 28, 1979, SE1. On collaborations between the INS and Los Angeles Police Department and the policing of the ethnic Mexicans and Central Americans in Los Angeles, see Max Felker-Kantor, *Policing Los Angeles: Race, Resistance, and the Rise of the LAPD* (Chapel Hill: University of North Carolina Press, 2018), 162–89.

82. Hernandez, "Deportation Didn't Last Long."

83. "The Raids Are Wrong"; Robert Scheer, "Illegal Aliens: Endless Cycle of Insecurity," *LAT*, Nov. 11, 1979, A1; Evan Maxwell, "INS Reexamines Plan for Raids," *LAT*, Oct. 26, 1979. In my oral history with INS and Border Patrol veteran Leo Soto, he expressed a similar sentiment, mentioning that even though an immigration official might not always agree with the law, it was his or her job to enforce it. Oral history with Leo Soto, El Paso, Texas, Aug. 9, 2012.

84. As quoted in Maxwell, "INS Reexamines Plan for Raids."

85. Larry Stammer, "INS Ends Raids on Illegal Aliens; 6,000 Seized in Week-Long Project," *LAT*, May 1, 1982, A30; Ronald Sullivan, "Nearly 1,000 Are Seized in a Job Sweep of Aliens," *NYT*, Apr. 27, 1982, A14; Crewdson, *The Tarnished Door*, 326–27. We should note that the INS had no evidence that such raids created jobs for unemployed US citizens. In this case, as in others, many workers crossed the border again to reunite with their families and resume their old jobs. See, for example, Jack Jones, "Cranston Demands Immediate End to INS Raids," *LAT*, Apr. 30, 1982, A3; Victor M. Valle, "Many Aliens Back on Jobs After Raids," *LAT*, May 6, 1982, SG1.

86. As quoted in Virginia Escalante, "Latinos Join to Condemn Raids," *LAT*, May 9, 1982, LB1.

87. As quoted in David Reyes, "Immigration Raids Spark Mixed Emotions," *LAT*, Mar. 4, 1984, OCA1.

88. Oral history with Álvaro Núñez Hernández and María Vela Morales (pseudonyms), Jalisco, México, Jan. 19, 2013 (translation by author). For similar accounts of migrants' constricted mobility in the United States, see Leo R. Chavez, *Shadowed Lives: Undocumented Immigrants in American Society* (Fort Worth, TX: Harcourt Brace Jovanovich, 1992), 159–73; Minian, *Undocumented Lives*, 83–86.

## Chapter 5: Fighting the Machine in the Streets and in the Courts

1. As quoted in File 20, Box 67, CHRCL.

2. Deposition of Arthur Gappert, Feb. 14, 1980, *Vallejo v. Sureck*, No. 2:78-cv-1912 (C.D. Cal. Dec. 27, 1978).

3. Deposition of Philip Smith, Assistant District Director for Investigations, Los Angeles District Office, INS, May 31, 1978, *Vallejo*, No. 2:78-cv-1912; Hand-drawn map of May 17, 1978, Sbicca factory raid and handwritten list of investigators involved, Box 70, CHRCL.

4. "Footwear for Women: Sbicca of California, Inc., South El Monte, California Report to the President on Investigation No. TEA-F-60 under Section 301(c)(1) of the Trade Expansion Act of 1962" (Washington, DC: United States Tariff Commission, 1974), A17–A18.

5. Deposition of Genoveva Ojeda-Alvarez (also known as Rosa Melchor López), Jul. 31, 1979, *Vallejo*, No. 2:78-cv-1912, CDC.

6. File 20, Box 67, CHRCL.

7. The apprehended workers ranged in age from seventeen to sixty. More than one-third were between seventeen and twenty-one, while one-quarter were older than thirty-five. The mean age was around 27.5, with the men being older (29) on average than the women (24.8), while the median age was 24. List of apprehended Sbicca employees, May 17, 1978, CHRCL. Calculations by author.

8. File 20, Box 67, CHRCL; Deposition of Philip Smith, May 31, 1978, *Vallejo*, No. 2:78-cv-1912, CDC; Robert Rawitch, "59 Aliens on Way to Border Returned by Judge's Order," *LAT*, May 19, 1978, D1.

9. Alex Aleinikoff makes a case for citizenship that includes "settled immigrants" and "those understood to *belong to* America." See T. Alexander Aleinikoff, *Semblances of Sovereignty: The Constitution, the State, and American Citizenship* (Cambridge, MA: Harvard University Press, 2002), 151–81. On denizenship and "the different ways ordinary people grapple with the idea" of citizenship, see David G. Gutiérrez, "The Politics of the Interstices: Reflections on Citizenship and Non-Citizenship at the Turn of the Twentieth Century," *Race/Ethnicity: Multidisciplinary Global Contexts* 1, no. 1 (Autumn 2007): 89–120. On the tension between citizenship's "inclusionary and exclusionary dimensions," see Linda Bosniak, *The Citizen and the Alien: Dilemmas of Contemporary Membership* (Princeton, NJ: Princeton University Press, 2006).

10. This definition of politics is borrowed from historian Steven Hahn's magisterial work on the African American freedom struggle. See Steven Hahn, *A Nation under Our Feet: Black Political Struggles in the Rural South from Slavery to the Great Migration* (Cambridge, MA: Harvard University Press, 2003), 3. On the long history of organizing to defend immigrants, see Buff, *Against the Deportation Terror*. On the history of interracial relations and political activism in Los Angeles and throughout California during the twentieth century, see Scott Kurashige, *The Shifting Grounds of Race: Black and Japanese Americans in the Making of Multiethnic Los Angeles* (Princeton, NJ: Princeton University Press, 2008); Allison Varzally, *Making a Non-White America: Californians Coloring Outside Ethnic Lines, 1925–1955* (Berkeley: University of California Press, 2008); Mark Brilliant, *The Color of America Has Changed: How Racial Diversity Shaped Civil Rights Reform in California, 1941–1978* (New York: Oxford University

Press, 2010); Shana Bernstein, *Bridges of Reform: Interracial Civil Rights Activism in Twentieth-Century Los Angeles* (New York: Oxford University Press, 2011).

11. On the politics of liberal foundations funding organizations like MALDEF, NCLR (recently renamed UnidosUS), and the NAACP, see Joan Roelofs, *Foundations and Public Policy: The Mask of Pluralism* (Albany: State University of New York Press, 2003): 121–55; Benjamin Márquez, "Mexican-American Political Organizations and Philanthropy: Bankrolling a Social Movement," *Social Service Review* 77, no. 3 (Sep. 2003): 329–46; Karen Ferguson, *Top Down: The Ford Foundation, Black Power, and the Reinvention of Racial Liberalism* (Philadelphia: University of Pennsylvania Press, 2013). On *Plyler v. Doe*, see Michael A. Olivas, *No Undocumented Child Left Behind: Plyler v. Doe and the Education of Undocumented Children* (New York: New York University Press, 2012); Motomura, *Immigration Outside the Law*, esp. 1–17; Minian, *Undocumented Lives*, 175–79; Sarah R. Coleman, *The Walls Within: The Politics of Immigration in Modern America* (Princeton, NJ: Princeton University Press, forthcoming), chapters 1 and 2. On Mexican Americans' struggle for educational equality before *Plyler*, see Guadalupe San Miguel Jr., *"Let All of Them Take Heed": Mexican Americans and the Campaign for Educational Equality in Texas, 1910–1981* (Austin: University of Texas Press, 1987).

12. Prior to cofounding CASA, Bert Corona, born in El Paso, Texas, in 1918, helped start and build the League of Spanish Speaking People in the late 1930s and the Mexican American Political Association in the late 1950s. Chole Alatorre, born in San Luis Potosí, Mexico, in 1927, immigrated to the United States with her husband and sister at age twenty-seven and soon became involved in union organizing. David G. Gutiérrez, "'Sin Fronteras?' Chicanos, Mexican Americans, and the Emergence of the Contemporary Immigration Debate, 1968–1978," *Journal of American Ethnic History* 10, no. 4 (Summer 1991): 17–18; Mario T. García, *Memories of Chicano History: The Life and Narrative of Bert Corona* (Berkeley: University of California Press, 1994); "Call to Action," 1974, Box 11, Folder 1, Bert Corona Papers (hereafter BCP), m248, SCSUL. On the systemic discrimination against Mexican Americans at the time, see "Mexican Americans and the Administration of Justice in the Southwest" (Washington, DC: Commission on Civil Rights, 1970). On CASA, including the organization's history, politics, gender relations, and internal split in 1975, see Ernesto Chávez, *"¡Mi Raza Primero!": Nationalism, Identity, and Insurgency in the Chicano Movement in Los Angeles, 1966–1978* (Berkeley: University of California Press, 2002), 98–116; Laura Pulido, *Black, Brown, Yellow, and Left: Radical Activism in Los Angeles* (Berkeley: University of California Press, 2006), 117–22, 173–79, 195–204. On the American Committee for Protection of Foreign Born, see Buff, *Against the Deportation Terror*.

13. "Call to Action," 1974.

14. The Rodino Bill passed the House, but, according to Daniel Tichenor, never even made it out of the Immigration Subcommittee of the Judiciary Committee in the Senate because the chairman, Senator James Eastland (Democrat, Mississippi), had close ties to southern agricultural interests and "supported a cheap and 'returnable' labor

supply from Mexico." Gutiérrez, "'Sin Fronteras?,'" 10–11; Tichenor, *Dividing Lines*, 224–31.

15. Del Olmo, "600 More Aliens Rounded Up in Continuing L.A.-Area Raids."

16. Press releases, May–June 1975, Box 31, Folder 11, CASA Papers, m325, SCSUL.

17. "Call to Action," 1974.

18. Slogans like "La union hace la fuerza" (Unity makes us strong), "Somos un pueblo" (We are one people), and "Un daño contra uno es un daño contra todos" (An injury to one is an injury to all) allowed these activists to connect the fight for immigrant rights to broader struggles. After all, they concluded, "Right now it is those workers without papers who are being attacked; tomorrow it might be those workers who dare to strike or those who dare to speak out against the terror of a police state." "Cesen Las Deportaciones!!," *El Inmigrante Militante*, Aug. 24, 1974, Box 22, Folder 7, CASA Papers, m325, SCSUL; "Despierta Chicano Defiende tu Hermano, Forum on Deportation," Feb. 1975, Doc. 10187, Reel 4, Section 10, CSLSC.

19. In March 1975, while CASA members attended a demonstration in Federal Plaza, the FBI and INS raided the law offices of Eiden, Rodríguez & Silbiger, who were members of CASA's legal committee as well as at the National Lawyers Guild. On May 20, 1975, at an antideportation rally in front of city hall, the FBI arrested CASA leader Raul Rodríguez, held him without bail, and interrogated him about his political activities in Mexico and the United States. Press releases, May–June 1975, Box 31, Folder 11, CASA Papers, m325, SCSUL. On the history of the National Lawyers Guild, two sympathetic sources are Victor Rabinowitz and Tim Ledwith, eds., *A History of the National Lawyers Guild, 1937–1987* (New York: National Lawyers Guild Foundation, 1987); Ann Fagan Ginger and Eugene M. Tobin, eds., *The National Lawyers Guild: From Roosevelt through Reagan* (Philadelphia: Temple University Press, 1988).

20. "Know Your Rights," circa 1977, JJM; "Que hacer si la migra te detiene en la fabrica o en la calle???," circa 1977–81, Box 10, Folder 11, BCP, m248, SCSUL.

21. "Know Your Rights," circa 1977, JJM.

22. "Know Your Rights," circa 1977, JJM. The INS understood that the "stay silent" strategy posed a threat to the deportation machine. As the acting district director in Los Angeles told Congress in 1973: "In those cases where the person remains mute at the outset, then of course we would be helpless. We would not be able to make an arrest again in that case." "Review of the Administration of the Immigration and Nationality Act," 7–8.

23. Flyer warning against signing voluntary departure, Box 11, Folder 1, BCP, m248, SCSUL. The earliest warning flyer of this sort that I found was from 1972, although it is possible that activists had developed this strategy prior to that. See, for example, "La forma de 'Salida Voluntaria,'" *Alambre, Revista Semanal*, No. 2 (Mar. 31, 1972), Box 31, Folder 12, CASA Papers, m325, SCSUL.

24. "Soledad y desamparo frente al interrogador de Inmigración," 1972, Box 16, Folder 13, BCP, m248, SCSUL (translation by author).

25. CASA, "Boletín Interno," May 18, 1976, 1, JJM (translation by author).

26. See, for example, the January 1974 ¡RAZA SÍ MIGRA NO! Immigration Conference, sponsored by La Raza Unida Party in Chicago, that included speeches from Bert Corona and other national figures, in addition to a movie screening, benefit dance, and other cultural activities; the February 1975 Despierta Chicano, Defiende tu Hermano, Forum on Deportation, hosted by the Comité Estudiantil del Pueblo in Los Angeles; and the March 1977 Victoria Obrera, Celebración Combativa carne asada in the Los Angeles area, organized by the Comite Obrero en Defensa de los Indocumentados en Lucha (CODIL). Flyer, "¡RAZA SÍ, MIGRA NO! Immigration Conference," Jan. 18–20, 1974, Doc. 10096, Reel 3, Section 10, CSLSC; Flyer, "Despierta Chicano Defiende tu Hermano, Forum on Deportation," Feb. 1975, Doc. 10187, Reel 4, Section 10, CSLSC; Flyer, "Victoria Obrera, Celebración Combativa," Mar. 13, 1977, Box 10, Folder 13, BCP, m248, SCSUL.

27. See, for example, the September 1975 meeting in Ciudad Juárez "to address the problem of campesinos and Mexican migrant workers in the United States." At the August 1980 International Conference on Undocumented Workers' Basic Rights, organized by Mexican political exile, CASA member, and labor organizer José Jacques Medina and held in Mexico City, attendees established an Undocumented Workers' Bill of Rights. "Minutes from Meeting in Ciudad Juárez, Sep. 5–7, 1975," Box 34, Folder 1, CASA Papers, m325, SCSUL; "Por Los Derechos Plenos de los Trabajadores Indocumentados, Conferencia Internacional," Aug. 15, 1980, JJM.

28. Gutiérrez, "'Sin Fronteras?,'" 25–28; José G. Pérez, "Chicanos Unite to Fight Carter Deportation Plan," *The Militant* 41, 42, Nov. 11, 1977, 1, 6–7. On other large gatherings, such as the May 1980 Chicano National Immigration Conference and Memorial March or the April 1981 Chicano National Immigration Tribunal, both held in San Diego, see Patiño, *Raza Sí, Migra No*, 222–49.

29. "President's Proposals on Undocumented Aliens," *INS Reporter*, Fall 1977, 24–27.

30. "Latino Leaders Rip Carter Deportation Plan," *The Militant* 41, 43, Nov. 18, 1977, 12; Peter Camejo, "Human Rights for Immigrants," *The Militant* 41, 46, Dec. 9, 1977, 20.

31. Vatican II, "Pastoral Constitution on the Church in the Modern World," *Gaudium et Spes*, Promulgated by His Holiness, Pope Paul VI, Dec. 7, 1965, http://www.vatican.va/archive/hist_councils/ii_vatican_council/documents/vat-ii_cons_19651207_gaudium-et-spes_en.html.

32. Father José L. Alvarez, et al., "Encuentro Regional de Pastoral Hispana del Noreste, 1974," Doc. 10156, Reel 4, CSLSC.

33. On religious institutions' defense of Mexicans and Central Americans in Los Angeles in the late twentieth century, see Sean Dempsey, "City of Refuges, City of Sanctuary," chapter 5 in *The Politics of Dignity: Religion, Human Rights, and the Making of Global Los Angeles* (Chicago: University of Chicago Press, forthcoming).

34. During the 1970s, labor unions' overall membership declined at the same time as women and nonwhite workers invigorated organizing efforts in certain sectors. For

more on these simultaneous transformations to the working class, see Jefferson Cowie, *Stayin' Alive: The 1970s and the Last Days of the Working Class* (New York: The New Press, 2010); Lane Windham, *Knocking on Labor's Door: Union Organizing in the 1970s and the Roots of a New Economic Divide* (Chapel Hill: University of North Carolina Press, 2017). On the history of Mexican and Mexican American labor organizing in the first half of the twentieth century, see Vicki L. Ruiz, *Cannery Women, Cannery Lives: Mexican Women, Unionization, and the California Food Processing Industry, 1930–1950* (Albuquerque: University of New Mexico Press, 1987); Zaragosa Vargas, *Labor Rights Are Civil Rights: Mexican American Workers in Twentieth-Century America* (Princeton, NJ: Princeton University Press, 2005).

35. As quoted in Joel Kotkin, "2 Labor Unions Aid, Organize Illegal Aliens," *WaPo*, Sep. 11, 1978, 1; Lisa Schlein, "Los Angeles' Garment District Sews a Cloak of Shame," *LAT*, Mar. 5, 1978, E3; Robert Lindsey, "Unions Move to Organize Illegal Aliens in the West," *NYT*, Jun. 3, 1979, 1.

36. As quoted in Lindsey, "Unions Move to Organize Illegal Aliens in the West."

37. As quoted in Schlein, "Los Angeles' Garment District Sews a Cloak of Shame."

38. The Mexican government forced Jacques Medina into exile because of his participation in the 1968 Mexican student movement. Handout, CODIL, 1976; José Jacques Medina to Bert Corona, Mar. 11, 1977, Box 10, Folder 13, BCP, m248, SCSUL; Juan Gómez Quiñones, *Mexican American Labor, 1790–1990* (Albuquerque: University of New Mexico Press, 1994), 221–24; José Jacques Medina, *De Mojado a Diputado: Memoria Gráfica y Documental* (México, DF: Movimiento Migrante Mesoamericano, 2009), 24–31; "Stop the Illegal Raids! Unite All Labor to Support Undocumented Workers!" *United Labor Action*, The Center for United Labor Action, Apr. 25, 1977, JJM. On undocumented agricultural workers organizing a successful 1977 strike at the family ranch of Arizona senator and former Republican presidential candidate Barry Goldwater, see Minian, *Undocumented Lives*, 159–67.

39. "Certificate of Arrival—For Naturalization Purposes, Francesco Sbicca" and "Petition for Naturalization, Francesco Sbicca," Jan. 22, 1920, Ancestry.com; "Obituary, Arthur Sbicca," *LAT*, Jan. 8, 2008; Testimony of Arthur Sbicca Sr. before the California Advisory Committee to the United States Commission on Civil Rights, Biltmore Hotel, Los Angeles (hereafter CACUSCCR), Jun. 16, 1978, Vol. II, 399–400.

40. *Sbicca-Del Mac v. Milius Shoe Co.*, 145 F.2d 389 (8th Cir. 1944).

41. As quoted in "City Gets First National Shoe Factory Branch," *LAT*, Jul. 24, 1943, A16; "Funeral Rites Set for Sbicca, Shoemaker," *LAT*, Nov. 15, 1953, A23; *Estate of Frank Sbicca, Deceased, Ernesta Sbicca and Arthur Sbicca, Executors, Petitioner, v. Commissioner of Internal Revenue, Respondent*, Reports of the Tax Court of the United States, Oct. 1, 1960, to Mar. 31, 1961, Vol. 35 (Washington, DC: US Government Printing Office, 1961): 96–107.

42. In the company's division of labor, Arthur served as the administrative head of the company, his brother Frank Jr. led the fashion and design team, and his brother Peter

ensured production ran smoothly. Frank Jr. left the firm in 1971 and started his own company in San Diego. "Shoe Plant Work Started," *LAT*, Oct. 21, 1956, E20; Sheldon L. Pollack, "Application for Building Permit—Division of Building and Safety, Department of County Engineer, County of Los Angeles," July 21, 1957, obtained from the City of South El Monte through a public records request by author, Feb. 2018; Nick Juravich, "City of Achievement: The Making of the City of South El Monte, 1955–1976," *KCET, East of East*, Apr. 28, 2014, https://www.kcet.org/history-society/city-of-achievement-the-making-of-the-city-of-south-el-monte-1955-1976; "Weddings: Sbicca-Meaglia," *LAT*, Aug. 19, 1946, A5; Arthur Sbicca, "Application for World War II Compensation—To Be Used by Honorably Discharged Veteran or Person Still in Service," Commonwealth of Pennsylvania, World War II Veterans' Compensation Bureau, May 19, 1950, Ancestry.com; "California, Voter Registrations, 1900–1968," Ancestry.com; "Six Men Here Honored by Italian Government," *LAT*, Nov. 5, 1957, B2; Julie Byrne, "Shoemakers Get Designs Off the Ground," *LAT*, Mar. 20, 1967, B1; "Footwear for Women: Sbicca of California, Inc., South El Monte, California Report to the President on Investigation No. TEA-F-60 under Section 301(c)(1) of the Trade Expansion Act of 1962," 3, A17; Testimony of Arthur Sbicca Sr., CACUSCCR, Jun. 16, 1978, 400–402. On the history of South El Monte and El Monte, see Jerry Gonzalez, *In Search of the Mexican Beverly Hills: Latino Suburbanization in Postwar Los Angeles* (New Brunswick, NJ: Rutgers University Press, 2017); Romeo Guzmán, Carribean Fragoza, Alex Sayf Cummings, and Ryan Reft, eds., *East of East: The Making of Greater El Monte* (New Brunswick, NJ: Rutgers University Press, 2020).

43. President Gerald Ford eventually broke the US Tariff Commission's two-two split decision, ruling in favor of Sbicca and directing the secretaries of labor and commerce to certify workers and former workers "as eligible to apply for adjustment assistance." "Footwear for Women: Sbicca of California, Inc., South El Monte, California Report to the President on Investigation No. TEA-F-60 under Section 301(c)(1) of the Trade Expansion Act of 1962," 4–7, A9–A18; "Notice to the Press," Office of the White House Press Secretary, Sep. 3, 1974, Box 1, White House Press Releases, Gerald R. Ford Presidential Library; Testimony of Arthur Sbicca Sr., CACUSCCR, Vol. II, Jun. 16, 1978, 404.

44. Arthur also touted the company's long history of employing immigrants, be they Europeans when the business was still based in Philadelphia, or Latin Americans in Los Angeles. "[We] know how they work and how they behave and how they act," he asserted. Testimony of Arthur Sbicca Sr., Jun. 16, 1978, CACUSCCR, Vol. II, 399–404.

45. Oral history with María Guadalupe González, El Monte, CA, Apr. 30, 2016 (conducted in Spanish; translated by the author); "Footwear for Women: Sbicca of California, Inc., South El Monte, California Report to the President on Investigation No. TEA-F-60 under Section 301(c)(1) of the Trade Expansion Act of 1962," A1–A5; "History of California Minimum Wage," State of California Department of Industrial Relations, accessed Feb. 28, 2018, https://www.dir.ca.gov/iwc/minimumwagehistory.htm.

46. Oral history with Jesse Gonzales, conducted over the phone, Jan. 25, 2018; Oral history with María Guadalupe González; Affidavit of David Hernández, Declaration in Support of Issuance of Temporary Restraining Order, May 17, 1978, *Vallejo*, No. 2:78-cv-1912, NLG-NIP.

47. To gain entry that morning, the service also used as leverage a $700,000 loan agreement between Sbicca and the federal Economic Development Administration that required employers to hire only US citizens and people with work permits, and gave immigration officials permission to check for compliance. Plaintiffs later challenged the constitutionality of such an agreement. Complaint for Injunctive and Declaratory Relief, May 17, 1978, *Vallejo*, No. 2:78-cv-1912, NLG-NIP; Oral history with María Guadalupe González; Oral history with Jesse Gonzales; "Sobre el Sindicato" questionnaire, File 20, Box 67, CHRCL; "Sobre el Sindicato" questionnaire, File 57, Box 68, CHRCL; Affidavit of Thomas J. Fineman, Declaration in Support of Issuance of Temporary Restraining Order, May 17, 1978, *Vallejo,* No. 2:78-cv-1912, NLG-NIP. On the company's and Arthur Sbicca's antiunion history, see In the Matter of Sbicca, Inc., and United Shoe Workers of America, Affiliated with the Congress of Industrial Organizations and Boot and Shoe Workers' Union, Local No. 141, Affiliated with the American Federal of Labor, Party to the Contract, Case Nos. C-1514 and R-1687— Decided March 5, 1941, "Decisions and Orders of the National Labor Relations Board," Vol. 30, Mar. 1, 1941 to Apr. 15, 1941 (Washington, DC: US Government Printing Office, 1942), 60–78; "NLRB Orders Vote for Shoe Workers," *Philadelphia Inquirer,* Mar. 7, 1941, 28; "Suit Asks Restraint on Mass Picketing of Plant," *LAT*, Oct. 18, 1957, 12; "Picketing Ban Denied," *LAT*, Oct. 29, 1957, 17; Economic Development Administration Loan Agreement with Sbicca of California, Inc., Jun. 25, 1976, included as part of Defendant's Submission, May 31, 1978, *Vallejo*, No. 2:78-cv-1912, Vol. I, CDC.

48. Joseph Sureck, INS, to Arthur Sbicca, Mar. 1977, CHRCL; Updated list of raids on Sbicca factory, May 1978, Box 70, CHRCL.

49. David Hernández also went to Sbicca that morning after a friend who worked there called to alert him about the situation. According to Gonzales, he got Schey's number from Linda Wong, an immigration attorney he had befriended who would also play a key role in the Sbicca cases. Oral history with María Guadalupe González; Oral history with Jesse Gonzales; Affidavit of David Hernández; Affidavit of Philip H. Smith, May 25, 1978, *Vallejo*, No. 2:78-cv-1912, CDC.

50. Résumé, Peter A. Schey, in author's possession.

51. "Complaint for Injunctive and Declaratory Relief," May 17, 1978, NLG-NIP; "Notes on May 6 Meeting on a Complaint Center," 1978, Box 13, Folder 4, BCP, m248, SCSUL.

52. Rodríguez spent part of his childhood shining shoes and selling chewing gum and newspapers in the streets to support his family. One of nine siblings, as an adolescent he spent a year studying to be a priest before crossing the border and returning to school. His mother and some of his siblings were also active in CASA and other Chicano movement organizations. Oral history with Mark Rosenbaum, Los Angeles, CA,

May 4, 2016; Oral history with Bill Blum, conducted over the phone, Apr. 22, 2016; "Petition for Naturalization, Antonio Hernández Rodríguez," May 16, 1962, U.S. Public Records Index, 1950–1993, Vol. 1, Ancestry.com; Oral history with Antonio Rodríguez, conducted over the phone, Jul. 12 and 20, 2016.

53. While Smith let Blum (who didn't speak Spanish) see the Sbicca workers, he didn't allow Rodríguez or Jesse Gonzales to speak with them. Oral history with Bill Blum; Deposition of Philip Smith, 4–10; Blum and Schey to All Concerned Officials of the INS, May 17, 1978, CHRCL.

54. 8 USC 1362 stated that "in any . . . deportation proceedings . . . the person concerned shall have the privilege of being represented . . . by such counsel . . . as he shall choose." 8 CFR 287.3 stated that "an alien arrested without warrant shall be advised of the reason for his arrest and his right to be represented by counsel of his own choice, at no expense to the Government." An alien "shall also be advised that any statement he makes may be used against him in a subsequent proceeding and that a decision will be made within 24 hours or less as to whether he will be continued in custody or released on bond or recognizance."

55. *Marquez v. Kiley*, 436 F. Supp. 100, 114 (S.D.N.Y. 1977), later reflected in 8 USC 1357(a)(1), quoted in Memorandum of Points and Authorities in Support of Motion for Temporary Restraining Order, May 17, 1978, *Vallejo*, No. 2:78-cv-1912, NLG-NIP. Underlining in original.

56. The complete list of named plaintiffs included Sbicca workers Arturo Vallejo, María Ceja, and Enriquez Santos, in addition to Schey, Rosenbaum, Blum, Jesse Gonzales, and David Hernández. Complaint for Injunctive and Declaratory Relief, May 17, 1978, *Vallejo*, No. 2:78-cv-1912, NLG-NIP.

57. As Schey described in his Memorandum of Points and Authorities, "Once physically removed from the United States, plaintiffs lose any administrative or judicial appeal rights that they may have to challenge defendant's actions in this case," per 8 USC 1105a. Under 8 USC 1105a(c), an "order of deportation . . . shall not be reviewed . . . if [the alien] has departed from the United States." Moreover, per 8 USC 1101(g), "any alien ordered deported . . . has left the United States, shall be considered to have been deported in pursuance of law." Thus, Schey concluded, "Plaintiffs will suffer irreparable injury unless this Court issues a temporary order halting their physical removal from the United States." Memorandum of Points and Authorities in Support of Motion for Temporary Restraining Order; Complaint for Injunctive and Declaratory Relief; Affidavit of Peter Schey, Declaration in Support of Issuance of Temporary Restraining Order, May 17, 1978, *Vallejo*, No. 2:78-cv-1912, NLG-NIP; Order to Show Cause and Temporary Restraining Order, May 17, 1978, *Vallejo*, No. 2:78-cv-1912, CDC.

58. It was unclear how many actually preferred voluntary departure, knowing that by doing so they might be able to return to United States soon thereafter and avoid an uncertain legal process, but some did. Order to Show Cause and Temporary Restraining Order, *Vallejo*; Modified Temporary Restraining Order, May 17, 1978, *Vallejo*,

No. 2:78-cv-1912, CHRCL; Deposition of Genoveva Ojeda-Alvarez, Jul. 31, 1979; Signed voluntary departure form, Rosa Melchor López, May 17, 1978; Declaration of Martín López Rocha, May 18, 1979, *Vallejo*, No. 2:78-cv-1912, CDC. For more on the INS coercing people into accepting voluntary departure, see Testimony of Barbara Honig, CACUSCCR, Jun. 15, 1978, Vol. I, 185–92.

59. Modified Temporary Restraining Order, *Vallejo*; "Quieren Abogado Gratis," Box 70, CHRCL; "Sbicca Addresses," JJM.

60. "Defending the Tortilla Curtain," *Wall Street Journal*, Sep. 24, 1984, 32.

61. Edwin Harwood, *In Liberty's Shadow: Illegal Aliens and Immigration Law Enforcement* (Stanford, CA: Hoover Institution Press, 1986), 67–68, 178; Testimony of Robert L. Miller, Jun. 15, 1978, CACUSCCR, Vol. II, 606–7.

62. Harwood, *In Liberty's Shadow*, 181–82.

63. Testimony of Judge Jay Segal, Jun. 15, 1978, CACUSCCR, Vol. II 488–89.

64. Testimony of Charles Gordon, Apr. 27, 1981, "Hispanic Immigration and the Select Commission on Immigration's Final Report," House of Representatives, Subcommittee on Census and Population, Committee on Post Office and Civil Service, 72–75. For a similar argument, see Peter H. Schuck, "The Transformation of Immigration Law," *Columbia Law Review* 84, no. 1 (1984): 66–68.

65. Bill Blum remembered that INS officials were "afraid that [the Sbicca] case would motivate greater numbers to ask for deportation hearings," with potentially far-reaching implications since "the machinery of administrative process is such that it would grind to a halt if everybody asked for a hearing. It would be very expensive. They would either have to be released on bond or they would have to be housed in pre-trial or prehearing detention facilities. It would be very expensive. So the machinery of deportation then, and I'm sure now also, just depends on most cases not going to trial." Mark Rosenbaum also noted that they knew Sbicca was a test case of sorts and the legal team was in touch with other immigration lawyers across the country—especially those with ties to the National Lawyers Guild. Oral history with Bill Blum; Oral history with Mark Rosenbaum.

66. The attorneys included Linda Wong, Edward Ortega, Gary Silbiger, William Snyder, Kenneth Leshen, Erica Hahn, and future federal judge Richard Paez. The law students from the People's College of Law included Carlos Holguín, Ben Holstrom, Chris Duran, Vicente Ulloa, Fred Nakamura, and Gina (last name unknown), among others. Addendum to Plaintiffs' Supplemental Memorandum in Opposition to Motion to Dismiss, Jul. 20, 1978, *Vallejo*, No. 2:78-cv-1912, CDC; Declaration of Carlos Holguín, Addendum to Plaintiffs' Supplemental Memorandum in Opposition to Motion to Dismiss, Exhibit F, Jul. 20, 1978, *Vallejo*, No. 2:78-cv-1912, CDC; "*Vallejo v INS*, Sbicca Legal Research," File 1, Box 67, CHRCL.

67. Oral history with Edward Ortega, Los Angeles, CA, Apr. 12, 2016.

68. Many workers returned to Sbicca. Despite its opposition to a unionized labor force, the company needed as much help as it could get after the loss of more than 15 percent

of its employees in a single day had resulted in a 40 to 50 percent drop in production. In June 1978, the secretary of the Southern California Shoe Manufacturers Association estimated that the industry employed 7,000 undocumented workers and urged legislators to change the law so that firms could fill their labor demand with workers who had permits. Testimony of Walter J. Gibson, CACUSCCR, Jun. 15, 1978, Vol. I, 267–69; Oral history with Mark Rosenbaum; Oral history with Antonio Rodríguez; Jacobo Rodríguez to Peter Schey and all interested attorneys, Jun. 7, 1978, Box 33, Folder 7, CASA Papers, m325, SCSUL; Defendants' Submission Re Status of Purported Class Members, Jun. 9, 1978, *Vallejo*, No. 2:78-cv-1912, CDC; Oral history with Jesse Gonzáles; García, *Memories of Chicano History*, 309; Testimony of Arthur Sbicca Sr., CACUSCCR, Jun. 16, 1978, Vol. II, 399–409.

69. Some of the initial organizations involved included the ILGWU, Teamsters for a Democratic Union, Committee Against Police Abuse, Comite de Igualdad, International Longshore and Warehouse Union, Third World Worker's Coalition of People's College of Law, National Lawyers Guild, American Civil Liberties Union, Retail Clerks Union, Coalition for Fair Immigration Laws & Practices, San Fernando Coalition, and Centro de Acción Social Autónomo. Oral history with Jesse Gonzales; "A Todos Los Trabajadores y Trabajadoras de 'Sibicca' [*sic*]" and "Structure of Committees," both found in Box 33, Folder 12, CASA Papers, m325, SCSUL; Members of the Sbicca Legal Defense Team, "INS Raids Sbicca Shoes—Mass Defense and Action Center Organized," *Immigration Newsletter*, National Lawyers Guild National Immigration Project, Vol. 7, No. 3 (Sep.–Oct. 1978): 1, 13; Bruce Bowman, "Sbicca Workers Winning—I.N.S. Reshuffling Deck," *Immigration Newsletter*, National Lawyers Guild National Immigration Project, Vol. 8, No. 1 (Nov. 1978–Feb. 1979): 7.

70. Discussing whether any tension existed between prioritizing the federal class action suit and individual cases, Mark Rosenbaum cautioned that "you had to be careful that you were not part of something that put a political agenda—no matter how much you believed in it and no matter how much it might change—over people's personal lives. You know, no lawyer ever had to spend a day in detention; and no lawyer ever had to take on the consideration that he or she might spend time in one of these hell holes of a detention center." Oral history with Mark Rosenbaum; Oral history with Bill Blum.

71. Oral history with Mark Rosenbaum; Oral history with Bill Blum; Oral history with Antonio Rodríguez; Oral history with Edward Ortega. *Woodby v. INS*, 385 U.S. 276 (1966) established the burden of proof on the INS to present "clear, convincing, and unequivocal evidence" of a person's deportability, as also described at the time in 8 CFR 242.14.

72. Oral history with Mark Rosenbaum; Oral history with Bill Blum; Oral history with Edward Ortega.

73. Oral history with Mark Rosenbaum; Oral history with Bill Blum; Oral history with Edward Ortega.

74. As Schey inferred, it's worth noting that in the months after the raid some Sbicca workers were deported via voluntary departure or decided to return to Mexico for different reasons. The vast majority, however, were still stuck in limbo in the labyrinthine immigration court system. At the time, only thirty-four of the sixty-five or more people had had hearings, with seventeen being dismissed, ten under appeal, and seven who accepted voluntary departure. Plaintiffs' Submission on the Current Status of Their Deportation Proceedings and Presence in the United States, Sep. 7, 1978, *Vallejo*, No. 2:78-cv-1912, CDC; In the Matter of Andres Cardona-Padilla, Respondent, In Deportation Proceedings, Sep. 5, 1978, *Vallejo*, No. 2:78-cv-1912, Vol. 8, CDC; In the Matter of Luis Manuel Cervantes-Cervantes, Respondent, In Deportation Proceedings, Aug. 25, 1978, *Vallejo*, No. 2:78-cv-1912, Vol. 8, CDC; "Record of Deportable Alien," File 11, Box 67, CHRCL; Bill Blum and Gina Lobaco, "Labor Has Joined Campaign to Eliminate Immigrant Sweeps," *LAT*, Nov. 26, 1978, J3; Jerry Ruhlow, "Unionist Promises to Assist Illegal Aliens," *LAT*, Mar. 11, 1979, C6; Bowman, "Sbicca Workers Winning—I.N.S. Reshuffling Deck," 5.

75. See, for example, *Almeida-Sanchez v. United States*, 413 U.S. 266 (1973); *International Ladies' Garment Workers' Union, AFL-CIO v. Sureck*, 681 F.2d 624 (9th Cir. 1982); *Illinois Migrant Council v. Pilliod*, 531 F.Supp. 1011 (N.D. Ill. 1982); *Blackie's House of Beef, Inc. v. Castillo*, 659 F.2d 1211 (D.C. Cir. 1981).

76. Testimony of Mr. Felipe Aguirre, Jun. 15, 1978, CACUSCCR, Vol. I, 259–60. An immigration lawyer expressed a similar sentiment around the same time: "Other agencies have specific regulations, but the immigration people are their own bosses. Each one, each immigration officer, is a little king. Each has tremendous discretionary power. No other agency in the government is like this—it's a zoo." Crewdson, *The Tarnished Door*, 122.

77. Oral history with Mark Rosenbaum. Legal scholars writing around the same time supported Aguirre and Rosenbaum's assertions that noncitizens lacked basic rights before the law. As Peter Schuck noted: "In a legal firmament transformed by revolutions in due process and equal protection doctrine and by a new conception of judicial role, immigration law remains the realm in which government authority is at the zenith, and individual entitlement is at the nadir." Schuck, "The Transformation of Immigration Law," 1.

78. Robert Rawitch, "Union Sues to Curb Raids on Garment District Aliens," *LAT*, Feb. 25, 1978, B12; Mark Stevens, "A union view of illegal aliens holding jobs in U.S.," *Christian Science Monitor*, Sep. 5, 1978, 7.

79. As an INS agent told the owner of a Valencia, California, factory that employed three hundred workers, "You have three choices. You can cooperate (in allowing a raid), or you can make us go to court which we don't like to do, or we'll harass your people at the gate." Grinder, "Reagan Policies on Immigration Shift into Full Swing"; Sbicca Search Warrant, US District Court for the Central District of California, for "the premises known as Sbicca of California, 2620 N. Rosemead Blvd., South El Monte, California, and

all appurtenances thereto, including but not limited to the central building itself and all parking lot areas surrounding the building," Los Angeles, CA, Jun. 5, 1974, Box 70, CHRCL; Testimony of Arthur Sbicca Sr., CACUSCCR, Jun. 16, 1978, Vol. II, 403–404.

80. Sbicca Search Warrant, Jun. 5, 1974, CHRCL.

81. Testimony of Robert L. Miller, CACUSCCR, Jun. 15, 1978, Vol. II, 588–91.

82. Testimony of Bernard Karmiol, CACUSCCR, Jun. 16, 1978, Vol. II, 559–61.

83. Testimony of Henry Fenton, Peter Schey, Mark Rosenbaum, Steve Hollopeter, and Bernard Karmiol, CACUSCCR, Jun. 16, 1978, Vol. II, 327–43, 467–72, 545.

84. Memorandum of Points and Authorities in Support of Motion for Temporary Restraining Order, May 17, 1978, *Vallejo*, No. 2:78-cv-1912, May 17, 1978, NLG-NIP. (Emphasis in original.) For more on this issue, see Testimony of Peter Schey, CACUSCCR, Jun. 16, 1978, Vol. II, 344–45.

85. From Maurice Roberts, "The Right to Representation in Immigration Cases," *La Luz* 7, no. 2 (Feb. 1978): 19. Quoted in Memorandum of Points and Authorities in Support of Motion for Temporary Restraining Order, *Vallejo*, No. 2:78-cv-1912, May 17, 1978.

86. 8 CFR 287.3, quoted in William Matthew Byrne Jr., Order, Dec. 27, 1978, 8–9, *Vallejo*, No. 2:78-cv-1912, CDC. Byrne cited *Navia-Duran v. INS*, 568 F.2d 803 (1st Cir. 1977) in support of this point.

87. To support his conclusion, the judge cited *Fuller v. United States*, 407 F.2d 1199, 1207 (D.C. Circ. 1967); *Moran v. United States*, 404 F.2d 663, 666 (10th Cir. 1968). Byrne, Order, 14. In a deposition the following year, INS Assistant Director Philip H. Smith, the officer overseeing the Sbicca raid, indicated that he agreed with Byrne. Responding to a question by Schey about "At what point were the persons taken into custody at Sbicca deemed to be under the arrest of the Immigration Service," Smith replied, "I would presume that the majority when they were taken into custody at the Sbicca plant." Exhibit "B," Deposition of Philip H. Smith, May 23, 1979, *Vallejo*, No. 2:78-cv-1912, Vol. II, CDC.

88. Byrne, Order, 14–16.

89. Jane Armbruster, "'Illegals' and the Courts," *NACLA*, XII, no. 6 (Nov.–Dec. 1978): 45–47.

90. Blum and Lobaco, "Labor Has Joined Campaign to Eliminate Immigrant Sweeps"; Harry Bernstein and Robert Williams, "INS Halts Almost All Factory Raids for Illegal Aliens," *LAT*, Oct. 11, 1978, A12; Harry Bernstein and Robert Williams, "Director of INS Denies Deemphasis on Arrests of Illegal Aliens in Southland," *LAT*, Oct. 12, 1978, E5. Officials stated that increased apprehensions at the border as a result of "intensified" antismuggling activities made up for the reduction in apprehensions from raids.

91. INS, "Deportable Aliens: Reports," USCISHOL. Calculations by author. The drop in apprehensions of Mexicans with long-term residence was even more pronounced when limited to those made by investigators: from 83,000-plus in 1977, to just over 61,000 in 1978, around 44,000 in 1979, and some 28,000 in 1980.

92. Bowman, "Sbicca Workers Winning—I.N.S. Reshuffling Deck," 6; Deposition of Charles C. Sava, Associate Commissioner of Enforcement, INS, Dec. 16, 1980, *Vallejo*, No. 2:78-cv-1912, CDC.

93. Bowman, "Sbicca Workers Winning—I.N.S. Reshuffling Deck," 7.

94. *INS v. Delgado*, 466 U.S. 210 (1984).

95. By that time, Rosa Melchor López, the young woman two agents had detained and pushed onto the bus that May morning, had become the lead plaintiff and the name of the case had changed to *Lopez v. INS*, No. 78-cv-1912 (C.D. Cal. June 4, 1992).

96. As quoted in Marvine Howe, "Legal Settlement Widens Rights of Detained Aliens," *NYT*, Jun. 12, 1992, D18; "Suspected Aliens Win Rights," *NYT*, Aug. 23, 1992, 31.

97. Oral history with Mark Rosenbaum; Oral history with Edward Ortega; Blum and Lobaco, "Labor Has Joined Campaign to Eliminate Immigrant Sweeps."

## Chapter 6: Deportation in an Era of Militarized Borders and Mass Incarceration

1. Derrick Jackson, "Mexicans Find True Home in Vermont," *Newsday*, Feb. 8, 1987, 15; "Alien Family: The Wait of a Lifetime," *NYT*, Jul. 5, 1987, 23.

2. Jackson, "Mexicans Find True Home in Vermont"; "Alien Family."

3. Jackson, "Mexicans Find True Home in Vermont"; Enrique Corredera, "Mexican Family Seeking Permanent Resident Status," *Burlington Free Press* (hereafter *BFP*), Jun. 24, 1987, 15; "Alien Family." On IRCA, see this chapter's section on "The Militarization of the Border and the Criminalization of Immigrants" as well as Tichenor, *Dividing Lines*, 242–88; Carolyn Wong, *Lobbying for Inclusion: Rights Politics and the Making of Immigration Policy* (Palo Alto, CA: Stanford University Press, 2006), 95–132; Minian, *Undocumented Lives*, 183–207; Coleman, *The Walls Within*, chapters 3 and 4.

4. "Alien Family"; Enrique Corredera, "Mexican Family Can Stay in U.S.," *BFP*, Feb. 17, 1988, 1, 10; Enrique Corredera, "Mexican Father Learns His Family Faces INS Hurdle," *BFP*, Aug. 22, 1988, 1, 10.

5. "Alien Family"; Corredera, "Mexican Family Can Stay in U.S."; Corredera, "Mexican Father Learns His Family Faces INS Hurdle."

6. After learning that only Mario benefited from IRCA, the Márquezes reluctantly left Vermont and moved to California in order to be closer to María's family. The final outcome of their case is unclear. "Alien Family"; Corredera, "Mexican Family Can Stay in U.S."; Corredera, "Mexican Father Learns His Family Faces INS Hurdle." For an ethnographic study of the challenges mixed-status families face, see Ruth Gomberg-Muñoz, *Becoming Legal: Immigration Law and Mixed-Status Families* (New York: Oxford University Press, 2017).

7. During Barack Obama's presidency, activists and the media paid considerable attention to the number of people authorities formally removed. "Deportations from US Hit a Record High," read a 2010 *New York Times* headline. Six years later, at the end of his second

term, ABC News claimed, "Obama Has Deported More People than Any Other President." But these reports missed the mark since they only referred to formal deportations and did not include voluntary departures. DHS, *YOIS: 2017*, 103; Julia Preston, "Deportations from US Hit a Record High," *NYT*, Oct. 7, 2010, A21; Serena Marshall, "Obama Has Deported More People than Any Other President," ABC News, Aug. 29, 2016, http://abcnews.go.com/Politics/obamas-deportation-policy-numbers/story?id=41715661.

8. Studies later found that widespread fraud most likely occurred in many of the 1.3 million SAW cases. Some have argued that IRCA should be understood in the context of other liberal immigration laws of the time, such as the Refugee Act of 1980, which created the federal Refugee Resettlement Program in the aftermath of the Vietnam War and increased the annual limit for refugees from 17,400 to 50,000. Massey, Durand, and Malone, *Beyond Smoke and Mirrors*, 89–91; Tichenor, *Dividing Lines*, 242–62; Wong, *Lobbying for Inclusion*, 95–101.

9. Oral history with Fernanda Camacho (pseudonym), Jalisco, México, Jan. 17, 2013; Oral history with Claudia Camacho (pseudonym), Jalisco, México, Jan. 21, 2013; Oral history with Gabriela Camacho (pseudonym), Jalisco, México, Jan. 18, 2013; Adam Goodman, "Family Matters," *The Pennsylvania Gazette*, Oct. 25, 2013, http://thepenngazette.com/family-matters/; Adam Goodman, "Mexican Migration, Family Separation, and US Immigration Policy since 1942," in *Forced Out and Fenced In: Immigration Tales from the Field*, ed. Tanya Golash-Boza (New York: Oxford University Press, 2017), 43–50; Minian, *Undocumented Lives*, 211–13.

10. Massey, Durand, and Malone, *Beyond Smoke and Mirrors*, 87–91.

11. Gary P. Freeman and Frank D. Bean, "Mexico and U.S. Worldwide Immigration Policy," in *At the Crossroads: Mexico and U.S. Immigration Policy*, ed. Frank D. Bean, Rodolfo O. de la Garza, Bryan R. Roberts, and Sidney Weintraub (Lanham, MD: Rowman & Littlefield, 1997), 34.

12. In 2006, federal officials consolidated the Alien Criminal Apprehension Program and Institutional Removal Program to create the Criminal Alien Program, or CAP. Kanstroom, *Deportation Nation*, 226–28; Ryan D. King, Michael Massoglia, and Christopher Uggen, "Employment and Exile: U.S. Criminal Deportations, 1908–2005," *American Journal of Sociology* 117, no. 6 (May 2012): 1797; Jonathan Xavier Inda, "Subject to Deportation: IRCA, 'Criminal Aliens,' and the Policing of Immigration," *Migration Studies* 1, no. 3 (2013): 292–310.

13. Kanstroom, *Deportation Nation*, 226–28; The Immigration Act of 1990 increased legal immigration levels, but it also increased border enforcement and provided funds to hire an additional 1,000 agents. See Tichenor, *Dividing Lines*, 244–46; Massey, Durand, and Malone, *Beyond Smoke and Mirrors*, 91–93.

14. Joseph Nevins, *Operation Gatekeeper and Beyond: The War on "Illegals" and the Remaking of the U.S.-Mexico Boundary*, 2nd ed. (New York: Routledge, 2010), 95–110; Zolberg, *A Nation by Design*, 402–10.

15. Massey, Durand, and Malone, *Beyond Smoke and Mirrors*, 73.

16. In 1992, 53.1 percent of Mexicans could not afford housing, clothing, transportation, health care, education, and food. Two decades later 52.3 percent could not afford those basic necessities. But, due to population growth, that meant that an additional 14 million-plus Mexicans lived in poverty in 2012 than had in 1992. Between 1991 and 2007 Mexico lost nearly 2 million agricultural jobs, spurring heightened levels of unauthorized migration. Mark Weisbrot, Stephan Lefebvre, and Joseph Sammut, "Did NAFTA Help Mexico? An Assessment after 20 Years," Center for Economic and Policy Research, Feb. 2014, 1–21; Zolberg, *A Nation by Design*, 383–84. For more on NAFTA's impact on Mexico, the United States, and migration, see Bill Ong Hing, *Ethical Borders: NAFTA, Globalization, and Mexican Migration* (Philadelphia: Temple University Press, 2010). On NAFTA and the North American economy's dependence on exploitative Mexican labor during the second half of the twentieth century, see Ronald L. Mize and Alicia C. S. Swords, *Consuming Mexican Labor: From the Bracero Program to NAFTA* (Toronto: University of Toronto Press, 2010); Gilbert G. González, *Guest Workers or Colonized Labor? Mexican Labor Migration to the United States* (Boulder, CO: Paradigm, 2006).

17. Tichenor, *Dividing Lines*, 244–46; Massey, Durand, and Malone, *Beyond Smoke and Mirrors*, 93–95; Daniel Martinez HoSang, *Racial Propositions: Ballot Initiatives and the Making of Postwar California* (Berkeley: University of California Press, 2010), 160–200.

18. William Safire, "Self-Deportation?," *NYT*, Nov. 21, 1994, A15.

19. Fred Alvarez, "'I Walk in Fear': A Family of Immigrants in Oxnard Will Split Up Rather Than Deal with the Uncertainty of Prop. 187," *LAT*, Nov. 20, 1994, 20; Fred Alvarez, "Going Home: Illegal Immigrant Returns to Mexico Amid Hopes, Fears," *LAT*, Dec. 18, 1994, 1; Robert Therrien, letter to the editor, *LAT*, Dec. 25, 1994, 8. On Mixtec migration to the United States, see Lynn Stephen, *Transborder Lives: Indigenous Oaxacans in Mexico, California, and Oregon* (Durham, NC: Duke University Press, 2007); Wayne A. Cornelius, *Migration from the Mexican Mixteca: A Transnational Community in Oaxaca and California* (San Diego: Center for Comparative Immigration Studies, University of California, San Diego, 2009).

20. As quoted in Nevins, *Operation Gatekeeper and Beyond*, 2–4, 111–14; Bill Ong Hing, "Operation Gatekeeper: The War against the *Alambristas* of the 1990s," in *Alambrista and the U.S.-Mexico Border: Film, Music and Stories of Undocumented Immigrants*, ed. Nicholas J. Cull and David Carrasco (Albuquerque: University of New Mexico Press, 2004), 80–81. For a comparative discussion of deportation, immigration control, and immigration's impact on "receiving" societies, see Jeannette Money, *Fences and Neighbors: The Political Geography of Immigration Control* (Ithaca, NY: Cornell University Press, 1999); Ellermann, *States against Migrants*.

21. Hing, "Operation Gatekeeper," 82; Massey, Durand, and Malone, *Beyond Smoke and Mirrors*, 93–95; Nevins, *Operation Gatekeeper and Beyond*, 6–7. Borders and walls did not need to act as impenetrable physical barriers in order to be effective. As political

theorist Wendy Brown has argued, the construction of border walls reflected the erosion, rather than affirmation, of nation-state sovereignty. Walls, Brown notes, "often function theatrically, projecting power and efficaciousness that they do not and cannot actually exercise and that they also performatively contradict." Similarly, as political scientist Peter Andreas has noted, "border control efforts are not only *actions* (a means to a stated instrumental end) but also *gestures* that communicate meaning." So, while US immigration enforcement "has failed to deter illegal border crossings significantly, it has nevertheless succeeded in reaffirming the importance of the border." Wendy Brown, *Walled States, Waning Sovereignty* (New York: Zone Books, 2010), 24–25; Peter Andreas, *Border Games: Policing the U.S.-Mexico Divide*, 2nd ed. (Ithaca, NY: Cornell University Press, 2009), 11. On the militarization of the border before 1994, see Timothy J. Dunn, *The Militarization of the U.S.-Mexico Border, 1978–1992* (Austin: University of Texas Press, 1996). For a longer history of the making of the border, see Juan Mora-Torres, *The Making of the Mexican Border: The State, Capitalism, and Society in Nuevo León, 1848–1910* (Austin: University of Texas Press, 2001); Kang, *The INS on the Line*; C. J. Alvarez, *Border Land, Border Water: A History of Construction on the US-Mexico Divide* (Austin: University of Texas Press, 2019); Mary E. Mendoza, "Unnatural Border: Race and Environment at the US-Mexico Divide" (Ph.D. diss., University of California, Davis, 2015). On how militarization and NAFTA have affected people living on the border, see Gilberto Rosas, *Barrio Libre: Criminalizing States and Delinquent Refusals of the New Frontier* (Durham, NC: Duke University Press, 2012).

22. From 1986 to 2000, linewatch hours increased from 2.4 million to 8.9 million. In addition to unauthorized migrants, the INS also focused its efforts and resources on controlling the movement of illicit drugs from Mexico to the United States. Statistics compiled by the Mexican Migration Project; Massey, Durand, and Malone, *Beyond Smoke and Mirrors*, 87–89, 96–98, 101–4. The Border Patrol's expansion is even more striking given that the overall federal government workforce shrank by over 10 percent from 1985 to 2002. See Ellermann, *States against Migrants*, 2–3.

23. Douglas A. Massey, Jorge Durand, and Karen A. Pren, "Why Border Enforcement Backfired," *American Journal of Sociology* 121, no. 5 (Mar. 2016): 1557–1600; Government Accountability Office, "Illegal Immigration: Status of Southwest Border Strategy Implementation" (Washington, DC: US General Accounting Office, 1999), 32.

24. Hing, "Operation Gatekeeper," 82–86; See also Karl Eschbach, Jacqueline Hagan, Nestor Rodríguez, Rubén Hernández-León, and Stanley Bailey, "Death at the Border," *International Migration Review* 33, no. 2 (Summer 1999): 430–54; Massey, Durand, and Malone, *Beyond Smoke and Mirrors*, 93–95, 112–36. On prevention through deterrence in the 1990s, see Timothy J. Dunn, *Blockading the Border and Human Rights: The El Paso Operation that Remade Immigration Enforcement* (Austin: University of Texas Press, 2009). For narrative, ethnographic accounts of the many dangers

migrants face, see Luis Alberto Urrea, *The Devil's Highway: A True Story* (New York: Little, Brown, 2004); De León, *The Land of Open Graves*.

25. "Border Trilogy Part 2: Hold the Line," *Radiolab*, Apr. 6, 2018, https://www.wnycstudios.org/story/border-trilogy-part-2-hold-line.

26. US Border Patrol, "Southwest Border Deaths by Fiscal Year, 1998–2018," accessed Aug. 1, 2019, https://www.cbp.gov/sites/default/files/assets/documents/2019-Mar/bp-southwest-border-sector-deaths-fy1998-fy2018.pdf.

27. Zolberg, *A Nation by Design*, 402–10.

28. Illegal Immigration Reform and Immigrant Responsibility Act of 1996 (hereafter IIRIRA), 110 Stat. 3009; Nancy Morawetz, "Understanding the Impact of the 1996 Deportation Laws and the Limited Scope of Proposed Reforms," *Harvard Law Review* 113, no. 8 (Jun. 2000): 1936–1962. On general trends in deportation since 1996, see Marc R. Rosenblum and Doris Meissner with Claire Bergeron and Faye Hipsman, "The Deportation Dilemma: Reconciling Tough and Humane Enforcement," Migration Policy Institute, Apr. 2014, 1–66.

29. IIRIRA, 110 Stat. 3009; American Civil Liberties Union, "American Exile: Rapid Deportations that Bypass the Courtroom," Dec. 2014, 1–148; Immigration Policy Center, "Removal without Recourse: The Growth of Summary Deportations from the United States," May 2014, 1–5; Jennifer Lee Koh, Jayashri Srikantiah, and Karen C. Tumlin, "Deportation without Due Process," 2011, https://www.nilc.org/wp-content/uploads/2016/02/Deportation-Without-Due-Process-2011-09.pdf.

30. Morawetz, "Understanding the Impact of the 1996 Deportation Laws and the Limited Scope of Proposed Reforms," 1950.

31. Kozuba's case prompted his wife, Laurie, to found Citizens and Immigrants for Equal Justice, an organization that fought against family separation in the aftermath of IIRIRA. As a result of their organizing and many years of fighting, Kozuba's deportation was eventually stayed. Mark Dow, *American Gulag: Inside US Immigration Prisons* (Berkeley: University of California Press, 2004), 171–74; Patty Reinert, "Two Texans Fight against Deportation," *Houston Chronicle*, May 6, 2001; "ACLU to Argue Crucial Immigrants' Rights Case before Supreme Court," Apr. 23, 2001, https://www.aclu.org/news/aclu-argue-crucial-immigrants-rights-case-supreme-court-tomorrow.

32. Spending on border control and interior enforcement increased as well, but only by 94 percent and 51 percent, respectively. Overall, detention and removal spending spiked more than 800 percent between fiscal years 1985 and 2002. Morawetz, "Understanding the Impact of the 1996 Deportation Laws and the Limited Scope of Proposed Reforms," 1936–1962; Jacqueline Hagan and Scott Phillips, "Border Blunders: The Unanticipated Human and Economic Costs of the U.S. Approach to Immigration Control, 1986–2007," *Criminology & Public Policy* 7, no. 1 (2008): 86–87; Nestor Rodríguez and Jacqueline Hagan, "Fractured Families and Communities: Effects of Immigration Reform in Texas, Mexico, and El Salvador," *Latino Studies* 2, no. 3 (2004):

329; "Immigration Enforcement Spending since IRCA," Migration Policy Institute, Nov. 2005, 7; US Citizenship and Immigration Services, "E-Verify History and Milestones," accessed Aug. 1, 2019, https://www.e-verify.gov/about-e-verify/history-and-milestones; Email correspondence between author and Marc Rosenblum, Deputy Assistant Secretary, Immigration Statistics, DHS, Jun. 11, 2019.

33. The language of "responsibility" included in the names of these two laws is important. Indeed, it aimed to shape how people in the United States conceptualized immigrants, citizens, and the state, in addition to who was "deserving" and who was "undeserving." Massey, Durand, and Malone, *Beyond Smoke and Mirrors*, 95–96; Kanstroom, *Deportation Nation*, 229; Daniel Denvir, *All American Nativism: How the Bipartisan War on Immigrants Explains Politics as We Know It* (New York: Verso Books, 2020). On the history of the relationship between immigration status and social policy, see Cybelle Fox, "Unauthorized Welfare: The Origins of Immigrant Status Restrictions in American Social Policy," *Journal of American History* 102, no. 4 (2016): 1051–74. Although it was part of the 1996 act, the federal government didn't enter into the first 287(g) agreement until 2002, when the state of Florida signed on. It wasn't until 2007–8, more than a decade after it was implemented, that the program took off and the federal government entered into another fifty-four agreements with state and local law enforcement agencies. On 287(g), see US Immigration and Customs Enforcement, "Delegation of Immigration Authority Section 287(g) Immigration and Nationality Act," accessed Jun. 11, 2018, http://www.ice.gov/factsheets/287g; Migration Policy Institute, "Key Immigration Laws and Policy Developments since 1986," Mar. 2013, https://www.migrationpolicy.org/research/timeline-1986.

34. Eight years before the 9/11 attacks, the 1993 bombing of the World Trade Center heightened fears about the connection between immigration and terrorism. Nicholas De Genova, "The Production of Culprits: From Deportability to Detainability in the Aftermath of 'Homeland Security,'" *Citizenship Studies* 11, no. 5 (2007): 421–48; Kevin R. Johnson, "September 11 and Mexican Immigrants: Collateral Damage Comes Home," *DePaul Law Review* 52 (2003): 849–70. On state terror and the connections between the Cold War period and the early 2000s, see Rachel Ida Buff, "The Deportation Terror," *American Quarterly* 60, no. 3 (Sep. 2008): 523–51. On social control and the punishment of immigrants in the post-9/11 United States, see Charis E. Kubrin, Marjorie S. Zatz, and Ramiro Martínez Jr., eds., *Punishing Immigrants: Policy, Politics, and Injustice* (New York: New York University Press, 2012).

35. Patrisia Macías-Rojas, *From Deportation to Prison: The Politics of Immigration Enforcement in Post-Civil Rights America* (New York: New York University Press, 2016), 68–69.

36. ICE, "ENDGAME: Office of Detention and Removal Strategic Plan, 2003–2012" (Washington, DC: DHS, Aug. 2003).

37. Amy Kaplan, "Homeland Insecurities: Reflections on Language and Space," *Radical History Review* 85 (2003): 90. Also cited in De Genova, "The Production of Culprits," 423.

38. Leti Volpp, "The Citizen and the Terrorist," in *September 11 in History: A Watershed Moment?*, ed. Mary L. Dudziak (Durham, NC: Duke University Press, 2003), 147–62.

39. According to Nicholas De Genova, after 9/11 "the Homeland Security State's real goal [was] *not to deport but to detain.*" De Genova, "The Production of Culprits," 433–36; John Ashcroft, Attorney General Prepared Remarks on the National Security Entry-Exit Registration System, Jun. 6, 2002, https://www.justice.gov/archive/ag/speeches /2002/060502agpreparedremarks.htm.

40. After controlling for inflation, the CBP budget increased by more than 75 percent between 2003 and 2016. De Genova, "The Production of Culprits," 421–48; Statistics from the Mexican Migration Project. On the INS/DHS's growing enforcement budget, see "Immigration Enforcement Spending since IRCA," Migration Policy Institute, Nov. 2005, 1–12. On the devastating impact the federal government's inability or refusal to pass immigration reform had on undocumented migrants, see Alicia Schmidt Camacho, "Hailing the Twelve Million: U.S. Immigration Policy, Deportation, and the Imaginary of Lawful Violence," *Social Text* 28, no. 4 (Winter 2010): 1–24.

41. Nadine Naber, "The Rules of Forced Engagement: Race, Gender, and the Culture of Fear among Arab Immigrants in San Francisco Post-9/11," *Cultural Dynamics* 18, no. 3 (2006): 240.

42. Motomura, *Immigration Outside the Law*, 50; Donald Kerwin and Kristen McCabe, "Arrested on Entry: Operation Streamline and the Prosecution of Immigration Crimes," *Migration Information Source*, Migration Policy Institute, Apr. 29, 2010, https://www.migrationpolicy.org/article/arrested-entry-operation-streamline-and -prosecution-immigration-crimes/; H.R. 6061, 109th Congress, Secure Fence Act of 2006, accessed June 11, 2018, https://www.govtrack.us/congress/bills/109/hr6061.

43. Apprehensions by ICE dropped during Obama's second term, in part because of an executive action recommending widespread prosecutorial discretion. DHS, *YOIS: 2017*, 91; Motomura, *Immigration Outside the Law*, 56–85, 113–44; Goodman, "A Nation of (Deported) Immigrants," 64–68. On who is removed and the question of discretion, see Marc R. Rosenblum and Kristen McCabe, "Deportation and Discretion: Reviewing the Record and Options for Change," Migration Policy Institute, Oct. 2014, 1–51. On the gap between legislation and implementation, see Ellermann, *States against Migrants*. Daniel Kanstroom argues that programs like Secure Communities and the rise in apprehensions by ICE can be attributed to a shift toward "post-entry social control." See Kanstroom, *Deportation Nation*; Daniel Kanstroom, *Aftermath: Deportation Law and the New American Diaspora* (New York: Oxford University Press, 2012).

44. Academics and authors also played an important role in spreading anti-immigrant ideas. People like Samuel Huntington, Pat Buchanan, Victor Davis Hanson, and Peter Brimelow all penned influential nativist texts in the 1990s and early 2000s. On rising xenophobia in recent decades, see Denvir, *All American Nativism*. On border militias, see Harel Shapira, *Waiting for José: The Minutemen's Pursuit of America* (Prince-

ton, NJ: Princeton University Press, 2013); Shane Bauer, "I Went Undercover with a Border Militia. Here's What I Saw," *Mother Jones*, Nov./Dec. 2016.

45. Adam Goodman, "The Long History of Self-Deportation," *NACLA Report on the Americas* 49, no. 2 (2017): 152–58; Mark Krikorian, "Fewer Immigrants, A Warmer Welcome: Fixing a Broken Immigration Policy," Center for Immigration Studies, Nov. 2003, 2; Kris W. Kobach, "Attrition through Enforcement: A Rational Approach to Illegal Immigration," *Tulsa Journal of Comparative & International Law* 15, no. 2 (2007–8): 156. Although it is impossible to quantify how many people have left in response to subnational self-deportation campaigns, scholars have shown that many undocumented immigrants remain in place, albeit under extraordinarily difficult circumstances. See, for example, Angela S. García, *Legal Passing: Navigating Undocumented Life and Local Immigration Law* (Oakland: University of California Press, 2019), 58–96; Alexandra Filindra, "The Myth of Self-Deportation: How Behavioral Economics Reveals the Fallacies behind 'Attrition through Enforcement'" (Washington, DC: Immigration Policy Center, 2012): 1–10.

46. María Cristina García, *Seeking Refuge: Central American Migration to Mexico, The United States, and Canada* (Berkeley: University of California Press, 2006), 1, 20–26. On the history of the externalization of migration control, see Zolberg, "The Archeology of Remote Control"; David Scott FitzGerald, *Refuge beyond Reach: How Rich Democracies Repel Asylum Seekers* (New York: Oxford University Press, 2019); Elliott Young, "Beyond Borders: Remote Control and the Continuing Legacy of Racism in Immigration Legislation," in *A Nation of Immigrants Reconsidered: US Society in an Age of Restriction, 1924–1965*, ed. Maddalena Marinari, Madeline Hsu, and María Cristina García (Urbana: University of Illinois Press, 2019), 25–44.

47. The Plan Frontera Sur proved to be ineffective and fizzled in the aftermath of September 11th. "U.S. Paid Mexico to Deport Illegal Latins," *Atlanta Constitution*, Oct. 27, 1983, 9A; "Agreement with U.S. to Stop Illegals Denied," Reuters, Mar. 23, 1989; Kirsten Gallagher, "Mexico Lays Out the Unwelcome Mat," *Orlando Sentinel*, Nov. 18, 1990, A1; Deborah Sontag, "Mexico's Position on Aliens Contradicted by Past Deeds," *NYT*, Jul. 15, 1993, A18; Ginger Thompson, "Mexico's Open Southern Border Lures Migrants Headed to U.S.," *NYT*, Aug. 5, 2001, 1; Ginger Thompson, "Mexico Worries about Its Own Southern Border," *NYT*, Jun. 18, 2006, A1.

48. Bill Frelick, "No Central Americans Need Apply," *LAT*, Jun. 25, 1991, B11. See also Ann Kimball, "The Transit State: A Comparative Analysis of Mexican and Moroccan Immigration Policies" (San Diego, CA: The Center for Comparative Immigration Studies, Working Paper 150, Jun. 2007), 44, 90.

49. Tracy Wilkinson, "Dreams Die on Mexico's 2nd Border," *LAT*, Jan. 1, 1994, A1.

50. Jenna M. Loyd and Alison Mountz, *Boats, Borders, and Bases: Race, the Cold War, and the Rise of Migration Detention in the United States* (Berkeley: University of California Press, 2018), 76–79; Sontag, "Mexico's Position on Aliens Contradicted by Past Deeds"; "INS 'Global Reach' Initiative Counters Rise of International Migrant Smuggling," INS Fact

Sheet, Jun. 27, 2001; Patrick J. McDonnell and Dina Bass, "INS Expands Its War on Smuggling of 'Human Cargo,'" *LAT*, Jun. 20, 1997; DHS, "US Immigration and Customs Enforcement, Operations and Support, Fiscal Year 2018 Congressional Justification," 89, accessed Aug. 1, 2019, https://www.dhs.gov/sites/default/files/publications/ICE%20 FY18%20Budget.pdf.

51. Suzanne Leone Fiederlein, "Responding to Central American Refugees: Comparing Policy Design in Mexico and the United States" (Ph.D. diss., University of Arizona, 1992): 88–104; Colin McMahon, "Mexico Tightens Guatemala Border," *ChiTrib*, Feb. 14, 1996.

52. Óscar Martínez, *The Beast: Riding the Rails and Dodging Narcos on the Migrant Trail*, trans. Daniela Maria Ugaz and John Washington (New York: Verso, 2013), 35, 72–73; US Embassy, Mexico, to Secretary of State, Washington, DC, Jan. 31, 2011, part of "Mexico's San Fernando Massacres: A Declassified History," National Security Archive, George Washington University, Washington, DC, http://www2.gwu.edu/~nsarchiv/NSAEBB /NSAEBB445/docs/20110131.pdf; International Crisis Group, "Easy Prey: Criminal Violence and Central American Migration," Latin America Report 57, Jul. 28, 2016.

53. The United States never offered TPS to Guatemalans. García, *Seeking Refuge*, 1, 20–26; Susan Bibler Coutin, "The Odyssey of Salvadoran Asylum Seekers," *NACLA*, Sep. 25, 2007, https://nacla.org/article/odyssey-salvadoran-asylum-seekers; Susan Bibler Coutin, *Exiled Home: Salvadoran Transnational Youth in the Aftermath of Violence* (Durham, NC: Duke University Press, 2016); Cecilia Menjívar, "Liminal Legality: Salvadoran and Guatemalan Immigrants' Lives in the United States," *American Journal of Sociology* 111, 4 (Jan. 2006): 999–1037; Cecilia Menjívar and Leisy J. Abrego, "Legal Violence: Immigration Law and the Lives of Central American Immigrants," *American Journal of Sociology* 117, no. 5 (Mar. 2012): 1380–1421; Leisy J. Abrego, "Legal Consciousness of Undocumented Latinos: Fear and Stigma as Barriers to Claims-Making for First- and 1.5-Generation Immigrants," *Law & Society Review* 45, no. 2 (2011): 337–69.

54. Jeffrey Passel, D'Vera Cohn, and Ana Gonzalez-Barrera, "Net Migration from Mexico Falls to Zero–and Perhaps Less" (Washington, DC: Pew Research Hispanic Center, 2012). In 2013, more authorized migrants came to the United States from China and India than from Mexico, marking the first time in decades that Mexico was not the top country of origin of recent immigrants to the United States. Muzaffar Chishti and Faye Hipsman, "In Historic Shift, New Migration Flows from Mexico Fall below Those from China and India," Migration Policy Institute, May 21, 2015, https://www.migrationpolicy .org/article/historic-shift-new-migration-flows-mexico-fall-below-those-china-and -india. On the history of refugee policy since the end of the Cold War, see María Cristina García, *The Refugee Challenge in Post-Cold War America* (New York: Oxford University Press, 2017).

55. INS/DHS, *YOIS: 1986–2017*; DHS, "ICE Enforcement and Removal Operations Report," Fiscal Year 2014, accessed June 11, 2018, https://www.ice.gov/doclib/about /offices/ero/pdf/2014-ice-immigration-removals.pdf. On immigration enforcement targeting Latino men in recent years, see Tanya Golash-Boza and Pierrette Hondagneu-

Sotelo, "Latino Immigrant Men and the Deportation Crisis: A Gendered Racial Removal Program," *Latino Studies* 11, no. 3 (2013): 271–92.

56. Elana Zilberg, *Space of Detention: The Making of a Transnational Gang Crisis between Los Angeles and San Salvador* (Durham, NC: Duke University Press, 2011).

57. "Stronger Neighbors—Stronger Borders: Addressing the Root Causes of the Migration Surge from Central America," United States Senate Committee on Homeland Security and Governmental Affairs, Ranking Member Thomas R. Carper, Minority Staff Report (Washington, DC, 2015), 1–46; Michael D. Shear and Jeremy W. Peters, "Obama Asks for $3.7 Billion to Aid Border," *NYT*, Jul. 8, 2014; DHS, *YOIS: 2014*, 113–14.

58. Mexico also carried out two-thirds of the 220,000 deportations from the United States and Mexico to El Salvador, Guatemala, and Honduras in fiscal year 2016. "Stronger Neighbors—Stronger Borders"; Secretaría de Gobernación, México, "Extranjeros Presentados y Devueltos," Boletín Estadístico 2014, 2015, and 2016, http://politicamigratoria.gob.mx/es_mx/SEGOB/Boletines_Estadisticos (accessed Mar. 6, 2017); International Crisis Group, "Easy Prey: Criminal Violence and Central American Migration" (Brussels, Belgium: International Crisis Group, Jul. 28, 2016): 34.

59. Lytle Hernández, *City of Inmates*.

60. On the growth of the carceral state and mass incarceration, see David Garland, *The Culture of Control: Crime and Social Order in Contemporary Society* (Chicago: University of Chicago Press, 2001); Bruce Western, *Punishment and Inequality in America* (New York: Russell Sage Foundation, 2006); Marie Gottschalk, *The Prison and the Gallows: The Politics of Mass Incarceration in America* (New York: Cambridge University Press, 2006); Ruth Gilmore Wilson, *Golden Gulag: Prisons, Surplus, Crisis, and Opposition in Globalizing California* (Berkeley: University of California Press, 2007); Christian Parenti, *Lockdown America: Police and Prisons in the Age of Crisis* (New York: Verso, 2008); Loïc Wacquant, *Punishing the Poor: The Neoliberal Government of Social Insecurity* (Durham, NC: Duke University Press, 2009); Alexander, *The New Jim Crow*; Marie Gottschalk, *Caught: The Prison State and the Lockdown of American Politics* (Princeton, NJ: Princeton University Press, 2014); Naomi Murakawa, *The First Civil Right: How Liberals Built Prison America* (New York: Oxford University Press, 2014); Elizabeth Hinton, *From the War on Poverty to the War on Crime: The Making of Mass Incarceration in America* (Cambridge, MA: Harvard University Press, 2016); Heather Ann Thompson, *Blood in the Water: The Attica Prison Uprising of 1971 and Its Legacy* (New York: Pantheon, 2016); Julilly Kohler-Hausmann, *Getting Tough: Welfare and Imprisonment in 1970s America* (Princeton, NJ: Princeton University Press, 2017); John F. Pfaff, *Locked In: The True Causes of Mass Incarceration and How to Achieve Real Reform* (New York: Basic Books, 2017); James Forman Jr., *Locking Up Our Own: Crime and Punishment in Black America* (New York: Farrar, Straus, and Giroux, 2017); Felker-Kantor, *Policing Los Angeles*; Stuart Schrader, *Badges without Borders: How Global Counterinsurgency Transformed American Policing* (Oakland: University of California Press, 2019).

61. Morawetz, "Understanding the Impact of the 1996 Deportation Laws and the Limited Scope of Proposed Reforms," 1944.

62. Jonathan Simon, "Refugees in a Carceral Age: The Rebirth of Immigration Prisons in the United States," *Public Culture* 10, no. 3 (1998): 577.

63. Heather Ann Thompson, "Why Mass Incarceration Matters: Rethinking Crisis, Decline, and Transformation in Postwar American History," *Journal of American History* 97, no. 3 (Dec. 2010): 703. For a comparative study of immigration detention in the United States and Europe, see Wong, *Rights, Deportation, and Detention in the Age of Immigration Control*, 109–43.

64. Pfaff, *Locked In.*

65. In 1991, for example, the INS's detention capacity was around 6,000, while the US general prison population hovered around 1 million people per day. Simon, "Refugees in a Carceral Age," 580.

66. Macías-Rojas, *From Deportation to Prison*, 63, 107–31.

67. Alina Das, "Immigration Detention: Information Gaps and Institutional Barriers to Reform," *University of Chicago Law Review* 80, no. 1 (Winter 2013): 137–38; David Manuel Hernández, "Pursuant to Deportation: Latinos and Immigrant Detention," *Latino Studies* 6 (2008): 43; Jennifer Chan, "Immigration Detention Bed Quota Timeline," National Immigrant Justice Center, Jan. 13, 2017, http://www.immigrantjustice.org/staff/blog/immigration-detention-bed-quota-timeline; Torrie Hester, "Deportability and the Carceral State," *Journal of American History* 102, no. 1 (Jun. 2015): 147; Detention Watch Network (DWN), "Immigration Detention 101," accessed June 11, 2018, https://www.detentionwatchnetwork.org/issues/detention-101; Transactional Records Access Clearinghouse (TRAC) Immigration, "New Data on 637 Detention Facilities Used by ICE in FY 2015," accessed June 11, 2018, http://trac.syr.edu/immigration/reports/422/; DHS, "US Immigration and Customs Enforcement, Operations and Support, Fiscal Year 2018 Congressional Justification," 136. On how the growth of immigration detention "helps to promote or reinforce widespread legal cynicism among immigrant detainees" because of the system's punitive nature and arbitrary legal outcomes, see Emily Ryo, "Fostering Legal Cynicism through Immigration Detention," *Southern California Law Review* 90 (2017): 999–1053.

68. Jenna Loyd and Alison Mountz's important work is essential in understanding the changing geography of detention during the Cold War. Loyd and Mountz, *Boats, Borders, and Bases*; James D. Sandefur, et al., to Rudolph W. Giuliani, Apr. 12, 1982, Box 53, "Oakdale," Records of the Department of Justice, RG60, NARA2; Simon, "Refugees in a Carceral Age," 577–607; Stephanie J. Silverman, "Immigration Detention in America: A History of Its Expansion and a Study of Its Significance" (Oxford: Centre on Migration, Policy and Society, Working Paper No. 80, 2010): 1–31. On the history of immigration detention, see also A. Naomi Paik, *Rightlessness: Testimony and Redress in U.S. Prison Camps since World War II* (Chapel Hill: University of North Carolina Press, 2016); Carl Lindskoog, *Detain and Punish: Haitian Refugees and the Rise of the World's Largest Immi-*

*gration Detention System* (Gainesville: University of Florida Press, 2018); Robert T. Chase, ed., *Caging Borders and Carceral States: Incarcerations, Immigration Detentions, and Resistance* (Chapel Hill: University of North Carolina Press, 2019); César Cuauhté-moc García Hernández, *Migrating to Prison: America's Obsession with Locking Up Immigrants* (New York: New Press, 2019); Jessica Ordaz, "The Rise of Immigration Detention: Labor, Migrant Politics, and Punishment in California's Imperial Valley, 1945–2014" (Ph.D. diss., University of California, Davis, 2017); and forthcoming work by Smita Ghosh, David Hernández, Brianna Nofil, Alexander Stephens, and Elliott Young. On the landscape of migrant detention and the importance of studying the built environment, see Sarah Lopez, "From Penal to 'Civil': A Legacy of Private Prison Policy in a Landscape of Migrant Detention," *American Quarterly* 71, no. 1 (Mar. 2019): 105–34.

69. Loyd and Mountz, *Boats, Borders, and Bases,* 189–94; Meredith Kolodner, "Immigration Enforcement Benefits Prison Firms," *NYT,* Jul. 19, 2006; Laura Sullivan, "Prison Economics Help Drive Ariz. Immigration Law," *NPR,* Oct. 28, 2010, http://www.npr.org/2010/10/28/130833741/prison-economics-help-drive-ariz-immigration-law; Michael Cohen, "How For-Profit Prisons Have Become the Biggest Lobby No One Is Talking About," *WaPo,* Apr. 28, 2015, http://www.washingtonpost.com/posteverything/wp/2015/04/28/how-for-profit-prisons-have-become-the-biggest-lobby-no-one-is-talking-about/; Bethany Carson and Eleana Diaz, "Payoff: How Congress Ensures Private Prison Profit with an Immigrant Detention Quota" (Austin, TX: Grassroots Leadership, Apr. 2015), 1–27.

70. Carson and Diaz, "Payoff," 7–8.

71. The GEO Group was known as Wackenhut Corrections Corporation until 2004. Its 2016 revenues represented a threefold increase from 2001 after adjusting for inflation. The GEO Group, Inc. "2016 Annual Report," p. 1, accessed April 2, 2018, http://www.snl.com/Interactive/newlookandfeel/4144107/2016-GEO-Annual-Report.pdf; Wackenhut Corrections Corporation, "Consolidated Statements of Income, Fiscal Years 2000–2002," accessed April 2, 2018, https://www.sec.gov/Archives/edgar/data/923796/000095014403012462/g85056a2e1ovkza.htm. CoreCivic, "2016 Annual Report," 54, accessed April 2, 2018, http://ir.corecivic.com/static-files/452022e9-1ced-4b2d-b4f3-3f7a254d9ebd.

72. Zusha Elinson, "More Detentions Boost Private Prisons," *Wall Street Journal* (hereafter *WSJ*), Jul. 3, 2018, A3; National Immigration Forum, "The Math of Immigration Detention," Aug. 22, 2013, https://immigrationforum.org/article/math-immigration-detention/. On the history of the detention bed quota, see Macías-Rojas, *From Deportation to Prison.* On DHS's fiscal year 2016 budget, see "Fact Sheet: Department of Homeland Security Fiscal Year 2016 Budget," Feb. 2, 2015, https://www.dhs.gov/news/2015/02/02/fact-sheet-dhs-fy-2016-budget. On the cost of detention, see Das, "Immigration Detention," 143–45.

73. Catherine E. Shoichet and Curt Merrill, "ICE Air: How US Deportation Flights Work," *CNN,* May 29, 2017, https://amp.cnn.com/cnn/2017/05/26/us/ice-air-deportation-flights-explainer/index.html (accessed Sep. 21, 2018).

74. Human Rights Watch, "Locked Away: Immigration Detainees in Jails in the United States," Sep. 1998, https://www.hrw.org/legacy/reports98/us-immig/.

75. Scholars and journalists have documented this at length. See, for example, Dow, *American Gulag*; Daniel Wishner, *Immigration Detention: Law, History, Politics* (New York: Cambridge University Press, 2012); Morawetz, "Understanding the Impact of the 1996 Deportation Laws and the Limited Scope of Proposed Reforms," 1943–1950; Daniel Zwerdling, "The Death of Richard Rust," *NPR*, Dec. 5, 2005, https://www.npr .org/ 2005/12/05/5022866/the-death-of-richard-rust; Nina Bernstein, "Officials Obscured Truth of Immigrant Deaths in Jail," *NYT*, Jan. 10, 2010, A1; "Deaths in Immigration Detention," *NYT*, n.d., accessed April 2, 2018, https://www.nytimes.com /interactive/projects/documents/deaths-in-immigration-detention; Detention Watch Network, "Immigration Detention 101."

76. Eligible class members were Salvadorans who entered the United States before Sep. 19, 1990, and Guatemalans who entered the country before Oct. 1, 1990. García, *Seeking Refuge*, 98–112; Susan Bibler Coutin, *Legalizing Moves: Salvadoran Immigrants' Struggle for U.S. Residency* (Ann Arbor: University of Michigan Press, 2000); Coutin, "The Odyssey of Salvadoran Asylum Seekers."

77. HoSang, *Racial Propositions*, 178–200.

78. Hispanics for Wilson, Press Release, Sep. 16, 1994, http://www.pocho.com/hispanics -for-wilsons-first-press-release-touting-self-deportation/; Robert Mackey, "The Deep Comic Roots of 'Self-Deportation,'" *NYT*, Feb. 1, 2012, https://thelede.blogs.nytimes .com/2012/02/01/the-deep-comic-roots-of-self-deportation/.

79. Guillermo Gómez-Peña, "The Self-Deportation Project, 1995," in *Dangerous Border Crossers: The Artist Talks Back* (London: Routledge, 2000), 95–97.

80. Alfonso González argues that the 2006 marches built on the activism of previous generations of Chicana/o and Central American activists. See Alfonso González, *Reform without Justice: Latino Migrant Politics and the Homeland Security State* (New York: Oxford University Press, 2014), 3, 21–74; Amalia Pallares and Nilda Flores-González, eds., *Marcha: Latino Chicago and the Immigrant Rights Movement* (Urbana: University of Illinois Press, 2010); Chris Zepeda-Millán, *Latino Mass Mobilization: Immigration, Racialization, and Activism* (New York: Cambridge University Press, 2017).

81. On undocumented youth activism and immigrant organizing, see Eileen Truax, *Dreamers: La Lucha de una Generación por Su Sueño Americano* (México, DF: Océano, 2013); Walter Nicholls, *The Dreamers: How the Undocumented Youth Movement Transformed the Immigrant Rights Debate* (Palo Alto, CA: Stanford University Press, 2013); Karma Chávez, *Queer Migration Politics: Activist Rhetoric and Coalition Possibilities* (Champaign: University of Illinois Press, 2013); Tania A. Unzueta Carrasco and Hinda Seif, "Disrupting the Dream: Undocumented Youth Reframe Citizenship and Deportability through Anti-Deportation Activism," *Latino Studies* 12, no. 2 (2014): 279–99; Cristina Beltrán, "'No Papers, No Fear': DREAM Activism, New Social Media, and the Queering of Immigrant Rights," in *Contemporary Latina/o Media:*

*Production, Circulation, Politics*, ed. Arlene Dávila and Yeidy M. Rivero (New York: New York University Press, 2014), 245–66; Amalia Pallares, *Family Activism: Immigrant Struggles and the Politics of Non-Citizenship* (New Brunswick, NJ: Rutgers University Press, 2015); Gabriela Márquez-Benitez and Amalia Pallares, "Not One More: Linking Civil Disobediences and Public Anti-Deportation Campaigns," *North American Dialogue* 19, no. 1 (2016): 13–22; Kevin Escudero, *Organizing while Undocumented: Immigrant Youth's Political Activism under the Law* (New York: New York University Press, 2020).

82. Memo, John Morton, Director ICE, Jun. 17, 2011, https://www.ice.gov/doclib/secure -communities/pdf/prosecutorial-discretion-memo.pdf; DHS, "Number of I-821D, Consideration of Deferred Action for Childhood Arrivals by Fiscal Year, Quarter, Intake, Biometrics and Case Status: 2012–2016 (June 30)," accessed June 11, 2018, https://www.uscis.gov/sites/default/files/USCIS/Resources/Reports%20and%20 Studies/Immigration%20Forms%20Data/All%20Form%20Types/DACA/daca _performancedata_fy2016_qtr3.pdf. On prosecutorial discretion, see Shoba Sivaprasad Wadhia, *Beyond Deportation: The Role of Prosecutorial Discretion in Immigration Cases* (New York: New York University Press, 2015). On the limitations of discretion and the costs of seeking mercy, rather than justice, in immigration law, see Allison Brownell Tirres, "Mercy in Immigration Law," *Brigham Young University Law Review* 2013, no. 6 (2014): 1563–1611. On the challenges young undocumented people face, see Roberto G. Gonzales, *Lives in Limbo: Undocumented and Coming of Age in America* (Berkeley: University of California Press, 2016).

83. Massey, Durand, and Malone, *Beyond Smoke and Mirrors*, 128–33; Laura Woldenberg and Bernardo Loyola, "Deportee Purgatory," *VICE* (May 13, 2013), http://www.vice .com/video/deportee-purgatory-video; Randal C. Archibold, "As Mexican Border Town Tries to Move On, Some Are Stuck in Limbo," *NYT*, Nov. 28, 2014; Adam Goodman, "Young U.S. Citizens Call on Obama to Reunite Families," *Dissent*, May 16, 2013, https://www.dissentmagazine.org/blog/young-u-s-citizens-call-on-obama-to -reunite-families; Miriam Jordan, "Hundreds of Veterans Were Deported, Rights Group Says," *WSJ*, Jul. 7, 2016. On family separation and the burden deportation places on children, see Joanna Dreby, *Divided by Borders: Mexican Migrants and Their Children* (Berkeley: University of California Press, 2010); Leisy J. Abrego, *Sacrificing Families: Navigating Laws, Labor, and Love across Borders* (Palo Alto, CA: Stanford University Press, 2014); Pallares, *Family Activism*; Jeremy Slack, Daniel E. Martínez, Scott Whiteford, and Emily Peiffer, "In the Shadow of the Wall: Family Separation, Immigration Enforcement and Security," Center for Latin American Studies, University of Arizona, Mar. 2013, 1–39; Luis H. Zayas, *Forgotten Citizens: Deportation, Children, and the Making of American Exiles and Orphans* (New York: Oxford University Press, 2015).

84. Jill Anderson and Nin Solís, *Los Otros Dreamers* (México, DF: Offset Santiago, 2014); Golash-Boza, *Deported*. On people's postdeportation experiences, see also Kanstroom,

*Aftermath*; Brotherton and Barrios, *Banished to the Homeland*; Boehm, *Returned*; Christine Wheatley, "Push Back: U.S. Deportation Policy and the Reincorporation of Involuntary Return Migrants in Mexico," *The Latin Americanist*, Dec. 2011, 35–60; Jeremy Slack, *Deported to Death: How Drug Violence in Changing Migration on the US-Mexico Border* (Oakland: University of California Press, 2019).

85. Reid J. Epstein, "NCLR Head: Obama 'Deporter-in-Chief,'" *Politico*, Mar. 4, 2014, https://www.politico.com/story/2014/03/national-council-of-la-raza-janet-murguia -barack-obama-deporter-in-chief-immigration-104217.

## Epilogue

1. Gregory Krieg, "14 of Trump's Most Outrageous 'Birther' Claims—Half from after 2011," *CNN*, Sep. 16, 2016, https://www.cnn.com/2016/09/09/politics/donald -trump-birther/index.html; "Full Text: Donald Trump Announces a Presidential Bid," *WaPo*, Jun. 16, 2015, https://www.washingtonpost.com/news/post-politics/wp/2015/06 /16/full-text-donald-trump-announces-a-presidential-bid; Eric Bradner, "Border Patrol Union Endorses Donald Trump," *CNN*, Mar. 30, 2016, https://www.cnn.com /2016/03/30/politics/border-patrol-union-endorses-donald-trump/index.html; "ICE Union Endorses Trump," *Politico*, Sep. 26, 2016, https://www.politico.com /story/2016/09/immigration-customs-enforcement-union-endorses-trump-228664. On the border wall replacing the limitless frontier as national symbol and reflecting the end of US expansionism and a reckoning with domestic racism, inequality, and extremism during Trump's presidency, see Greg Grandin, *The End of the Myth: From the Frontier to the Border Wall in the Mind of America* (New York: Metropolitan Books, 2019).

2. Franklin Foer, "How ICE Went Rogue," *The Atlantic*, Sep. 2018.

3. Donald J. Trump, "Executive Order: Enhancing Public Safety in the Interior of the United States," Jan. 25, 2017, https://www.whitehouse.gov/presidential-actions /executive-order-enhancing-public-safety-interior-united-states/; Donald J. Trump, "Executive Order: Border Security and Immigration Enforcement Improvements," Jan. 25, 2017, https://www.whitehouse.gov/presidential-actions/executive-order-border -security-immigration-enforcement-improvements/; Donald J. Trump, "Executive Order: Protecting the Nation from Foreign Terrorist Entry into the United States," Jan. 27, 2017, https://www.whitehouse.gov/presidential-actions/executive-order -protecting-nation-foreign-terrorist-entry-united-states/. On immigration policy and enforcement actions since Trump took office, see Shoba Sivaprasad Wadhia, *Banned: Immigration Enforcement in the Time of Trump* (New York: New York University Press, 2019).

4. "Press Briefing by Press Secretary Sean Spicer," Feb. 21, 2017, https://www.whitehouse .gov/briefings-statements/press-briefing-press-secretary-sean-spicer-022117/.

5. Daniel González, "Deported Arizona Mom Makes New Life in Mexico," *The Arizona Republic*, Feb. 9, 2018, https://www.azcentral.com/story/news/politics/immigration/2018/02/09/deported-arizona-mom-guadalupe-garcia-de-rayos-1-year-later-life-mexico/308079002/; Gene Johnson, "Immigrant Daniel Ramirez Medina 'Hopeful for Future' of Dreamers as He's Freed from Tacoma Detention," *Seattle Times*, Mar. 29, 2017, https://www.seattletimes.com/seattle-news/seattle-area-dreamer-released-from-immigration-detention-center/; Alan Gómez and David Agren, "First Protected DREAMer Is Deported under Trump," *USA Today*, Apr. 18, 2017, https://www.usatoday.com/story/news/world/2017/04/18/first-protected-dreamer-deported-under-trump/100583274/; Goodman, "The Long History of Self-Deportation," 152–58; Foer, "How ICE Went Rogue."

6. Heather Long, "Private Prison Stocks up 100% since Trump's Win," *CNNMoney*, Feb. 24, 2017, https://money.cnn.com/2017/02/24/investing/private-prison-stocks-soar-trump/index.html; The GEO Group, Inc., 2007 and 2017 Annual Reports, accessed Oct. 5, 2018, http://investors.geogroup.com/FinancialDocs; Elinson, "More Detentions Boost Private Prisons"; Mark Collette, Joshua Fechter, and Bill Lambrecht, "Companies Earn Billions to Shelter Immigrant Children," *San Antonio Express-News*, Jun. 29, 2018, https://www.expressnews.com/business/local/article/Companies-earn-billions-to-shelter-immigrant-13038840.php; Chan, "Immigration Detention Bed Quota Timeline"; Robert Moore, "In El Paso, Border Patrol Is Detaining Migrants in 'a Human Dog Pound,'" *Texas Monthly*, Jun. 11, 2019, https://www.texasmonthly.com/news/border-patrol-outdoor-detention-migrants-el-paso/; "Currently Detained Population by Arresting Agency as of 6/22/2019," Detention Management, ICE, accessed Oct. 5, 2018, https://www.ice.gov/detention-management. For a brief history of for-profit immigration detention, see Livia Luan, "Profiting from Enforcement: The Role of Private Prisons in U.S. Immigration Detention," *Migration Information Source*, Migration Policy Institute, May 2, 2018, https://www.migrationpolicy.org/article/profiting-enforcement-role-private-prisons-us-immigration-detention. To get a sense of the inhumane conditions detained immigrants are forced to endure, see Human Rights First, "Ailing Justice: New Jersey: Inadequate Healthcare, Indifference, and Indefinite Confinement in Immigration Detention," Feb. 2018, https://www.humanrightsfirst.org/sites/default/files/Ailing-Justice-NJ.pdf; Department of Homeland Security, Office of the Inspector General, "Management Alert—Issues Requiring Action at the Adelanto ICE Processing Center in Adelanto, California," Sep. 27, 2018, https://www.oig.dhs.gov/sites/default/files/assets/2018-10/OIG-18-86-Sep18.pdf.

7. Jonathan Blitzer, "Trump's Public-Charge Rule Is a One-Two Punch against Immigrants and Public Assistance," *New Yorker*, Sep. 28, 2018, https://www.newyorker.com/news/dispatch/trumps-public-charge-rule-is-a-one-two-punch-against-immigrants-and-public-assistance; Department of Justice, Office of Public Affairs, "EOIR Announces Largest Ever Immigration Judge Investiture," Sep. 28, 2018,

https://www.justice.gov/opa/pr/eoir-announces-largest-ever-immigration-judge
-investiture; Transactional Records Access Clearinghouse, "Immigration Court's
Active Backlog Surpasses One Million," accessed Sep. 18, 2019, https://trac.syr.edu
/immigration/reports/574/; Donald J. Trump (@realdonaldtrump), "We cannot
allow all of these people to invade our Country. When somebody comes in, we must
immediately, with no Judges or Court Cases, bring them back from . . ." Twitter, Jun.
24, 2018, https://twitter.com/realDonaldTrump/status/1010900865602019329.

8. Julie Hirschfeld Davis, "Trump Plans to Cap Refugees Allowed into US at 30,000, a
Record Low," NYT, Sep. 17, 2018, A6; Katie Benner and Caitlin Dickerson, "Sessions
Shrinks Path to Asylum," NYT, Jun. 11, 2018, A1; Susannah George and Colleen Long,
"Trump Refugee Policy Leaves Thousands Stranded Outside US," Associated Press,
Oct. 7, 2018, https://apnews.com/e1dbfda873d34c81af5bbe033acd2472; Michael D. Shear
and Zolan Kanno-Youngs, "US Cuts Refugee Program Again, Placing Cap at 18,000
People," NYT, Sep. 27, 2019, A16. On Trump's demonizing rhetoric, see Julie Hirschfeld
Davis, Sheryl Gay Stolberg, and Thomas Kaplan, "In Vulgar Terms, Trump Disparages
Some Immigrants," NYT, Jan. 11, 2018, A1; Julie Hirschfeld Davis, "Trump Rants on
Unauthorized Migrants: 'These Aren't People, These Are Animals,'" NYT, May 16,
2018, A13; Tom Newton Dunn, "Migrants 'Harm UK,' Donald Trump Says Britain Is
'Losing Its Culture Because of Immigration," The Sun, Jul. 12, 2018, https://www
.thesun.co.uk/news/6766947/donald-trump-britain-losing-culture-immigration/;
Ellen Cranley, "Trump Says 'Thieves and Murderers' Are Coming into the US as He Re-
sponds to Outrage over Immigration Policy," Business Insider, Jun. 18, 2018, https://
www.businessinsider.com/trump-thieves-and-murderers-coming-into-the-us
-immigration-2018-6; Eli Rosenberg, "'The Snake': How Trump Appropriated a Radical
Black Singer's Lyrics for Immigration Fearmongering," WaPo, Feb. 24, 2018, https://
www.washingtonpost.com/news/politics/wp/2018/02/24/the-snake-how-trump
-appropriated-a-radical-black-singers-lyrics-for-refugee-fearmongering/.

9. Department of Justice, Office of Public Affairs, "Attorney General Announces Zero-
Tolerance Policy for Criminal Illegal Entry," Apr. 6, 2018, https://www.justice.gov/opa
/pr/attorney-general-announces-zero-tolerance-policy-criminal-illegal-entry; Julia
Preston, "Zero Tolerance Lives On," The Marshall Project, Sep. 14, 2018, https://www
.themarshallproject.org/2018/09/14/zero-tolerance-lives-on; Comment from Border
Patrol on zero tolerance, Jun. 18, 2018, https://assets.documentcloud.org/documents
/4519977/June-18-2018-Comment-From-Border-Patrol.pdf. On the longer history of the
"deportation to prison pipeline," see Macías-Rojas, From Deportation to Prison.

10. Despite then–DHS secretary Kirstjen Nielsen's repeated denials, signed memos released under the Freedom of Information Act later showed that the administration
purposefully used family separation as a deterrent measure. According to Amnesty
International, US officials divided some 8,000 "family units" in all during 2017 and
2018. Philip Bump, "Here Are the Administration Officials Who Have Said that Family
Separation Is Meant as a Deterrent," WaPo, Jun. 19, 2018, https://www.washingtonpost

.com/news/politics/wp/2018/06/19/here-are-the-administration-officials-who-have-said-that-family-separation-is-meant-as-a-deterrent/; Caitlin Dickerson and Ron Nixon, "White House Weighs Separating Families to Deter Migrants," *NYT*, Dec. 21, 2017, A15; Caitlin Dickerson, "Over 700 Children Taken from Parents at Border," *NYT*, Apr. 20, 2018, A1; Michael D. Shear, Abby Goodnough, and Maggie Haberman, "In Retreat, Trump Halts Separating Migrant Families," *NYT*, Jun. 20, 2018, A1; Ryan Devereaux, "The US Has Taken More Than 3,700 Children from Their Parents—And Has No Plan for Returning Them," *The Intercept*, Jun. 19, 2018, https://theintercept.com /2018/06/19/children-separated-from-parents-family-separation-immigration/; Cora Currier, "Prosecuting Parents—And Separating Families—Was Meant to Deter Migration, Signed Memo Confirms," *The Intercept*, Sep. 25, 2018, https://theintercept.com /2018/09/25/family-separation-border-crossings-zero-tolerance/; Amnesty International, "USA: 'You Don't Have Any Rights Here': Illegal Pushbacks, Arbitrary Detention & Ill-Treatment of Asylum-Seekers in the United States," 2018, 1–72.

11. Devin Miller, "AAP a Leading Voice against Separating Children, Parents at Border," *AAP News*, Jun. 14, 2018, http://www.aappublications.org/news/2018/06/14/washington 061418; Ron Nixon, "Official Likens Shelters to Summer Camp," *NYT*, Jul. 31, 2018, A13; Ginger Thompson, "Listen to Children Who've Just Been Separated from Their Parents at the Border," *ProPublica*, Jun. 18, 2018, https://www.propublica.org/article /children-separated-from-parents-border-patrol-cbp-trump-immigration-policy; Dan Barry, Miriam Jordan, Annie Correal, and Manny Fernandez, "Scrubbing Toilets and No Hugging: A Migrant Child's Days in Detention," *NYT*, Jul. 14, 2018, A1; Cedar Attanasio, Garance Burke, and Martha Mendoza, "Attorneys: Texas Border Facility Is Neglecting Migrant Kids," *AP*, Jun. 21, 2019, https://apnews.com/46da2dbe04f54adbb 875cfbc06bbc615; Melissa Sanchez, Duaa Eldeib, and Jodi S. Cohen, "As Months Pass in Chicago Shelters, Immigrant Children Contemplate Escape, Even Suicide," *ProPublica Illinois*, Sep. 6, 2018, https://www.propublica.org/article/chicago-immigrant -shelters-heartland-internal-documents; Graham Kates and Angel Canales, "A 10-Year-Old Migrant Girl Died Last Year in Government Care, Officials Acknowledge," *CBS News*, May 22, 2019, https://www.cbsnews.com/news/migrant-children-death-a -10-year-old-migrant-girl-died-last-year-in-government-care-officials -acknowledge-exclusive/. On the detention of asylum-seeking families in the United States, see Ingrid Early, Steven Shafer, and Jana Whalley, "Detaining Families: A Study of Asylum Adjudication in Family Detention," American Immigration Council, Aug. 2018, 1–45. On the trauma migrant children faced even after being released from detention and placed with foster parents, see Miriam Jordan, "A 5-Year-Old Migrant's Heartache: 'When Will I See My Papa?,'" *NYT*, Jun. 7, 2018, A1.

12. Jeremy Raff, "ICE Is Pressuring Separated Parents to Choose Deportation," *The Atlantic*, Jul. 6, 2018, https://www.theatlantic.com/politics/archive/2018/07/how-ice-pressures -separated-parents-to-choose-deportation/564461/; Sarah Stillman, "Migrants Say They Are Still Being Threatened with Child Separation," *New Yorker*, Jun. 26, 2018, https://

www.newyorker.com/news/dispatch/migrants-say-they-are-still-being-threatened
-with-child-separation; Adam Cox and Ryan Goodman, "Detention of Migrant Families as 'Deterrence': Ethical Flaws and Empirical Doubts," *Just Security*, Jun. 22, 2018,
https://www.justsecurity.org/58354/detention-migrant-families-deterrence-ethical
-flaws-empirical-doubts/; Adam Isacson, "Southwest Border Data Shows 'Zero Tolerance' Didn't Deter Migrants after All," *WOLA*, Jul. 5, 2018, https://www.wola.org
/analysis/southwest-border-data-shows-zero-tolerance-didnt-deter-migrants/.

13. Though formal deportations have increased since 2017, they have not exceeded the
record highs seen during the middle years of the Obama administration. DHS, *YOIS:
2018*, 103.

14. The history of xenophobic fear mongering dates back well before the federal government took control of immigration enforcement in the late nineteenth century.
During the last century alone there are numerous examples of public officials relying on fear, including Doak and Visel in the 1930s and Swing in the 1950s (see chapter 2), Chapman in the 1970s (see chapter 4), Tanton and his network of organizations
since the 1970s (see chapters 4 and 6), and Wilson and Huntington in the 1990s (see
chapter 6). In addition to Trump's own anti-immigrant politics, he has surrounded
himself with other far-right nativists like Stephen Miller, Steve Bannon, Jeff Sessions, Julie Kirschner, Ken Cuccinelli, Kris Kobach, and others. On the senior administration officials behind the draconian immigration policies discussed in this
epilogue, see Emily Bazelon, "Department of Justification," *NYT Magazine*,
Feb. 28, 2017, https://www.nytimes.com/2017/02/28/magazine/jeff-sessions-stephen
-bannon-justice-department.html; Jason Zengerle, "How America Got to 'Zero Tolerance' on Immigration: The Inside Story," *NYT Magazine*, Jul. 16, 2019, https://www
.nytimes.com/2019/07/16/magazine/immigration-department-of-homeland
-security.html.

15. Interview transcript, "Bob Woodward and Bob Costa with Donald Trump, Corey
Lewandowski, Press Secretary Hope Hicks and Donald Trump Jr. Also Present, at the
Old Post Office Pavilion Trump Hotel, March 31, 2016, beginning at noon," https://www
.washingtonpost.com/wp-stat/graphics/politics/trump-archive/docs/donald-trump
-interview-with-bob-woodward-and-robert-costa.pdf. On fear during Trump's presidency, see Martha C. Nussbaum, *The Monarchy of Fear: A Philosopher Looks at Our Political Crisis* (New York: Simon & Schuster, 2018); Bob Woodward, *Fear: Trump in the
White House* (New York: Simon & Schuster, 2018).

16. Julia Carrie Wong, "'Psychological Warfare': Immigrants in America Held Hostage
by Fear of Raids," *The Guardian*, Feb. 18, 2017, https://www.theguardian.com/us-news
/2017/feb/18/us-immigration-raids-fear-trump-mexico.

17. Testimony of Thomas D. Homan, Acting Director of ICE, "Immigration and Customs Enforcement & Customs and Border Protection FY18 Budget Request," before
House Committee on Appropriations, Jun. 13, 2017.

18. Noelle Phillips, "Jeanette Vizguerra Leaves Sanctuary after 86 Days Avoiding Immigration Authorities," *Denver Post*, May 12, 2017, https://www.denverpost.com/2017/05/12/jeanette-vizguerra-arturo-hernandez-garcia-stay-deportation/; Laurie Goodstein, "Immigrant Father Shielded from Deportation by a Philadelphia Church Walks Free," *NYT*, Oct. 11, 2017, A17; Goodman, "The Long History of Self-Deportation," 152–58.

19. Alexandra Hall, "America's Dairyland and Trump in the Rearview Mirror as Workers Return to Mexico," Wisconsin Public Radio and the Wisconsin Center for Investigative Journalism, Jun. 18, 2017, https://www.wisconsinwatch.org/2017/06/americas-dairyland-and-trump-in-the-rearview-mirror-as-workers-return-to-mexico/. For other examples of self-deportation, see Brittny Mejia, "'It's So Hard Right Now': For a Mother Who Self-Deported to Mexico, Days of Feeling Lost," *LAT*, Feb. 7, 2018, http://www.latimes.com/local/california/la-me-ln-family-struggles-mexico-20180207-htmlstory.html; Emily Green, "As DACA Debate Drags On, Some DREAMers Are Moving Back to Mexico Voluntarily," *NPR*, Apr. 17, 2018, https://www.npr.org/2018/04/17/603352038/as-daca-debate-drags-on-some-dreamers-are-moving-back-to-mexico-voluntarily; Mike Schneider, "Facing Deportation, US Marine's Wife Leaves for Mexico," *Associated Press*, Aug. 3, 2018, https://apnews.com/32bb7d14fa6e4802b65c82905fb0d959. Wisconsin dairy farmers reported that their business entirely depended on immigrant labor. One farmer with around 1,000 head of cattle said losing her workers was her "worst nightmare" and would essentially force the farm to cease operation. Alexandra Hall, "Under Trump, Wisconsin Dairies Struggle to Keep Immigrant Workers," Wisconsin Public Radio and the Wisconsin Center for Investigative Journalism, Mar. 19, 2017, https://www.wisconsinwatch.org/2017/03/under-trump-wisconsin-dairies-struggle-to-keep-immigrant-workers/. See also "These Undocumented Wisconsin Parents 'Live with Fear Every Day,'" *PBS NewsHour*, Jul. 3, 2017, https://www.pbs.org/newshour/show/undocumented-wisconsin-parents-live-fear-every-day; Foer, "How ICE Went Rogue."

20. Claire Galofaro and Juliet Linderman, "Immigrants Wait in Fear after Raids; Trump Takes Credit," *Associated Press*, Feb. 12, 2017, https://apnews.com/ec63f4f9bfb5450d82d8f9861b7ebc77; Emily Baumgaertner, "Immigrants Abandon Public Nutrition Services," *NYT*, Mar. 6, 2018, A17; Helena Bottemiller Evich, "Immigrants, Fearing Trump Crackdown, Drop Out of Nutrition Programs," *Politico*, Sep. 3, 2018, https://www.politico.com/story/2018/09/03/immigrants-nutrition-food-trump-crackdown-806292; Pam Fessler, "Deportation Fears Prompt Immigrants to Cancel Food Stamps," *NPR*, Mar. 28, 2017, https://www.npr.org/sections/thesalt/2017/03/28/521823480/deportation-fears-prompt-immigrants-to-cancel-food-stamps; Hall, "Under Trump, Wisconsin Dairies Struggle to Keep Immigrant Workers"; Katherine Hernandez, "Fearing Deportation, Food Vendors Are Leaving New York City's Streets," *NPR*, Jan. 12, 2018, https://www.npr.org/sections/thesalt/2018/01/12/577462634/fearing-deportation-food-vendors-are-leaving-new-york-city-s-streets; Heidi Glenn, "Fear of

Deportation Spurs 4 Women to Drop Domestic Abuse Cases in Denver," *NPR*, Mar. 21, 2017, https://www.npr.org/2017/03/21/520841332/fear-of-deportation-spurs-4-women-to-drop-domestic-abuse-cases-in-denver; Cora Engelbrecht, "Fewer Hispanics Report Domestic Abuse. Police Fault Deportations," *NYT*, Jun. 3, 2018, A12.

21. Robert Samuels, "After Trump's Immigration Order, Anxiety Grows in Florida's Farm Fields," *WaPo*, Feb. 27, 2017, https://www.washingtonpost.com/politics/after-trumps-immigration-order-anxiety-grows-in-floridas-vegetable-fields/2017/02/25/1539c4be-f915-11e6-be05-1a3817ac21a5_story.html; Catherine E. Shoichet, "ICE Raided a Meatpacking Plant. More Than 500 Kids Missed School the Next Day," *CNN*, Apr. 12, 2018, https://www.cnn.com/2018/04/12/us/tennessee-immigration-raid-schools-impact/index.html; Thomas S. Dee and Mark Murphy, "Vanished Classmates: The Effects of Local Immigration Enforcement on School Enrollment," Stanford Center for Education Policy Analysis, CEPA Working Paper No. 18-18, Sep. 2018, http://cepa.stanford.edu/wp18-18; Sarah Elizabeth Richards, "How Fear of Deportation Puts Stress on Families," *The Atlantic*, Mar. 22, 2017, https://www.theatlantic.com/family/archive/2017/03/deportation-stress/520008/. See also Nomaan Merchant, "Hunger, Fear, Desperation: What Came of an Ordinary ICE Raid," *Associated Press*, Jul. 9, 2018, https://www.apnews.com/2349feae4c134107ae927d9d7e797759; Dustin Blitchok, "Fear and Anxiety in Pontiac over Presence of Immigration Agents," *The Oakland Press*, Feb. 19, 2017, https://www.theoaklandpress.com/news/nation-world-news/fear-and-anxiety-in-pontiac-over-presence-of-immigration-agents/article_ffc6be3d-243e-5798-924c-afa48428569a.html; David Schaper, "Anxiety Grows over Anti-Immigrant Actions: 'We Feel They Are after Us,'" *NPR*, Jul. 5 2018, https://www.npr.org/2018/07/05/626241032/anxiety-grows-over-anti-immigrant-actions-we-feel-they-are-after-us; David Nakamura, "Amid Immigration Setbacks, One Trump Strategy Seems to Be Working: Fear," *WaPo*, Apr. 30, 2017, https://www.washingtonpost.com/politics/amid-immigration-setbacks-one-trump-strategy-seems-to-be-working-fear/2017/04/30/62af1620-2b4e-11e7-a616-d7c8a68c1a66_story.html; Samantha Artiga and Petry Ubri, "Living in an Immigrant Family in America: How Fear and Toxic Stress Are Affecting Daily Life, Well-Being, & Health," Kaiser Family Foundation, Dec. 13, 2017, https://www.kff.org/disparities-policy/issue-brief/living-in-an-immigrant-family-in-america-how-fear-and-toxic-stress-are-affecting-daily-life-well-being-health/; Lisseth Rojas-Flores, Mari L. Clements, J. Hwang Koo, and Judy London, "Trauma and Psychological Distress in Latino Citizen Children Following Parental Detention and Deportation," *Psychological Trauma: Theory, Research, Practice, and Policy* 9, no. 3 (May 2017): 352–61; Foer, "How ICE Went Rogue"; Zayas, *Forgotten Citizens*.

22. Glenn Thrush and Maggie Haberman, "Giving White Nationalists an Unequivocal Boost," *NYT*, Aug. 15, 2017, A1; Ryan Devereaux, "US Citizenship and Immigration Services Will Remove 'Nation of Immigrants' from Mission Statement," *The Intercept*, Feb. 22, 2018, https://theintercept.com/2018/02/22/u-s-citizenship-and-immigration-services-will-remove-nation-of-immigrants-from-mission-statement/.

## Note on Sources and Language

1. DHS, *YOIS: 2018*, 103.
2. DHS, *YOIS: 2018*, 103. The immigration bureaucracy has frequently changed the terms used to refer to different expulsion mechanisms. One could argue that the agency's creation of categories like removals, returns, and voluntary departures is part of a larger effort to sanitize the terminology. Since 2006, for example, the word *deportation*—with all of its negative connotations of state coercion and power—does not appear at all in DHS's *Yearbook of Immigration Statistics*. DHS, *YOIS*, 2006–2018.
3. DHS, *YOIS: 2005*, 95; DHS, *YOIS: 2003*, 146.
4. INS, *Statistical Yearbook*, 1978–2001.
5. The USCIS History Office and Library also lists "reship foreign" under "Deportation." On "reship foreign," see chapter 1n59. "Keywords for Case Files," Records and Correspondence (INS)—INS (RG 85) Historical Subject File Index Project, Vertical Files, USCISHOL.
6. DHS, *YOIS: 2018*, 103.
7. G.J.L. Coles, "Working Group on Mass Expulsion: Report," International Institute of Humanitarian Law, San Remo, Italy, Apr. 16–18, 1983, 4. A few years later, another group of experts made a similar declaration: "Mass expulsion results from the use of coercion, including a variety of political, economic and social measures which directly, or even more so indirectly, force people to leave or flee their homelands for fear of life, liberty and security." International Law Association, Preamble to the Declaration of Principles of International Law on Mass Expulsion, 62nd Conference, Seoul, Aug. 24–30, 1986. On the variety of coercive mechanisms states rely on to expel people, see Guy S. Goodwin-Gill, *International Law and the Movement of Persons between States* (Oxford: Clarendon Press, 1978), 201; Jean-Marie Henckaerts, *Mass Expulsion in Modern International Law and Practice* (The Hague: Martinus Nijhoff, 1995); Walters, "Deportation, Expulsion, and the International Police of Aliens," 265–92; Matthew J. Gibney, "Asylum and the Expansion of Deportation in the United Kingdom," *Government and Opposition* 43, no. 2 (2008): 146–67.
8. A notable exception is Heyman, "Putting Power in the Anthropology of Bureaucracy," 261–87.
9. AR 1944, Table 24A; AR 1945, Table 37; AR 1946–50, Table 29; AR 1960, 64; AR 1970, 98; INS, *Statistical Yearbook: 1978*, 75; INS, *Statistical Yearbook: 1982*, 196; INS, *Statistical Yearbook: 1989*, 130.

# INDEX

Page numbers in italics refer to illustrations and tables.

## Politics and Society in Modern America
William H. Chafe, Gary Gerstle, Linda Gordon, and Julian E. Zelizer, Series Editors

For a full list of books in this series see: https://press.princeton.edu/series/politics-and-society-in-modern-america